A QUANTITATIVE TOUR OF THE SOCIAL SCIENCES

Social scientists become experts in their own disciplines but aren't always familiar with what is going on in neighboring fields. To foster a deeper understanding of the interconnection of the social sciences, economists should know where historical data come from, sociologists should know how to think like economists, political scientists would benefit from understanding how models are tested in psychology, historians should learn how political processes are studied, psychologists should understand sociological theories, and so forth.

This overview by prominent social scientists gives an accessible, nontechnical sense of how quantitative research is done in different areas. Readers will find out about models and ways of thinking in economics, history, sociology, political science, and psychology, which in turn they can bring back to their own work.

A QUANTITATIVE TOUR OF THE SOCIAL SCIENCES

Edited by

ANDREW GELMAN
Columbia University

JERONIMO CORTINA
University of Houston

CAMBRIDGE
UNIVERSITY PRESS

CAMBRIDGE UNIVERSITY PRESS
Cambridge, New York, Melbourne, Madrid, Cape Town, Singapore, São Paulo, Delhi

Cambridge University Press
32 Avenue of the Americas, New York, NY 10013-2473, USA

www.cambridge.org
Information on this title: www.cambridge.org/9780521680035

First published 2009

Printed in the United States of America

A catalog record for this publication is available from the British Library.

Library of Congress Cataloging in Publication data
A quantitative tour of the social sciences / [edited by] Andrew Gelman, Jeronimo Cortina.
p. cm.
Includes bibliographical references and index.
ISBN 978-0-521-86198-4 (hardback) – ISBN 978-0-521-68003-5 (pbk.)
1. Social sciences – Methodology. 2. Social sciences. I. Gelman, Andrew.
II. Cortina, Jeronimo. III. Title.
⌐ H62.Q365 2009
300.72–dc22   2008054986

ISBN 978-0-521-86198-4 hardback
ISBN 978-0-521-68003-5 paperback

Para Zacky, Jacobito, Jacinto, y Camilo

Contents

Preface: Learning to Think Like a Social Scientist

MOTIVATION FOR WRITING THIS BOOK

This book has been created as a one-stop introduction to quantitative empirical social science for busy students. It originated as lecture notes from a one-semester class taught by five professors, with three weeks each of history, economics, sociology, political science, and psychology. Rather than emphasizing common features of all social sciences, we pull out examples that demonstrate the distinctive ways of working within each area. What does it mean to think like an economist? Or like a sociologist, political scientist, psychologist, or historian? We hope that students, in reading this book and working through its examples, will develop some social science literacy in these different ways of thinking, which in turn should improve their understanding of their individual areas of study.

We focus on quantitative models and methods for two reasons. First, quantitative skills are difficult and are in demand, both within and outside academia. Hence, students should be motivated to learn the relevance of quantitative ideas in the study of society. Second, by centering on quantitative approaches, we give a common theme to the book so that students can see how a core group of ideas is applied in different ways to different problems.

MATHEMATICAL LEVEL

This book is not limited to students with a statistical or methodological focus; we think that all social science students would benefit from it, and we are careful to place technical terms in social science contexts.

A unique feature of the book is that we work with quantitative models and methods, but the material is presented in an almost entirely nontechnical fashion. In contrast to books on research methods, ours is a book on *social science*, and we consider the quantitative methods as tools for understanding social phenomena. By reading the book, a student will develop an understanding of the ways in which working social scientists use quantitative models and methods.

The statistical and mathematical ideas considered in different parts of the book are presented intentionally at different levels of complexity. The history chapters discuss the sources of quantitative historical and economic data and the diverse efforts required to collect and understand this information. In contrast, the chapters on economics focus in depth on a particular area – time series econometrics – to illustrate general issues of evaluating social science hypotheses using quantitative data. The next part of the book, on sociology, begins with a general introduction to social science modeling and then continues with several examples of research indicating the use of statistical models – including how research proceeds when a hypothesized model does *not* fit the data. The political science part has a similar structure, and as with the earlier parts, there is extensive discussion of the practicalities of collecting and evaluating historical data. The psychology part presents a number of theories from social and cognitive psychology along with a discussion of the possibilities of evaluating these theories using empirical data. The book concludes with a discussion and an example of causal inference in social science research.

USING THIS BOOK IN A COURSE OR FOR INDEPENDENT STUDY

We expect that the primary audience for this book will be undergraduates in social science survey courses, junior and senior social science majors, and beginning graduate students. All these students should be interested in an overview of the social sciences with a focus on research methods, whether to learn about methods that they can use in their own senior theses or research projects or simply to get a better understanding of how quantitative knowledge is achieved in these areas.

We envision the use of the book in three sorts of classes. First, it can be a main text (or one of a small set of texts) in a general social science course. Second, it can serve as a supplementary text in a course on quantitative methods in any of the social sciences. For example, in a quantitative methods course in sociology, economics, or political science, it would give students a broad view of the different social sciences in a serious, scholarly, yet easy-to-read format. An instructor can assign this book, along with some homework assignments and focused reading, to give the students a taste of the different quantitative perspectives in the social sciences. The third audience we see for this book consists of students taking social science overview courses in professional programs such as law, public policy, and business.

ACKNOWLEDGMENTS

This project originated from a course that we designed specially for the Quantitative Methods in Social Sciences program at Columbia University. The professors were experienced teachers who enjoyed having an opportunity to give an overview of quantitative methods within their field for a general audience. We thank everyone at Columbia who has helped design and administer the QMSS program, including (in alphabetical order) Peter Bearman, Anthony Cruz, Daphne Estwick, David Krantz, Steven Laymon, Gillian Lindt, Eduardo Macagno, Henry Pinkham, Seymour Spilerman, Tanya Summers, Beatrice Terrien-Somerville, Francis Tuerlinckx, Cynthia Van Ginkel, Greg Wawro, Chris Weiss, and Danielle Wolan. We thank Jorge Balan of the Ford Foundation for arranging funding for supporting the QMSS program in various ways, including helping to support the costs of transcribing these lectures. We also thank Hayward Alker and Jennifer Hill for helpful discussions, Chandler Sims and Amalia Mena for helping to put this book together, Charles Stockley for his immense effort in transcribing dozens of hours of lectures, and the National Science Foundation and the Columbia University Applied Statistics Center for financial support. Lauren Cowles and her colleagues at Cambridge University Press have provided crucial motivation and assistance in putting together the final version of this book. We are eternally grateful to our spouses, Carolina and Daniela, for their love and support. Finally, we thank the past, current, and future students who have motivated this work and continue to motivate us to combine insights from the different social sciences to study the problems of people in social settings.

About the Contributors

Charles Cameron is a professor of political science at Princeton University. He has been a Fellow at the Brookings Institution, and his book *Veto Bargaining* won the Fenno Prize from the American Political Science Association. He works on applied formal theory and empirical tests of game-theoretic models of politics as applied to legislatures, courts, and elections.

Richard Clarida is a professor of economics at Columbia University and has published more than 25 articles on topics ranging from exchange rates to public investment. He has served on the staff of the President's Council of Economic Advisors and as the U.S. assistant secretary of the treasury for economic policy.

Jeronimo Cortina is an assistant professor of political science at the University of Houston. He specializes in political behavior, immigration, and quantitative methods. His work has been published in scholarly and policy journals such as the *American Politics Research Journal, Foreign Affairs in Spanish*, and the *Harvard Journal of Hispanic Policy*.

Andrew Gelman is a professor of statistics and political science, director of the Applied Statistics Center, and founding director of the Quantitative Methods in Social Sciences program at Columbia University. His books include *Bayesian Data Analysis, Teaching Statistics: A Bag of Tricks,* and *Data Analysis using Regression and Multilevel/Hierarchical Models*. He has also published more than 200 research articles in statistical theory, methods, computation, and applications in various topics in social and environmental sciences.

Emanuele Gerratana received his Ph.D. thesis in economics at Columbia University on the topic of competing mechanisms and common agency. He has also written on family effects of youth unemployment in Italy. He is currently on the faculty of economics at Koc University in Istanbul.

Heidi Grant completed her Ph.D. in psychology at Columbia University and is on the faculty of psychology at Lehigh University, doing research in social psychology and motivation.

E. Tory Higgins is the Stanley Schacter Professor of Psychology at Columbia University and has received several awards for his research in social psychology, including the Thomas M. Ostrom Award for outstanding contributions in social cognition, the William James Fellow Award for Distinguished Achievements in Psychological Science from the American Psychological Society, and the American Psychological Association Award for Distinguished Scientific Contributions.

Herbert S. Klein is a professor of history at Stanford University. He has written 15 books, including *The Atlantic Slave Trade, Bolivia: The Evolution of a Multi-Ethnic Society* and *Transicao Incompleta: Brasil desde 1945*, along with more than 125 articles in six languages on topics including comparative social and economic history, international migrations, and demographics of the late colonial to modern periods.

Marta Noguer completed her Ph.D. in economics at Columbia University on the topic of capital flows, technology diffusion, and economic growth. She currently is at the Research Department of la Caixa in Barcelona.

Seymour Spilerman is the Julian C. Levi Professor of Social Sciences and director of the Center for the Study of Wealth and Inequality at Columbia University. He is a Fellow of the American Association for the Advancement of Science and has published more than 70 articles on diverse topics such as occupational attainment, intergenerational financial linkages, racial disorders, and mathematical sociology.

Charles Stockley received his Ph.D. in history at Columbia University on the topic of British economic policy in the 1960s and was previously assistant vice president at Morgan Bank and a vice president at Commodities Corporation.

Elke Weber is a professor of psychology and management and director of the Center for Decision Sciences at Columbia University. She has served as president of the Society for Mathematical Psychology and the Society for Judgment and Decision Making and as a member of a National Academy of Sciences committee on the human dimensions of global change. Her research topics include cross-individual and cultural differences in risk taking.

PART I. MODELS AND METHODS IN THE SOCIAL SCIENCES

Andrew Gelman

1. Introduction and Overview

WHAT THIS BOOK IS ABOUT

The seven parts of this book cover different examples of quantitative reasoning in social science applications, along with interspersed discussions on the role of quantitative theories and methods in understanding the social world. We are trying to show how researchers in different social sciences think about and use quantitative ideas. These approaches vary across the different disciplines, and we think that the best way for a student to get a broad overview is to see how quantitative ideas are applied in a variety of settings.

Hence, we focus on applications, including combat in the First World War, demographics in nineteenth-century Mexico, forecasts of economic conditions by the Federal Reserve, racial disturbances in the 1960s, voting in congressional committees, Pavlovian conditioning, and the effect of migration on solidarity. Each part of the book has several examples, with discussion of the theories used to explain each phenomenon under study, along with the data and models used to describe what is happening. We thus hope to give a general perspective of how these models and methods are used in the social sciences. It is not the usual straightforward story of the form, "Here are some data, here's the model, and look how well the method works." Rather, we explore the strengths but also the limitations of the models and methods in the context of the real problems being studied. Mathematical models and statistical methods can be powerful – you can fit a linear regression model to just about anything – but one needs some sense of what the models mean in context.

The style of the book is conversational and episodic. We do not intend to cover every mathematical model and every statistical method, but rather to give a specific sense of the diversity of methods being used. We believe that the reader of this book or the student in a course based on this book will gain a broader view and some specific tools that he or she can use in attacking applied problems with a social science dimension. This can be especially valuable for a student trained in a specific social science who has only a vague sense of what ideas are used in other fields. A psychological view can be important in understanding a problem that was thought of as pure economics, political scientists need to appreciate the strengths and weaknesses of their sources of historical data, social psychologists need to comprehend the large-scale studies of sociologists, economists need to think seriously about the workings of governments, and so forth.

Just to be clear: This is not a statistics or a research methods book but rather a social science book with a quantitative focus. We certainly think that social science students need to learn some statistics, and we see the book's ideas as complementing that study. We do discuss linear regression (in Part III) and Poisson models (in Part IV), but we focus on how these answer (or fail to answer) the substantive questions in the particular applications considered. We also discuss some purely mathematical models (for example, game theory in Chapter 3 and decision theory in Chapter 20).

GOOD SOCIAL SCIENCE IS INTERDISCIPLINARY

We don't attempt to define social science except to say that whatever it is, it is studied from different perspectives by historians, economists, sociologists, political scientists, and psychologists. Everybody has his or her own turf, and that's fine, but as a student – or, for that matter, as a practitioner – it's good to know your way around the farm. To some extent, this already happens – quantitative political scientists learn economics, economists use results from cognitive psychology, and just about everybody should learn some history. In this book, we're trying to lay out some concepts in each of the social sciences that can be part of everybody's toolkit in understanding the social world.

We focus on quantitative methods because that's a common ground, an objective reality on which we can all agree – or, where we disagree, we can focus our disagreements on specific questions that, at least in theory, can be answered by hard data. This point arises in Part II of the book; for example, ideas about families that many of us take for granted are associated with demographic patterns in Europe hundreds of years ago. In Part III, there's a discussion of some methods used to assess how much information different economic actors have in predicting exchange rates, and Part IV describes a model for promotion of employees within a large corporation. Different methods can be used to attack similar problems. In political science there's a lot of research on the topic of bargaining, which can be studied quantitatively by looking, for example, at how legislators vote on different issues and to what extent these votes are consistent with political ideology. Part VI discusses several different kinds of theories used to explain decisions and behavior. Some of these theories are more quantitative than others, and it is important to understand under what circumstances such theories can be tested. This issue arises in all the social sciences.

Why do the social sciences use such different methods? One reason is that people study different phenomena in different fields; for example, a discrete Markov transition model[1] might be reasonable to describe changes in a person's

---

[1] In a "discrete Markov model," a person can be in one of several *states* (for example, 1, 2, or 3, corresponding to "unemployed," "underemployed," or "employed"). The person starts in a particular state, and then at each of a sequence of time points (for example, every month), he or she can stay in the same state or switch to a different state, with specified "transition probabilities" corresponding to each pair of states. Examples of Markov models appear in Parts IV and V of this book, and they can

employment status but inappropriate for modeling gradual changes in public opinion. Another reason for the differences might be personal tastes, traditions, and even political ideology. In any case, if you can understand and communicate in these different fields, you can move to integrate them in solving applied problems, which are never confined to a single academic discipline. Part VII, the last part of this book, provides a more comprehensive, although by no means exhaustive, discussion of causal inference in the social sciences.

CONTROVERSIES IN ESTIMATING THE DOLLAR VALUE OF A LIFE

Mathematical and statistical models can be extremely effective in studying social situations, especially when many methods are used and none is relied on entirely. To take just one case, the economist Peter Dorman wrote a book in 1996 on workers' compensation and valuing human life. The value of a life has long been a contentious topic. From one perspective, it seems immoral to put a dollar value on lives, but in practice this must be done all the time, in settings ranging from life insurance to building code regulations to the cost of air bags in automobiles. For workers' compensation (insurance payments for on-the-job injuries), it is sometimes suggested that dollar values be set based on workers' own valuations of job risks, as revealed by the "risk premium" – the additional amount of money a person will demand in order to take on a risky job. This risk premium can itself be estimated by statistical analysis – for example, running a regression of salaries of jobs, with the level of risk as a predictor variable. In his book Dorman discusses the history of economic analyses of this problem, along with problems with the current state of the art. (For one thing, jobs with higher risks pay *lower* salaries, so the simplest analysis of risks and salaries will "show" that workers actually prefer riskier jobs. An appropriate analysis must control for the kind of job, a perhaps impossible task in practice.)

But what really makes Dorman's book interesting is that he includes historical, political, and psychological perspectives. Historically, workers' compensation has been a government solution to a political struggle between unions and management, so nominal dollar values for risks have been set by political as well as economic processes. In addition, psychologists have long known that attitudes toward risk depend strongly on the sense of responsibility and control over the dangers, and it should be no surprise that people are much less willing to accept new risks than to tolerate existing hazards. Dorman puts all this together, along with some theoretical economic analysis, to suggest ways in which labor,

---

apply to entities other than persons (for example, a plot of land could be unused or used for residential, agricultural, industrial, commercial, or other purposes, and it can move between these states over time). Such models can be relevant for studying the progress of individual persons or chains of events, but they are generally less appropriate for studying gradual behavior of aggregates. For example, one might consider modeling public opinion in the United States as supporting the Democrats or the Republicans or as balanced between the parties. Such a characterization would probably not be as useful as a time-series model of the continuous proportion of support for each of the parties.

management, and government could negotiate reasonable compromises in assignment of risks.

Dorman's particular interdisciplinary approach is controversial, however. In many different studies, economists have attempted to refine the regressions of wages on risk (these attempts are considered an example of "hedonic regression," so called because they estimate individuals' preferences or judgments about what will make them happiest) to adjust for differences among the sorts of people who take different jobs (see, for example, Costa and Kahn 2004; Viscusi 2000).

As Dorman points out in his book, these questions are politically loaded, and he and others are necessarily giving their own perspectives. But I still believe that the quantitative analyses are useful as long as we are able to evaluate their underlying assumptions – both mathematical and historical.

FORECASTING AS A SOCIAL SCIENCE PROBLEM AS WELL AS A STATISTICAL PROBLEM

I'd like to try to separate the details of a statistical forecasting model from what we learn simply from the existence of a successful forecast. This general idea – that quantifying your uncertainty can reveal the underlying structure of a system – is important in all the observational social sciences, most notably economics, and also is used in engineering in the area of quality control.

Forecasting is an important – in some ways fundamental – task in economics, as discussed in Part III. In addition to its importance for practical reasons (for example, to estimate costs and set prices), the limits of your ability to forecast tell you how much information you have about the underlying system that you are studying. More precisely, the predictive error of your forecast reflects some combination of your ignorance and inherently unpredictable factors (which will always occur as long as humans are involved). Economists sometimes talk about an ideal forecast, which is not a perfect, zero-error prediction but rather is the most accurate prediction possible given the inherent variation in a system between the current time T_0 and the time T_1 about which you are trying to forecast.

To put it another way – this may be a familiar idea if you've studied linear regression – the residual error or unexplained variance represents the variation in the outcome that is not explained by the predictors. For example, a regression of income on job category, years of experience, and an interaction between those predictors will not be perfect – that is, its R-squared will be less than 100% – which makes sense since other factors affect your income (in most jobs). From a social science perspective, the very fact that the regression predictions are accurate only to a certain level is informative, because it tells us how much other factors affect income in this particular society. Statistically, this is one of the ideas motivating the analysis of variance, which involves studying how important different factors are in explaining the variation we see in the world. In addition, the coefficients in a regression model can tell a story by revealing which predictors carry information, which is discussed in detail at the end of Chapter 9.

To return to time-series forecasting, if a variable can be accurately predicted two years ahead of time, then intervening factors during those two years cannot be important in the sense of affecting the outcome. What is more common is that a forecast several years in advance will have a large error variance, but as the time lag of the forecast decreases, it will become increasingly accurate – but with some limit on the accuracy, so that a very short term forecast (for example, of tomorrow's prices) will still not be perfect.

From a social science point of view, the situations and time lags where a forecast has large errors provide an opportunity to try to understand the intervening variables that make a difference. (A similar point comes up in Part IV, where data on racial disturbances do *not* follow a Poisson model, motivating a search for further understanding.) We consider this in more detail for election forecasting.

There are many ways to predict the outcomes of elections. In the following discussion we focus on U.S. congressional and presidential elections, but the same ideas apply to other contests in the United States and other places where elections are held regularly. You can forecast two years ahead of time, or three months before the election, or one week before, or on election night. Each of these forecasts can be useful for different purposes, and each uses different information. For example, to forecast an election two years early, you'll use past election results, forecasts of the economy in two years, and general political knowledge such as that the president's party often does poorly in off-year elections. Three months before the election the candidates are known, so you can include information on candidate quality. You also have some information from polls, such as presidential approval ratings and answers to the question "Who would you vote for?" as well as more reliable economic data. These forecasts have received a lot of attention in the economics and political science literature (studies by Ray Fair [1978], Steven Rosenstone [1983], Bob Erikson and Chris Wlezien [1996], James Campbell [1996], Michael Lewis-Beck and Tom Rice [1992], and others) because of their inherent interest and also because of the following paradox: The final months of election campaigns sometimes feature dramatic reversals, but if elections can be accurately forecast three months ahead of time, this seems to allow little room for the unexpected. As Gelman and King (1993) put it, why do pre-election polls vary so much when elections are so predictable? In this setting, the very existence of a forecasting model has political implications.

To continue briefly with the election forecasting example, the next step is prediction on election night itself. Partial information – the election results from the first precincts and states to report – can be used to forecast the whole. Time-series forecasts are used in an interesting way here: From a previously fitted model, you can get a forecast for each precinct and state. As actual election returns come in, you can see where each candidate is performing better or worse than predicted and then make inferences about the forecast error – and, from there, the actual election results – in the rest of the country. The important fact, from a modeling standpoint, is that these cross-sectional errors are in fact correlated and that correlation is part of the model used to make the forecast.

Although interesting as a statistical problem and important to news organizations, election night forecasting is not particularly interesting from a political or economic perspective. It is certainly no surprise that elections can be forecast from partial information, and, in any case, you can always just wait for the morning to find out who won. An exception was the 2000 election, where forecasting models had a sort of afterlife, being used, among other things, to show the implausibility of Patrick Buchanan's vote total in Palm Beach County, Florida (see, for example, Adams 2001).

The example of election forecasting illustrates how similar statistical models can have different social science implications. U.S. presidential elections can be forecast fairly accurately months ahead of time. This implies that campaigns, in aggregate, have little effect and in some ways seems to imply that our vote choices are less the product of free will than we might imagine. Social scientists found similar results decades ago (Converse 1964): From a series of opinion polls they found that voters' preferences were very stable, even across generations; people inherit their political views much as they inherit their religion (or, for that matter, their height and body type). In contrast, the accuracy of election night forecasts, based on a decomposition of vote swings at the national, regional, state, and local levels, is somewhat reassuring in that these forecasts reinforce the idea that the United States is a single political entity but with local characteristics. Once again, similar results have been found in public opinion polls: Page and Shapiro (1992) use the term "parallel publics" to refer to the phenomenon that national changes in opinion tend to occur in parallel throughout different segments of the population. Similar models are used for tracking information in other social sciences but to different ends: for example, the study of individual judgment and decision making in psychology and the study of information flow and communication in economics.

OVERVIEW OF THE BOOK

This book is about mathematical models; ways of understanding quantitative data; concepts of probability, uncertainty, and variation; and sources of historical and current data – all applied to the understanding and solution of social problems. With parts on each of five social sciences – history, economics, sociology, political science, and psychology – we teach by example some of the different ways in which researchers analyze social phenomena using mathematical ideas and quantitative data.

Although this is not a statistics textbook, we refer throughout to the use of statistical methods. Our focus is on the social problems being modeled. Also, we are not attempting to present a unified quantitative view of the social sciences; rather, we favor a more pluralistic approach in which different methods are useful for different problems. This book is intended to make the reader comfortable with the kinds of quantitative thinking used in the different social sciences.

In the next two chapters, I'll present some specific examples in which quantitative modeling or analysis has had an impact. My focus will be on how the mathematical or statistical methods link to the underlying social science. The rest of the book, as noted previously, is divided into separate parts for each of the major social sciences. The parts have little overlap, which is intentional: We want you to see the different perspectives of the different social sciences.

We continue our tour of the social sciences with history. Much of our understanding of history (including the recent and immediate past) is based on numbers, ranging from national statistics on populations, trade balances, public health records, and voting records to data that are important for particular studies such as those on dietary consumption, television ratings, and sports attendance. (In between are data sources such as national opinion polls, which are privately collected but used for public policymaking.) In addition, nonnumerical data can be summarized quantitatively; for example, in the study of a historical debate, contemporary newspaper articles for and against the issue can be counted. Part II of this book begins with a discussion of the historical uses of statistics and then considers various primary sources of quantitative historical data. The lecture material is best supplemented with two kinds of exercises: first, those in which students must collate some historical data (for example, from city property records or old newspapers) and, second, those in which they must read secondary sources and summarize a scholarly debate about some quantitative question with historical implications (for example, the number of people living in the Americas in 1492).

We then move to economics, which is increasingly important in a variety of settings, from private-sector decision making (for example, deciding how seriously a consumer products company should take its sales forecasts) to cost-benefit analyses such as evaluating how much the population is willing to pay for public parkland. Part III begins with a general discussion of the difficulties of understanding and using economic data and then presents three examples of analysis of time series of interest and exchange rates. The focus is not on the particular statistical models being used, but rather on the way in which economic concepts are encoded into the models. All the analysis is done using simple least squares or two-stage least squares, and the key concerns are the predictor variables in the equations and the interpretation of the coefficients. One thing all these examples have in common is that they use macroeconomic data to study the flow of information, which is a major theme in modern economics. Doing the exercises for Part III is a good way to learn data analysis on the computer, starting with simple downloading and plotting of time-series data and then fitting some simple time series and regression models. For the model-fitting exercises, it is important to interpret the coefficients in the model in terms of the motivating economic questions in order to have a good understanding of the theoretical implications of the model

Part IV covers sociology, which in many ways is the most flexible and interdisciplinary of the social sciences. At the theoretical level, sociologists consider a variety of models for social interactions and the roles of individuals in groups, with no single underlying set of principles (unlike in economics). In addition, sociologists often invent new methods of analysis to study unusually structured data (for example, on social networks). Part IV begins with a general discussion of social science theories and the ways in which a single phenomenon can be understood from different theoretical perspectives. It then presents two examples of models for discrete events in which quantitative data are used to understand violent incidents in race relations. For these examples, we discuss the challenges of modeling as well as accurately summarizing historical data. Finally, there is a discussion of models for promotion of employees within large organizations. This sort of analysis can be useful in a wide variety of contexts when studying the fates of individuals within a large social structure. The mathematical ideas used in sociology, such as Markov chains and the Poisson distribution, are not extremely complex, but they are new to many students (who are more likely to be trained in linear regression models). Hence, the exercises for the chapters in Part IV are focused on these models. For example, in one assignment you must come up with a set of count data to which you must fit the Poisson distribution and then comment on any lack of fit of the model.

We continue with Part V on political science, which encompasses both the particular study of individual governmental processes and the general study of political behavior. At a practical level, anyone trying to solve a problem – inside or outside of government – should be aware of the presence of governments at local, state, and national levels, whether as means for solving the problem or as arenas for competing possibilities. More generally, political science – the study of ways to work around conflict – is also relevant in nongovernmental settings. Along with economics, political science as a field can be highly quantitative due to the availability of vast amounts of numerical data (particularly in more industrialized countries) on taxes and spending, voting, and opinion polls. At the same time, political theory can be highly mathematical. Part V contains detailed discussions about how social theories can be constructed so that they can be testable using empirical data. This is followed by specific examples of linear regressions and more sophisticated methods using game theory and Markov chains to model political decision making and voting in committees.

Part VI focuses on psychology, which is both a cognitive and a social science – that is, it studies people's internal processes as well as their interactions with others. Psychology is clearly necessary, at some level, for understanding all social phenomena, since they all are ultimately based on human actions. For example, the laws of micro and macroeconomics and the observed regularities of politics require some sort of consistent behavior, either of individuals or in the aggregate. Part VI starts with a general discussion of theories of human behavior and how these theories can be tested or disproved. It continues with descriptions of some mathematical models of decision making, which in turn suggest where classical economics might be relevant to describing individual behavior and where it might fail. A useful exercise in Chapter 18 is to compare the predictions that several different psychological theories would each make about an actual experiement. Chapter 20 presents some exercises on decision making and the combination of information.

The book concludes with Part VII, a discussion of causal inference in the social sciences. It focuses on the ever-present issue of causal versus spurious relations and discusses the example of estimating the effects of migration on solidarity in migrant-sending communities.

Our chapters go back and forth between general discussions of social science modeling and applied examples that are designed to allow class discussion. The material can be used as a starting point to explore the variety of mathematical and statistical models used in social science, with the ultimate goal of enriching your understanding of the complexities of the social world.

2. What's in a Number? Definitions of Fairness and Political Representation

A key starting point of quantitative social science is *measurement* – which encompasses direct observations from personal interviews and field observations, large-scale data collection efforts such as surveys and censuses, structured observations in designed experiments, and summary measures such as the Consumer Price Index. All these form the raw material for larger social science studies, and it is easy to get lost in these analyses and forget where the numbers came from and, even more importantly, what they represent.

We illustrate the choices involved in numerical measurements in the context of a subject of general interest – how people are represented in a political system – that can be studied both at a theoretical and an empirical level. I want to make the case that quantitative summaries can be helpful, as long as we are aware of the choices that must be made in summarizing a complex situation by a single set of numbers.

We want our political system to represent the voters and treat them fairly. At the simplest procedural level, this means giving a vote to each citizen and deciding elections based on majority or plurality rule. In practice, however, we are not all represented equally by the government, and as long as there is political disagreement, there will be some dissatisfaction. It would be appealing to have a mathematical definition of the amount of citizen "representation." Unfortunately, different measures of representation can interfere with each other, as we discuss with examples from national elections in the United States.

WHAT IS THE MEANING OF POLITICAL REPRESENTATION?

The United States is a representative democracy, and we vote for people who represent us: congressmembers, the president, state legislators and governors, and local officials. Indirectly, through our elected representatives, we vote for the justices of the Supreme Court and other persons in appointed positions.

What does it mean for us to be represented in this political system? For one thing, everyone's vote counts equally, and as a consequence of two Supreme Court rulings in the 1960s, most legislatures are set up so that the number of people living in each district is about the same.[1] (Two important exceptions are the Electoral College and especially the U.S. Senate, both of which overrepresent small states.)

The right to vote could be thought of as a "procedural" aspect of democracy, but what about actual outcomes? Representation can be of individuals or of groups, and both of these perspectives are relevant. For example, suppose you lived in a country where 90% of the voters got what they wanted in the sense that their favored candidates for Congress won. So, 90% of the people are happy on election night (at least for the congressional elections). That's real representation, right? Well, maybe not.

In this scenario, you'll have very few, if any, close elections. For example, maybe the Democrats get 95% of the vote in one district; the Republicans get 88% in another, and so forth. If 90% of the voters get what they want, this can happen mathematically only if almost all the districts have landslide elections. Then, all the seats are "safe," so the congressmembers have no reason to fear the voters. If they fear us, they'll respect us; otherwise, they can ignore us, and then we have no influence at all! (I don't mean to be cynical here. I assume that most politicians are trying to do what's best for the country, but if they think the election might be close, then they will probably worry a bit more about what *we* think is best for the country, too.)

Electorally, to get the benefit of two-party competition, you need competition in the individual districts, not just in the country as a whole. Hence, there is a whole theory of "pivotal votes" (see Gelman, Katz, and Bafumi 2002 for an overview).

How close are actual elections? Figure 2.1 shows histograms of the Democratic share of the two-party vote for elections to the U.S. House of Representatives in 1948 and 1988. Each histogram represents 435 districts and, as you can see, many are noncompetitive (that is, far from 0.5), especially in 1988. This has been studied in different ways (see, for example, Gelman and King 1994), and there has been a trend in the United States in the past few decades for legislative elections to be less close. Much but not all of this trend can be attributed to an increase in incumbency advantage – it's worth about 10% of the vote to be a sitting member of Congress (see Cox and Katz 1996, Erikson 1971, and Gelman and King 1990, among others). Politicians are not stupid, and when they see elections that are less close, they are less worried about keeping the voters happy.

An exception was in 1994, when there was a big swing to Newt Gingrich and the Republicans. But, even then, in most of the country the elections were not close. For example, I was living in Berkeley, California, at the time, and there was no way that a Republican would win there. Poll results sometimes find that most Americans are dissatisfied with Congress as a whole, but they like their local representative; this is sometimes taken as a paradox, but it makes sense, given that most congressional elections are not close (see Figure 2.1).

So far, we've considered three senses of representation: having equal votes, being satisfied with electoral outcomes, and having your vote have the potential to make a difference. Other measures are possible that are perhaps more important politically.

[1] In their book *The End of Inequality*, Stephen Ansolabehere and James Snyder (2008) discuss the changes in U.S. politics that have occurred since congressional and state legislative districts were required to be drawn with equal populations.

U.S. Congressional Districts in 1948

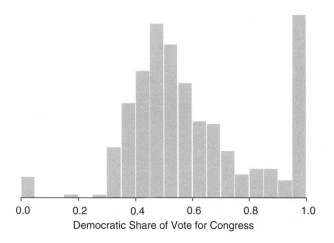

Democratic Share of Vote for Congress

U.S. Congressional Districts in 1988

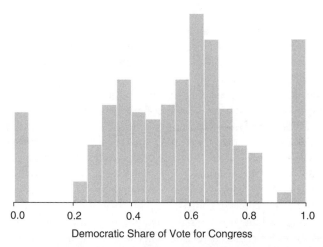

Democratic Share of Vote for Congress

Figure 2.1. Democrats' share of the two-party vote for the 435 elections to the U.S. House of Representatives in 1948 and 1988. (The spikes at the extremes of the graphs represent uncontested elections.) There were relatively few close elections (that is, with vote shares near 0.5) in 1988.

For example, instead of asking if your vote is influential, we could ask if your money is influential. Given the effort put into campaign fund-raising, it is reasonable to suppose that individuals and groups that give more money are better represented by politicians.[2]

---

[2] Thomas Ferguson, in his 1995 book *Golden Rule*, backs this claim with data on campaign contributions from different industries over several decades of elections.

Table 2.1. *Some comparisons of the U.S. population to the U.S. House of Representatives in 1989 and 2006*

	Proportion in U.S. population		Proportion in House of Representatives	
	1989 (%)	2006 (%)	1989 (%)	2006 (%)
Catholic	28	24	27	30
Methodist	4	7	14	12
Jewish	2	1.3	7	6
Black	12	12	9	10
Hispanic	10	15	4	6
Female	51	51	6	16
Under 25	30	34	0	0

Sources: Adapted from King, Bruce, and Gelman (1995); US Census Bureau http://www.census.gov/popest/estimates.php; http://womenincongress.house.gov/data/wic-by-congress.html?cong=109; www.adherents.com; Congressional Research Service (CRS) Report "Black Members of the United States Congress: 1870–2005" available at http://digital.library.unt.edu/govdocs/crs/permalink/meta-crs-7142; http://www.senate.gov/reference/resources/pdf/RS22007.pdf

A completely different notion of representation is demographic: Do your representatives look like you? Table 2.1 shows some data from the U.S. Congress: Representation varies greatly by religious and ethnic group. The most extreme case, lack of representation of the under-twenty-fives, is a consequence of the minimum age requirement in the Constitution.

A related issue is representation by occupation: Many congressmembers are former lawyers and businesspeople and some are former teachers, but not many are former janitors. My colleague from the Netherlands thought it surprising that in the United States, even the Democrats rarely nominate labor union officials for elective office. He said that in Europe, it is considered unseemly for left-wing parties to run white-collar candidates and that such politicians are called "saloon socialists." I said, that's funny, "saloon" sounds pretty down-to-earth. He replied, oh, that's right, it's "salon" socialists.

Another thing to look at is the representation of your political views. Suppose you support abortion rights, a missile defense system, and a higher minimum wage. If all these policies are being implemented, maybe you should feel happy whether or not the candidates you vote for actually win. One could measure this sort of representation using opinion polls and compare the average satisfaction levels of different groups in the population.

FAIRNESS AND REPRESENTATION

What about the representation of political parties? Most of Europe uses proportional representation: If a party gets, say, 20% of the vote, it is given 20% of the seats in the legislature. In some countries, a party that gets only 2% of the votes still receives 2% of the seats. Other countries have a threshold of 5% before a party gets representation; they don't want every group with 1% of the vote to have a representative, screaming, putting chewing gum in the elevators, and generally causing problems in the legislature.

The United States does not have proportional representation. There's a separate election in each congressional district, and whoever wins that election goes to Congress. In theory, a party could get 49% of the vote and still get zero representation – if it got 49% in every district in the country. More realistically, a party could get 45% of the vote and only 40% of the seats or 20% of the vote and no seats. Suppose some unfortunate third party gets 20% of the vote in every district. In one district, the Democrat might receive 42% and the Republican 38%. In another, the Democrat might win 60% while the Republican ties with the third party at 20%. Regardless, the third party loses out.

Some people consider the lack of proportionality to be a defect in our system, with the 20% of the votes that went to the third party wasted, since they did not lead to any representation. Of course, you could also consider the 38% for the Republican candidate as wasted or consider all votes for any losing candidate as wasted. For that matter, you can consider extra votes for a winning candidate as wasted, too – did that person really need 60% of the vote? – but it seems particularly tough on that third party, since *all* of its votes are wasted.

But proportional representation has a problem too: Small changes in the vote produce only small changes in seats for the political parties. This is a problem because swings in votes between national elections are typically only about 5%. In the American (or British) system, a 5% swing in votes can easily produce a 10% swing in seats – enough to possibly change which party controls the legislature. This gave Newt Gingrich and the Republicans control of the House of Representatives in 1994. You might not have been happy with that particular outcome, but it's reassuring that a change in votes has the power to change who rules Congress. Under proportional representation this can happen too, but in a more subtle, less voter-controlled way: Perhaps some minor party increases its vote share from 10% to 15%, and then it can make a deal with another party, ultimately changing the government. The change in votes has an input, but not so directly: The proportional representation system with multiple parties is more like a pinball game where the voters shoot the ball, and then the parties keep it bouncing all by themselves.

VOTES

Amid all this discussion of rules, we shouldn't forget the people being represented. A congressional district in the United States has nearly 700,000 people (the number varies slightly from state to state), of whom perhaps 500,000 are eligible voters (over age eighteen, citizens, nonfelons). So, you can win your very own seat in Congress with 250,000 voters, or 100,000 voters if the turnout is 40%. If the turnout is below 20%, then if you can convince the right 50,000 people to vote for you, you can represent all 700,000 people in the district. According to the Constitution, the elected legislator represents everyone who lives in the district, including those who could not vote, did not vote, or voted for the losing candidate.

But obviously, a politician will be less concerned with the people who did not vote for him or her, whatever the reason.

For that matter, my friends in other countries say that they should get to vote for the president of the United States also, since he has such a large effect on their lives.

INHERENT BIASES OF THE POLITICAL SYSTEM

As we have seen, even if our political system is working perfectly as designed, not all individuals and groups will be treated equally. Children don't get to vote and can't hold political office, even though they are nominally represented in the government. Voters in small states are vastly overrepresented in the U.S. Senate. Votes for minor parties are generally wasted (at least in their direct effects), and, as we have seen, proportional representation creates other problems. And as long as campaigns need money, rich people and better-funded groups can expect disproportionate representation of their political views.

Looking at representation in terms of decisive votes creates other paradoxes. If you want politicians to fight for your vote, then elections have to be close (or at least potentially close), but when an important election actually is close (such as the 2000 presidential election), half of the people will feel unrepresented.

Two other systematic biases that have been studied by political scientists are the "tyranny of the majority" and the "median voter" rule. Majority rule has always been considered dangerous since, for example, 51% of the people could get together and vote to tax the other 49% into poverty (which worried conservatives during the New Deal in the 1930s). The founders of the U.S. Constitution created various checks and balances to slow this trend down, but it is still something of a mystery why the majority in a democratic system is not more tyrannical. Perhaps one reason is that most people do not trust politicians enough to lend them this power.

The median voter rule was formulated by Harold Hotelling in 1929 as an application of a theorem in economics and was developed further in a book by Anthony Downs (1957). We illustrate the basic idea in Figure 2.2: The curve represents the distribution of voters in the electorate, ranging from far left to far right, and the usual positions of the Democratic and Republican candidates are indicated by D and R, respectively. Suppose that any voter will choose the candidate who is ideologically closest to him or her. Then all the voters to the left of the D position will go for the Democrat, all the voters to the right of R will side with the Republican, and the voters in the middle will go for whichever is closest.

In this scenario, the Democrat will gain votes by moving to the right – he or she will still get all the voters on the left and will also gain some votes in the center. Similarly, the Republican should move to the left. Ultimately, the only stable position for the candidates is for them both to be at the position of the median voter (labeled M in Figure 2.2). If either candidate deviates from this position, the other can move to the median and get more votes. This explains why presidential candidates tried to sound moderate. It's not that there are no voters at the extreme; it's just that these extreme voters have nowhere else to go. (In 2000, 2004, and 2008, all the minor-party candidates together got less than 5% of the vote.)

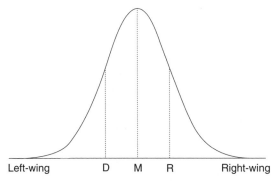

Left-wing   D   M   R   Right-wing

Figure 2.2. Sketch of the theory of voter competition leading to the rule of the median voter. The curve represents the political ideologies of the voters (it is drawn as a bell-shaped curve for convenience but in general can be any distribution). D and R indicate the initial positions of the Democratic and Republican candidates. If all voters turn out and the two candidates have complete ideological flexibility, then they will both end up at the median voter's position, M.

Getting back to representation, this theory suggests that the median voter is strongly represented by the political system, whereas voters away from the center have no representation. This translates into less representation for groups such as African Americans and other ethnic minorities whose political views are far from the center.

In real life, however, Democrats and Republicans do not occupy the same point at the center of the political spectrum, and so the median voter rule does not tell the whole story, as in fact is indicated by the differing initial positions of D and R in Figure 2.2. The differences between parties can be studied in various ways; Figure 2.3 shows some data based on votes in the House of Representatives in 1992. The 435 members of Congress were ranked from left to right based on their roll-call votes (Poole and Rosenthal 1997), and this is plotted versus the liberalness or conservativeness of their districts, as measured by an adjusted version of Bill Clinton's share of the presidential vote in 1992. (The polarization between the two political parties is discussed further in Part V of this book.)

Figure 2.3 shows that Democratic and Republican politicians differ greatly in their ideologies (as measured by their actions in Congress), even after controlling for the political slants of their districts. There are many reasons for this; our point here is that the median voter rule gives some insights into political representation, but it is not completely borne out by the data. Another way to study the influence of median and extreme voters, which we won't get into here, is to look at survey results to see where the positions actually taken by elected politicians fall on the spectrum of public opinion.

DIFFERENT PERSPECTIVES ON REPRESENTATION

Definitions of representation can be categorized in several ways. First, there is the distinction between procedure and outcome. The laws may treat everyone equally, but differences in resources can translate into differences in political power. Second,

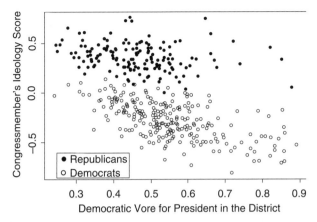

Figure 2.3. Ideology scores (high values are conservative, low values are liberal) for congressmembers in 1992 plotted versus the Democratic proportion of the two-party presidential vote in their districts. (The presidential vote has been corrected for home-state advantage and other effects to yield an estimate of the party's political strength in the district.) Congressmembers in more Democratic-voting districts tend to be more liberal, but there is a dramatic difference between the ideologies of the Democrats. This ideological gap implies that the median voter (see Figure 2.2) is not completely dominant.

one can distinguish between electoral outcomes and ultimate satisfaction with policy. Representation requires political participation at many steps in the political process (see Verba, Schlozman, and Brady 1995). And one can study many levels of government, including local, state, and national, as well as quasi-governmental organizations such as public corporations. We're used to thinking of government as one thing and private enterprise as another, but there's a lot of discussion in the social sciences about how these categories blur. On the one hand, areas of government can act like private businesses – sometimes in a good way, by serving customer demand and allocating resources, and sometimes less beneficially to the public interest, for example by charging the taxpayer for no-bid construction projects. On the other hand, large corporations and labor unions are like governments in that they must balance many different internal interests, and on a personal level they can provide a promise of security that is one of the traditional functions of government. Business, consumer, or special-interest lobbying groups are generally unelected but claim to represent interests in the political process. Internationally, nongovernmental organizations such as the World Bank serve some of the roles of government, but it is not always clear whom they represent.

More fundamentally, representation can be defined in relative or absolute terms. Fairness requires that any person or group be represented just as much as any other, but on an absolute scale it is possible for all the citizens of a country to be more or less represented by its political system. (And, to return to our earlier concerns, it is possible for people to get what they want politically without representation or for well-represented groups to be dissatisfied.)

What's best for you individually might not be best for your group. For example, maybe you would rather not pay taxes, but if nobody pays taxes, we're all in trouble. This is also true of representation. We'd all like to have more influence over government policy, but at some point it's mathematically impossible – there are more than 300 million of us, and we can't all be decisive. And, as we discussed in the context of proportional representation, a system that seems fair in one way can reduce representation in others. Political theorists have been struggling with these questions for millennia (see Beitz 1990 for a review).

From the standpoint of quantitative social science, it is interesting to see how empirical data, in conjunction with theoretical ideas, can be used to get a better perspective on some issues of representation. Once we go beyond the search for a single numerical measure of fairness, we can study how our institutions represent us, both individually and as groups. When crunching numbers, it's easy to get stuck worrying about relatively minor aspects of the political system, such as gerrymandering and the allocation of congressional seats, and forget about more systematic ways in which people get more or less of a say in their collective institutions.

3. The Allure and Limitations of Mathematical Modeling: Game Theory and Trench Warfare

We conclude the first part of this book with a critical overview of an application of mathematical theory to a problem in history – a game-theoretic model that was developed more than twenty years ago to describe some surprising behavior in the trenches in the First World War. As we shall see, the model is appealing because it seems to bring some sense to a scary and confusing subject. However, ultimately, I find this particular analysis unconvincing, and I'll talk about why such a model, if wrong, was so persuasive. This is an important step in social science analysis, inside or outside the academic setting: If you're going to claim that you're right and other people are wrong, you'd better also explain why those other people (who were generally not fools) got it wrong. Scholarly journals are littered with proudly "counterintuitive" findings that are counterintuitive for the simple reason that they are wrong and most people's intuition is right.

THE PRISONER'S DILEMMA: A GAME-THEORETIC MODEL APPLIED TO SOCIAL INTERACTIONS

Mathematical theory can be a powerful tool for understanding social phenomena but can also mislead, as I'll illustrate with an example from my undergraduate thesis, which was in political science. At the beginning of my senior year in college, I reviewed a list of potential advisors and found one who worked on game theory – I was a physics and mathematics major, minoring in political science, and game theory seemed like a good topic. My advisor handed me *The Evolution of Cooperation*, a then-recent book on game theory, society, and evolution, written by Robert Axelrod (1984). Nowadays, books on evolution and social science – sociobiology – are commonplace, but this book, written by a political scientist and published in 1984, was one of the first and was extremely well received in the general and scholarly press.

I'll describe this example in detail to illustrate how mathematical ideas – in this case, of game theory – can be applied to real social and historical problems. In addition to illustrating the power of mathematical modeling, this example shows some of its weaknesses. (I would summarize Axelrod's book as a valuable theoretical argument with fundamental flaws in its applications.) Finally, we'll explore the political implications of explaining human actions quantitatively. Is it possible to use mathematics to gain insight without surrendering the political equivalent of free will?

The fundamental problem Axelrod was studying is *cooperation*. From a psychological or economic point of view, why do people cooperate with each other (instead of acting purely selfishly, which would give them short-term benefits, at the very least)? A historian might study cooperation as it has existed in past societies, and a sociologist might consider the settings in which individuals assume cooperative and noncooperative roles. From a political science perspective, the natural question is how to *promote* cooperation – behavior that is essential to the functioning of any political system to avoid a Hobbesian war of all against all. (In the 1640s, Thomas Hobbes wrote *Leviathan*, the classic analysis of political life arising from a brutal state of nature.)

From a game-theoretic standpoint, cooperation has always been viewed as a puzzle, and this puzzle has been given various names. The "free rider problem" refers to the logical motivation of any individual to sit lazily while the heavy lifting is done by others. In a political context, free riding might mean avoiding voting, paying taxes, or military service. The "tragedy of the commons" (Hardin 1968) describes what happens when people behave selfishly – for example, consuming more than their fair share of resources or polluting a common water supply – under the expectation that they might as well act selfishly, since others will do so if they do not. A classic example is overfishing; any given fisher will want to catch as many fish as possible, but if this happens, then all the fish will be caught and everybody loses. Both the free rider problem and the tragedy of the commons have the following properties: (1) if everyone behaves cooperatively, then they will all do well, (2) any individual will do even better by behaving selfishly, but (3) if all (or even many) individuals behave selfishly, all will suffer – even the selfish ones. Social scientists often refer to this as a "prisoner's dilemma game" by analogy to a different cooperation problem that we will not go into here (see the Axelrod book for details if you'd like, or Maurer and Tucker [1983] for the history of the term, which is due to Albert Tucker).

Table 3.1 shows a formal expression of the shared-commons or prisoner's dilemma. The key question here is, why do people cooperate at all in situations like this or, to reframe it more constructively, how can we develop social systems to encourage cooperation? In the long term, cooperation makes sense, but in the short term, it pays to not cooperate. How can cooperative short-term behavior occur? Several answers have been suggested. People are more comfortable cooperating with people they know, and this has been studied experimentally by economists and psychologists (see Dawes, De Kragt, and Orbell 1988). In situations where cooperation is important (for example, in a business) or even a matter of life and death (for example, in the military), it is considered crucial to create a team spirit.

However, in other settings, most notably in the economic sphere (recall the overfishing example), the incentives to not cooperate are so strong that psychological motivation does not seem enough. Cooperation can then be enforced through governmental action or private binding agreements (which themselves typically require governmental presence to be enforceable). Economists refer to these situations where cooperative behavior requires outside enforcement as

Table 3.1. *Game-theoretic expression of the prisoner's dilemma*

Payoff matrix for Player 1				Payoff matrix for Player 2			
	Player 2 cooperates?				Player 2 cooperates?		
		Yes	No			Yes	No
Player 1	Yes	+5	−10	Player 1	Yes	+5	+10
cooperates?	No	+10	−5	cooperates?	No	−10	−5

This table expresses the so-called prisoner's dilemma in a game-theoretic framework. Each of two players has the option to cooperate or not, and their payoffs are determined by the actions of both players.

First, consider Player 1's payoff matrix: He or she has no control over Player 2's action. If Player 2 *cooperates*, Player 1 will do better by not cooperating (thus giving a payoff of +10 rather than +5). If Player 2 *does not cooperate*, Player 1 will do better by not cooperating (thus giving a payoff of −5 rather than −10). Thus, whether or not Player 2 will cooperate, Player 1 is better off not cooperating.

Now look at Player 2's payoff matrix: This player also is better off not cooperating, no matter what Player 1 does. So, the optimal action for each player is to not cooperate.

But now consider both payoff matrices together. If both players do not cooperate, then they will each get a payoff of −5. But if they both cooperate, then they would each get +5. Here is the dilemma: If each player acts in his or her best interest, then they will both be worse off. However, if the two players can communicate in some way, then they can perhaps agree in advance and get the benefits of cooperation.

"externalities." (For elaboration on this concept, see, for example, *The Economist's View of the World* by Steven Rhoads [1985].)

Axelrod's interest was slightly different, however. Rather than study settings where cooperation is automatic or where it needs outside enforcement, he was interested in intermediate scenarios in which cooperative behavior was risky and unstable but developed anyway. This seems to describe many human interactions: When the rules break down, people can act brutally, but stable societies are greased by a layer of trust.

In his book, Axelrod made a three-part argument. First, at the level of pure game theory, he argued – and presented evidence for the claim – that a strategy called "tit for tat" (TFT) was effective in a game consisting of repeated plays of the prisoner's dilemma. (The TFT strategy is defined as follows: Begin by cooperating, and then at each step do what your opponent did in the previous step.) Second, Axelrod argued that this strategy was effective in important real-life settings where these games arise. His central example was the behavior of soldiers in trench warfare in the First World War (an example perhaps chosen because it is well documented and was a relatively stable system for years, which would presumably allow things to settle into equilibrium states if there were any). The third step of Axelrod's argument was evolutionary: Because TFT was effective, it would be natural for organisms that developed this strategy to survive and reproduce; hence, one would expect this strategy to prevail in nature. But there's an interesting twist here: In this game scenario, TFT becomes more effective as more players use it. The evolutionary process thus has an accelerating aspect: Once the strategy becomes commonly used in a population, it can become dominant. As we will discuss, TFT can be viewed as a strategy of cooperation, hence the title of Axelrod's book, *The Evolution of Cooperation*.

AXELROD'S APPLICATION OF THE PRISONER'S DILEMMA TO TRENCH WARFARE

Axelrod looked at trench warfare in the First World War, which, as detailed in the fascinating 1980 book by Tony Ashworth (*Trench Warfare, 1914–1918: The Live and Let Live System*), had ongoing examples of cooperative behavior amid a violent, anticooperative structure. The soldiers in the two opposing armies can be considered as two players in a game, in which at each step a player can cooperate by *not* shooting at the other side. Axelrod's basic argument goes as follows: At each step, a player is better off if he does not cooperate (that is, if he shoots), since this has the chance of eliminating an enemy soldier. However, if both sides were somehow to agree to cooperate, then they would both be better off, since none of them would be shot. Empirically, the two sides *did* in fact cooperate despite the many obstacles placed in their path. I'll briefly describe the story of the trench warfare cooperation (as related by Ashworth in great detail) and then return to the game-theoretic analysis.

The First World War started in the summer of 1914 when the Germans invaded Belgium. By the late fall of that year, the war on the Western Front (France and Belgium) had stabilized and the two sides (the Germans and their allies on one side, the French and British and their allies on the other) were facing each other behind trenches. The soldiers were expected to shoot at each other from the trenches but in many instances avoided doing so, and Christmas 1914 featured many instances of the two sides meeting peacefully between their front lines. As described by Ashworth, the commanders on both sides did not like this and ordered the soldiers to shoot at each other. At some point, this pattern also switched to cooperation in many places, with soldiers shooting to miss on purpose (and at the same time demonstrating their ability to do harm by aiming at precise targets). Throughout the war, the commanders tried different strategies – for example, rotating troops more quickly in and out of the front lines – to stop the troops from getting friendly with the enemy. The most effective strategy appeared to be sending the soldiers on raids into the enemy trenches. This put them in a kill-or-be-killed situation in which cooperation was essentially impossible.

This pattern – soldiers who do not want to fight and commanders who force them to do so – has been reported throughout history, as has been noted by example, officers in the Napoleonic Wars stood behind their troops with bayonets to force them toward the enemy. In the Second World War, a famous study by Colonel S. L. A. Marshall estimated that only one-quarter of the U.S. soldiers in a position to fire their rifles actually did so (although this finding has been questioned; see Spiller 1988). This behavior has been attributed to fear and a sense of isolation, as well as simple self-preservation, since firing your gun can make you a target.

Now we return to Axelrod's argument, which is an attempt to explain theoretically the cooperation described by Ashworth. Given the immediate risks of cooperation, how did the soldiers so often develop cooperative social structures without the possibility of binding agreements? Axelrod suggests that they were following the TFT strategy: starting by cooperating and then continuing to cooperate as long as cooperation took place on the other side. In the trench warfare example, this means: Do not shoot until your opponent shoots. If your opponent shoots, shoot back, but then stop shooting if he stops.

In the terminology of game theory, TFT works because trench warfare is a "repeated-play" game. In a single play, the dominant strategy is noncooperation – that is the essence of the tragedy of the commons or the prisoner's dilemma. But when the game is played repeatedly, it is beneficial to establish a pattern of cooperation, a point that Axelrod illustrated with a simulation in which, out of a large selection of game strategies, TFT performed best. The simulation was performed in an "evolutionary" way, with the more successful strategies "reproducing" to reflect the popularity of success, and TFT performed even better as time went on and the alternative, noncooperative strategies diminished in the population.

To summarize the argument: Soldiers spontaneously developed cooperation strategies despite the short-term advantages of shooting at the enemy. This behavior is "explained" or at least can be modeled by a repeated-play prisoner's dilemma game, in which cooperative strategies will grow to dominate. With a large population of such players, the norm of cooperation becomes stable, to the extent that, in the First World War, commanders had to actually change the rules of the game (for example, by forcing soldiers to make raids) in order to eliminate cooperative behavior. This argument is appealing because it explains otherwise baffling behavior (how did the soldiers develop the norm of cooperation without the ability to communicate directly or make agreements?) and also, from a moral point of view, it gives some hope that cooperation might be possible in a hostile world.

WHY TRENCH WARFARE IS ACTUALLY *NOT* A PRISONER'S DILEMMA

Having presented Axelrod's argument, I'd like to tell you why I think it's wrong. The key assumption in his model is that an individual soldier benefits, in the short term, from firing at the enemy. (In the notation of the payoff matrices displayed earlier, to cooperate is to avoid firing, and the model assumes that, whatever the soldiers on the other side do, you are better off firing, that is, not cooperating.) Thus, elaborate game-theoretic modeling is needed to understand why this optimal short-term behavior is not followed. In fact, however, it seems more reasonable to suppose that, as a soldier in the trenches, you would do better to *avoid* firing: Shooting your weapon exposes you as a possible target, and the enemy soldiers might very well shoot back at the place where your shot came from (a point mentioned by S. L. A. Marshall). If you have no short-term motivation to fire, then cooperation is completely natural and requires no special explanation. This is an example of a sophisticated mathematical model being created to explain behavior that is perfectly natural. In fact, if any games are being played, they are between the soldiers and the commanders on each side of the front line, with many of the soldiers avoiding combat and the commanders trying to enforce it.

If the explanation of cooperative behavior in the trenches is indeed so obvious, then how could a researcher as clever and well read as Axelrod get it so wrong (and how could his book have been so widely praised)? To start with, in any theoretical formulation there is a natural bias toward conventional roles. In game theory, it is usual to think of the two sides in a war as opponents. And, indeed, in the grand strategy of the First World War, this might be reasonable (although even this is complicated, since it has been argued that France lost the war by winning it). But on the front line, it is not at all clear that shooting an individual German would help a given British soldier.

Another reason why Axelrod might have been led to construct his complicated model is that, historically speaking, cooperation among soldiers on opposite sides of a battle has been unusual, and thus an elaborate explanation might seem to be required. However, this does not really address the question of whether his fundamental assumptions are reasonable. From the perspective of game theory, other models such as coordination games might be more appropriate (see, for example, Snidal 1985). In fact, the very stability of cooperation in First World War trenches, and the fact that the commanders had to devise elaborate schemes to thwart it, argues for the claim that joint cooperative behavior was a stable solution to the "game" for soldiers on both sides, and thus it was no prisoner's dilemma at all.

Maybe I've convinced you that Axelrod was wrong, maybe not – if you're interested, you should read his book and judge for yourself. In any case, we have a debate: Some scholars characterize trench warfare as a prisoner's dilemma game and attribute cooperation to its evolutionary benefits in repeated-play games. Others model trench warfare as a setting in which both sides benefit in the immediate sense from cooperation, so that no subtle game-theoretic models are needed to explain it (although, as a practical necessity, some coordination is needed to establish the exact forms of cooperation, as described by Ashworth). More realistically, any serious model would have to allow for individual variation in behavior at the level of the individual soldiers and of groups: Some entire sectors of the front featured cooperation and others did not.

POLITICAL IMPLICATIONS OF THE HISTORICAL STUDY

Does this matter? How does a difference in opinion about game theory affect our understanding of military or social behavior? In some ways, not at all – we are all trying to explain the same facts. But, of course, I would like to argue that the mathematical model and its interpretation do matter. As always, arguments about history are often really about the present and the future. If you really believe the prisoner's dilemma and the TFT story, then you are characterizing the soldiers on the two sides of the First World War as fundamentally opponents, who avoided shooting at each other only because of long-term calculations based on repeated encounters.

Looking toward the future, how can we achieve more cooperation in real-life tragedies of the commons such as environmental devastation and international arms races? Axelrod's logic suggests that we should look for ways to set up these situations as repeated-play games so that participants have long-term motivations to cooperate. A more skeptical approach might be to set up immediate gains from cooperation and to watch out for outside agents (such as the commanders in the trench warfare example) who have motive and opportunity to disrupt the cooperative behavior.

We conclude our discussion of this example with a question: What are the political implications of Axelrod's theory? At one level, the theory looks "liberal," both in the so-called classical or nineteenth-century sense of respecting individual action (that is, in contrast to classical "conservative" political theory, which favors tradition) and in the more recent American sense of supporting cooperative behavior. The story goes as follows: It's a cold world out there, with payoff matrices that favor noncooperation, but with multiple plays of the prisoner's dilemma game, if everyone acts in his or her long-term interest, virtue (in the sense of cooperation or, in the warfare setting, nonviolence) will be rewarded. This appears to be an intriguing synthesis of classical and modern liberal ideas.

However, in another sense, Axelrod's game-theoretic model is fundamentally conservative, because it accepts the assumption that the soldiers on the two sides of the trenches had an immediate motivation to shoot at each other. His recommendation for cooperation and peacemaking is to accept existing conflicts and work within their structure, rather than to suggest, as a liberal might, that these conflicts exist only because the commanders of the armies are exercising unchecked power.

I don't mean to imply any claim about Axelrod's personal beliefs here. His book was, and perhaps continues to be, influential, and I suspect that one reason for its success is that it appears to supply a theoretical and empirical justification of the liberal idea of cooperation. Since at least the days of Machiavelli and continuing to the present time, political theory has often leaned toward the position that individuals and nations must pursue their own self-interests (see Miller 1999 for a perspective from psychology). From this perspective, Axelrod's argument came as a welcome relief: a rigorous justification of altruistic behavior. But, at least in the trench warfare example, his logic is unnecessarily complicated, and in fact cooperation may have occurred for much more direct reasons.

In summary, some carefully documented history of the First World War revealed the surprising fact that soldiers on the Western Front routinely avoided fighting. This finding inspired quantitative modeling. The evolutionary repeated-play formulation of the prisoner's dilemma is a model – a logical story expressed in mathematics – showing how cooperative behavior can arise and thrive in an initially hostile environment. The model is interesting in its own right, but before applying it to warfare or other conflict settings, one should check whether its basic premise applies. If cooperation (not fighting) has short-term benefits – as it often does – then the prisoner's dilemma does not apply.

CRITICAL COMMENTS

A collegial element of academic research is that you can send an article to a high-quality peer-reviewed journal and get anonymous comments from experts in the field. I sent this chapter to the journal *Sociological Theory* and heard back from three reviewers. I will share with you the substance of the reviewers' comments on my anti-Axelrod thesis, along with my responses to their criticisms. The comments were valuable, and by including this give-and-take here in the book, I hope to show how social science research proceeds through critical exchanges.

The first reviewer agreed with my analysis of individual-level motivations and behavior of soldiers but pointed out that Axelrod's game-theoretic analysis is at the level of battalions rather than individual soldiers. That is, it is in a battalion's interest to reduce the numbers of the enemy; hence, a prisoner's dilemma arises at that level. This reviewer referred me to articles by Gibbons (1998) and Prendergast (1999) on incentives within organizations as a pointer toward a more careful study of the relations between the soldiers and their commanders on each side.

The second reviewer picked up on my statement that soldiers in the trenches have no short-term motivation to fire because enemy soldiers might very well shoot back at the place where the shot came from. The reviewer concludes that "soldiers develop an interest in developing cooperative strategies because the game is repeated. This is the thrust of Axelrod's argument."

The third reviewer objected to my arguments about the political implications of Axelrod's model. Without accepting or rejecting the political arguments, the reviewer wrote, "cut the stuff about the politics of Axelrod's theory – who cares, since it has no impact on whether he is right or wrong."

RESPONSE TO CRITICISMS

I will now sketch my reply to these comments. This reply cannot be seen as definitive – for one thing, the anonymous reviewers have not had a chance to reply back – but I hope it gives some sense of the ways in which different social scientists can have different perspectives on a single problem.

For a game to be a prisoner's dilemma in an interesting sense – for it to be worthy of the extended treatment of Axelrod, for example – the gain from not cooperating must be meaningfully bigger than the gain from cooperating. The "dilemma" arises because the player – the "prisoner" – recognizes that it would be in both players' interest to cooperate, but noncooperation is irresistible (at least from a short-term logical standpoint) because of its greater payoff. For example, in Table 3.1 earlier in this chapter, noncooperation gives a consistent 5-point benefit to either player, no matter what the other player does.

In contrast, an individual soldier on the Western Front had a *negative* gain from shooting – that is, not cooperating – because by shooting, the soldier would expose himself personally to enemy fire. For a battalion, the gain from shooting was arguably positive – a small chance of weakening the enemy position – but small compared to the risk of being shot at. Tables 3.2 and 3.3 illustrate hypothetical payoff matrices in these games. For the single soldier, Table 3.2 shows no benefit from noncooperation and thus no decision dilemma. For the battalion, Table 3.3 shows a slight dilemma, with noncooperation giving a benefit of 0.1 at any point. In this case, a small amount of coordination is required to secure mutual cooperation, and Axelrod's analysis is somewhat relevant. Point taken. However, I would argue that the prisoner's dilemma aspect of this situation is small, especially given that,

Table 3.2. *Possible payoff matrix for soldiers on the Western Front in the First World War (Player 1: British soldier, Player 2: German soldier)*

Payoff matrix for Player 1				Payoff matrix for Player 2			
		Player 2 cooperates?				Player 2 cooperates?	
		Yes	No			Yes	No
Player 1	Yes	+5	−10	Player 1	Yes	+5	+4.9
cooperates?	No	+4.9	−10.1	cooperates?	No	−10	−10.1

Noncooperation hurts the other player and also slightly hurts oneself. Hence there is no prisoner's dilemma; mutual cooperation is a dominant short-term and long-term strategy.

Table 3.3. *Possible payoff matrix for battalions on the Western Front in the First World War (Player 1: British battalion, Player 2: German battalion)*

Payoff matrix for Player 1				Payoff matrix for Player 2			
		Player 2 cooperates?				Player 2 cooperates?	
		Yes	No			Yes	No
Player 1	Yes	+5	−10	Player 1	Yes	+5	+5.1
cooperates?	No	+5.1	−9.9	cooperates?	No	−10	−9.9

Noncooperation hurts the other player but slightly helps oneself. Here there is a prisoner's dilemma, but of a very weak form. It would take only a small amount of caution for a player to resist the short-term benefit of 0.1 in order to reach the desired point of mutual competition.

for the individual soldier, it is still less risky to simply not shoot (in the absence of coercion from his commanders). Axelrod in his book did recognize the importance of coercion, but I think he was too tied to the prisoner's dilemma perspective to step back and consider the payoffs for the individual soldier.

The second reviewer claimed that reluctance to shoot – a soldier not firing because it puts him at risk of the enemy firing back at him – is exactly an instance of the repeated-play prisoner's dilemma game described by Axelrod. As emphasized previously, for a game to be a prisoner's dilemma, the *immediate gain* from noncooperation must be positive. That is, there must be a short-term temptation to not cooperate, which will be moderated only by strategic considerations. For an individual soldier in a trench, it was a short-term risk to stand up and shoot, hence no prisoner's dilemma. According to Ashworth's book, that was how things were until the rules of the game were changed by forcing soldiers to make raids on the enemy trenches.

Finally, the third reviewer criticized my speculations about the political motivations and implications of Axelrod's model. Here, all I can say is that different people care about different things. The reviewer cared only "whether [Axelrod] is right or wrong," whereas for me, given that I am already skeptical about the applicability of this particular model to trench warfare, I would like to understand why the model was so well received and what its implications are for resolving future conflicts. Given the popularity of Axelrod's book and the fact that I am no expert on trench warfare, you are welcome to come to the parsimonious conclusion that he was right and I was wrong (thus agreeing with the second reviewer of my article) or that he was right and so am I, but we are describing different problems (thus agreeing with the first and third reviewers). In a theoretical and historical study such as this, it is difficult to come to any more definitive conclusion. This is one reason why game theorists often like to study experimental results (typically on college students) so that hypotheses can be formulated, tested, and sometimes rejected and revised. But that is beyond the scope of our example here.

IDEAS FROM SEVERAL SOCIAL SCIENCES

The trench warfare example is appropriate for this book because it brings together ideas from several social sciences. To start with, the analysis relies on a detailed *historical* study of soldiers in the First World War. The game-theoretic model falls under the category of *political science*, but similar models are used in *economics* to study strategies in commercial interactions. More realistic models of battlefield behavior rely again on historical studies but also on *sociological* concepts of the roles of soldiers and their interactions with officers. Finally, the reactions of individual soldiers are essentially *psychological*, involving decisions and trade-offs as well as more immediate reactions related to personal safety and group cohesion. All these concerns underlie Axelrod's book, along with my criticism of it and the reviewers' criticism of my work in turn.

FURTHER READING FOR PART I

On the Topics Discussed in this Part of the Book

My discussion of workers' compensation, the value of a life, and hedonic regression was drawn from Dorman (1996); other work on this topic includes the article by Dorman and Hagstrom (1998) and, for a less skeptical view of the use of wage differentials to estimate risk preferences, Viscusi and Aldy (2003) and Costa and Kahn (2004).

For more on election forecasting, see Rosenstone (1983), Campbell and Garand (1999), Wlezien and Erikson (2004), and the references therein. Gelman and King (1993) discuss some of the political implications of the existence of accurate election forecasts. Page and Shapiro (1992) consider the stability of public opinion in the United States.

The material in Chapter 2 on fairness and political representation comes from Gelman (2002); see Beitz (1990) for a more theoretical perspective on the topic and Verba et al. (1995) for empirical evidence of aspects of inequality in political participation in the United States. For more on political polarization and the relevance of median voter arguments to modern American politics, see chapters 8 and 9 of Gelman et al. (2008).

Chapter 3, most of which appears as Gelman (2008), is an extended discussion of Axelrod (1984), a book with a clear description of the prisoner's dilemma model and its motivation. The historical work underlying the trench warfare example comes from Ashworth (1980). For further background on game theory, *Games and Decisions* (Luce and Raiffa 1989) remains my favorite book. More generally,

Miller (1999) criticizes the assumption of selfishness that is implicit in many social science models of rational behavior. For a stronger view, see Green and Shapiro (1994) along with the discussions, from various perspectives, in the volume edited by Friedman (1996). Edlin, Gelman, and Kaplan (2007) presents our own attempt to model rational political behavior (in this case, voting and political participation), explicitly removing the assumption that rationality requires selfishness. See also Quiggin (1987) and Fowler (2006).

On Social Science in General

In recommending some readings in the individual social sciences, we recognize that these few sources can only give an incomplete picture of a vast and changing landscape. The following books are focused on individual social sciences, but with a common focus on ways of learning from observation and ways of evaluating social science theories and models:

- *In Defense of History* (Evans 2000) is a readable overview of controversies within the historical profession, with an extensive list of references of its own.
- *The Economist's View of the World* (Rhoads 1985) gives a political scientist's view of the strengths and weaknesses of economists' way of thinking, and as such serves as a handy introduction to both fields.
- *Invitation to Sociology* (Berger 1963) considers and compares several different approaches to understanding social interaction.
- *How to Think Straight about Psychology* (Stanovich 2004) discusses the successes and failures of different schools of psychological thought.

I also recommend *Judgment under Uncertainty* (edited by Kahneman, Slovic, and Tversky 1982), which has some great examples of interdisciplinary work, centered on cognitive psychology but with implications for other social sciences.

On Statistical Methods in the Social Sciences

The Statistical Sleuth by Ramsey and Schafer (2001) is a good place to start learning about data analysis. For practical advice on fitting models in R and Stata (our preferred statistical packages), we recommend *An R and S-Plus Companion to Applied Regression* by John Fox (2002) and Rabe-Hesketh and Everitt's (2003) *Handbook of Statistical Analyses Using Stata*. For more depth on regression modeling and analysis of variance, you could look at the book by Gelman and Hill, *Data Analysis Using Applied Regression and Multilevel/Hierarchical Models* (2007). I also recommend two influential and thought-provoking books on statistical graphics by William Cleveland (1985, 1993): *The Elements of Graphing Data* and *Visualizing Data*.

Moving from data analysis to data collection, the book by Groves and his colleagues (2004), *Survey Methodology*, offers a comprehensive overview of the topic; if you have specific statistical questions on the design and analysis of survey data, you can turn to Sharon Lohr's (1999) *Sampling: Design and Analysis* for specific statistical questions on the design and analysis of survey data. Don Campbell and Julian Stanley's (1963) book, *Experimental and Quasi-Experimental Designs for Research*, remains an excellent overview of the design and analysis of experiments and observational studies. *News That Matters* by Shanto Iyengar and Donald Kinder (1987) is an interesting example of an experiment applied to an area that is usually studied observationally.

Finally, a key challenge in social science research is connecting qualitative and quantitative methods. Books such as Babbie's (2003) *The Practice of Social Research* review both qualitative and quantitative research methods.

All seven parts of the present book illustrate the interplay between qualitative and quantitative ideas. So far, we have discussed applying cost-benefit calculations to life and death; probabilistic forecasting to capture uncertainty in economics and politics; numerical measures of fairness; and game-theoretic models of the non-zero-sum nature of combat. The remaining parts of this book focus to different extents on the qualitative sources underlying our social science data and the models and methods used to understand them.

Exercises for Part I

1. Drawing from an example in a recent news article, show how you could have set up models to forecast this outcome one day, three weeks, two months, and two years before it occurred. Describe the data sources you would need to make these forecasts. What problems might you encounter in setting up these forecasts?
2. Consider different definitions of representation in some social setting other than elected government. It should be a setting with which you are familiar (for example, your high school, your place of work, your child's Scout troop, a professional organization to which you belong). Identify the people with a stake in this organization and list as many different ways as you can think of that they are represented.
   How could you measure the representation of different individuals and groups in your organization?
3. Find an article in the popular or scholarly press that contains quantitative historical data. Answer the following questions: Which person or what group benefits most from the data as presented? Could the data be collected in a different way to alter the conclusions of the article? If no numerical data were presented, how would or could that affect the conclusions of the article?
4. Drawing from an example in a recent news article, show how you could cast a situation as a problem of the commons or a prisoner's dilemma. Is it a single-play or a repeated-play game? Who are the players in the game, what is the payoff matrix, and what would be a tit-for-tat strategy in this scenario?

What strategies are being applied by the players in the real-life "game"? Would tit-for-tat be effective?

PART II. HISTORY

Herbert S. Klein and Charles Stockley*

* Stylistically, first-person singular is used in the text to maintain the lecture format even though that both authors contributed equally to the development of this part.

4. Historical Background of Quantitative Social Science

QUANTIFICATION AND THE RISE OF THE WEST

The origins of quantification in social thought reach far back into history. Numbers are found in the classical Greek texts as well as in traditional Indian, Chinese, and Islamic texts, but the sort of quantitative analysis that we are particularly interested in is a European invention that has flourished in the past few centuries and whose roots go back to the Middle Ages. I'll be referring to an interesting work by Alfred Crosby (1997), who asks, why do we count, and do Europeans count differently from everybody else? Did they start at a different time than everybody else, and if so, why? Crosby studies quantification in Western society from 1250 to 1600, and he incidentally sheds light on another of the great debates in history: Why did Europe conquer or expand over the rest of the world? It should not have occurred. Europe in 1500 was not the wealthiest area in the world, nor was it the most advanced area economically, nor did it have the most advanced technology at the time. It was in fact a relatively backward zone of world civilization. Nonetheless, Europeans conquered the world's sea lanes and became the dominant world powers until the twentieth century. Europeans did not merely touch on areas of the world unknown to them and then move on. After all, the Chinese had junks trading on the East African coast long before the Portuguese reached the West African coast. The big difference was that unlike the voyagers from other civilizations, once the Europeans arrived, they just kept coming, and if the Portuguese faltered, the Spanish were right behind them, and if the Spanish faltered, the English, the French, and the Dutch were behind them. The Europeans drew maps, published accounts, and generally made their information about routes, peoples, and trading activity available first to their own nationals and then to all others, always keeping careful log books and detailed accounts. That they continued to expand upon each discovery after 1400 and eagerly adapted to innovations probably had a lot to do with their state and their economic organization, but it also had to do with their way of quantifying and visualizing the world.

Historians have provided various answers to the question of why Europeans, after 1500, began to spill out of their little corner of Eurasia and spread across the face of the globe. Some economic historians say that Europe's high savings rate was the driving factor. Other historians highlight the peculiarities of the political organization of Europe. Crosby (1997) argues that equally fundamental was the fact that the Europeans had a different worldview. Their take on reality was quite different from everyone else's. He goes through music and art, and even looks at Scholasticism and finds much of interest there, like the origin of the index and of the footnote. Most importantly, he looks at how people counted. He points out that the Europeans invented almost nothing. Our numbers are Arabic; the zero is Indian. Nevertheless, the Europeans became addicted to counting and to mechanical toys too: Crosby devotes a good deal of space to the discussion of the mechanical clock, which, of course, wasn't even invented in Europe. The windmill was one of the few native European mechanical innovations, but the Europeans, nevertheless, went all out in the application of new technologies, even if they had been invented elsewhere. Crosby argues that this is evidence that the Europeans had begun to look at the world differently from other civilizations. The introduction of perspective in painting, he finds, is another clue that the European worldview tended toward the mathematical, measurable, and precise. At about this same time, the Europeans abandoned the Roman numerical system in favor of the Arabic. Crosby sees these changes in techniques as outward signs of an epochal cultural and intellectual change.

Crosby's book does not, of course, resolve the debate over why the Europeans spread over the globe and why they came to be technologically superior, but it nonetheless gives the interesting argument that the key change was in how Europeans came to see the world as measurable, quantifiable, and, ultimately, amenable to the manipulations of ever more ingenious technological innovations. Perhaps there is a uniquely Western way of perceiving the world. This interest in cataloging, categorizing, and organizing the world seemed for centuries to set Europe apart from the rest of the world and give it an advantage.

THE POLITICS OF NUMBERS: AN EXAMPLE
FROM THE AFRICAN SLAVE TRADE

But what of the numbers used in historical research? Can historians resolve issues through numerical analysis? I will argue that they can. Let me begin with a major contemporary debate about how many Africans crossed the Atlantic. This question is the occasion for a sometimes acrimonious and often highly politicized debate. The numbers range from about 10 million to about 100 million or even higher. These numbers have all sorts of political implications and often serve as background to many contemporary debates on race and ethnic politics in the United States. Can we derive some coherent set of numbers? One way has been to use known population growth rates to estimate what must have been the original populations of Africans in various parts of the New World. This estimation, based on birth and death estimates for slave and free colored populations, along with some preliminary work on shipping, was used by Philip Curtin (Curtin 1969) to generate a roughly 10 to 12 million population migration figure.

Many historians rejected these numbers as too low, and the debate raged for years without serious resolution. But in the past several decades, historians were able to generate enormous datasets of actual voyages from African,

European, and American archives. From the surviving archives, you can estimate what mortality was like on the voyages by having information on those who left Africa and the numbers who died during the crossing. We know the volume of shipping, and its change over time and by route, and so we can use average numbers for missing data and thus estimate the total number of migrants. We now know almost exactly – within a small margin of error – how many Africans came across the Atlantic in the slave trade. Intensive research has been devoted to this question since the late sixties. Almost every important archive in the world has been exploited. We even have a CD containing all the known voyages, and these voyages are estimated to be about 60% of all the voyages that took place. This allows us to calculate with great accuracy how many slaves crossed the Atlantic. In the end, while Curtin's estimations have been changed by route and by century, the overall number of roughly 10–12 million crossing the Atlantic remains the same. Unfortunately, it turns out that for political reasons, the number derived this way is unacceptable to many. Both the total number and the mortality suffered are just not high enough to serve their appointed political agenda. Therefore, the number is usually inflated by adding on "unknowns" about which no one has any data and whose elasticity seems unbounded. In particular, two unknowns are added in this case: mortality on arriving at the coast and mortality from the arrival in America through, say, the first six months in the New World. We currently have no reliable data for these two quantities, and they have therefore been the subject of politically motivated and intellectually questionable manipulations so that the number that we know to be pretty close to the actual number is doubled, tripled, or further increased to arrive at a politically endorsable number. This is a case where attempts to resolve one historical problem have led to new historical debates and to new issues (for example, mortality on land before and after crossing the Atlantic) that only quantitative analysis can resolve.

Another closely related debate in which I am directly involved is mortality in the slave trade. The typical textbook probably refuses to discuss mortality in the slave trade or the numbers that I and researchers of various nationalities have established. Why? The mortality of around 8% in the late eighteenth and early nineteenth centuries, which has been established through careful research, sounds too low and would offend the sensibilities of politicians, who insist, erroneously I think, that the victim status of black Americans would be somehow diminished if it were known that Africans didn't die in droves during the Atlantic crossing. But the fact of the matter is that 8% mortality during an approximately one-month period is very high. If you were to study, say, a French village in the eighteenth century and found such a level of mortality in one month, you would think that the Black Death had passed through.

The lesson here is that one must be aware of the political freight that some historical questions bring with them and that numbers derived through historical research can have larger political implications. Sometimes it's not good enough simply to tackle a politically sensitive question with scientific objectivity. One has to be conscious of groups that might take offense at the cold light shed on the subject by a rigorous examination of the facts as best we can ascertain them. I am reminded of the famous line near the end of John Ford's film *The Man Who Shot Liberty Valance* in which the newspaperman says, "When the legend becomes fact, print the legend." Sometimes it seems that, for many, the emotional cost of giving up cherished myths outweighs the alleged benefits of objective knowledge. I say this to caution you against thinking that you'll be loved if you expose as myth that which everybody had long thought to be the truth.

Were there Jews in the slave trade? Most definitely there were, just as there were lots of Protestants, Catholics, Muslims, and Africans of numerous religious persuasions. Currently, we estimate that less than 1% of slave ship owners were Jews. Nonetheless, that there were Jews at all in the slave trade has made for an explosive and in many regards puzzling, even distressing, political debate in the United States. Somehow, for some, the fact that there were any Jews in the slave trade is thought to make all Jews suspect for the trade, though the same presumption of guilt is not made for Catholics or Protestants. It was after all an English slave trader, John Newton, who later became a minister and wrote the hymn "Amazing Grace."

Quantitative researchers must remain wary of those who misuse numbers to push some ideological agenda, often focusing on some isolated set of numbers without regard to their context. So again, bear in mind that in the social sciences you'll find that, unlike in the pure sciences, numbers and facts are rarely neutral. There is almost always some political context in which our numbers fit, and there is therefore almost always someone eager to take offense or to misconstrue.

NUMBERS AND THE RISE OF COMPLEX SOCIETIES

How does one go about doing quantitative historical research, and where can the numbers be found? Almost every complex society that we know of produced numbers. They counted men, provisions, land, taxable wealth, and so on. There were Asian censuses long before those found in Europe. We have detailed record keeping for almost every known society, including societies that had no written records. In the Incan Empire, for example, numbers were vital, yet no writing existed. Here was a complex society with huge public granaries and state-maintained roads. The Incans were able to mobilize substantial numbers of troops over long distances and keep them in the field for long periods of time. Their armies were so ingeniously supplied that the Incans were not dependent on the harvest cycle to dictate the time limits in which troop mobilization could take place. This certainly distinguished them from many ancient peoples whose armies could take the field in strength only during certain seasons of the year. Some of the historical literature sees the system of public granaries as a kind of precursor of the socialist utopia since an ecological crisis in zone A could, and apparently would, be resolved by shipping grain from zone B or C so that the agricultural wealth of the empire would be more or less evenly distributed.

The Incans kept all of their records; we just can't read them. We know where the records were kept. They were on string tied to a piece of wood. They are called *Quipus*. These *Quipus* are knotted strings often laid out in different colors, and many museums in Europe and North America have one. They appear to have been mnemonic devices for statisticians and accountants who kept the records of armies, food resources, and even labor obligations, They also served for professional storytellers or chroniclers, who repeated the histories of the famous conquests and of the famous noble houses that were also recorded by these knots and strings. Once you start searching through the archives of almost any complex society, you will find that all of them had to create censuses of some kind, often, if for no other reason, to determine how many men there were of military age. The provision of public granaries was likewise common in older complex societies where food production was subject to great year-to-year variability due to climate. This usually implied some sort of record keeping of yearly crop production. These societies had to know how much grain they had, how many storage facilities were needed, and how much could be levied in taxes. Taxation, of course, becomes fundamental to all complex societies where there are various classes of useful non-food-producing specialists, such as warriors, teachers, artisans, or adminis-trators, who must be fed by the surplus taxed in large part from the agricultural sector. Tribute and taxes must be registered or recorded in some form.

This kind of census material has come down to us on tablets, papyri, or even carved stones. Though archeologists find it, often they can't read it. My point is that all complex societies must generate these quantifiable records in some form. This material is there for the researcher to gather and subject to statistical analysis – that is, if it can be can read.

Still, producing these materials is one thing but using them for analytical purposes is another. The administrative class in these societies surely did use these materials to further and maintain social organization. Let me mention the Witt-fogel thesis of "hydraulic civilizations" (Wittfogel 1957), in which the need for irrigation to maintain food production led to an ever more complex organization of societies, including bureaucrats and proto-engineers who were necessary to keep the system of dams and water diversion up and running. Complex organi-zation of this sort, again, requires the centralized gathering and keeping of information. I might add that Wittfogel was trying to address the fascinating question of why complex societies arise in the first place. Are they a response to military threat, a by-product of religious movements, or, as Wittfogel argued, an adaptation to the need of early agricultural societies to dominate river valleys and create irrigation systems? For whatever reason complex societies arose, it seems to be universally true that they gathered quantitative information for administra-tive purposes, and this information, if it can be deciphered, can be of immense use to the social scientist who studies these societies.

When the Spanish conquered the New World, they tried to preserve traditional Indian land tenure and legal structures. In so doing, the Spanish fell heir to all the preexisting accommodations and disputes over land and water rights. These appear in the earliest colonial documents, where the Spanish authorities are often called upon to adjudicate disputes between Indians. There you see awareness on the part of the natives of traditional quantities and allocations: One group might argue that from time immemorial they have had the right to a given amount of water that is now being infringed upon by a second group. This tends to show with some conclusiveness that the organization of pre-Columbian societies was based on systems of measurement and quantification.

Another example of how a complex society used quantification comes to mind: A few years back, we had a Ph.D. student here (at Columbia University) who was studying the Ottoman Empire. She studied the detailed records left behind of the inhabitants of military colonies that had been planted by the Ottomans throughout the Near East. The authorities in Constantinople wanted records kept of this useful class of people. Back at the center of the empire, they wanted to know about these people's marriages, their land ownership, and their production of offspring so that there would be a record of who and what could be mobilized for military purposes in each area.

QUANTIFICATION IN EARLY MODERN EUROPE: THE FIRST SOCIAL STATISTICS

Quantification, though it seems to be generally present in all complex societies, was taken to new heights of sophistication by Europeans, and we see from Crosby that Europe's fascination with numbers goes back at least to the late Middle Ages. We find cadastral (real estate) surveys of great complexity in early Renaissance Europe – for Florence, for instance. Of course, there were many sophisticated cadastral surveys in other non-European societies too, but in Europe a certain passion for measurement and enumeration became evident early on. All sorts of social statistics came to be produced from an early date. For example, the Council of Trent in the 1560s decreed that all Catholics anywhere in the world were to be formally registered. They had hitherto been informally registered, of course, parish by parish, in a rather haphazard fashion. Every birth, every confirmation, every marriage, and every death was from then on to be recorded. An analogous registration of the faithful occurred in the Protestant world at around this time. So, from the sixteenth century on, we have vital statistics for Europe that the historian can go back to and study, lending a quantitative underpinning to his or her conclusions about early modern European society. Thus, well before the first Western European periodic census taken in the eighteenth century, a vast array of quantitative material was being produced in all European societies and their overseas colonies.

The first person we know of who tried to use some of the available quantitative materials to study society in a systematic way is John Graunt, whose *Natural and Political Observations Made Upon the Bills of Mortality* is a pioneering work of social statistical research. Graunt, who is often called the "father of demography," lived from 1620 to 1674 and was a London draper merchant and a Fellow of the Royal Society from its foundation. In 1662, he published the first crude life tables of which we know, basing them on the "London bills of mortality." The city of London recorded the age, time of death, and cause of death, if known, of everyone who died in London. Graunt tried to find systematic patterns in these data by trying to weigh the effects of variables like age and seasonality on mortality, while at the same time estimating the effects of immigration from the countryside to London.

Graunt was followed by a series of Dutch thinkers like Christian Huygens, John DeWitt, and John Huddle, all of whom were interested in the possibility of raising money from the offering of life annuities, and in fact, the Dutch government in the seventeenth century did begin to offer life annuities based on life-expectancy tables. They were sufficiently successful in using this method for raising revenue that in the next century, life annuities were offered by other

European governments. Thus, we see that parallel to the scientific revolution there was a promising new field called "political arithmetic" that was compiling and analyzing social statistics. The guiding idea of political arithmetic was that, just as in the newly successful physical sciences, one could look at society, measure and quantify, and thereby find patterns as fixed and predictable as that of the transit of Venus. It was hoped to be possible to harness the European vogue for measuring and quantifying to the service of governments enmeshed in the dynastic struggles of early modern Europe. As a result, the new disciplines of demography and historical demography were founded and in time took on a life of their own.

THE BEGINNINGS OF THE MODERN SOCIAL SCIENCES

These early developments in the social sciences, or more particularly in historical demography, are brought together in a broad theoretical model by the English political economist Thomas Malthus, whose *Essay on the Principle of Population* (Malthus 1798) pulls together what was known at the time about the forces driving population growth. Malthus predicted that population growth would always tend to outstrip the means of subsistence – a prediction that was proved spectacularly wrong over the next 200 years. For our purposes, however, it doesn't matter so much that Malthus was wrong as that the methods he used and furthered pointed the way to the modern study of social statistics as we know it today. What has fascinated demographers from the beginnings of the science to our time is that human populations seem to respect certain predictable limits: There can be only so much mortality. There can be only so much reproduction. Within those limits changes can occur, but changes can be predicted based on what we know of this generation – witness the present debate over the solvency of Social Security, which depends on patterns of reproduction and mortality now and in the recent past that will tell us the likely size of the working and dependent populations a generation hence.

Demography was not the only social science whose origins stretch back to seventeenth-century England. Indeed, it seems that the English were rather pre-cocious in the early advancement of the social sciences, for it was another Englishman, Gregory King of London (1648–1712), who appears to have been the first to attempt to study systemtically the wealth of nations. If Graunt was the father of demography, then I suppose we can call Gregory King the "father of national income accounting." In the late seventeenth and early eighteenth centuries, there were a number of European thinkers like King who were questioning the tenets of mercantilism and seeking ways of discovering how much wealth a nation possessed and, in general, what were the ways that nations became rich. King, who was also a noted genealogist and engraver, compiled his *Natural and Political Observations and Conclusions Upon the State and Condition of England* in 1696, although it was not published until 1801 (King 1936). This work, which presents all sorts of statistical information on wealth, landholding, industry, and commerce, gives us the best picture we have of the population and wealth of England near the end of the seventeenth century.

What makes the work of Gregory King and those who followed in his foot-steps in the eighteenth century different from the sort of census material that, in

England at any rate, goes back to the Domesday Book of the eleventh century, is that these proto–social scientists were not compiling data on population and wealth for administrative purposes, as census takers had done for centuries; instead, they were using these materials to analyze society. Governments had previously used censuses to judge potential manpower for their armies, or to see if there was potential for more taxation or at least for more revenues from the old taxes. For example, in the Spanish colonial empire, the government produced enormous historical tomes devoted to the quantitative analysis of the economies of the colonial world. The Spanish were interested in knowing, for instance, why taxes might be falling in zone A, or whether they should move their treasury to zone B, or whether this or that trade should be taxed or not. By the eighteenth century, however, there were thinkers outside the ranks of government administrators who, for philosophical reasons, were convinced that there should be order to be found and measured in human society analogous to the order found and measured in the physical world. Their interests might only incidentally touch on the number of possible recruits or on where revenue might be raised, but the real impetus behind their work was scientific curiosity about society itself.

Carrying on this new line of social inquiry, the eighteenth-century French Physiocrats led by François Quesnay (1694–1774) were committed to the application of a priori principles of reason and natural law to human affairs. To them, mercantilism was based less on natural law and more on raison d'etat. The economic reforms they advocated they thought more "natural" than the wide-ranging controls of the mercantilist economy. In short, this school of thinkers is emblematic of the trend to treat human affairs as a subset of the natural order being unveiled by scientific inquiry in the natural sciences. Classical economics, which dominated economic thinking until the 1930s, is a descendant of the physiocratic avowal of laissez-faire as the natural order of human economic relations. Adam Smith's *Wealth of Nations* of 1776 pulled together many strands of social thought current in the eighteenth century including, obviously, a physiocratic strand. The work of Smith was carried further in the next century by David Ricardo, Jean-Baptiste Say, John Mill, and his son John Stuart Mill, so one can say that economics was really the first established modern social science.

What had been achieved by the eighteenth century, then, was the idea that quantities or data from the study of society could be analyzed just as data in the physical sciences were analyzed. Here we find the first inklings of the idea that, for the social scientist, the wealth of historical material to be found in archives and censuses could be searched to uncover regularities, even laws, of development for human society.

For the sake of brevity, I'll have to skip over much intellectual and social thought that was important and just briefly touch on two nineteenth-century figures who were very important for the development of the social sciences, Auguste Comte (1798–1857) and Charles Darwin (1809–1882). Comte was much influenced by earlier thinkers such as David Hume and the Comte de Saint-Simon. The school of thought he founded, called "positivism," was the font of modern sociology as well as of social history and helped launch the systematic study of social trends over time. The impact of Darwin was, of course, even more revolutionary and pervasive. Darwinism firmly established humans as a part of the natural order and as a subject worthy of scientific study. In the wake of Darwin and Comte, human history came to be viewed less from metaphysical or theological heights. To understand humanity, it wasn't sufficient to read the Scriptures or Church Fathers; one had to gather and analyze data, just as in the other sciences.

THE DEMOGRAPHIC TRANSITION IN EUROPE, INDUSTRIALIZATION, AND THE SOCIAL QUESTION

In the course of the nineteenth century, the collection of data on society by governments, by private institutions, and by individuals expanded greatly. It is considered part of modernity systematically to generate, analyze, and publish great amounts of material on society. By the middle of the nineteenth century, most of the modernizing parts of Europe and America had a central statistical or census bureau. For instance, in Latin America, with which I'm most familiar, the first central statistical bureaus date from around the 1840s, and by the 1880s practically every country had one. In the industrializing countries of Europe, the enhanced gathering of statistics went hand in hand with the unprecedented upheavals of urbanization and internal migration. These upheavals followed hard on the so-called demographic transition (see Figure 4.1), which began in the late eighteenth and early nineteenth centuries, and which took the population of the world and the rate of population growth to levels never before sustained, until finally growth rates and population leveled off again in the late nineteenth century.

When one adds to this mix of rapidly expanding populations the yeast of an urban industrialization that in many cases in one generation created an urban proletariat out of legions of uprooted rural migrants, one gets a potentially explosive social brew about which governments and concerned individuals thought it prudent and necessary to gather data. After all, debates in the late nineteenth century over the "social question" were usually based on some quantifiable information about social conditions in the rapidly expanding cities. Governments wanted numbers to underpin decisions about public health and accommodations and to answer questions about pauperization or long-term unemployment or underemployment. For instance, in Great Britain, conditions of public health in the rapidly burgeoning cities were studied as early as the 1840s under the auspices of the Poor Law Commission Secretary Edwin Chadwick, with the help of Southwood Smith, a follower of Jeremy Bentham. Later in the century, large amounts of data on the urban poor of London's East End and York's slums were privately collected and published by Charles Booth and Seebohm Rowntree, respectively. All of these sorts of materials, whether generated privately or officially, are of use to economists, demographers, sociologists, and social historians.

THE PROFESSIONALIZATION OF HISTORICAL STUDIES

History per se is a relative latecomer to the social sciences, although it was among the first to be established within the universities. By the nineteenth century, historical data were commonly used to build models of social and economic development. For instance, the Comtean positivists as well as the political

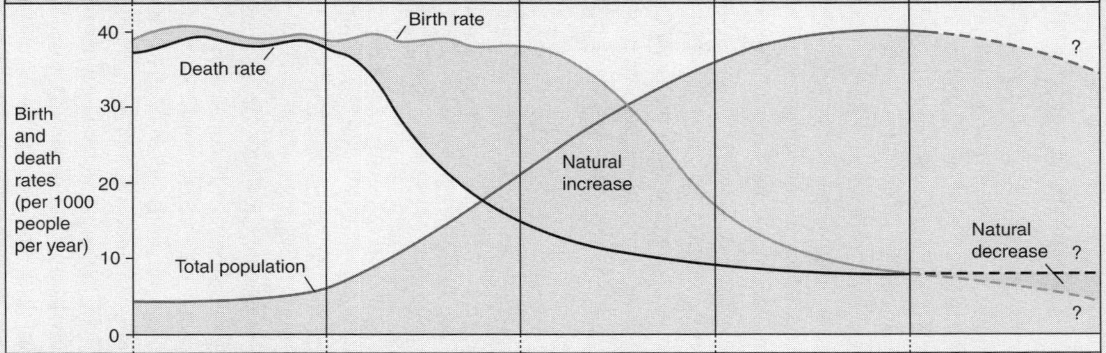

Figure 4.1 Diagram of the demographic transition.

Stage	1	2	3	4	5 ?
	High stationary	Early expanding	Late expanding	Low stationary	Declining?
Examples	A few remote groups	Egypt, Kenya, India	Brazil	USA, Japan, France, UK	Germany
Birth rate	High	High	Falling	Low	Very low
Death rate	High	Falls rapidly	Falls more slowly	Low	Low
Natural increase	Stable or slow increase	Very rapid increase	Increase slows down	Stable or slow increase	Slow decrease
Reasons for changes in birth rate	Many children needed for farming. Many children die at an early age. Religious/social encouragement. No family planning.		Improved medical care and diet. Fewer children needed.	Family planning. Good health. Improving status of women. Later marriages.	
Reasons for changes in death rate	Disease, famine. Poor medical knowledge so many children die.	Improvements in medical care, water supply and sanitation. Fewer children die.		Good health care. Reliable food supply.	

Source: David Waugh, *Key Geography for GCSE* (Cheltenham, UK: Nelson Thomas, 2002; ISBN: 978-07487-6581-2). Reprinted with permission of the author and the publisher.

economists were wont to use historical examples. But history itself was often thought, both then and now, more a branch of belles-lettres than of science. The nineteenth-century German school of historians emanating from the seminal figure of Leopold von Ranke (1795–1886) was the first to establish history as a profession complete with professional canons of inquiry that gave history at least the patina of scientific objectivity, and the professionalization of the study of history first occurred in Germany with the school of Ranke. By the late nineteenth century, Rankean methods had spread to the United States. Johns Hopkins was the first university where faculty and graduate students devoted their efforts solely to advanced research and where history was taught according to the Rankean canons. Columbia University and the University of Chicago also soon thereafter founded graduate schools where the German historical tradition found a home. In fact, the German tradition dominated historical studies in the United States until World War II. In this tradition there is a systematic handling of original sources, often much of it quantitative data. If you look at the doctoral dissertations and master's theses, which were then published as series by universities like Columbia or Johns Hopkins, you'll find that many of them are quantitative in nature. For instance, work with which I am quite familiar is the early histories of free colored people in the United States under slavery. Some of the earliest scholars in this field were black, and they wrote some of the pioneering studies. They did a systematic analysis of the number of free colored persons in each state of the Union, what sorts of jobs they had, where they lived, and so on. Using quantitative data from census materials, these scholars produced the best social history we have of the free colored population in the United States, and most of it was produced before the First World War. Also, many early urban quantitative studies were done under the influence of German scholars, many of whom migrated to the United States, while many of the first Americans to earn Ph.D.s did so at German universities.

QUANTIFICATION AND THE *ANNALES* HISTORIANS

This systematic use of original sources, some of them quantitative in nature, to reconstruct and understand the past, though of German origin, was taken to new levels of sophistication by the French, who often combined geographical studies with historical studies. The rise of modern geography was to have a pervasive influence on the study of history thanks to the importance of French scholarship. In 1929 Marc Bloch and Lucien Febvre founded a journal called the *Annales d'histoire économique et sociale* dedicated to broadening the traditional scope of history via the incorporation of techniques drawn from the other, and allegedly more rigorous, social sciences like economics and geography. Around that journal grew the *Annales* school, which for decades exerted enormous influence on the historical profession by combining meticulous scholarship with an interdisciplinary approach. Under the dominant influence of Febvre's student, Fernand Braudel, the *Annales* school tended to divide historical forces into various strata. According to Braudel, at the most basic level were "*les forces de profondeur*" or "*la longue durée*," that is, deep structural forces imposed on a society by such elemental factors as geography, demography, climate, or fertility of the land. Influenced by these deep structures were more transient institutions such as the slowly changing creations of human culture: religion, political institutions, economic and social structures. Finally, there were what Braudel called "events" or "*l'histoire événementielle*" as experienced by individuals, which were profoundly influenced by both the deep and more transient structures. It was obvious then that any historian wanting to understand any historical phenomena had to begin by understanding the basic structures in which they occurred.

What we see, then, is that during the interwar period, especially after the triumph of National Socialism, the leadership in historical studies slips away from Germany, and it is in France where the sort of historical research we are concerned with here – that is, rigorous quantitative history, history aspiring to be social science – finds an especially congenial home in the *Annales* school. The *Annales* journal, renamed after World War II *Annales: économies, sociétés, civilisations*, became without question the leading journal for advanced historical studies in the world. Of course, the seeds planted by German scholars in the United States in the late nineteenth and early twentieth centuries still continued to flourish, and German rigor even to some extent penetrated into Great Britain, but Germany had ceased to be the pace-setter.

The crowning and most influential work of the *Annales* approach to history appeared after World War II with the publication in 1949 of Braudel's *The Mediterranean and the Mediterranean World in the Age of Philip II* (Braudel 1996), a large part of which was sketched out by Braudel while he was a prisoner of war in Germany. Braudel's innovation was to look at the "complex totality" of the Mediterranean world and try to see how the Mediterranean environment conditioned social and economic structures from the Levant to the Pillars of Hercules.

The development of historical studies along the lines advocated by the *Annales* school was without doubt very fruitful for the development of quantitative historical studies. The French produced an enormous amount of data on sixteenth, seventeenth, and eighteenth-century population change in France. Since France and England were at the forefront of the demographic transition, which at first stabilized population growth at a level higher than heretofore was thought possible, these demographic studies are of particular interest to those trying to determine what happened to mortality and fertility rates during this key period and why.

The *Annales* school also produced large time series of price data going back centuries. In particular, price series of wheat were generated by scholars such as Ernest Labrousse, and were used in attempts to explain the origins of ancien régime subsistence crises and even of the Great Revolution itself (see Labrousse 1933, 1944). Figures 4.2 and 4.3 show some examples.

Eventually, however, a reaction to the *Annales* method set in, especially as it related to quantitative research. The French historian Pierre Chaunu, whose doctoral dissertation consisted of a count of the number of ships leaving Seville for the New World in the sixteenth century, in the 1960s wrote a famous article that maintained that there was a difference between what he called "serial history" and quantitative history (Chaunu 1964). His point was that numbers and statistical analysis have been overrated as tools for historical understanding. Chaunu thought that one might visualize the data but saw little point in analyzing them statistically. In other words,

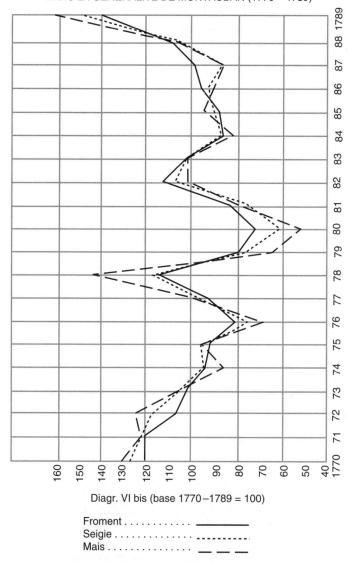

CONCORDANCE ET DISCORDANCE SPECIFIQUES
DE LA VARIATION DES PRIX DES DIVERSES CEREALES
DANS LA GENERALITE DE MONTAUBAN (1770 – 1789)

Diagr. VI bis (base 1770–1789 = 100)

Froment . . . . ────────
Seigie . . . . ----------
Mais . . . . ── ── ──

Prix empruntes aux etals des diverses subdelegations de la generalite de Montauban,
arch. dep. Lot, C 295 a 322 el 324 a 335.

Figure 4.2. Time series of historical prices of grain.
Source: Labrousse. (1944)

he found value in charts and graphs but not in other statistical methods. Chaunu's
article sparked a rebellion against the *Annales* among some French historians, who
subsequently took the graphical presentation of historical material to the level of a
high art in factor analysis studies (see Figure 4.3) but who declined to apply other

CONCORDANCE TENDACIELLE DES VARIATIONS ANNUELLES DE PRIX
ENTRE GENERALITES VOISINES (1756 – 1700)

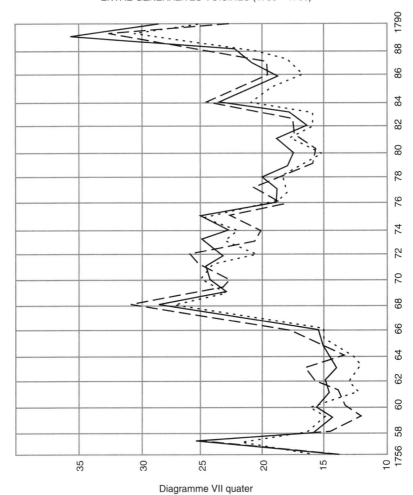

Diagramme VII quater

Prix du froment au setier de Paris dans les generalites de:

Hainaut . . . .   ——————
Flandres . . . .   ·············
Soissons . . . .   — — — —

Figure 4.3. Time series of historical prices of grain.
Source: Labrousse.(1944)

statistical methods to further analyze their data. In more recent times, French historical studies, which seem to have an inordinate amount of influence in the Anglophone world, have moved away from the quantitative social and economic studies of the *Annales* and have concentrated instead on things like *mentalités* (a type of historical reconstruction of the mental landscape of previous eras, also pioneered by the *Annales*) and cultural studies. While this trend is only one among many within the current French historical school, it has become a far more dominant theme of study in the Anglo-Saxon historical tradition.

There is, of course, a place for *mentalités* and cultural studies in history. They were included by the *Annales* in what were called *civilisations*, which were to be accorded a place for study along with *économies* and *sociétés*. My objection is to the study of the *mentalités* of individuals to the exclusion of the cultural, social, economic, and ecological structures that surely to a large degree condition them. It is unhistorical simply to turn away from numbers as if they are not representative of historical realiies. In the humanities, for better or more likely for worse, we are now deep into the so-called postmodern era. Anyone who has been away from the study of the humanities for the past twenty years or so might come back to them and find the intellectual landscape unrecognizable. Postmodern thinking formally rejects the intellectual tradition from which the social sciences originally sprung. Further, it rejects the idea that what traditional social science has called knowledge is anything other than a manifestation of "the will to power" or a strategy of social, racial, or sexual oppression. To be referred to as a "positivist" in the historical profession today is to be dismissed as a sort of intellectual dinosaur. The use of numbers to do history has now been deemed a rejection of reality, a hiding behind a cloak of quantification by a historian whose bad faith has prevented him or her from seeing the postmodern realities of knowledge and power.

HISTORICAL DEMOGRAPHY AND FAMILY RECONSTITUTION

There is one area of quantitative historical research that I haven't talked about and that is important and rather unusual, as well as advanced. It grew out of the *Annales* school among demographers and historians who were interested in creating basic demographic indices for the period before the first gathering of usable vital statistics. This turned out to be a very fruitful intellectual exercise first in France and then in England. It started with Louis Henry, a demographer by training, who wrote the *Manuel de Démographie Historique* (Henry 1967). His method for reconstructing vital statistics from surviving parish registers is called "family reconstitution." As I mentioned before, from about the mid-sixteenth century on, every parish in Europe, Catholic and Protestant alike, maintained parish registers containing information on births, baptisms, marriages, and deaths. Henry conceived of a way to use those registers to get basic indices of vital statistics on fertility and mortality. To work properly, the method required a set of special circumstances: One had to have a closed population, that is, one without significant in- or out-migration. This condition by and large held for the closed peasant society of ancien régime France, so Henry and his coworkers were able to do a massive reconstruction of the population statistics for early modern France. This material was eventually included in the Princeton Office of Population Research's model life tables as a result of a mutually beneficial exchange between historians and demographers. Even the United Nations picked up on Henry's techniques as a way to construct indices of vital statistics for less-developed contemporary societies since centralized registrations of births and deaths usually postdate censuses in most societies. In fact, in most societies, it is not until the late twentieth century that good vital statistics have been available, so if one wants to study historical population trends, alternative ways of modeling are necessary.

In Britain, Peter Laslett and his followers applied Henry's methods to British data, and his Cambridge Group for the History of Population and Social Structure is probably the most productive quantitative historical research team ever created. Beginning in the early sixties, the Cambridge Group hired local historians, who were given model sheets on which to record data taken from their local parish registers. The result was a demographic history of Britain from the late 1500s to the 1900s tracing key variables such as mortality and fertility (Laslett 1984; Wrigley and Schofield 1989).

We know that in modern times for most societies it was the mortality rate that first stabilized, while the birth rate remained very high until people realized that mortality had stabilized and too many children were being born. It appears that it was the English who then first began to control fertility on a systematic basis beginning in the late nineteenth century. But before the twentieth century, most nations of Europe underwent explosive population growth. Many of us are here in the United States due to the overpopulation of Europe as a result of this so-called demographic transition, which began in Western Europe and gradually moved to Eastern and Southern Europe until finally reaching the Third World in the mid-twentieth century with the introduction there of modern sanitation techniques and drugs like penicillin. In the nineteenth century, high rates of population growth were maintained for a number of generations and emigration of excess population was openly encouraged in many countries. Today, high rates of population growth in developing countries often endure for only a couple of decades before subsiding or being subject to limitation by law, as in China. Of course, in the nineteenth and early twentieth centuries, there were more outlets for surplus populations since most borders were open for the movement of labor as well as capital. Today, it's mostly capital that is allowed to cross borders without restrictions. For much of the nineteenth century and into the early twentieth century, comparative wages seemed to determine the flow of labor and immigration. There have been a number of studies of this trend. The market price for labor obviously can't fulfill its function of distributing labor resources globally when legal restrictions are placed on immigration. For instance, during the 1920s, many restrictions were placed on immigration to the United States, although since the 1960s there have been fewer restrictions. On the other hand, at least in the United States, there have never been significant restrictions on the movement of capital except for a brief period in the 1960s and early 1970s. Other nations in the twentieth century were far less liberal than the United States in terms of both capital controls and restrictions on immigration. However, in recent decades, the free flow of capital has become the norm. People speak of globalization today not realizing that there was a time before the First World War when there were almost no restrictions on the movement of labor and capital and when most major countries maintained currencies easily convertible into one another or their equivalent in precious metal. Gold was in effect a global currency.

WHITHER QUANTITATIVE HISTORICAL STUDIES?

What is the state of quantitative historical research in North America today? I remain a social science historian, while all the departments of history with which

I've been associated have moved more and more toward the humanities. On the other hand, other related disciplines, political science for instance, have become more quantitative and theoretical. Economic history has now found a home in the economics department and even the New Institutional Economics in mainstream economics has developed a distinctly historical interest, and much social history has migrated to sociology departments. Although much interesting work is being done on re-creating popular perceptions through original legal and other records, most of the cultural history being done in major history departments is based on inverting elite records to get at "everyday forms of resistance" and "agency" of oppressed peoples, totally abandoning class and structural analysis. Moreover, there has developed a political antipathy to quantitative analysis that is difficult to understand. Quantitative analysis is rejected as an inherently conservative enterprise; at the same time, explicit hypothesis testing is seen as simply positivistic and with no utility for historical analysis, which supposedly thrives only on the unique experience. This does not prevent cultural historians from proclaiming that they believe in theory, but with no coherent agreed-upon set of issues to test and no means to formally reject any hypothesis, it is difficult to see how this strain of historical research, now totally dominant, can lead to any significant advances in research.

The sort of modeling that goes on in the other social sciences is largely absent in history. Historians are usually not good at modeling. They may use a model, but they don't articulate it very well. They don't state their hypotheses clearly. They at least think they value empathy over cold numbers, but often they are merely working with unspoken assumptions that could be modeled and that might make their arguments clearer and might serve to clarify their own thinking. The root of the problem seems to me to be that historians are very naive about methodology. Historians do have a methodology, but they seem unaware of it. In my opinion, too many historians think like lawyers and pile on evidence to make their case while ignoring both the biases of their sources and data that do not fit their argument. To make a full historical analysis, the quality of the sources must be examined and the cases that do not fit the argument must be explained. Finally, the data and hypotheses should be articulated in such a way that later historians can use this material, even to make alternative arguments or reject the hypotheses of the original work.

Summing up, I don't find much promise in the direction taken by historical studies in the past quarter of a century. I think much has been lost by the cession of large portions of our discipline to political science, sociology, and economics, while in compensation we have added cultural studies modeled on what is done in the English and comparative literature departments. I don't think this has been a fruitful trade, and I look forward to the time when a reaction against this postmodern trend will set in and historians will reclaim at least some of the ground ceded to their more quantitatively oriented sister disciplines. After all, much of the historical data that sociologists or economists rely on were first compiled and used by historians. There is a legacy here to be reclaimed.

5. Sources of Historical Data

OFFICIAL GOVERNMENT STATISTICS

Chapter 4 laid out the evolution of the use of numerical data by historians up to our time. Let me stress that presently only a small minority of historians uses quantitative methods of some kind, and I would guess that fewer than half of those use them with any sophistication. Historians by and large blanch at mathematical equations and have now largely left to economists and sociologists the application of more advanced quantitative methods to social data. As I mentioned in Chapter 4, economic history is no longer done in history departments but in economics departments and in business schools, where some fine institutional histories have been produced. Likewise, as mentioned, the sociology department has taken over from historians most quantitative social history except for demographic history, which is still done by a small band of specially trained historians. This is where we left off in Chapter 4, where I described what quantitative history was in earlier times and what it has become today, when history is without a doubt the weakest of the social sciences in using quantitative methods. There are very few areas where historians have been innovative in the use of quantitative methods. Some original programming has been done. For instance, the Soundex Index for linking records was developed by historians. This is a rather complex computer program that lets you link similar-sounding names from different lists, say, "Smythe" and "Smith." It then can tell you the probability that these are the same person. The use of census data is possibly the most sophisticated quantitative field of study presently for historians, who, using these samples, have furthered demographic, social, and economic history. The Minnesota Population Center at the University of Minnesota has online public use samples of the U.S. census from 1850 to 2000 called IPUMS, which stands for Integrated Public Use Microdata Series. The compilers of this series have created a common record layout and coding schemes, with IPUMS assigning uniform codes for all samples to facilitate their analysis.

In general, however, historians are hardly in the vanguard when it comes to quantitative research. Also, we often lack many of the variables that would be necessary to establish causation or correlation. We might have three or four out of, say, fifteen or twenty of the pieces of information that would be necessary to make a model of cause and effect. Historians are usually loath to use the more advanced statistical methods that might allow them to get around at least some of the problems of missing data.

Let's talk about some of the places where you can get historical data. First of all, let me emphasize that this sort of data exists in vast quantities. If we start with government publications alone, we have sets of data sometimes going back to the eighteenth century. For instance, from the late eighteenth century we have national censuses from Europe and North America, as well as state and provincial censuses in most American countries. For the United States, at least most of the eastern states had local state censuses in the nineteenth century that often asked quite different questions from the national census. Also, among early government publications are parliamentary papers with eighteenth-century statistics on trade, colonies, and slaving. For the nineteenth century there are parliamentary blue books studying various industries, like coal or textiles. Subjects as diverse as Gypsies in the Austro-Hungarian Empire were covered by nineteenth-century censuses. The rather fascinating detailed Gypsy occupational census dates from the 1890s.

Beginning in the early decades of the nineteenth century, there are official statistical bureaus for many of the governments in Europe and the Americas. There is a mass of nineteenth-century statistical material, especially for the second half of the century. By the 1850s, most governments had ministries of the interior, agriculture, and industry. Each of these bureaus set about gathering statistical material on the subject under its control, and often these materials were published in both a monthly *Bulletin* and an *Annual*. A good guide through the maze of all this government publication material is Gregory Gerould's survey from 1932. This impressive volume lists every bulletin and every serial published by every ministry in every foreign country that produced this material. What these bulletins contain depends on what the particular ministry was interested in. In Latin America, the earliest bulletins cover foreign trade. From not long after these nations became established in the 1820s, we have statistics covering imports and exports in some detail. Also, some of the earliest publications treat expenditure on public works like bridges and railroads. Railroads in particular get detailed treatment of the amount of subsidies, the mileage built, and the cost of materials.

Starting in the last quarter of the nineteenth century, many governments began to generate statistics on social conditions. As a result of rapid urbanization and the social changes wrought by industrialization, what was then called the "social question" engaged the labors of many investigators and statisticians. Most governments were naturally quite concerned about the class conflict that appeared to increase as traditional social structures gave way to new, and perhaps at first bewildering, patterns of work and habitation. We have from most countries a steady flow of statistics on social indicators like crime and strike activity dating from the late nineteenth century. For example, Argentina has superb strike statistics from about the 1870s to the 1920s indicating the cause of the strike and the number of workdays lost. The nineteenth century is also the century that gave us the asylum and the penitentiary. Often modeled on the famous prototype located at Elmira, New York, penal institutions began to flourish in the nineteenth century as older penal models based on physical punishment or exile gave way, largely under Benthamite influence, to allegedly more humane efforts to reform and rehabilitate the criminal. The state had an interest in finding out how many and whom it was incarcerating, their color, their social origins, and their employment or lack thereof. The statistics produced for these purposes can be used in various unanticipated ways by social scientists.

In countries of heavy immigration like the United States, crime statistics often became a quite politicized part of the debate over the social question since it was argued by many that unrestricted immigration by non-Anglo-Saxon or non-Germanic stock was directly correlated with an increase in crime and with the rise of dangerous fringe political groups like anarchists. The U.S. Congress set up special fact-finding committees to study immigration, and hence we have statistics on everything from immigrant family savings patterns to immigrant educational achievement (see the voluminous Dillingham Commission Reports from the 1910s, which are available online at http://library.stanford.edu/depts/dlp/ebrary/dillingham/body.shtml). State legislatures also commissioned special committees to find out facts about immigrants.

Urbanization and immigration of masses of laborers were just two unsettling features of the rapidly industrializing late-nineteenth-century U.S. economy. Another disturbing concomitant of industrial growth for which the U.S. Congress commissioned statistical information was industrial concentration. Appearing as an unmistakable trend in the U.S. economy starting in the 1880s and, of course, still of concern in our own time, industrial concentration had far-reaching consequences for the nation's economic structure and aroused fears of monopoly. Congress answered with various fact-finding efforts followed by installments of antitrust legislation beginning in 1890 with the Sherman Antitrust Act. Congress wanted to know about restraint of trade, price-fixing, and unfair or monopolistic business practices and commissioned studies to gather information. For an example of the kind of statistical materials gathered by the U.S. Congress, on this subject, see "Hearings on Economic Concentration" (1964–6) produced by the Senate Judiciary Committee's Subcommittee on Antitrust and Monopoly. In addition to statistics gathered for Congress, one can find much interesting information on industrial concentration in U.S. Census publications such as the *Twelfth Census of the United States, Manufactures, Vol. VIII* (1900).

With the recent development of the Internet, a great deal of historical statistical material has now been made freely available by national governments and international agencies. For example, the United Nations Population division and several of its regional branches have made an enormous effort to publish demographic data from 1948 to the present (see its *Demographic Yearbook 1997-Historical Supplement*, found at http://unstats.un.org/unsd/demographic/products/dyb/dybhist.htm; and, for example, the United Nations Economic Commission for Latin America and the Caribbean has published life tables for all the Latin American countries at http://www.eclac.cl). There have also been some extraordinary efforts to make historical data available from given government agencies. Just recently, for example, the Brazilian Census Bureau (Instituto Brasileiro de Geografia e Estatística) has made available all the published statistics (several hundred tables) of data taken from the publications of all the agencies of the federal government from 1900 to 2000 and has made these approximately 1,000 tables available in Excel files (see IGBE, "*Conteúdo Historórico: Estatísticas do século XX*," at http://www.ibge.gov.br/). Both the U.S. Census Bureau and Statistics Canada, Canada's national statistical agency, have made available online their published "Historical Statistics" volumes. For the United States, go to http://www. census.gov/prod/www/abs/statab.html; also useful for quick reference is the mini-series recently provided by the U.S. Census Bureau at http://www.census.gov/ compendia/statab, which also contains the original two-volume set of historical statistics. For Canada's historical statistics see http://www.statcan.ca/bsolc/english/ bsolc?catno=11–516-X). The federal censuses of the United States since 1790, along with numerous state censuses, are available online from the University of Virginia Library (see http://fisher.lib.virginia.edu/collections/stats/histcensus/). Recently, I and a Brazilian economist put together an Internet guide to the social and economic history of Brazil, which describes the enormous quantity of statistical material that is now online for Brazilian historical questions (Klein and Luna 2004).

PUBLICLY AVAILABLE NONOFFICIAL DOCUMENTS

Another source of statistics, one that might not at first seem obvious, is news-papers. For example, I have seen excellent studies of slavery based on the descriptions of runaway slaves in newspaper advertisements. These advertise-ments almost always gave detailed descriptions of the slave, usually describing his or her skills and language abilities. Advertisements for the sale of slaves also gave detailed descriptions, as well as prices. I have even used early-nineteenth-century newspapers to analyze the mortality of slaves in the Atlantic slave trade for slave ships arriving at the port of Rio de Janeiro in the 1820s (Klein 1978). In fact, newspapers are a good source for prices of all sorts of goods, as well as the exchange rate of the local currency. Newspapers are also a good alternative source for government reports. In many countries prior to the systematic publication of government statistics, often newspapers were the outlets for the publication of official reports. Reviewing the Brazilian newspapers from about 1820 to 1860, I found government trade statistics published in much greater detail than in any other source. I was particularly interested in coffee exports to the United States, and I was able to find information on the regions and ports from which coffee exports originated. Some of the newspapers from port cities also had daily shipping registries. There was information on arrivals, departures, goods for sale, kinds of ships, available shipping, ports of departure, destinations, tonnage, and national flags.

Very good regional economic studies have been done using price information from newspapers, where it was customary to list the local prices of most basic commodities on a daily or weekly basis. The economic historian Nicolás Sánchez-Albornoz and the economist Daniel Peña Sánchez de Rivera have put a lot of this price material together and subjected it to statistical time series analysis in order to analyze the correlation of regional price movements before the arrival of the railroad. Of course, the railroad changed the structure of internal markets dramatically by reducing transportation time and costs and thus unifying markets via arbitrage. Before the railroad, for instance, price movements in Barcelona might correlate more with those in Seville than with those in a town in its own interior, thanks to the ease of communication by sea relative to that by land (Peña Sánchez de Rivera and Sánchez-Albornoz 1983). I am also reminded of a study of Bolivian tin miners that correlated the gleaning of residual tin by poor part-time miners to the price, as available by radio, of tin in London. If the price in London rose high enough, it was worth the trouble to root around in the piles of refuse for lower-quality tin ore and, in effect, steal small amounts of tin from the company for sale on the market (Godoy 1990). Once the world's markets were connected by rail and ship, global centers like London determined the price of a nonperishable commodity the world over, and even illiterate miners were sophisticated enough to respond to the price signal.

As we have seen, historical data can be used to develop, test, and extend economic or social theories, but usually the data are not just sitting there waiting to be plucked. It takes real work as a historian to go through the mass of newspapers or census materials. In addition to the uses we have just seen, newspapers are a source for numerous other events. Part IV of this book has an example of the use of newspapers as the source of information on lynchings in the American South. Also, crimes, fires, and other catastrophes might be counted, coded, and analyzed using newspapers as the source.

Another source of information that you might not think of immediately is almanacs. From about the 1830s on, most countries produced commercial almanacs with lists of merchants. They are somewhat like modern Yellow Pages in that merchants are listed by trade and the more prominent ones might pay extra for a more visible listing. Often these almanacs also threw in for free a list of government officials or even their salaries, usually with a grab bag of other statistics, for instance, on climatology.

From about the 1880s on, perhaps as an adjunct to the rise of nationalism, national biographical dictionaries were published in most of the Western countries. These dictionaries have well served historians interested in prosopography, that is, in the biographical study of elites. There have been, for instance, prosopographical studies of missionaries and of the aristocracy that focus on their career patterns and mortality rates. Using these biographical dictionaries, you might be able to study, say, the education levels of government officials. The Jesuit order in particular kept, for every province in which the order was active, massive biographical dictionaries of its members, from which career path studies, among other things, may be made. One student of mine did a study of how the age at which a clergyman might reach the rank of bishop near Cuzco determined his career pattern. If he got to that level by the time he was twenty-nine or thirty, he had the potential to be an archbishop in some big city, perhaps even back in the metropolis. If he got there when he was over forty, it meant, instead, that he was near the end of his career and was being put out to pasture. My student showed this by following the career paths of about fifty bishops.

I want to warn you that much of the data have biases, and you should adjust for these biases whenever the phenomena studied are not the result of a random selection. It's always important to understand who produced the dataset and for what reason. Are the numbers really neutral? Are they systematically biased? How were they collected? One should always be concerned with the provenance of any written record and be aware of how its provenance might bias it. In writing an article about an Indian uprising in Chiapas in 1712, I relied on the standard chronicle of the time that laid out the causes of the revolution. The chronicle blamed the rebellion on the old bishop for being too conservative. The new bishop was portrayed as trying in vain to defuse the explosive situation bequeathed to him. For that article I was more interested in the consequences of the revolt than in the causes, but when someone did go back to look at the causes and examine the source material with a more critical eye, he found that the standard chronicle was little more than propaganda. It had actually been the new bishop, by changing the policies of his conservative predecessor, who had provoked the rebellion, but this had been obscured by the fact that the new bishop had better public relations, so to speak (Klein 1966). My point is again that one must be aware of biases in the presentation and the production of data. Always take into account the source of your data and weigh possible motives for falsification or manipulation. Also, remember that the data that have survived may not be representative of the whole population under study. If, say, data from twelve textile firms have survived from 1840 because they went into bankruptcy, and data from other similar firms have been lost, one is dealing with data that survived due to some accident, and one must show why these data might still be representative. This is a problem historians have to deal with all the time since it is impossible to go back and do random sampling. Often historians, being very naive statisticians, ignore this problem and produce work whose biases, originating from self-selecting data, make their results difficult to accept. For instance, the study of *mentalités* must by necessity be based in large part on the written records of contemporaries, but since, especially in past eras, only the elite would have left written records, we are dealing with obviously nonrepresentative sources. These sources can still be useful even to get at nonelite views if they are carefully weighed and analyzed. Moreover, data produced for one reason can be used for another. The mortality on the slave ships arriving in Rio de Janeiro from Africa in the 1820s was recorded for tax purposes, so that the captains who had their total number of slaves recorded when they left Africa did not have to pay import taxes for any slaves who were not landed. These data produced for tax purposes have turned out to be one of the best sources available on the mortality in the Atlantic slave trade. Moreover, the bias in the source would have been to overstate mortality for tax evasion reasons, but even so, I biased the dataset against low numbers by excluding all voyages where no deaths were reported.

Also, bear in mind that I have been describing only about publicly available documents that you should be able to find at a good university library. Once one gets to the late nineteenth century, the statistical material is very abundant and in many ways comparable to what we have today. There also tended to be uniformity of collection patterns among nations. That is, most nations agreed about what were the important numbers to collect.

PRIVATE OR CONFIDENTIAL RECORDS THAT BECOME PUBLIC

Often via the judicial system, private information becomes publicly available. For instance, we have nineteenth-century employment records from bankrupt companies. Once the company goes into receivership, many of its records then fall into the public domain and eventually get deposited in public archives. The same is true of companies that are nationalized. Whether the company is purchased or seized by the state, records often become public that were never meant to see the light of day. Sometimes the fact that these records were never meant to be published indicates that they are in fact less biased and more reliable than comparable documents that were prepared for publication. I am reminded of a controversy I've been involved in over the reliability of Royal Treasury records prepared for the Spanish Crown. These documents were not prepared for historians. The Crown, quite simply, wanted to know how much money it was getting and how much it was spending. Of course, officials could cook the books so that they could steal from the Crown, but the Crown tried in every way possible to double-check the authenticity of the accounts. Thus, the numbers produced were not some fantasy or propaganda exercise to show that little money was being made out of the empire and that the Spanish were governing the colonies for the love of the natives. On the contrary, these documents, since they were never meant for publication, are quite likely a fairly accurate record of the amounts flowing in and out of the Royal Treasury (see Klein 1998). After all, to function as propaganda a document has to be published, and the Royal Treasury accounts were published only after the revolutions that expelled the Spanish from most of the New World. They were never intended to enter the public domain.

I hope I have given you some ideas on where to search for data for historical quantitative studies. As you can see, the published material available in both print and now on the Internet is both abundant and, for the most part, easily accessible. Chapter 6 discusses difficulties in interpreting agreed-upon data, and Chapter 7 covers less accessible archival sources and unpublished materials in general.

6. Historical Perspectives on International Exchange Rates

HISTORY AND SOCIAL SCIENCE

Before we take a look at an example drawn from twentieth-century economic history, let me recapitulate and expand a bit on what was said in Chapter 5 about the general question of history and quantification and on history's place in the social sciences. We've already seen that today history is the least quantitative of the social sciences. Most history Ph.D. candidates study neither mathematics nor statistics as part of their training to be a historian, and history retains many of the peculiarities that come with its position as the first social science to have more or less uniform professional standards inculcated by training at the university level. The principles governing the professional historian's inquiries are still largely those laid down by the German school of Leopold von Ranke (1795–1886) in the early nineteenth century, and the wellsprings of the Rankean method are to be found in classical philology, which emphasized textual criticism and the close reading of original documentary sources, although, as mentioned in Chapter 5, this did not at all rule out the inclusion of quantitative material.

The superiority of the methods of the hard sciences was not so obvious in Ranke's time, and Ranke can certainly be excused for taking as his model classical philology, which had been enormously successful in its pursuit to establish the ur-texts of the ancient authors. In fact, the methods of German historicism were, with much justification, in their time considered scientific compared to the amateurism that had characterized historical studies previously. However, "scientific" history as practiced by the Rankean school wasn't really scientific by today's standards, and later attempts, often under the influence of Comtean positivism, to integrate methods from the natural sciences with the Rankean tradition provoked a countervailing reaction. The scientific pretensions of historical positivism were given a thorough critique in the theories of *Geisteswissenschaften,* most notably associated with the name of the German philosopher Wilhelm Dilthey (1822–1911). *Geisteswissenschaften,* which might be literally translated as "sciences of the spirit" but is often translated as "the human sciences," sought to put history firmly back in the camp of the humanities and contrasted the *Verstehen* ("understanding") needed by the historian with the *Erklären*

59

("explaining") practiced by the scientist. The proper methods for the study of humanity were *Einfühlung* ("empathy") and *Erlebnis* ("lived experience"), not quantification and scientific methodology. The natural sciences were "nomothetic" in character, that is, they were capable of finding deterministic laws, while history was "idiographic," dealing with the individual and unique and not subject to any mechanistic law (Dilthey 1883, 1989; see, e.g., Pinson 1966: 258, 259 and passim).

It is tempting, but perhaps an oversimplification, to characterize those who have sought to take history in the direction of quantification and the natural sciences as having come from a French Enlightenment genealogy stretching back to eighteenth-century *philosophes* such as Turgot (1727–81) or Condorcet (1743–94), while, by contrast, the strain in German historicism that emphasizes the unique and individual stretches back to a German counter-Enlightenment tradition associated with Johann Gottfried von Herder (1744–1803) (cf. Berlin 2000: 168ff.). Professional historical studies entered the university, by and large, under the aegis of German historicism, and most professional historians, for better or for worse, still bear the stamp of this *déformation professionelle*.[1]

It should be evident from this brief glimpse at the nineteenth-century beginnings of the historical profession that the tension within the guild between those wanting to keep history closer to the humanities and those attempting to incorporate the latest in scientific methodology, including quantification, is of long standing. It didn't crop up with the rise of postmodernism, although postmodernism has certainly been a major factor in reorienting historical studies. Generally speaking, history, unlike, say, economics or political science, has rebuffed efforts to bring in the methods of science, most notably, for our purposes, quantitative modeling, and has hewed closer to the methods and trends in the humanities than to those in the social and natural sciences. For instance, a generation or so ago, there was a brief frisson of excitement among historians over cliometrics, which sought to apply neoclassical economic theory and the methods of econometrics to the study of history. Robert Fogel and Douglass North, two of cliometrics' foremost practitioners, subsequently won the Nobel Prize for their pioneering work in bringing sophisticated quantitative methods and economic theory to bear on historical questions. Fogel, for instance, focused on some classic questions of American economic history like "How much did the railroads contribute to economic growth in the nineteenth century?" (Fogel 1964) and "Was the southern slave economy economically viable?" (Fogel and Engermann 1974),

---

[1] The Marshallian tradition is so dominant in economics today that we take it for granted that economics is the most mathematical of the social sciences, and even most economists may not be aware that there was once an alternative tradition in economics that sprang from German historicism and rejected the general application of the abstract theorizing of classical economics. The German school of economics, two of the most famous exponents of whom were Wilhelm Roscher (1817–94) and Friedrich List (1789–1846), emphasized the particularities of time, place, and institutions and doubted that what the classical economists took to be the universally applicable laws of the market were relevant to every time and place. In the United States, economists such as Thorstein Veblen (1857–1929) carried on the traditions of the German historical school. Veblen's idea of "conspicuous consumption," put forward in *The Theory of the Leisure Class* (1912), challenged the classical notion that the market's outcomes were rational and efficient.

while North emphasized the importance of social, legal, and political institutions for economic development (see, e.g., North and Thomas 1973). Nonetheless, their methods and many of their conclusions were, by and large, rejected by the historical profession. Economic history using econometrics and economic theory is rarely done in university history departments but rather has a foothold in economics departments. Quantitative historians are now more likely to have been trained as economists in economics departments rather than as historians in history departments.

In short, quantitative methods have never really caught on with historians. In addition to the institutional bias that these methods have encountered in history departments, there is something to be said for the argument that the farther you go back in time, the less reliable the data are, which makes quantitative methods quite often difficult, if not impossible, to apply. Also, if history is indeed idiographic, that is, dealing with unique events and facts, how are statistical methods to be applied? After all, you can't appeal to the law of large numbers or the central limit theorem when dealing with something unique, that is, with one observation. But then again, if we have only one observation, is any sort of true understanding possible? It could be argued, in fact, that, unless an observation is a draw from a larger population of which we have at least some knowledge of other examples generated by the same process, understanding – at least scientific understanding – is not possible and that statistical reasoning merely formalizes this intuition. Every historical event may indeed be unique in the sense that we can't go back and rerun the process that generated it. However, I'm not sure that trying to grasp this uniqueness is a superior path to knowledge compared with trying to uncover the event's connections to other events in an overall process unfolding over time, and quantitative methods are best suited for uncovering whatever relationships hold in dynamic processes of this sort. If one believes that history is or at least should be a social science, I see little alternative to adopting econometric methods, but most historians have resisted this conclusion, or rather, perhaps what they are resisting is the admission that history is a social science.

So, is there, in fact, much scope for quantification in history or should we just leave all that to the economists and political scientists? Personally, I think it a shame that more time and effort aren't spent training historians to use quantitative tools. Although I wouldn't want to see studies based on primary documents done in the Rankean tradition disappear, there are wide swaths of social, economic, political, and even cultural history that, with a little imagination, might be amenable to the use of modern quantitative methods, which, especially since the advent of the personal computer, would allow historians to execute sophisticated studies with far less difficulty than a generation ago.

Furthermore, as was pointed out previously, many historians already use a sort of naive modeling, a sort of modeling that dare not speak its name since the model is never explicitly stated. After all, if you think of some of the classic ways in which the historical process has been conceived by historians, behind most of them there is some sort of model that could be expressed mathematically. For instance, the ancient Greeks saw history as cyclical. What they had in mind resembles the periodic functions like sine and cosine. Other historians have charted the rise, decline, and fall of civilizations. This process would bring to mind the growth and decay modeled by differential equations. I'm not suggesting that one should generally seek to fit history to a sine wave or a differential equation. That would, most likely, be replacing one sort of naiveté with another. Rather, I'm suggesting that behind even some of the most common historical schemas lie models that might gain some clarity from being expressed mathematically. When done judiciously, mathematical modeling in the social sciences has the power to clarify, sharpen, and, hopefully, enlighten, although, as we shall see in the example I will go over, it is probably too much to hope that our mathematical models will give us definitive answers to very complex social questions. As much as a historian might dream of answering some historical question for all time, the reality is that, even with sophisticated quantitative methods, history will still be "an argument without end," as Pieter Geyl (1946: 4–5) put it, but at least it will be clearer what we're arguing about and what we mean when a hypothesis can't be rejected given our data. It will also mean that we can advance to ever more sophisticated questions. Proving that slaves were held in America for economic profit, which is now finally accepted by all scholars, still does not answer the question of whether slavery made economic sense for the society at large or whether it was more efficient than free labor – an ongoing argument among economic historians.

WHAT DO WE MEAN BY MODELING?

So, assuming that there is a place for quantification in history, what are we trying to do exactly when we try to model some process that we hypothesize as operating on society or the economy in a past time? First, let me say that a historian's data need not necessarily be time series data; he or she may encounter cross-sectional or even panel data. Suppose that we have a dataset in front of us. At the most basic level, the question we'll want to ask and then try to answer is whether there is an identifiable process that generated the data. Do the data have some underlying structure or are they just white noise? Assuming there is some discernible process at work generating the data, our goal will be to use mathematical or statistical methods to separate the process's signal from its noise the same way that any scientist might. Our problem as social scientists is that there is usually a lot of noise, often a huge amount.

Our methods are predicated on the assumption that it is the process's signal, not the noise, that tells us the real truth about the underlying process, and there are various statistical techniques (you will no doubt soon encounter one of them called "least squares regression") that are good for separating signal from noise. A method such as least squares regression, if we use it correctly, will divide our process into a systematic part and a random or white noise part. For those of you who are familiar with linear algebra, least squares will divide the process into two orthogonal pieces: a projection and an error vector.

Generally speaking, a model seeks to apply a set of restrictions on the joint distribution of the predictor and outcome variables. For instance, the classical regression model is a set of joint distributions satisfying the Gauss–Markov assumptions (Hayashi 2000: 4). It is not my goal here to go into the details of the quantitative methods that you will learn elsewhere, and so I'll end my excursus on the use of statistics and mathematics to build models. But I do think it is important to know and remember what, at the most general level, this modeling is supposed to accomplish since sometimes this goal gets lost as a student becomes immersed in the particulars of various statistical methods.

AN EXAMPLE DRAWN FROM ECONOMIC HISTORY

I have referred to the difficulties a social scientist might have in separating the signal of the process under study from its noise. The example we'll go over here illustrates some of the difficulties we might encounter since it is often not at all clear what signal our data is giving us. You'll learn more elsewhere about the problems of endogenous explanatory variables and things of that sort. Here my more modest goal is to illustrate, at an intuitive and nontechnical level, how difficult it can sometimes be to figure out what the data are trying to tell us and how you'll likely find these difficulties manifested by interpretations of the data that are strongly influenced by important recent events such as the Great Depression, World War II, or the great inflation of the 1970s. This is not necessarily a bad thing. It is only natural that we should try to draw lessons from these sorts of seminal events. However, these changing interpretations should caution us that truth in the social sciences is often an elusive thing. What I want to say here is that, although quantification and mathematical modeling are powerful and essential tools in our search for knowledge, they are tools that are only as good as the judgment of the researcher using them, and a researcher's judgment is, for better or worse, often influenced by recent events. I repeat: This is not necessarily a terrible thing. I think a social scientist, unless he or she is studying, say, Merovingian France, is quite properly involved in the search for solutions to the great social and economic problems of the day. It was no accident that the dominant economic paradigm in the mid-twentieth century, Keynesianism, was conceived in response to the mass unemployment of the 1930s. After all, the return of mass unemployment was the overriding preoccupation of the generation that had seen the lives ruined by the economic catastrophe of the Great Depression. It was likewise no accident that monetarist arguments began to look more attractive when, in the 1970s, inflation took the place of mass unemployment as the major preoccupation of economists and policymakers. Nonetheless, it is hard to square these shifting paradigms with the ideal that some of you might have of the social scientist standing above the fray and revealing timeless truths. I don't mean, at the beginning of your studies, to pour cold water on your ambitions to solve by quantitative methods all the great social and historical questions, but rather to forestall the disappointment you might feel later on in your studies when it becomes clear that answering these complex questions is not so easy and that the answers favored at any time seem to have some reference to the defining events in the recent past.

However, one might want to cast this process of continual reassessment in a more positive light and say that important recent events often fruitfully stimulate a reassessment of the data and sweep away stale interpretations. After all, this sort of reassessment happens in the hard sciences too. If it didn't, then Newton would have had the last say and there would have been no need for Einstein. Many times consensus interpretations of one generation have been shown to be untenable by the work of another generation. For instance, the Marxist interpretation of the French Revolution once held sway among historians. The Great Revolution was supposed to be all about the rising bourgeoisie and a waning feudal system, but once historians like Alfred Cobban (1964) and François Furet (1978) began to point out how little the facts of the case fit the Marxist schema, the old interpretation collapsed. Was it any accident that this reinterpretation came along during the post-1956 period, that is, after the full revelation of the horrors of Stalinism and after the crushing of the Hungarian uprising by Soviet tanks? These political events occasioned for many a reassessment of "actually existing socialism," and this reassessment included a raft of Marxist assumptions – including those about the French Revolution – with which so many intellectuals had grown comfortable.

Let's take a look at some descriptive statistics taken from an essay by Michael Bordo called "The Bretton Woods International Monetary System: A Historical Overview" (Bordo and Eichengreen 1993: 3–98). As we examine these statistics, I want to focus on the interesting correlations they suggest and their limitations when it comes to drawing conclusions on causation. Let's look at these statistics and see what we can glean from them.

Across the top of Table 6.1 are listed the various international monetary regimes from 1881 to 1989. Down the side are listed various macroeconomic variables like inflation or real per capita growth. Bordo's intention is to correlate economic performance, as measured by various macroeconomic statistics, with the different monetary regimes of the past century or so. We have no information here about the transmission mechanism by which good or bad economic performance results from the implementation of a certain monetary regime. I also caution you that a few of the numbers seem erroneous. For instance, Bordo gives the mean for inflation for the United States from 1946 to 1970 as 2.4%, which is lower than both the 2.8% mean for 1946–58 and the 2.6% mean for 1959–70. This obviously can't be right, but it's probably just a typo, or maybe the numbers are drawn from different data series that calculate inflation slightly differently. The overall conclusion is not affected.

Bordo's statistics for the period prior to 1939 include two gold standard periods: one before the outbreak of World War I, the classical gold standard, and one from the interwar period lasting for a brief period in the 1920s and 1930s that is often described as a "gold exchange" standard since key currencies like the dollar or the pound sterling were often held as central bank reserves as well as gold. The interwar statistics Bordo presents are a mixed bag since, as well as the gold exchange years, they also include the turbulent aftermath of World War I, which lasted until the major currencies were stabilized against each other in the mid-1920s; the period after the summer of 1931, when the gold exchange standard was still only selectively in force; and the years 1936–8, when the gold exchange standard had vanished almost completely (see, e.g., Eichengreen 1992). The Bretton Woods regime is likewise divided into two periods: Before 1959, exchange controls prevented the system from working as originally envisioned, but after 1958, exchange controls were loosened on current account[2] transactions,

---

[2] The current account is the account that includes all sales and purchases of currently produced goods and services, income on foreign investments, and unilateral transfers (Salvatore 1995: 741).

Table 6.1. *Descriptive statistics of selected open economy macro variables, the G-7 countries, 1881–1989 (M = mean, SD = standard deviation over the years in each column)*

	Gold Standard 1881–1913		Interwar 1919–38		Bretton Woods: Preconvertible 1946–58		Bretton Woods: Convertible 1959–70		Floating Exchange 1974–89		Bretton Woods Total, 1946–70	
	M	SD	M	SD	M	SD	M	SD	M	SD	M	SD
A. Inflation PGNP[a]												
United States	0.3	(3.1)	−1.8	(7.6)	2.8	(3.5)	2.6	(1.5)	5.6	(2.4)	2.4	(2.6)
United Kingdom	0.3	(3.1)	−1.5	(7.8)	4.6	(2.5)	3.4	(1.5)	9.4	(6.1)	3.7	(2.2)
Germany	0.6	(2.6)	−2.1	(4.7)	2.1	(6.2)	3.2	(1.8)	3.3	(1.3)	2.7	(4.0)
France	0.0	(5.0)	2.2	(9.1)	5.6	(5.1)	5.5	(3.6)	8.8	(3.2)	5.6	(4.1)
Japan	4.6	(5.5)	−1.7	(7.3)	4.2	(5.7)	5.5	(1.0)	2.6	(2.4)	4.5	(4.6)
Canada	0.4	(1.4)	−1.9	(6.0)	2.1	(3.1)	3.5	(1.1)	7.9	(3.0)	2.7	(3.0)
Italy	0.6	(3.2)	−1.1	(11.7)	5.9	(16.0)	3.8	(2.1)	12.9	(4.6)	3.8	(11.5)
Mean	1.0	(3.4)	−1.1	(7.7)	3.9	(6.0)	3.9	(1.8)	7.2	(3.3)	3.6	(4.6)
Convergence	1.0	(1.0)	1.0	(1.5)	1.3	(2.9)	0.9	(0.6)	2.9	(1.2)	0.9	(2.0)
B. Real per Capita Growth[a]												
United States	1.8	(5.0)	0.2	(8.1)	1.8	(3.4)	2.9	(1.9)	2.1	(2.7)	2.0	(2.8)
United Kingdom	1.1	(2.4)	1.2	(4.5)	2.1	(2.2)	2.3	(1.4)	1.5	(4.2)	2.1	(1.8)

(continued)

Table 6.1. (*continued*)

	Gold Standard 1881–1913		Interwar 1919–38		Bretton Woods: Preconvertible 1946–58		Bretton Woods: Convertible 1959–70		Floating Exchange 1974–89		Bretton Woods Total, 1946–70	
	M	SD	M	SD	M	SD	M	SD	M	SD	M	SD
Germany	1.7	(2.9)	2.6	(8.5)	7.3	(3.9)	3.6	(2.6)	2.2	(1.9)	5.0	(3.3)
France	1.5	(4.6)	1.3	(7.2)	4.6	(2.7)	3.9	(1.3)	1.7	(1.5)	3.9	(2.2)
Japan	1.4	(3.8)	2.0	(6.1)	7.3	(2.8)	8.9	(2.4)	3.5	(1.1)	8.1	(2.7)
Canada	2.3	(2.8)	0.2	(8.8)	1.9	(3.2)	3.8	(1.1)	1.6	(2.6)	2.5	(2.6)
Italy	1.0	(4.1)	0.9	(4.7)	5.2	(4.4)	5.8	(1.9)	2.5	(2.2)	5.6	(3.3)
Mean	1.5	(3.7)	1.2	(6.8)	4.3	(3.2)	4.5	(1.8)	2.2	(2.3)	4.2	(2.7)
Convergence	0.3	(0.8)	0.7	(1.5)	2.1	(0.6)	1.7	(0.5)	0.5	(0.7)	1.8	(0.4)
C. Monetary Growth												
United States	6.1	(5.9)	0.6	(8.6)	6.4	(8.3)	7.0	(1.5)	8.6	(2.4)	6.3	(5.8)
United Kingdom	2.1	(1.7)	0.8	(4.7)	1.7	(2.9)	5.5	(2.9)	13.5	(5.6)	3.2	(3.2)
Germany	5.7	(4.7)	1.3	(10.1)	17.6	(5.6)	10.9	(4.7)	5.7	(4.5)	12.8	(6.0)
France	2.2	(3.5)	6.4	(8.5)	14.7	(7.2)	8.6	(6.6)	8.8	(3.4)	11.5	(7.5)
Japan	5.8	(10.8)	0.5	(9.7)	18.2	(18.5)	14.6	(2.5)	5.7	(6.2)	17.3	(15.9)
Canada	7.4	(5.3)	1.1	(4.7)	5.0	(3.9)	9.4	(4.3)	11.0	(5.5)	6.0	(4.0)
Italy	3.2	(3.1)	3.6	(6.2)	15.9	(10.5)	12.4	(2.0)	13.4	(4.9)	13.3	(7.8)

Mean	4.6 (5.0)	2.0 (7.5)	11.4 (8.1)	9.8 (3.5)	9.5 (4.6)	10.1 (7.2)
Convergence	1.8 (2.0)	1.7 (2.0)	6.0 (3.7)	2.5 (1.4)	2.7 (1.1)	4.2 (2.8)

D. Short-Term Interest Rate

United States	4.8 (0.9)	3.5 (2.0)	2.0 (0.9)	4.8 (1.6)	8.9 (2.6)	3.4 (1.9)
United Kingdom	2.8 (0.8)	3.0 (1.8)	2.3 (1.8)	5.8 (1.6)	11.2 (2.1)	4.0 (2.5)
Germany	3.2 (0.9)	4.8 (1.6)	4.1 (1.1)	4.0 (1.7)	5.9 (2.4)	4.0 (1.5)
France	2.5 (0.6)	3.1 (1.4)	3.2 (1.5)	5.1 (1.9)	10.3 (2.6)	4.2 (1.9)
Japan	2.4 (0.5)	2.0 (0.5)	6.8 (0.8)	5.9 (0.4)	5.2 (2.0)	6.5 (0.8)
Canada	N.A.	0.9 (0.4)	2.2 (1.3)	4.8 (1.3)	9.2 (3.4)	2.9 (2.0)
Italy	N.A.	N.A.	N.A.	N.A.	N.A.	N.A.
Mean	3.2 (0.7)	2.9 (1.3)	3.5 (1.2)	5.1 (1.4)	8.5 (2.5)	4.2 (1.8)
Convergence	0.7 (0.2)	0.9 (0.4)	1.3 (0.2)	0.5 (0.2)	1.9 (0.3)	0.8 (0.3)

E. Long-Term Interest Rate

United States	3.8 (0.3)	4.2 (0.6)	3.0 (0.4)	5.0 (1.1)	10.4 (2.1)	3.9 (1.3)
United Kingdom	2.9 (0.2)	4.1 (0.7)	3.9 (0.8)	6.6 (1.3)	12.1 (2.8)	5.2 (1.8)
Germany	3.7 (0.2)	6.9 (1.8)	5.9 (0.5)	6.7 (0.7)	7.8 (1.5)	6.3 (0.7)
France	3.2 (0.3)	4.6 (0.8)	5.8 (0.5)	5.7 (1.0)	10.9 (2.4)	5.7 (0.8)
Japan	N.A.	N.A.	N.A.	7.0 (0.1)	7.1 (1.8)	7.0 (0.1)
Canada	3.5 (0.4)	4.7 (0.8)	3.8 (0.8)	5.9 (1.0)	10.3 (2.3)	4.5 (1.5)
Italy	4.2 (0.5)	5.9 (0.6)	6.3 (0.4)	5.7 (0.7)	13.7 (3.3)	6.0 (0.7)
Mean	3.6 (0.3)	5.1 (0.9)	4.8 (0.6)	6.1 (0.9)	10.3 (2.3)	5.5 (1.0)
Convergence	0.3 (0.1)	0.9 (0.3)	1.2 (0.1)	0.6 (0.3)	1.7 (0.3)	0.9 (0.5)

Table 6.1. (continued)

	Gold Standard 1881–1913		Interwar 1919–38		Bretton Woods: Preconvertible 1946–58		Bretton Woods: Convertible 1959–70		Floating Exchange 1974–89		Bretton Woods Total, 1946–70	
	M	SD	M	SD	M	SD	M	SD	M	SD	M	SD
F. Real Short-Term Interest Rate[b]												
United States	4.8	(2.0)	3.8	(6.7)	−1.2	(4.7)	2.4	(0.4)	2.5	(2.8)	0.3	(3.9)
United Kingdom	2.9	(2.3)	4.2	(7.1)	−2.4	(3.3)	2.3	(1.1)	1.3	(5.1)	−0.1	(3.4)
Germany	2.4	(2.3)	5.1	(5.2)	3.0	(3.6)	1.6	(1.5)	2.5	(1.9)	2.2	(2.6)
France	2.8	(6.4)	1.2	(14.7)	−3.3	(6.9)	1.2	(1.4)	2.1	(2.8)	−0.9	(5.2)
Japan	−1.5	(5.5)	1.4	(8.8)	2.7	(2.8)	0.5	(1.1)	1.4	(3.5)	1.9	(2.5)
Canada	N.A.		−0.8	(1.3)	0.1	(3.4)	2.0	(0.7)	2.5	(3.2)	−0.3	(4.2)
Italy	N.A.		N.A.		N.A.		N.A.		N.A.		N.A.	
Mean	2.3	(3.7)	2.5	(7.3)	−0.2	(4.1)	1.7	(1.0)	2.0	(3.2)	0.5	(3.6)
Convergence	1.5	(1.8)	1.9	(2.7)	2.1	(0.9)	0.6	(0.3)	0.5	(0.7)	1.0	(0.6)
G. Real Long-Term Interest Rate[b]												
United States	3.7	(2.2)	4.6	(6.8)	−0.7	(4.4)	2.5	(0.7)	3.9	(3.8)	0.8	(3.6)
United Kingdom	3.0	(2.5)	5.4	(7.1)	−0.8	(2.6)	3.2	(1.0)	2.2	(3.7)	1.1	(2.8)
Germany	2.9	(2.4)	6.9	(6.0)	4.3	(4.4)	4.3	(1.0)	4.4	(0.9)	4.3	(2.8)
France	3.5	(6.5)	1.0	(15.1)	−1.2	(6.2)	1.8	(1.0)	2.7	(3.1)	0.4	(4.4)
Japan	N.A.		N.A.		N.A.		1.7	(1.3)	2.0	(4.2)	1.7	(1.3)

Canada	3.5	(0.4)	4.7	(0.8)	3.8	(0.8)	3.0	(0.6)	3.6	(2.8)	1.3	(3.8)
Italy	4.2	(0.5)	5.9	(0.6)	6.3	(0.4)	2.2	(2.2)	0.5	(5.3)	−0.4	(12.1)
Mean	3.5	(2.4)	4.8	(6.1)	2.0	(3.1)	2.7	(1.1)	2.7	(3.4)	1.3	(4.4)
Convergence	0.4	(1.4)	1.3	(3.6)	2.9	(1.9)	0.7	(0.4)	1.1	(1.0)	1.0	(2.2)
H. Nominal Exchange Rate												
United States							0.7	(0.8)			0.7	(0.8)
United Kingdom	0.2	(0.2)	6.8	(7.9)	3.6	(8.3)	1.4	(3.9)	10.1	(4.7)	2.4	(6.3)
Germany	0.2	(0.1)	3.9	(9.5)	2.4	(5.3)	1.3	(2.1)	9.3	(8.2)	1.8	(3.8)
France	0.3	(0.2)	17.8	(16.9)	4.4	(11.3)	1.1	(3.3)	10.7	(7.8)	2.5	(7.7)
Japan	2.9	(4.5)	6.7	(8.9)	22.0	(42.6)	0.2	(0.2)	8.8	(9.5)	15.9	(37.2)
Canada	0.0	(0.0)	2.6	(3.4)	2.2	(2.0)	0.8	(1.9)	3.7	(2.4)	1.6	(1.9)
Italy	1.4	(1.5)	13.6	(20.1)	14.1	(27.4)	0.2	(0.2)	10.9	(9.0)	7.4	(20.6)
Mean	0.8	(1.1)	8.6	(11.1)	8.1	(16.1)	0.8	(1.8)	8.9	(6.9)	4.6	(11.2)
Convergence	0.9	(1.3)	4.8	(4.9)	6.6	(12.6)	0.4	(1.2)	1.8	(2.3)	4.0	(10.1)
I. Real Exchange Rate[c,e]												
United States[d]							1.7	(1.0)			1.7	(1.0)
United Kingdom	1.7	(1.5)	6.5	(6.9)	4.7	(7.1)	2.5	(3.5)	9.4	(4.3)	3.5	(5.5)
Germany	2.4	(1.2)	5.8	(9.2)	3.8	(7.3)	1.9	(1.8)	8.8	(8.2)	2.8	(5.1)
France	4.3	(5.0)	8.9	(6.9)	6.2	(7.7)	2.5	(2.9)	9.2	(7.7)	4.1	(5.6)
Japan	6.6	(5.6)	7.8	(7.2)	4.4	(4.3)	2.1	(1.2)	9.6	(8.9)	3.0	(1.5)
Canada	2.6	(2.2)	3.2	(2.8)	2.4	(2.3)	1.2	(1.7)	3.8	(2.0)	2.4	(2.3)
Italy	2.1	(1.7)	13.3	(16.9)	13.1	(25.2)	2.4	(1.6)	8.6	(7.8)	8.0	(18.7)

(continued)

Table 6.1. (*continued*)

	Gold Standard 1881–1913		Interwar 1919–38		Bretton Woods: Preconvertible 1946–58		Bretton Woods: Convertible 1959–70		Floating Exchange 1974–89		Bretton Woods Total, 1946–70	
	M	SD	M	SD	M	SD	M	SD	M	SD	M	SD
Mean	3.3	(2.9)	7.6	(8.3)	5.8	(9.0)	2.0	(2.0)	8.2	(6.5)	3.6	(5.7)
Convergence	0.9	(1.6)	2.4	(3.2)	2.6	(5.4)	0.4	(0.7)	1.4	(1.9)	1.4	(3.7)

Note: For inflation, the standard deviation of the forecast error based on a univariate regression is shown in parentheses. The forecast error is calculated as the standard error of estimate of the fitted equation $\log(P_t) = a + b \log(P_t - 1)$, where P_t is the price index in year t.

[a] Mean growth rate calculated as the time coefficient from a regression of the natural logarithm of the variable on a constant and a time trend.

[b] Calculated as the nominal interest rate minus the annual rate of change of the CPI.

[c] Absolute rates of change.

[d] Trade-weighted nominal and real exchange rate starting in 1960.

[e] Calculated as the nominal exchange rate divided by the ratio of foreign to the U.S. CPI.

Source: Michael D. Bordo and Barry Eichengreen, eds., *A Retrospective on the Bretton Woods System: Lessons for International Monetary Reform, National Bureau of Economic Research Project Report.* Chicago: University of Chicago Press, 1993. © 1993 by the National Bureau of Economic Research. Reprinted with permission.

Table 6.1 reproduces the table from pages 7–11 of Bordo's chapter. We follow with Figure 6.1, which reproduces Bordo's graphs of the postwar balance of payments in Britain, Germany, and the United States, to show the increasing instability just before the Bretton Woods system was abandoned in 1973. The graph seems to show a turning point around 1968 in the stability of the system, and if we were doing an in-depth study of the monetary history of this period, we might want to focus on the events of that year. If we had, say, monthly data for the period 1959–71 and had estimated some parameters using linear regression, we might want to split our data into two parts at 1968 and try a Chow test for parameter stability. In addition, Figure 6.1 reveals the increased volatility of short-term capital movements after the move to convertibility in 1958 and, in particular, the big and very destabilizing move in short-term capital out of the dollar after 1969. Figures 6.2 and 6.3 show the average and variation of inflation and per capita growth for the G-7 countries during the interwar year and afterward.

although there was still an array of controls on the movement of capital, which still found ways of moving in spite of the controls. All of these previous regimes were mostly characterized by more or less fixed exchange rates, but after 1973, the Bretton Woods system was replaced by a system under which the major currencies floated in value against each other.

Looking at this statistical material, it is clear that up to 1989, the period of the best economic performance coincided with the period of Bretton Woods convertibility from 1959 to 1970,[3] but can we say that the economic performance was superior *because* of the move to convertibility in 1959, or, at least, that the liberalization of payments was one of a number of causes? In short, do we treat the liberalization of payments as an explanation for the high and steady growth we see in the statistics or is the liberalization of payments itself something that can be explained within our model? What I mean is, assuming we've constructed a model that relates, say, economic growth to the openness of the monetary regime, should we treat the monetary regime as a given outside of our model or as something determined within our model? At first blush, you might assume that the monetary regime can safely be treated as exogenous, but this is quite possibly not the case. Liberalization of payments on the international account might be a by-product of economic prosperity. After all, it is much easier to build a political coalition behind openness to the international economy when the economy is growing briskly and businesspeople and politicians are optimistic about their country's prospects in international competition.

For this reason, it is not so simple to treat liberalization of payments as an exogenous explanatory variable in our growth model – at least, not in an ordinary least squares framework. My guess is that the liberalization of payments was an

---

[3] Bordo makes the Bretton Woods period look a bit better than it would have had he included the years 1971–3, which were characterized by the disintegration of the Bretton Woods system and the transition to floating rates.

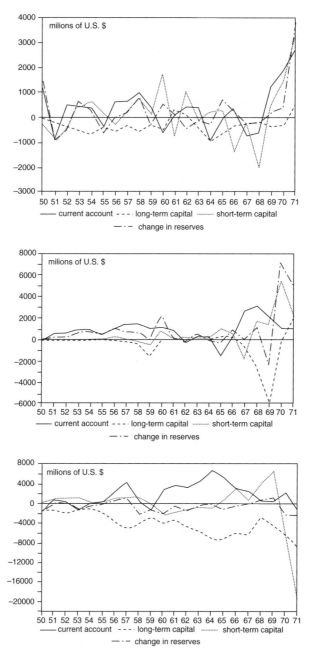

Figure 6.1. Balance of payments for the United Kingdom, Germany, and the United States during the period after World War II and before the abandonment of the Bretton Woods regime. From Michael D. Bordo and Barry Eichengreen, eds., *A Retrospective on the Bretton Woods System: Lessons for International Monetary Reform, National Bureau of Economic Research Project Report,* Chicago: University of Chicago Press, 1993. © 1993 by the National Bureau of Economic Research. Reprinted with permission.

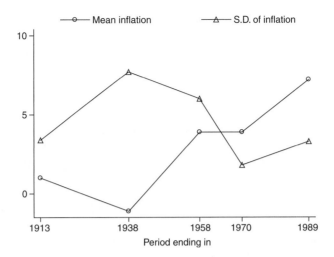

Figure 6.2. Mean and standard deviation for inflation for five periods in the G-7 countries: 1881–1913, 1919–38, 1946–58, 1958–70, and 1974–89 (wartime periods 1914–18, 1939–45 excluded). Note the deflationary bias of the interwar years and the inflationary bias afterward. Also, note the volatility of inflation, as measured by the standard deviation, during the interwar years and the increasing volatility after 1970. Graph constructed with data from Michael D. Bordo and Barry Eichengreen, eds., *A Retrospective on the Bretton Woods System: Lessons for International Monetary Reform, National Bureau of Economic Research Project Report.* Chicago: University of Chicago Press, 1993. © 1993 by the National Bureau of Economic Research. Reprinted with permission.

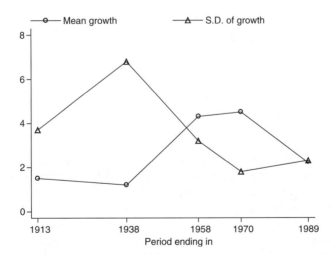

Figure 6.3. Mean and standard deviation for real per capita growth for five periods in the G-7 countries: 1881–1913, 1919–38, 1946–58, 1958–70, and 1974–89 (wartime periods 1914–18, 1939–45 excluded). Contrast the low and volatile growth of the interwar period with the high and stable growth of the postwar period up to the 1970s. Graph constructed with data from Michael D. Bordo and Barry Eichengreen, eds., *A Retrospective on the Bretton Woods System: Lessons for International Monetary Reform, National Bureau of Economic Research Project Report.* Chicago:. University of Chicago Press, 1993. © 1993 by the National Bureau of Economic Research. Reprinted with permission.

important factor in the long boom of the sixties since this is what economic theory tells us should be the case, but this is a hypothesis that is hard to prove from the data. We find here, just as we'll very often find generally in the social sciences, that the social scientist's empirical evidence is usually much harder to interpret than evidence from the physical sciences. For example, I think one could probably make a good contrary argument that the liberalization of payments in the 1950s and 1960s had destructive side effects and that it was at least one of the origins of the monetary instability that eventually sank the whole Bretton Woods system by the early 1970s. Since the pursuit of independent and domestically oriented full-employment policies was common to most of the industrialized world, the only way these independent monetary and fiscal policies could have possibly remained compatible with the fixed Bretton Woods exchange rates would have been through strict exchange and capital controls. Even though capital controls were maintained after 1958, liberalized payments on current accounts allowed currency speculation via "leads and lags" on payment for traded goods. For instance, if a merchant wanted to short the pound versus the D-mark, he would wait as long as possible to convert his D-mark receivables into sterling. Also, after the reopening of the London commodity markets in the early 1950s, one could effectively buy or sell sterling versus the dollar via commodity arbitrage. For example, a long position in London cocoa, denominated in pounds, and an equivalent short position in New York, dollar- denominated cocoa would create a synthetic short sterling position. So, was the liberalization of payments associated with the period after 1958 a good thing or a bad thing? A balanced answer would be that in the short run it gave much greater scope to monetary instability. For instance, the pound sterling was under chronic and serious balance of payments pressure for years after de facto convertibility of the currency had been achieved in the 1950s, and by the late 1960s the dollar's gold par value was increasingly in doubt. On the other hand, it is quite likely that the long-run gains due to the liberalization of both trade and payments have been substantial. The arguments from economic theory showing the gains in efficiency from an international division of labor are very persuasive. However, coming up with a model that demonstrates this from our historical data might be tricky.

In the social sciences in general and in economic history in particular, rarely does one have the equivalent of a controlled experiment in which an event A is introduced into the experiment that will allow one to say that this event is almost beyond a doubt the cause of effect B. We can't go back, rerun the period 1959–70 with a different monetary regime, and see what would have happened. As discussed previously, an attempt to explain the connection between the liberalization of payments and the excellent macroeconomic performance of the late Bretton Woods period can't rule out the possibility of reverse causation, that is, the possibility that the improving economic performance and increasing economic stability in the 1950s allowed a return to convertibility. Was the liberalization of payments while retaining fixed exchange rates caused by an improving economy rather than a cause of the economy's improvement? In the former case, the liberalization of payments would be an endogenous variable. In general, the possible difficulties created by treating the liberalization of payments as an exogenous variable make it hard to argue with complete confidence that a regime of fixed exchange rates and liberalized payments was a cause of the dozen years of superior economic performance from 1959 to 1970.[4]

No doubt the data are suggestive and provide us with important information, but as Bordo himself writes:

These data are limited. Although they show excellent performance for the convertible Bretton Woods regime, they do not tell us why it did so well – whether it reflected a set of favorable circumstances or the absence of aggravating shocks, or whether it reflected stable monetary policy by the key country of the system, the United States, or whether it masked underlying strains to the system. They also do not tell us whether the system was dynamically stable, that is, whether it would endure, or whether it was just a flash in the pan of history. (Bordo 1993: 27–8)

After all, if the system worked so well, why did it crumble so quickly in the early 1970s and why, during much of those twelve years, were there repeated sterling balance of payments crises and a sterling devaluation, followed later in the period by dollar balance of payments crises – not to mention a franc devaluation and two D-mark revaluations? In fact, it is certainly possible to maintain that the original system no longer functioned at all after March 1968, when the free market price for gold was separated from the official price of $35 at which central banks dealt among themselves. Also, we would, of course, have to control for other explanatory variables: Couldn't one argue that the low energy prices during the 1960s as compared to the oil shocks of the 1970s were even more important to good economic performance than relatively fixed exchange rates and liberalized payments? Where do the diffusion of technological improvements and improved managerial methods fit in, and how should we control for them? In short, there is a tangle of causes and effects to sort out here, and one can't rule out relationships among our variables like simultaneity and feedback, but we won't go into this topic further at this point.

My main point here is that in the social sciences, it is often very difficult to choose definitively between conflicting arguments over cause and effect. Usually we can show that, say, two variables are correlated, but to go further and say that one caused the other is often difficult and sometimes impossible. It could be that a third variable unknown to us or difficult to measure caused the behavior of both the variables we are looking at (see, e.g., Mishkin 1995: chap. 27). My point here will probably not be news to any of you who have taken a basic statistics or econometrics course, but it is nonetheless always worth bearing in mind since it is a difficulty often encountered in empirical work.

A BRIEF LOOK AT THE HISTORY OF THE INTERNATIONAL MONETARY SYSTEM

Let's take a brief tour of the history of the international monetary system over the past century or so, and we'll see how accepted wisdom about monetary regimes

---

[4] Of course, if we think that the explanatory variable of interest is not exogenous, we might want to try other estimation techniques such as instrumental variables estimation and two stage least squares. In Part III of this volume, there is a more in-depth discussion of this problem. Instrumental variables and two-stage least squares are discussed in standard textbooks on the subject such as Wooldridge (2000).

was heavily influenced by financial and monetary events fresh in the minds of policymakers and their advisers. One theme of twentieth-century monetary history was the debate over the relative merits of fixed versus floating exchange rates, and after generations of experience and argument, it is still not possible to say with any certainty whether a regime of fixed exchange rates is better than one of floating rates. There are reasonable arguments on both sides of the issue and "the lessons of history" can, I think, be cited in support of both sides. At least until a few years ago, there seemed to be a consensus that floating exchange rates probably served large economies like the United States best, while small countries seeking to import capital for development or seeking a stable role as a supplier of goods to large, developed economies like the United States were probably best off with a currency peg[5] or fixed exchange rate. A stable exchange rate for small economies would serve both to facilitate capital flows from the industrialized countries, where investors would want to be assured of the rate at which they could reconvert their capital to their home currency if so desired, and ensure that a developing country's exports were offered at stable prices in their main markets. This would all work out very well if these countries could hold their exchange rate fixed in the face of large capital inflows and outflows. However, in the 1990s there was a series of currency crises involving failed attempts to maintain a system of fixed exchange rates or currency pegs. First, within the industrialized world there was the crisis within the European Monetary System in 1992; then there was the Mexican peso crisis of 1994 and the Thai crisis of 1997 and its subsequent spread to Malaysia, Korea, Russia, Brazil, and beyond. Argentina even tried a currency board (see, e.g., Hanke, Jonung, and Schuler 1994) linked to the dollar, which, in effect, relinquished Argentina's control over its own monetary policy to the Federal Reserve Board of the United States. You perhaps recall reading in the newspapers about the dismal fate of the Argentine currency board and the economic turbulence that caused its abandonment. On the other hand, the European Monetary Union, an ambitious attempt at establishing a unified currency covering most of the European subcontinent, seems so far to have been a success.

Recent history seems to have an overwhelming weight in the deliberations of policymakers concerned with our international financial and monetary architecture. That is nothing new. As I stressed previously, social science data rarely lead us to incontrovertible conclusions. Often we judge as best we can from our data and allow recent experience to revise our judgments. After all, recent experience gives us new data to work with, and especially in the case of annual time series that don't go back very far, these new data might give us a new and better understanding of whatever process we're looking at. Even for the G-7 countries, macroeconomic data from more than, say, fifty or sixty years ago might not be reliable and might have been intermittently gathered. (For two provocative articles illustrating the problems of relying on old data series, see Romer 1986a, 1986b.)

Let's look at other historical examples, which we can illustrate from our data table drawn from Bordo's (1993) article. Look first at the data for the gold standard period. The low inflation and steady economic growth of the period make

---

[5] Generally speaking, currency peg implies an exchange rate that, though generally maintained at a defined par value, might be adjusted periodically to correct for balance of payments disequilibria.

it unsurprising that after the gold standard system was disrupted by World War I, an attempt was made to reestablish it in the 1920s. The 1919 *First Interim Report* of the Cunliffe Committee in the United Kingdom pretty much took it for granted that the gold standard was the natural and logical choice of monetary system. The report attributed the smooth balancing of international accounts in the pre-1913 period both to the price-specie-flow mechanism[6] and to the judicious raising or lowering of the bank rate by the Bank of England – both considered key features of the prewar gold standard (Eichengreen 1992: 35). Despite the now rather famous misgivings of John Maynard Keynes, most thought the return to the fixed sterling-gold rate as set by Isaac Newton early in the eighteenth century would be a first step to restoring the prosperity of the prewar world. They were to be quickly disabused of their illusions.

Now take a look again at Bordo's Table 6.1 and focus on the economic performance of the G-7 group of capitalist economies in the interwar period. Of the periods shown, the interwar period without question shows the worst economic performance. By the time negotiations for a new monetary system began during World War II, the interwar gold exchange standard was widely blamed for at least some of the economic problems of the interwar period – problems that doubtless contributed to the economic, social, and political disasters of the 1930s. Even though the new gold exchange standard can be said to have begun to function only in 1925 with the return of the United Kingdom to the gold standard – and it was effectively dead after the September 1931 decision to float the pound – it lingered on during the Great Depression in countries such as France and Belgium, where it seems to have exacerbated the manifold problems of the slump. Within a short period, Keynes's misgivings about the gold standard had come close to being the accepted wisdom rather than a minority view. To the British delegation at Bretton Woods, led by Keynes himself, any attempt to restore the old-fashioned gold standard was anathema. However, at American insistence, gold did continue to play a role in what evolved into a de facto dollar standard after World War II since during this period the dollar was fixed at $35 per ounce of gold, and the other currencies were in turn pegged to the dollar.

As social scientists looking at our data, how do we explain how the gold standard of the pre–World War I period correlated with good and relatively steady economic performance, whereas the interwar gold exchange standard was in effect during the period of the worst cyclical downturn ever recorded? Well, first of all, we would emphasize that there had also been very severe business contractions in the 1890s and in 1907 under the old gold standard, although these declines were never as steep or long-lived as the slump beginning in 1929. Also, we would want to highlight other factors that made it difficult or impossible ever to really

---

[6] The first explanation of the price-specie-flow mechanism is usually attributed to David Hume, who in 1752 refuted the doctrines of the mercantilists by demonstrating that a country losing gold in international trade will have its price level reduced relative to that of a country gaining gold. This price reduction will make the first country's goods more attractive in international trade, thereby eliminating or even reversing the loss of gold. In this way, the interaction between prices and the flow of gold (specie) and goods will maintain an equilibrium without any need for tariffs or government intervention (see Hume 2006).

reestablish a gold standard that had the stability of the one operating before World War I. By the 1920s, the political and economic landscape was so altered that any fixed-rate monetary system would have probably been too inflexible to handle the shocks. For one thing, the price level after the war never returned to pre-1913 levels despite the severe deflation of the early 1920s. Without a revaluation of gold in terms of the dollar and the pound, there was perhaps not enough of the metal on hand to support the higher price level. That the price level seemed to be too high relative to the amount of gold available was the impetus behind the decision at the Genoa Conference of 1922 to formally acknowledge the use of foreign exchange – in effect, pounds and dollars – as gold equivalents in international reserves – hence the name gold *exchange* standard rather than gold standard. In addition, the Bank of England, which had the largest vested interest in maintaining an open and stable system of international trade and payments, was left in a precarious position because world gold reserves not only seemed scarce but also were maldistributed. Britain had to support a weakened balance of payments with a very thin gold reserve, while the lion's share of gold reserves was in France and the United States, neither of which felt obliged to put the interests of the international system above its own domestic interests. Besides, during this period France was steadily embroiled with Germany and often at odds with Great Britain over the question of German reparations. This state of affairs tempted France to use its gold hoard as a political weapon and weakened the international cooperation between central banks upon which the prewar system had depended. We must add to the mix the political fact that during the interwar period the power of labor and socialist parties had increased manyfold compared to the period before 1913. The power of these parties and their orientation toward maintaining wages and employment cast doubts on whether, in a crunch, sufficient deflationary measures would be taken to maintain the external value of the currency (see, e.g., Eichengreen 1992).

As should be clear from our example so far, the economic historian is usually confronted with a complex reality where politics, economics, and social conflict interact and create a multitude of confounding variables that make the interpretation of the empirical data less than straightforward. Often our empirical data, which might not even be very good, can take us only so far, and we must rely on judgment and experience to make sense of the phenomena we are examining.

This brings me back to my discussion of how important recent historical experience often is in helping to forge a consensus over what is the best interpretation of ambiguous or even conflicting social science data. This, in turn, explains why conclusions from history or economics that seem firmly established in one generation often are overturned and revised by a later generation.

To continue with our example: As the interwar gold exchange standard withered and finally disappeared in the 1930s, some key currency rates like sterling/dollar and sterling/franc were left to float against each other, often in volatile fashion. Other important currencies such as the German Reichsmark ceased to be freely negotiable in the international foreign exchange market due to strict capital and exchange controls. Chaos in the foreign exchanges during the 1930s was accompanied by moves at least partly, and in some cases almost wholly, to withdraw from the international system. Rising tariff barriers and autarkic economic programs were common. It was in reaction to this interwar monetary experience that the new post–World War II monetary system was conceived. Look yet again at the interwar data in Table 6.1: Economic performance was poor and also quite volatile, as measured by the standard deviations. This economic stagnation, even regression, during this period galvanized and reoriented economic thinking so that the liberal orientation – liberal in the old sense of minimal state intervention – that had up to that point dominated was swept away or at least largely revised. The consensus reaction to the monetary disasters of the interwar period was perhaps best expressed in Ragnar Nurkse's *International Currency Experience*, published under League of Nations auspices in 1944.

As Bordo explains (1993: 29, 30), Nurkse examined the interwar gold exchange standard and diagnosed its failure as due to the reluctance of the main central banks to follow "the rules of the game." What Nurkse meant was that, in order to shield the domestic economy against foreign economic disturbances that might be transmitted by the gold standard, central banks largely offset the loss or gain in international reserves on their balance sheets by the addition or subtraction of a similar amount of domestic assets, thereby maintaining the money supply they considered proper to keep up the level of domestic activity while ignoring the external imbalances that might be perpetuated. This practice is known as "sterilization." Let me give an example of what Nurkse meant: In the 1920s, the United States persistently ran balance of payments surpluses, which means that gold tended to flow into the United States. Since the Federal Reserve feared the inflationary effects that this increase in liquidity might cause, it attempted to neutralize them by selling government securities from its portfolio to sop up the extra liquidity. Had the Fed allowed the economy to inflate in line with the inflow of gold, as in theory the rules of the game dictated, the U.S. balance of payments would have returned to equilibrium and relieved at least some of the balance of payments pressure on Britain. Instead, the United States continued to accumulate gold and shirked its responsibility for maintaining international equilibrium.

However, Nurkse didn't state that the failure of the interwar gold exchange standard could be remedied with floating exchange rates. On the contrary, he wrote:

If there is anything that inter-war experience has clearly demonstrated, it is that paper currency exchanges cannot be left free to fluctuate from day to day under the influence of market supply and demand. . . . If currencies are left free to fluctuate, speculation in the widest sense is likely to play havoc with exchange rates – speculation not only in foreign exchanges but also, as a result, in commodities entering into foreign trade. (Quoted in Bordo 1993: 29)

Nurkse's proposal was meant to correct the deflationary bias he attributed principally to the sterilization policy of the largest gold reserve–holding countries, the United States and France. He also wanted to avoid the destabilizing speculative flows of hot money in the foreign exchange markets. Basing his suggestions on his interpretation of the interwar experience, Nurkse wanted the new monetary system to have pegged rates that might be adjusted in cases of persistent balance of payments disequilibria.

He also wanted exchange rates set by international agreement rather than by resort to unilateral "beggar-thy-neighbor" devaluations. He envisioned the norm as no controls for payments on current account, although he advocated capital controls to prevent destabilizing speculation in foreign exchange. The deflationary bias of the interwar gold exchange standard was to be avoided by imposing discriminatory exchange controls for "scarce" currencies. Nurkse's ideas were very close to those of Keynes and Harry Dexter White (Bordo 1993: 30), who were, respectively, the British and U.S. representatives at Bretton Woods, and I think Nurkse's perspective can fairly be said to represent a consensus view at the time of the mistakes of the interwar period and of how their repetition might be avoided.

But was this consensus view necessarily correct, or did it gain ascendancy merely because it seemed to make sense of the recent past and because it had the advantage of being backed by the not inconsiderable prestige of Keynes? As early as 1953, Milton Friedman was questioning the consensus view that speculation in the interwar period was destabilizing and that floating exchange rates were unworkable (Bordo 1993: 30, 31; Friedman 1953). He reexamined the same data as Nurkse and saw the cause of sharp currency fluctuations when the gold standard was not in force (1919–25 and 1931–9) not in wild speculation but in a variable that Nurkse had overlooked – destabilizing changes in government policy. Speculators had merely responded rationally to the new information on government policy changes, and they helped facilitate the adjustment of the currency to its proper level in light of these changes. Another pillar of the consensus – that rampant sterilization of changes in central bank holdings of international assets was responsible for the miserable failure of the interwar gold exchange standard – was called into question in 1959 by Arthur Bloomfield, who found that central bank practice in the interwar period was not too different from that before the war (Bloomfield 1959; Eichengreen 1992: 36). In other words, Bloomfield found that there had been a good deal of sterilization of changes in international reserves even under the classical gold standard before World War I.

The minority of economists (for the most part, monetarists like Friedman or adherents of the Austrian school such as F. A. Hayek) who remained outside the consensus that had helped forge the new post–World War II monetary arrangements was consigned to the wilderness until seemingly vindicated by events. The collapse of the Bretton Woods system in the late 1960s and early 1970s, as well as other manifestations of the inadequacies of the postwar Keynesian consensus, suddenly turned Hayek and Friedman from eccentrics into Nobel Prize winners (awarded 1974 and 1976, respectively). Yet again, we see how quickly the accepted wisdom in economics can be cast into doubt by events. Around 1970, President Richard Nixon announced that "We're all Keynesians now" at about the same time that the Keynesian consensus was beginning to come apart. By the late 1970s, monetarist advisers taught or inspired by Friedman were being sought out to make policy in much of the industrial world and even as far afield as Chile. By then, the dollar was already floating against all the other major currencies, as had been advocated by Friedman since the early 1950s, and central banks were either targeting various measures of money growth or at least contemplating doing so. A sort of monetarist counterrevolution had set in.

It is difficult to say that there was ever a monetarist consensus – certainly the doctrines of monetarism were never as widely accepted as those of Keynesianism – perhaps for the simple reason that monetarism's heyday passed so quickly. Monetarism's eclipse can, I think, be ascribed principally to two factors: Monetarism in practice proved to be unwieldy, even impossible to operate, since the financial innovations of the 1980s made the definition of "money" very plastic. In addition, it was probably these same financial innovations that caused the velocity of money – treated as a constant by most monetarists – to become very unstable, thereby making the effects of money growth very unpredictable. The Federal Reserve now targets the federal funds rate.

I hope we haven't lost my point in the thicket of my example. I don't want you to take away from this discussion the cynical conviction that in the social sciences there is no truth but only passing fashions. On the contrary, I mean only to inculcate a certain modesty as to what social scientists and in particular historians can prove with our data. Even data that are incomplete or hard to interpret can often provide useful information. Awareness of history should certainly serve to keep us from delusions of grandeur since, as even my brief examples have I hope shown, one generation's accepted wisdom is often considered folly by the next. Moreover, even though economic historians are more apt to rely on data and quantitative analysis and take for their model the harder sciences, at the end of the day the interpretation of data often involves a use of judgment. This is especially the case if you are dealing with time series data that might not go back far enough in modern form to give reliable parameter estimates or that might have to be constructed from incomplete or imperfect sources. Still, I can't help but believe that this is far better than making arguments that are unconstrained by the available data or that seem naive with regard to most basic principles of statistical reasoning. It is certainly possible to make a fetish out of quantification and thereby come up with answers that are nonsense, but the tendency in the historical profession has been in the other direction, so that historians haven't fully taken advantage of what can be done with quantitative methods.

FURTHER READING

Mainstream works of history, whether academic or otherwise, rarely employ quantitative methods that go much beyond descriptive statistics. However, history using econometric methods is found as a subfield in many economics departments. The field of cliometrics or the new economic history had its heyday in the 1960s and 1970s. After around 1980, much of the initial enthusiasm died. A good, brief recounting of cliometrics' rise and decline can be found in chapter 8 of Pat Hudson's *History by Numbers* (2000). Typical of the disillusionment with cliometrics that had set in by the mid-1980s is Robert Solow's remark (quoted by Hudson [2000]): "As I inspect some current work in economic history, I have the sinking feeling that a lot of it looks exactly the kind of economic analysis I have just finished caricaturing: the same integrals, the same regressions the same substitution of *t*-ratios for thought."

Two of the best-known and controversial books that tried to apply econometric methods to history are Robert W. Fogel's *Railroads and American Economic*

Growth: Essays in Econometric History (1964) and Fogel and Stanley L. Engermann's *Time on the Cross: The Economics of American Negro Slavery* (1974). Generally speaking, cliometrics was criticized for trying to import neo-classical economic assumptions such as rational consumers, profit-maximizing entrepreneurs, and functioning markets to times and places where they did not apply and for ignoring the particularities of social and cultural institutions and customs that couldn't easily be fit into the stylized facts of an econometric model. In addition, in some cases counterfactual assumptions were made and data extrapolations constructed that seemed, if anything, to make these studies even more subjective than traditional history, despite the scientific pretensions. Historians of the New Institutional Economics school tried to remedy some of these defects by making their study that of social and especially legal institutions that were necessary prerequisites to a functioning market economy. One of the better-known books in this vein is Douglass C. North and Robert P. Thomas's *The Rise of the Western World: A New Economic History* (1973). All in all, most historians are unimpressed by more recent claims that econometric methods have now become sophisticated enough to overcome many of the problems of the first generation of econometric history, though this is argued by H. F. R. Crafts in a working paper entitled "Quantitative Economic History" (1999).

Econometrics itself has an interesting history, and those interested in it might want to read Mary S. Morgan's *The History of Econometric Ideas* (1990). As for a synoptic work of reference, the reader might want to dip into one or two of the five volumes of *The Oxford Encyclopedia of Economic History* (Mokyr 2003).

7. Historical Data and Demography in Europe and the Americas

Where can one go to find datasets relevant to historical research? As far as ferreting out data goes, this is one area where historians have made a real contribution to quantitative studies in the social sciences. For it is historians who have mined the many and varied sources of quantitative data from the prestatistical age, and it is mostly historians who have found and used published sources of social and economic data from the period before 1900. As far as published data goes, the first place you should look is your library's social science data collection. Many universities are part of the University of Michigan consortium, which means that virtually all of the social science datasets that are publicly available can be downloaded in your library without too much trouble. That includes all sorts of exotic things that you wouldn't think of as having a historical element. For example, I know that the Roper collection is available for public opinion surveys going back to the 1930s. Enormous amounts of historical data are likewise available on the Internet. I myself, for instance, placed a large amount of data on the Atlantic slave trade that is available online from the University of Wisconsin. We also have, as I mentioned in Chapter 6, IPUMS, the public use sample of the U.S. census from 1850 to 2000. Using these materials, the historian can do time depth studies and observe how a certain variable changes over time. If you want to learn more about IPUMS, try the website at http://www.ipums.org.

I want to begin this chapter with the observation that historians tend to view things diachronically rather than synchronically, that is, they tend to look at causal factors over time. They want datasets that stretch over time, and the analysis of time series should be their natural terrain. However, as I've stressed, historians often lack knowledge of the mathematical methods that are needed for the advanced analysis of datasets. With what you're learning in your other courses, I trust this won't be an impediment for you once you've found your data.

I've already given you a survey of published sources. Now I'm going to go over some unpublished primary sources that may be of use to you. At some point, you might be interested in answering questions for which you'll need to generate your own datasets. First of all, there are unpublished records created by the state itself. A good example of this would be cadastral (real estate) surveys, usually done at the national or provincial level (see Figure 7.1 for an example of a page from one of these surveys).

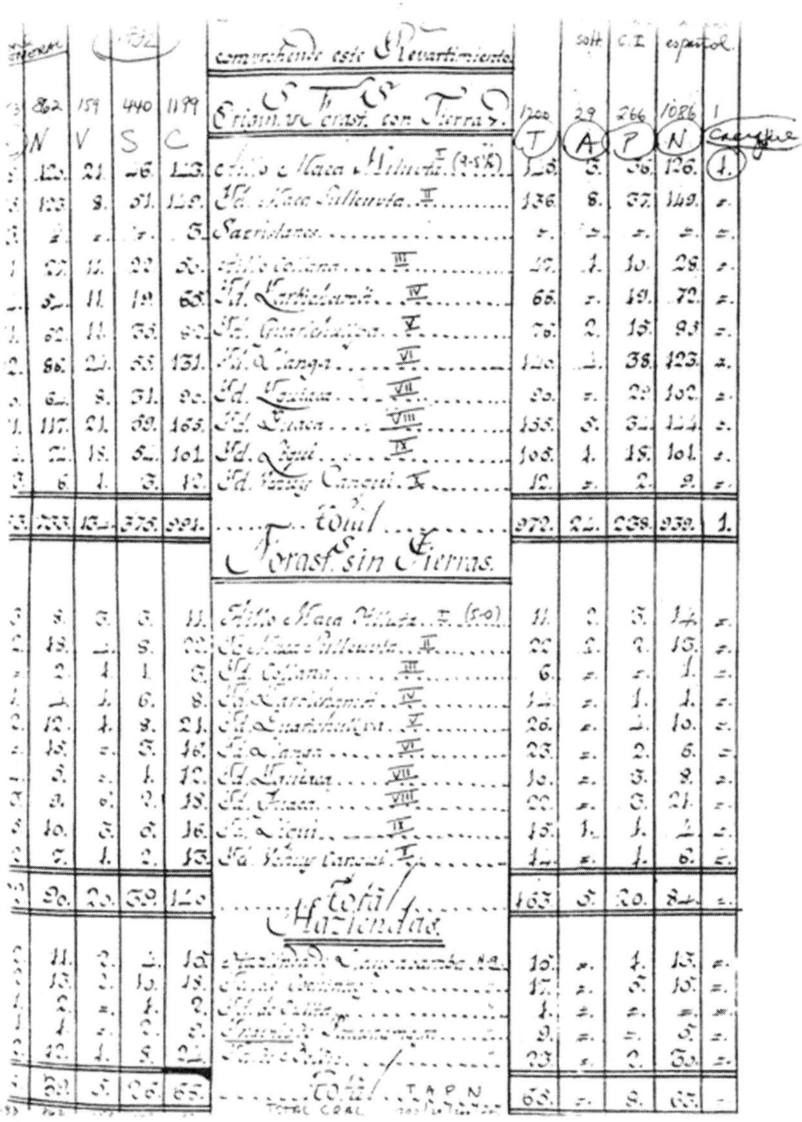

Figure 7.1. Truly raw data from a New World cadastral survey.

A friend of mine looked at the entire island of Puerto Rico, which had a cadastral survey every five years from about the 1870s to the 1950s. Nobody had ever done anything with these surveys until he and his team processed this huge amount of data (see Ayala and Bergad 2002). One interesting question they looked at was the impact of American capital on the sugar industry. These surveys began under Spanish rule for tax assessment purposes and were continued after the Spanish-American War, so we should be able to compare conditions before and after the Americans came. Did sugar become more profitable after the Americans arrived? Did land prices increase? Did small landholders lose or gain during the period of sugar expansion? These sorts of questions should be answerable.

Other unpublished sources in government archives are lists of taxable persons. If you went to the Municipal Records Building in New York City, for instance, you would find excellent tax records for the period up to about the mid-nineteenth century, which include the personal property of renters and the value of real estate of owners of property for New York City. I did an essay using this material and was able to show changing patterns of income distribution by neighborhood. Of course, at that time, almost all of New York City was south of Fourteenth Street, even south of Canal Street. North of that area was farmland. However, certain districts had begun to be developed. There was an odd combination of high-value property next to low-value tenement property, whereas in the older districts there had been a more even distribution of income. These materials are in the archives in downtown New York on Chambers Street and can answer many questions one might pose about the wealth of the colony and later of the city. What's unusual and especially useful about these archives is that, as mentioned before, the personal property of both renters and homeowners is inventoried. Also, this material can be tied in with other government-generated data – with census material, for example. My article tied in material from the 1790 census (see Klein and Willis 1985).

Wills and testaments are also important sources of social data. In the United States there have been several studies using wills and testaments, but this material is often a bit complicated and difficult to use since you're always capturing a snapshot, so to speak, of a person at the end of his or her life. Also, the material is biased insofar as people who are poor tend not to leave wills and testaments, so that we are left with records only from those wealthy enough to have property to leave behind. Nonetheless, scholars have tried to use wills and testaments to answer questions about distribution of wealth in the United States and how it has changed over time (see Jones 1980). Has inequality increased or declined? Since usually we have few good records of wealth until fairly recently, we often have to rely on this kind of material and try to adjust for inherent biases. Incidentally, the first household survey of wealth in the United States was not done until 1962. Before that date, estimates of average household wealth, concentration of wealth, and the change in its distribution over time depend on estate data, which are generated only from estates large enough to pay the estate tax. From this small and biased sample of, say, the top 5% of the richest households, scholars have tried to work back to the overall wealth distribution of the entire population. Of course, we are talking about wealth here. Income, which is a yearly rate of flow, is available from census data and is not the same thing as wealth, which is the measure of a stock rather than a flow. Income distribution and wealth distribution are highly politicized issues in most modern countries. Today, government data are usually available on both. Which of the two, wealth or income, is more important to look at is an interesting question to which I don't know the answer: Is someone better off with $50,000 in income and $200,000 in assets or with $70,000 in income and $100,000 in assets? In the United States, the distribution of wealth appears to have become much more concentrated in the past twenty-five years after its concentration had declined in the period from about 1920 to 1980. It's quite possible that some of this increased concentration of wealth in the past twenty-five years is due to deliberate government policy. For instance, the tax code has become less progressive and capital gains taxes have diminished. These are the sort of questions that one can try to answer with data on wealth or income. For example, you might want to try to ascertain whether the rate of increase in the concentration of wealth stayed the same or perhaps even increased after the new tax law of 1993 brought back more progressivity to the tax code, or whether the latest tax revisions of the twenty-first century have increased inequality, as many have argued. If wealth concentration continued to increase at the same rate or at an increasing rate even after controlling for the changes in government policy, one might want to argue that other factors, such as the runup in stock prices or structural changes in the U.S. and world economies, have been more decisive in increasing wealth concentration than government policy.

Business records are also an extraordinarily good source of information, but most of this material is, of course, unpublished, and the trick is getting access to it. For the nineteenth century, studies have been done using these kinds of records to determine the level of pay by skill level, or by sex and age, or by length of service on the factory floor. One can also look at upward mobility over an employee's lifetime. There have also been studies using bank lending records. For instance, I know of a sociology professor who got access to loan records from the nineteenth century for New Hampshire banks, where he found the same sort of insider dealing that occurs in some developing countries today, such as Mexico. The owners of the banks made loans to themselves with inadequate or nonexistent collateral. This worked out fine as long as times were good, but in a downturn they often went under along with their banks (Beveridge 1985).

A classic study was done on bank records from Newburyport, Massachusetts, in the nineteenth century. It turns out that if you look at the wealth of residents of English descent and compare it to the wealth of those of Irish descent, a curious thing is found. The Irish Catholics were wealthier than the Anglo-Protestants. The Irish, it turned out, were investing a large proportion of their income in housing and real estate. They got their children into the labor market early and invested the resulting income stream in housing. The Protestants, in contrast, tended to be renters and to keep their children in school, forfeiting the possible income from their labor. Stephan Thernstrom, the author of this interesting study (Thernstrom 1970), based his work on materials from the savings and loan records of the Newburyport banks, which clearly showed the different patterns of savings and expenditure based on ethnicity. The Irish were willing to sacrifice the future mobility of their children in order to contribute right away to family wealth in the form of home ownership. Often the first generation or two in this country were willing to sacrifice their own consumption and forgo education in order to provide a firm economic base for later generations.

If one were interested in pursuing this question of the savings patterns of various ethnic groups in the nineteenth century, bank records might be supplemented with publicly available materials from congressional committees that investigated the question in the late nineteenth century and found that, among the new immigrant groups, the Italians were the biggest savers. For example, many of the buildings on the Columbia University campus were built by immigrant Italian laborers, who were a common source of manpower in the early twentieth century not only in the United States but also in Argentina, where they were called *golondrinas* or "swallows" because of the impermanence of their stay. At the turn of the twentieth century, these laborers would come to the United States, live together in cheap all-male housing, contract their labor out to the local *padrone*, save their money, and send remittances back to the native country, all the while usually planning eventually to return to the native country themselves. We see the same pattern among immigrants today. For example, some Chinese immigrants in New York City, both legal and illegal, are willing to forgo consumption, perhaps live together with other immigrants in one room and contract their labor to a neighborhood boss, who might get them a job, say, in a kitchen. They are willing to make these sacrifices in order to save enough money to send back to their families in China – mainly to invest in the home country but perhaps to help bring the rest of their family here. This is a rather classic work and savings pattern among immigrants. The immigrant issue is just as pertinent today as it was at the beginning of the twentieth century. The 2000 census showed that New York City has more immigrants, that is, more nonnative-born people, than at any time in the city's history. By the way, there is an interesting online study of New York City's Emigrant Industrial Savings Bank in the 1850s. The study used the bank's records to look at the mostly Irish customers of the bank, analyzing their savings patterns and particularly their behavior in the bank panic of 1854 (see http://ideas.repec.org/p/fth/dublec/98–2.html).

Another place to look for nonpublished material is in the records of public institutions like hospitals. From these records we can generate datasets to answer interesting questions of a social science nature. Hospital records, for example, may tell us about the incidence of diseases, treatment policies, and death rates. From hospital records we may be able to tell that some persons were discriminated against because of their class, gender, or ethnicity or that some immigrant groups were more prone to be hospitalized for some disease than others. The definition of disease is not as straightforward as one might think, and the World Health Organization has been constantly changing and updating definitions of diseases up to the most recent period. Asylums have become a growth area in scholarship ever since Foucault made it fashionable by, in effect, stating that mental illness was a social construct, not a biological state (Foucault 1965, 2001). Researchers now look at records from these institutions to see how insanity was defined, as well as the social and economic background of the patients and their changes over time. One student did a study of people who were brought before the Inquisition because they claimed that they were talking to God or that the Devil had possessed them the night before or some such religious fantasy (see Jaffary 2004). In our culture, we would, of course, assume that these people were mentally ill, but the Inquisition didn't seem to think so and usually took reports of conversations with God or possession by evil spirits pretty matter-of-factly. The shamans of Amerindian societies we would consider stark raving mad. They walk around spouting gibberish and seeing visions. But in Indian societies they are accorded a place of honor, and even though they may be barely functional, Indian society finds ways for them to get by. There also seem to be national styles in diseases. For example, Argentines seem to complain of liver problems, whereas Americans have headaches. Latin Americans usually don't have headaches, but they might have *"susto"* or "fright." There also seem to be fashions in diagnoses. In the late nineteenth century, all sorts of female complaints were lumped under hysteria. Epstein-Barr syndrome was recently a popular diagnosis. Now I hear that it's out. There are often all sorts of vague malaises that some group wants defined as a disease.

Criminal statistics have also been a growth area in scholarship, thanks also, at least in part, to Foucault's work in this area (see Foucault 1975). Property damage and murder seem to be the only crimes on whose definition people from different societies can agree. Other crimes seem to be culture bound. The same act may be a crime in one society; a misdemeanor in another, and no crime at all in yet another, and even within the same society, attitudes toward crime change over time. After all, only in the past forty years or so in our own society have the margins of permissible behavior been widened to the extent that, say, a man walking around in women's clothes is not considered criminally deviant. The statute books are full of behaviors that were once considered crimes but are no longer prosecuted, or are prosecuted so rarely that it makes headlines when these laws are enforced: for instance, the controversy in the 1990s over the sodomy laws in Georgia. Also, there are debates about the incidence of crime. If the police force is no good, it may appear that the crime rate is low when actually it's not; and, conversely, a good police force that catches a high percentage of the criminals may cause the incidence of crime to seem higher. There are also national styles in incarceration. In the United States, we put more people in prison and for longer periods of time than anywhere else I can think of. The correlation of criminal statistics with ethnicity has also been popular. Most white-collar crimes are obviously committed by well-educated middle- and upper-class persons. Blacks and recent immigrants are often overrepresented in crimes of violence and against property. Sex differences in types of crime are also quite pronounced.

As I've said, vital statistics were generally in the hands of the church up to the twentieth century. Many good church records are available; probably the most famous ones are those of the Mormon Church. From the foundation of their church, the Mormons have believed that families are eternal. Mormons can rejoin their family after death, and dead ancestors can accept the Mormon gospel. The Mormons incorporate as many people as possible into the church by doing genealogical studies. If someone becomes a Mormon, he or she can get all of his or her ancestors into the church via genealogical studies. For this reason, the Mormon Church has paid for the largest collection of parish registers, birth registers, and vital statistics of all kinds from every country in the world for which they are available. These microfilms are kept in Salt Lake City in bombproof shelters, though a lot of this material is now online at www.familysearch.com. These records are available to anyone who wants to do research. Near Lincoln Center in New York City is a Mormon reading room; there, one can put in an order, pay a fee to have the microfilm shipped there, and then examine any of the film. I, in fact, was able to get the Mormon Church to microfilm the parish register of the Archbishopric of La Paz, Bolivia. I convinced a monsignor, who was in despair over the advanced state of decay of his parish registers, to ask the Mormon Church to commit all the material to microfilm. The Mormons sent down professional microfilmers and did the whole job. Theirs is a truly extraordinary collection of records, which even includes things like tax records or conscription records that the Mormons might not have been interested in but that they had to microfilm as a condition for being allowed to microfilm the vital statistics material they wanted.

As an interesting sidelight on church parish registers, when Christian children are baptized, they receive godparents. These persons are usually listed in the parish registries, sometimes along with information on what they do, where they live, their literacy, and (in South America) their color. Here we can glean a lot about friendship patterns as well as occupation, literacy, and ethnicity. Much recent work on slave friendships and class alliances has been done using these godparenthood records (see, for example, the classic study Carmagnani 1972; and, most recently, Góes 1993).

In Chapter 4, I said that historical demographers had been the first to develop the techniques for constructing vital statistics indices from parish church materials. Before we look at the displays, let me refresh your memory on what they did. As you may remember, this historical demographic work goes back to the 1940s and 1950s and was pioneered by Louis Henry. These demographers sought to put together vital statistics in pre–vital statistics eras, which generally means any era before 1900. In 1950, when United Nations representatives went around the world in an attempt to do the first census for every known society, they also wanted to research historical trends about such things as mortality, fertility, and age structure. The UN was faced with the same problem as the French demographers, that is, how to generate life tables from alternative datasets. Parish registers in Catholic countries proved to be the most useful, especially birth, death, and marriage books. What you see in Figure 7.2 is called a "family reconstitution."

How is a family reconstitution done? You take a parish. It has to be a closed parish without a lot of in- and out-migration, so usually you are dealing with a rural parish. You then list every birth, every death, and every marriage. You take these three lists to create what is called a "marriage register" like the one in Figure 7.2 that I created for a town in Chiapas, Mexico, using parish records from 1792. I was lucky in this case. I found a small parish, which is unusual in Mexico, and the natives were for the most part Mayan speakers located in a frontier area where almost no one migrated out or in. Once I had collected all the materials, I got to work creating the lists. First, we see that Pascuala Lopez was married to Juan Gomez. We know that she was born on June 5, 1774, and died on November 7, 1816. For the purposes of family reconstitution, we are most interested in her. What we want to find out is her birth rate. We know that in this community there was no impediment to marriage. In other words, it was not like a Scandinavian or North American pattern of delayed marriage, where marriage is put off until the prospective husband has enough income to support the family and where sexual restraint is used to prevent pregnancy before there is sufficient income. In this community in Chiapas, people traditionally got married and had children as early as possible.

We need to know the girl's age at the time of her marriage in order to get good data on her reproductive cycle. Next, we try to find the children of Pascuala and determine when they were born and when they died. We see that Pedro was born on October 24, 1795. He died within a few months. For Pascuala's daughters Isabela and Filipa, we find their dates of birth but no death register, and so we

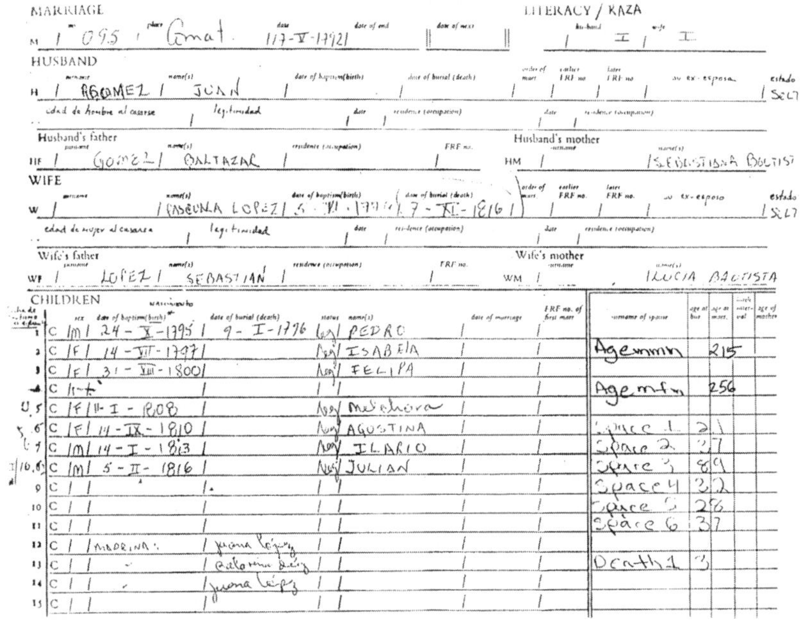

Figure 7.2. Family register based on parish data from Chiapas, Mexico, around 1800.

assume that they survived. Incidentally, at the bottom, we listed "*Madrina*," which means "godmother," and the father's name, which is extra information that is not necessary for our current purposes of estimating fertility but may be useful for linking to other records in dealing with other issues. An essential item for our fertility study is knowing whether, for both the man and the woman, this was their first marriage. Remarriage presents special problems. These Indian women of Chiapas were in fact very unusual in that they had low widowhood rates, which is not the norm in most premodern societies, where women tended to remain widowed more often than men since the men tended to remarry. However, many of these Chiapas women had access to land and therefore were still attractive mates even when widowed. In the case we're looking at, the man and the woman were both marrying for the first time. The age of the woman when she married was 215 months, and she had her first child at age 256 months. We also need to calculate the spacing between the children, which is 21 months, 37 months, 89 months, 32 months, 28 months, and 37 months. The spacing of the children and the time between marriage and first birth are our key data for calculating fertility and contraception if it was practiced. There are various models worked out by the French demographers in which you can fit these patterns. They constructed life tables encompassing all known fertility patterns so that now, when you study a society, if you know you have X level of mortality and Y level of fertility, you should have a certain age structure for the population based on the life tables. If another society has $X + 10$ level of mortality and $Y - 5$ level of fertility, it gives you a different age structure.

Pascuala's fourth child, who came 89 months after the third, makes me think that we might have made a mistake and either missed a child or perhaps one wasn't registered. The more typical pattern for a fertile woman for whom there are no impediments to bearing children and no form of birth control is for the spacing between the first children to be less and then for the spacing gradually to lengthen as she approaches the end of her childbearing years, typically in her early forties. You can estimate how long the woman was fertile by calculating the length of time between the first child and the last. There are also methods that one can apply for estimating the number of stillbirths. Cultural patterns of lactation will also influence fertility. If there is on-demand lactation, then there will be a long period of infertility after each birth, in some cases lasting as long as three years. Also, in the premodern period, about half of all children died before their fifth birthday.

Historical demography has been successful in establishing life tables for premodern societies using just the kind of parish record material presented in Figure 7.2. I warn you that it is tedious work, taking hundreds of hours. The Cambridge School in England, which I mentioned in Chapter 4, overcame the manpower shortage by sending students to train local amateur historians to gather this material from their local parish registers. As a result, we have a complete demographic reconstruction of England from about 1500 until official records began to be kept in the nineteenth century. Also, there are many limitations on what communities can be used. In Latin America, for instance, the reconstruction I did for this parish in Chiapas is one of the few ever done because of the mobility of the population in most areas in the region.

One interesting result that became evident from this research was that there was a particular European family model. No one was aware of this European peculiarity until demographers uncovered it. The Malthusian idea was that people were incapable of controlling their fertility and, as a result, would tend to reproduce up to the limits dictated by the food supply. Ultimately, population would be held in check only by periodic subsistence crises. It turns out that there are few societies for which the Malthusian model holds. In Europe, social and cultural norms served to check fertility and, for the most part, avoid a tendency toward a state of disequilibrium between population and food supply. The European pattern was characterized by keeping fertility within the bounds of marriage, that is, there was a low rate of illegitimacy. The highest marital fertility rates known are from European data. However, marriage in Europe tended to be delayed, so a woman bore no children during her early fertile years. Marriage was usually put off until the economic resources for rearing a family were in place. In fact, we find that the rate of marriage for the population is a function of economic conditions. For example, when the price of wheat went up, the number of marriages went down.

There were also mechanisms for completely withdrawing some women and men from the marriage market. Monasteries, for instance, appear to have attracted more novices in bad economic times, and spinsterhood was a more or less recognized status for women in Protestant countries. Men were discouraged from marrying unless they first had the means to support a family. As long as births were confined to marriage, all these mechanisms served to limit reproduction, as evidenced by the low European rate of illegitimacy: fewer than 10% of births. The upshot was that in bad economic times, fewer marriages occurred since men did not have sufficient resources. As a result of the shortage of eligible men, more and more women were consigned to a nunnery in Catholic countries or to spinsterhood in Protestant ones. The European family model clearly anticipated and forestalled Malthusian conditions by reducing the population before a subsistence crisis developed. The necessity to husband resources with a view to marriage is often cited as a reason why the European savings rate was so high, which could, in turn, explain why Europe was in the forefront in financial, commercial, and industrial innovations. Once Europeans married, however, usually in their late twenties, their marital fertility rate was very high. This European family model was discovered while doing these family reconstitutions, which revealed late marriages and short spacing between children. Don't forget that infant mortality was, of course, very high, so a high proportion of children did not survive to adulthood. All in all, the European marriage pattern was an ingenious response to European conditions of periodic shortage and famine. It acted as an automatic social stabilizer by minimizing marriages, and thus fertility, during hard times.

For reasons that are not quite clear, the European family model began to change in the eighteenth century. The main index of this change is the rise in the illegitimacy rate. Suddenly, the secular rate of illegitimacy, which had held at less than 10%, increased. This occurred from the last quarter of the eighteenth century in France, England, and Scandinavia. It appears that at that time, age-old social prohibitions broke down. The usual explanation is that this demographic change was a response to an expanded resource base. Often it is argued that the breakdown of the old system was a result of the spread of potato and maize cultivation, which provided an abundant and alternative source of food. It is also worth noting that European rates of birth outside of marriage were quite high in the American colonies in the period when they were extremely low in Europe itself. In the seventeenth century, when Spain had an illegitimacy rate well below 10%, elite women in La Paz, Bolivia, had illegitimacy rates of over 40% (see López Beltrán 1989). The Old World social and cultural controls on sexuality no longer functioned in the New World, where resources were more abundant and sexual mores more permissive, and by the late eighteenth century, as illegitimacy rates began to increase in Europe, the mechanism of fertility control by late marriage ceased to work there too. Of course, other societies have mechanisms to control natality. There are, for example, taboos against sexual activity during religious holidays or controls over the age at which sexual activity is initiated, but none seemed so finely tuned to reducing natality during times of economic crisis as the European pattern.

We know that mortality decreased in the late eighteenth century and the beginning of the nineteenth century. This set the stage for the demographic transition in European history of which I spoke in Chapter 4. Eventually, the rate of population increase for all of Europe rose to over 1% per year until finally, by the late nineteenth century, it began to level off for a variety of reasons: There were housing crises in some areas. The increasing importance and expense of education may have deterred some parents. Also, the new pension systems that were slowly being established meant that one no longer had to depend on one's children for sustenance in old age. In our modern industrial society, unlike in traditional agricultural society, children cost money rather than contribute to family income.

As you can see, as the result of much painstaking work on the part of historians, we have an accurate picture of the demographic evolution of Europe from at least the sixteenth century to the present. We know from what happened in Europe what can be expected to occur as, in the recent past, the demographic transition has spread beyond Europe into the so-called Third World. Nevertheless, it is worth stressing that the historical model of one period does not necessarily explain all later historical patterns. Thus, the demographic transition, which took generations to evolve in most European countries, happened much more quickly in most Third World countries. The slow development of modern sanitation in the rising urban centers of the developing world from the mid-twentieth century was accompanied by the massive introduction of antibiotics, all of which reduced mortality at a faster rate than Europe had experienced and led to much higher growth rates from populations accustomed to very high fertility rates – sometimes even higher than those that Europeans experienced in the pretransition period in nineteenth-century Europe. By the 1950s, many Latin American countries were experiencing growth rates of over 3% per annum, a figure unheard of in Western Europe. But this abrupt increase in the rate of population growth occurred without the structural changes that Europe went through. Europe's changeover to a higher rate of population growth was probably made possible by an increased food supply. In many Third World countries this condition did not apply, and the increase in population that has resulted from the decline in infant mortality has often led to increased social problems. As European cities grew in the nineteenth century, there were usually quick and effective responses to problems of sanitation and water supply, so that by the later nineteenth century, mortality in the city was no worse than that in the countryside. Third World countries today often have cities that have grown so rapidly that improvements in infrastructure have not kept pace. Obviously, if fertility had stayed the same and mortality continued to decrease sharply, population growth rates would have been well above 3% per annum in many parts of the world. Growth rates like these inevitably cause a shock to the social order, and via the social order to the political system. Fortunately, after the 1960s, the worldwide spread of modern contraceptives had an impact in most Asian and American countries, and in many of them, the widespread use of contraceptives was sometimes accompanied by active state family planning. China even introduced a one-child policy. Thus, the populations of many developing countries have reacted more quickly to increased population pressure than they did in nineteenth-century Europe. Usually within one generation fertility dropped sharply, at a rate far exceeding the European experience. The Brazilian and Mexican growth rates, for example, quickly decreased from 3% to below 2% between the 1950s and 2000. All of this suggests that even well-defined historical patterns based on long-term, well-defined demographic conditions can change with the introduction of new and different variables. This is worth keeping in mind when one examines even phenomena that seem to replicate past experiences.

Exercises for Part II

Pick one of the following themes that are debated in quantitative history and discuss the substantive points of contention and how these relate to specific quantitative questions. Also, discuss what data sources are used in the different references.

1. *Was Southern slave labor more efficient than Northern free labor?*

   Robert W. Fogel and Stanley L. Engerman, "Explaining the Relative Efficiency of Slave Agriculture in the Antebellum South," *The American Economic Review* 67, no. 3 (June 1977): 275–96. Gavin Wright, "The Efficiency of Slavery: Another Interpretation," *American Economic Review* 69, no. 1 (March 1979): 219–26. Paul A. David and Peter Temin "Explaining the Relative Efficiency of Slave Agriculture in the Antebellum South: Comment," ibid.: 213–18. Thomas L. Haskell, "Explaining the Relative Efficiency of Slave Agriculture in the Antebellum South: A Reply to Fogel–Engerman," ibid.: 206–7. Donald F. Schaefer and Mark D. Schmitz, "The Relative Efficiency of Slave Agriculture: A Comment," ibid.: 208–12 . Finally, see their "Reply," ibid. 70, no. 4 (September 1980): 672–90. And for general background to the debate, see Paul A. David et al., *Reckoning with Slavery: A Critical Study in the Quantitative History of American Negro Slavery* (New York: Oxford University Press, 1976).

2. *Did Southern slave owners breed slaves for sale?*

   Richard Sutch, "The Breeding of Slaves for Sale and the Westward Expansion of Slavery, 1850–1860," in *Race and Slavery in the Western Hemisphere, Quantitative Studies*, ed. Stanley L. Engerman and Eugene D. Genovese, 173–210. (Princeton, NJ: Princeton University Press, 1975). Robert W. Fogel and Stanley L. Engerman, "The Myth of Slave Breeding," in *Time on the Cross: The Economics of American Negro Slavery*, vol. 1, 78–86 (Boston: Little, Brown, 1974).

3. *Did higher fertility among U.S. slaves mean better treatment compared to other slaves?*

   Herbert S. Klein and Stanley L. Engerman, "Fertility Differentials between Slaves in the United States and the British West Indies: A Note on Lactation Practices and Their Possible Implications," *William and Mary Quarterly* 3rd. Ser., 35, no. 2 (April 1978): 357–74. Robert W. Fogel, "Demographic Issues in the Struggle Against Slavery," in *Without Consent or Contract: The Rise and Fall of American Slavery*, 116–26 (New York: W. W. Norton, 1989). C. Vann Woodward, "Southern Slaves in the World of Thomas Malthus," in *American Counterpoint: Slavery and Racism in the North– South Dialogue* (New York: Oxford University Press, 1983).

4. *How many people lived in the Americas before 1492?*

   Woodrow Borah, "The Historical Demography of Aboriginal and Colonial America: An Attempt at Perspective," in *The Native Population of the Americas in 1492*, ed. William B. Denevan, 13–34 (Madison: University of Wisconsin Press, 1976) Rudolph A. Zambardino, "Mexico's Population in the 16th Century: Demographic Anomoly or Mathematical Illusion," *Journal of Interdisciplinary History* 11, no. 1 (1980): 1–27.

5. *Did the frontier lead to equality?*

   J. R. Kearl, Clayne L. Pope, and Larry T. Wimmer, "Household Wealth in a Settlement Economy: Utah, 1850–1870," *Journal of Economic History* 40, no. 3 (September 1980): 477–96. Gary B. Nash, *Class and Society in Early America* (Englewood Cliffs, NJ: Prentice-Hall, 1970).

6. *Did the profits from slavery and slaving finance the Industrial Revolution?*
   Robin Blackburn, *The Making of New World Slaver : From the Baroque to the Modern, 1492–1800*, chap. 9 (New York: Verso, 1997). Stanley L. Engerman, "The Slave Trade and British Capital Formation in the Eighteenth Century: A Comment on the Williams Thesis," *The Business History Review* 46 (1972):430–43.

7. *How many Africans crossed the Atlantic?*
   Philip Curtin, *The Atlantic Slave Trade, A Census* (Madison: University of Wisconsin Press, 1969). Herbert S. Klein, *The Atlantic Slave Trade* (New York: Cambridge University Press, 1999).

For those whose interests run more to modern European history:

1. *Were the European empires assembled in the late nineteenth century important for stabilizing European capitalism or not? Can the theories of imperialism be reconciled with the numbers for the movements of goods, capital, and labor?*
   "The Economic Theory of Imperialism" in Winfried Baumgart, *Imperialism: the Idea and Reality of British and French Colonial Expansion, 1880–1914* (Oxford: Oxford University Press, 1982). J. A. Hobson, *Imperialism. A Study* (New York: Cosimo, reprint 2006. 1st ed. 1902). Vladimir Lenin, *Imperialism, the Highest Stage of Capitalism* in *Collected Works, Vol. 19* (New York: International Publishers, 1942). Hans-Ulrich Wehler, *The German Empire, 1871–1918* (Leamington Spa: Berg, 1989). D. K. Fieldhouse, *The Theory of Capitalist Imperialism* (London: Longmans, 1967). Wolfgang Mommsen, *Theories of Imperialism* (Chicago: University of Chicago Press, 1980).

2. *After World War I, Germany was saddled with a large bill for reparations. What was Germany's capacity to pay? Were the obstacles to payment political or economic?*
   William C. McNeil, *American Money and the Weimar Republic*, esp. chap. 4 (New York: Columbia University Press, 1986). John Maynard Keynes, *The Economic Consequences of the Peace* (London: Macmillan, 1920). Etienne Mantoux, *The Carthaginian Peace, or the Economic Consequences of Mr. Keynes* (New York: Scribner, 1952). Karl Bergman, *The History of Reparations* (London: E. Benn, 1927). David Felix, "Reparations Reconsidered with a Vengeance", *Central European History* 4 (1971): 231–55. Stephen A. Schuker, "American Reparations to Germany, 1919–1933," in *Die Nachwirkungen der Inflation auf die deutsche Geschichte, 1924–1933*, ed. Gerald D. Feldman and Elisabeth Muller Luckner (Munich: Oldenbourg, 1985).

3. *The end of the Weimar Republic and the beginning of the Nazi dictatorship was one of the great turning points of twentieth-century history. Many argue that economic discontent was crucial to Weimar's demise. What was the economic room for maneuver for the Brüning government in the decisive years*

of the onset and spread of the worldwide Depression? Do the numbers show that high wages were an insuperable structural difficulty of the Weimar economy?

Knut Borchardt, "Constraints and Room for Maneuver in the Great Depression of the Early 30s," in *Perspectives on Modern German Economic History and Policy*, 143–60 (Cambridge: Cambridge University Press, 1991). J. Baron von Kruedener, ed., *Economic Crisis and Political Collapse: The Weimar Republic 1924–1933* (New York: Berg, 1990).

4. *Accepted wisdom has always stressed the importance of the Marshall Plan for restoring Europe's prostrate economies after World War II. Might the statistics be read differently to argue that Europe's own contribution to recovery has been too downplayed?*

Alan Milward, *The Reconstruction of Western Europe, 1945–1951* (Berkeley and Los Angeles: University of California Press, 1984). Michael Hogan, *The Marshall Plan: America, Britain, and the Reconstruction of Western Europe, 1947–1952* (Cambridge: Cambridge University Press, 1987). Lucrezia Reichlin, "The Marshall Plan Reconsidered," in *Europe's Postwar Recovery,* ed. Barry Eichengreen, 39–67 (Cambridge: Cambridge University Press, 1995).

PART III. ECONOMICS

Richard Clarida and Marta Noguer*

* Stylistically, first person singular is used in the text to maintain the lecture format.

8. Learning from Economic Data

The use of statistics and econometrics in economic applications is a broad field. Rather than try to cover a representative sample or even an unrepresentative sample of the different statistical applications in economics, I will pick one area where basic statistical and regression results are very useful and then work through a number of examples of applications within that area. These applications and examples I think you will find interesting and timely; in addition, they will nicely illustrate some of the things we will cover later on. They also have some special interest for me.

CONTROLLED EXPERIMENTS ARE RARE

Let's talk about some issues that come up in many applications of statistical and econometric tools when they are applied to economics. These are issues that provide a challenge for doing statistical or empirical work in economics. The main issue that we have to confront in economics is that we rarely have controlled experiments in which we can analyze the effect of the change in one variable on another variable. I say "rarely" because there are occasional exceptions. A basic paradigm of classic statistical analysis that is very prevalent in experimental psychology, as well as in medical and clinical applications, is the idea of testing a hypothesis about the effect of a certain drug or treatment by experimenting on one group of patients while using another group as a control. The control group should be as similar as possible to the treated group. The goal is to be able to draw some conclusion about the efficacy of the treatment by comparing the treated group with the control group.

Unfortunately, we almost never have a controlled experiment in economics. There are a few exceptions. For instance, we have a branch of economics called "experimental economics." There is a class of propositions from classical economics that happens to lend itself quite well to empirical testing, and this is the work that experimental economists do. These experiments are quite similar to those done in social psychology. In particular, this field is valuable for those parts of economics dealing with financial markets and the behavior of the participants in auctions or that of people who can choose to either cooperate or compete with each other in a game-theoretic setting. In these circumstances, we have learned quite a bit from the use of controlled experiments, and there is a small but growing group of economists who aver that the use of controlled experiments is the only way to go. They believe that in many cases economists should abandon the statistical work that they actually do and move toward the laboratory and controlled experiments.

The only firsthand knowledge that I have of this field is not in the field of economics. When I was an undergraduate, I was very interested in psychology and I took several courses in social psychology. In those days (and I am sure it is still true today), in order to get your grade in social psychology, you had to show up for some of the experiments that social psychologists conducted. The experimental subjects were usually the students taking social psychology courses. The second course I took required me to take part in ten experiments, or about one a week. To me it was fascinating, and at that time it was a controversial area of social psychology. Not being a social psychologist, I am not sure if it is still controversial or not. In those days, you see, there was a big debate over the ethics of deceiving the people who were participating in the experiments. There were some classic and notorious deceptions involved. Of the two most famous ones, I suppose, there was one in which people were told that they were to help people learn a series of numbers by administering an electric shock to the person on the other side of the glass whenever he or she gave a wrong answer. The experimental subject was told that the farther he or she moved the handle on the lever, the more intense would be the shock, and it was up to the subject to decide on the dose of electricity. What the social psychologists were looking for were basic patterns of aggression according to age and gender. It was fascinating, but it was a huge deception because the person on the other side of the glass was not really being shocked at all. There was a similar experiment called the "Zimbardo prisoner experiments," conducted in the summer of 1971 at Stanford University, in which college students were asked to be prison guards for a weekend (see http://www. prisonexp.org for more information).

At any rate, in economics we also do controlled experiments, but they are rarely controversial in the way that those fondly remembered social psychology experiments from my undergraduate days were. Economists' experiments usually involve some people sitting in a room or at computer terminals and playing a game in which, even if they cannot communicate with each other, if they cooperate they each get a big payoff, but if they compete with each other they get only a small payoff. (This is related to the repeated prisoner's dilemma game described in Chapter 3 of this book.) The purpose of the experiments is to see whether, if the game is repeated, the participants learn to cooperate even without direct communication. In another version, an experimenter might simulate the financial markets by giving a few of the participants inside information and then seeing how long it takes for the information to be reflected in prices.

However, aside from these sorts of experiments, we almost never have controlled experiments in economics. When we make inferences and test theories in economics, we are looking at data generated in a world over which we typically have no control. One appeal of economic history for many people is that economic history can provide natural experiments, or so they argue. Historical events are, of course, not controlled in the laboratory, but nonetheless, there are dramatic historical incidents that give us the closest approximation we can get to controlled experiments. One will occasionally see discussions of historical episodes and of the use of the data from these episodes to draw inferences germane to a current economic theory. There is a branch of labor economics that uses these so-called natural experiments. An example of a natural experiment might be, two cities that are next to each other and are similar in almost every respect. Then at some point a change is introduced in one of the cities, say a change in the educational system. The idea is to see if the introduction of this change makes the formerly identical cities different and, if so, in what way.

Another example of this use of natural experiments is the attempt in the United States in 2001 to do a real-world experiment on the effect of school vouchers on student achievement. The basic idea, as I understand it, was to have people apply for these vouchers, and since the supply of vouchers was limited and more people would apply for them than could get them, the selection of who would get the vouchers was done at random. This random selection was, of course, very important in that it provided a control against a common problem in these sorts of experiments: that of sample selection bias. A lot of what drives the power of statistics is the idea that the sample that we're looking at has been taken randomly or perhaps independently over time. In many economics applications that is a very difficult assumption to make. The absence of randomness in sample selection gives you a biased selection. How would sample selection bias be an issue in a study of the efficacy of school vouchers? Suppose that there are two factors that influence success in school: the quality of the school and the amount of time that parents devote at home to helping their children with their homework. It is quite likely that the parents who are willing to spend more time helping their children with their homework are also more likely to be the parents who are willing to go to the trouble of filling out applications for school vouchers. If you let the voucher applicants "self-select" – rather than have the treatments assigned by the experimenters – then you will never know whether it was the voucher program or the unobserved parental input that was responsible for the improved performance.

This sort of thing happens all the time in economics. Over a wide range of applications, you will run into the problem of having some unobservable characteristics that tend to be correlated with whether an observation is in the sample. Another example of selection sample bias that comes up is in the context of financial data. Very often when people deal with financial data, they run into a problem called "survivor bias": When you are looking at the historical returns of securities and you want to have a matched sample, you look at securities for which prices are available for a certain time period. In other words, the firms must have survived over the entire period. For example, suppose you're looking at returns for the period 1940 to 1990. Usually, for the whole time period, you'll look only at firms that have been around for that entire period. That introduces potential bias if the firms that are in your sample part of the time are different from the firms that are in your sample for the whole time. In financial data there may be a very good reason why those two sets of firms may be different. The usual reason why a firm in your sample in 1940 may not be there in 1990 is that the firm went bankrupt. If you're hypothesizing something about the behavior of firms in general, you have to be careful when using a sample that ultimately will include only those firms well managed or well capitalized enough to have survived for the fifty years. That might be fine if your theory is about how well-managed and well-capitalized firms do something. However, typically you would not want to theorize only about well-managed or well-capitalized firms. You would want your sample to include firms of all types to control for good management or ample capitalization. Obviously, if you restrict yourself to firms that have survived the entire sample period, you open yourself up to survivor bias, a serious form of sample selection bias.

Another interesting example, which comes up more often in a macroeconomic context, is similar to survivor bias. This involves the idea of convergence – that is, the idea that poor and rich countries' living standards, though they may be very different today, will become more similar or converge over time. There is a large body of theoretical economics that makes predictions about convergence, and now there is a growing branch that predicts that convergence will not occur. This is clearly an interesting question. A paper by William Baumol, one of the giants of economics in the past forty or fifty years, called "Productivity Growth, Convergence and Welfare: What the Long-Run Data Show" (1986), presents the evidence for convergence by taking a group of countries with similar living standards and then going back forty or fifty years to show that back then their living standards were not so similar. He concludes that they have converged, that is, that countries that started off with very different levels of income now have similar levels of income. By contrast, economists like J. Bradford De Long have contended that Baumol (1986) is asking the wrong question or, rather, that the problem is that Baumol's sample of countries is tainted by survivorship bias. Baumol (1986) draws conclusions from regressions of growth since 1870 on 1870 productivity for sixteen countries covered by Maddison (1982). In his paper "Productivity Growth, Convergence and Welfare: Comment" (1988), De Long points out that the only way to avoid survivorship bias is not to start out by selecting just the countries that are rich today (Maddison's sample of countries). You have to look at all countries, not just the successful ones. If you redo Baumol's experiment by including all countries in your sample, you'll discover that Baumol's findings are valid only for those countries that are rich today (see Figure 8.1).

To sum up, we rarely have controlled experiments. Sometimes we look for natural experiments, but we must always be conscious of the problems of selection bias that this might present – in particular, survivorship bias.

ENDOGENOUS, EXOGENOUS, AND PREDETERMINED VARIABLES

So, what do we generally do when we apply statistical methods to economic problems? What we look at in economic applications are collections of variables. These might measure the amount people consume, the amount of money they have in the bank, the level of interest rates set by the Federal Reserve, the rate of inflation, and so forth. An almost unlimited array of economic variables can be and have been studied in different contexts. What we will do in this chapter is to stress the distinction between variables that are endogenous, exogenous, and predetermined. These concepts are important throughout economics, but they are particularly important in the branch of economics we will discuss here: time series economics.

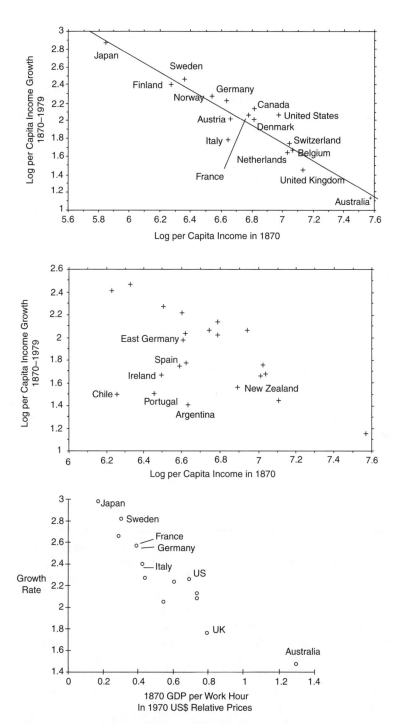

Figure 8.1. De Long (1988) on Baumol (1986). Reprinted with permission of the author and the publisher.

Let's give some rough definitions by putting some variables we might look at into various categories. In any economic application that you might think of, there will be some variables: an outcome variable on the left side of the equation and one or more predictors on the right side. These variables can be endogenous, exogenous, or predetermined.

An "endogenous variable" is one that your theory seeks to explain. It's nice if you are looking at many variables and there's only one that you seek to explain; the rest of them are exogenous. In the ideal world of econometrics and statistical textbooks, a theory usually has one endogenous variable and possibly a large number of exogenous variables. Then, under some assumptions that we will go over later, even though we do not really have controlled experiments in economics, we can proceed as if we do because exogenous variables take on the role of the experimental control. A lot of work that was done historically in applying statistics to economics served to kid either yourself, your students, or whoever was reading your papers that you had found one variable that you wanted to explain, say, how much people consume or how much money they have in the bank, while all the other variables were exogenous.

But what exactly do we mean by an "exogenous variable"? An exogenous variable has several important characteristics, the first of which is that it is not explained within your model. Anything that happens to that variable is outside of the model. A second feature, which is probably, at a deeper level, just a restatement of the first, is that if there are any mistakes in your model, those mistakes are completely unrelated to any exogenous variables past, present, or future. Suppose we have a theory. The theory makes predictions and sometimes the predictions are in error, but the key concept for exogenous variables is that any of these errors are, at least in a statistical sense, unrelated to any past, present, or future of your exogenous variables. Any variables of which this is true are strictly exogenous. In that world, even though we cannot do controlled experiments, by selecting appropriate exogenous variables, we can get pretty close to a controlled experiment.

Now there is just one problem here, and it is big: In the applications that I am going to talk about in this chapter and in most of the applications that anyone works on in time series economics, there are no exogenous variables. They do not exist. In fact, if you think seriously – as we will – about the economics of our examples, the economics itself will tell you that exogenous variables do not exist. We have theories that are interesting to us and make interesting predictions about things like consumption or money holding or stock prices, but they are theories for which there are no exogenous variables. The corollary to this is to say that everything is endogenous at some level. This is especially true in statistical work involving economic time series.

There is a third category of variables that is similar to and often confused with exogenous variables but is different in an important way. We are speaking of variables that are predetermined. A "predetermined variable" is one that helps to explain the endogenous variable but, more importantly, one whose current level and history are unrelated to the errors you made in your theory. So, a predetermined variable is one that helps to explain the endogenous variable and is one whose entire history is unrelated to the mistakes you are making in the theory. But is this not the same as an exogenous variable? Well, there is one difference that may seem small, but it is of crucial importance. A predetermined variable has a history that is unrelated to your mistakes, but an exogenous variable has both a history and a future unrelated to your mistakes. In many applications, what you will find is that mistakes are unrelated to history but influence the future. One thing about time is that you cannot stop it. It keeps going forward. Many economic applications have the property that mistakes today influence the so-called predetermined variables in the future. However, it turns out that this is not so bad since some smart people have figured out ways to do statistical inference in a world in which the variables we have to control for are predetermined and not exogenous. We will go into this later.

So, endogenous variables are the variables you want to explain: how much money someone will save, how much he will consume, and so on. Exogenous variables are on the wish list of the researcher. You would like to find variables that explain the endogenous variables but are unrelated to the errors in the model. Finally, predetermined variables are variables that can also explain your endogenous variables and whose history is unrelated to your mistakes but whose future values can influence your mistakes.

ANALYZING TIME SERIES

Let me make a few more observations. I have mentioned a good bit about economic time series. We will define these more carefully in a little while but, loosely speaking, when we talk about time series, we have at least one endogenous variable that we want to explain and perhaps a collection of predetermined variables that help explain it. We are looking at a series of observations of our data that are measured at certain points over calendar time. So, the simplest example of a time series application would be a theory that has one variable you want to explain, say, consumption in each period t, with t usually being a month or a year. Let's say that my theory is that consumption (C) in a month equals b times income per month, but I realize that in some months I consume more than my income and in some months less, so that there is some mistake in this equation, which we call the "error term" or the "residual." So, in this case, I am explaining C_t, my endogenous variable, by one variable X_t (income), and that, perhaps, is my predetermined variable. Given this one predetermined variable and this one endogenous variable, my theory says that consumption this month is proportional to income on average, but that some months I consume more than this fraction and some months less (Figure 8.2).

Why have we called income a predetermined variable and not an exogenous variable? Well, imagine a story in which I have some private information because I know more about my job prospects than the econometrician, and suppose that, in months that I am consuming more than my income, it is due to my boss's having told me that I am going to get a raise. In that case, the error term would be larger because of my expectation of more income in the future, so X would be predetermined and not exogenous. You might think of some sort of controlled experiment to test this theory with only exogenous variables. The researcher could assign each of the subjects an income level and not give any advance information of changes in income levels. In that case, X is exogenous since the experimenter

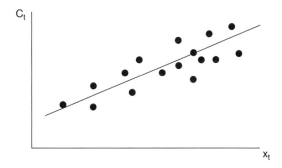

Figure 8.2. Hypothetical data and model explaining consumption.

selects it. But economists do not select incomes this way. We observe incomes that people select either by supplying labor or by other means, and certainly we must recognize that people have more information about their income than we economists do.

What we have just shown you would be a time series application. You can also see a cross section, that is, data on a number of individuals at a point in time. There would be no time dimension here since all of our data would be drawn from individuals at the same time. What we have is a cross-sectional dimension – say, the consumption of many people in some year joined with observations on their incomes. We can use this cross section to estimate the common fraction of income they consume. Of course, each equation will have its error term, so that there will be an error for person 1, for person 2, and so on. You can argue that under certain circumstances the error terms will not be related to the variables, although that can be problematic. The key point to remember here is that to make any kind of inference about an unknown parameter, one must have either a time dimension to one's data or a cross-sectional dimension. Clearly, if all you have is data on one person in one year, you have nothing. You can even combine cross-sectional and time series analysis, which is called "panel analysis." Here you have a cross-sectional dimension within time periods. For our purposes, we will not talk much about either cross sections or panel studies.

As I mentioned previously, our plan is to look at some data first, before we go on to study the mathematical analysis. When I am doing a statistical project, I try to spend as much time looking at the data as I do trying to explain them. One incredible advantage that we have now that we did not have just twenty years ago is that there has been an enormous revolution in statistical work due to personal computers and the Internet. For example, a small laptop today has more power than any college student outside of perhaps MIT or Caltech had access to just twenty years ago. In those days, you would have to sit in a big sterile-looking room with an air conditioner humming. You would do your little program, which you would have to type into a card puncher – not into the computer itself. At that time, IBM made not only the computers but the keypunch cards too. Every card had one line of instructions. Today, when you do a line of program, you just put it on the screen; in those days, you had to submit these cards and every card had a line of program. Some lines of program were so long that you had to continue them on another card. You would put two or three rubber bands around them and then submit them to a person standing behind a window. That person's job was to queue your program behind those of others who had submitted theirs earlier. When it was your turn, your cards would be inserted in the machine; the computer would run your program, and a loud printer would print out the results, which would then be stacked up so that, in the end, it was like going to pick up your laundry. The most frustrating thing would be that you might have eighteen pages of code, and if one column was missing on one card, the whole program would blow up. You would not know this for four hours, even if it took the program only four seconds to run, because many other people would be ahead of you. Then you would have to completely debug your program and start all over. So, you can see why people did not do much of this sort of work at that time. But now you can sit anywhere and do this sort of work. I usually get my deskwork out of the way while commuting in on the train in the morning.

SOME SAMPLE APPLICATIONS

The goal of this and the next two chapters is to impart some basic knowledge of how economists use statistical methods to do their work. We need not concern ourselves too much with the details but rather with what we can learn from the general approach. The first application we consider comes from a very interesting article, "Federal Reserve Information and the Behavior of Interest Rates" (2000), by Christina Romer and David Romer. The purpose of the article is to see whether the Federal Reserve has superior information or superior abilities to process information relative to the private sector. In particular, the researchers assess the hypothesis that the private sector uses the information it has in an efficient way, if not in the best way. In other words, they test for the rationality of private sector forecasts and then look at the relation between the interest rates that the Federal Reserve sets and its ability to *forecast* inflation versus the private sector. Is there anything the private sector could learn from the information the Fed has about inflation by looking at the policies the Fed follows?

The second article we will get to is one by Robert Cumby and Frederic Mishkin called "The International Linkage of Real Interest Rates" (1986). This article explores the hypothesis that interest rates in different countries are linked in the international capital markets. In particular, it tests whether interest rates adjusted for inflation are equalized across different capital markets. Obviously, interest rates themselves are not equalized across *capital markets*, and we'll look at some data on interest rates. For instance, short-term interest rates at the end of July 2007 in the United States were over 5%, while in Japan they were less than 1% and, in Europe, between 2.5% and almost 6%. The hypothesis we'll be looking at later is that these differences in interest rates are entirely explained by differences in inflation – or, more precisely, expected inflation. So, the way to explain that U.S. interest rates are a point or so lower than those in Europe is to say that expected inflation in the United States is also a point or so lower. The same goes for Japan. If our interest rates are 5 points higher than in Japan, it should be because the expected inflation differential between the two countries is about 5%. This is an interesting hypothesis, and we will go over it in Chapter 10.

The third article we will talk about is one I wrote with two coauthors, Mark Gertler and Jordi Galí called "Monetary Policy Rules in Practice" (1998), in which we proposed a hypothesis that tries to explain the way central banks conduct monetary policy. We tested our data by using some of the econometric methods that we are going to talk about.

Right now, let me give a simple example of why it is important to be humble whenever one does empirical work in economics. Very basic and important things that policymakers and firms need to know are actually difficult to know. One thing that they need to know is the relation between the amount that they actually produce and their long-run ability to produce. This is a very important issue for the Fed right now because the Fed has models with which it estimates productive capacity, and it has used these models for decades. The models are based on the same methods that we will discuss in the next two chapters, and they show the productive capacity of the economy growing over time as more machines and workers are added and as technology improves. But what the Fed is concerned about more than our capacity to produce is the gap between actual production and capacity. Even though in textbooks we might treat the economy's capacity to produce as known and observed, it is really not. The Fed has to estimate it. A significant development of the past few years has been that these estimates, based on our historical data, have broken down. The historical patterns suggest that, given how rapidly the economy was growing in the middle to late 1990s, we should have had high inflation in the United States. We had essentially four consecutive years of economic growth in excess of 4%. This was from a base where the Fed thought the economy was at capacity. Unless you think that the economy's capacity to produce is increasing at 4% a year, that rapid growth was outstripping capacity and should have resulted in inflation.[1] It did not result in inflation – or at least not much inflation – and this led the Fed to believe that it needed to rethink its models of the underlying economy. The surprising growth of the economy in the late 1990s had some people talking of the "new economy." Sometimes, however, it can be difficult to sort out disturbances from shifts in the economy's potential to produce output. We will see some examples.

TEMPORAL DEPENDENCE

Now we will look at some time series of interest. We will focus on "temporal dependence" – that is, local *correlation* or "stickiness" in the series. Let's look, for example, at the plot of U.S. ten-year interest rates over time (Figure 8.3). We see some temporal dependence, and if we test the hypothesis that the observations are independent draws, it will be clearly rejected.

Let's look at another example, the "nominal exchange rate" between the U.S. dollar and the U.K. pound (Figure 8.4).

---

[1] The argument behind this statement is the following: Capacity is understood as the economy's long-run ability to produce. If aggregate demand is growing at a faster pace than aggregate capacity to produce, producers will be forced to raise wages in order to get more workers or more hours per worker and this will be translated into higher prices, at some point in time, so that firms continue to make profits. These higher prices will yield inflation.

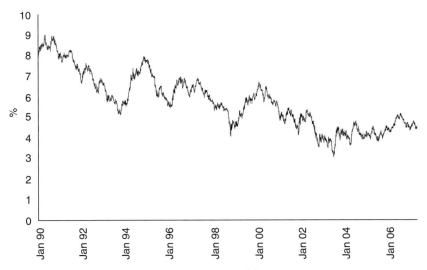

Figure 8.3. U.S. ten-year real interest rates.

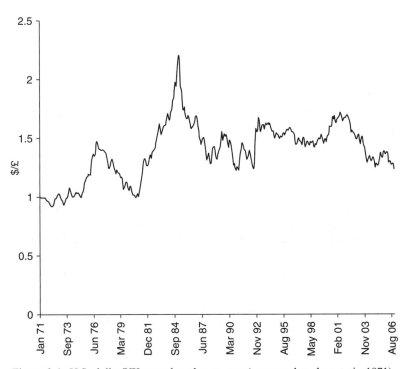

Figure 8.4. U.S. dollar/UK pound exchange rate (compared to the rate in 1971).

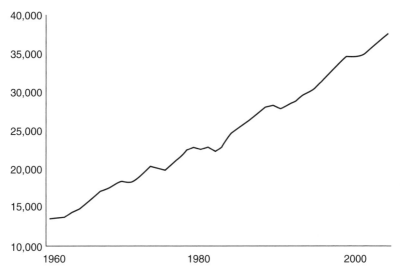

Figure 8.5. U.S. per capita GDP (inflation-adjusted) over time.

Observing this plot, we can see that there is one part of the series that never dies out in expectation. In real time series data we will usually also observe trends. They reflect another type of temporal dependence. Let's take a look at the time series of gross domestic product (GDP) per capita (Figure 8.5).

We see a growing *trend* in GDP per capita. However, during some years it grows very rapidly, whereas in others it slows down. We observe downturns from 1990 to 1991. There was a recession then. Except for this short period, U.S. income per capita grew continuously for eighteen years. This turns out to be a new pattern because, before the 1990s, there were four years of recession and four years of expansion. So, there are basically two important types of temporal dependence: temporal dependence on the deviation to the trend and temporal dependence on the mean of the series. We will label the "cycle" as the deviation of the series from the trend.

Temporal dependence makes it more difficult to make inferences from the underlying distribution of the series. Time series usually exhibit temporal dependence; however, they can be expressed as the sum of other variables (random shocks) not exhibiting temporal dependence. We will use that property to make inferences from time series.

9. Econometric Forecasting and the Flow of Information

Before considering examples, let me introduce some background material on statistical models for economic time series. The level of a series today is equal to the level of the series plus some independent draw from a distribution, and, if the series is a random walk, it can also be rewritten as saying equivalently that the level of the series today is just a simple sum of all past disturbances or increments to the series. For a random walk, the series is just the sum of random variables that themselves are an independent draw from the same distribution. We saw in the previous chapter that this same basic idea can also be applied to a series with more general and elaborate temporal dependence, but the idea throughout is that the series, even if that series itself exhibits this dependence, is the sum of variables that do not. It is the ability to write it that way that enables us to make inferences and to estimate things that we need to estimate.

We write the random walk this way, saying that the expected product of these random variables is ε_t and that ε_{t-j} is 0. This means that these residuals or disturbances are unrelated to the history of the series, but they certainly are not unrelated to the future. In particular, it is not the case that the expectation of the disturbance today and the realization of the series in i periods in the future is equal to zero. In general, for a random walk this will not be the case. This is the difference, then, between what we call the "property of orthogonality" and independence. So, we say that the product of these "error terms" historically is 0 but the product of the error terms in the future is not 0, and that means that those error terms are not independent.

What happens if you sum a collection of variables that themselves exhibit no temporal dependence? Start with draws from a common distribution for 100 periods with a mean of 0: Sometimes the values are positive; sometimes they are negative. Sometimes they are big; sometimes they are small. However, there is no tendency for there to be long runs of either positive or negative values because each draw is independent of the previous one. Now create a new variable that is a sum of current and past draws from this distribution, with a weight of one-half on the lag value of the series. That means we will be adding up past shocks, but we will be applying a weight of less than 1 to them. You see some tendency here for this series to be smoother than the shocks that are input, and then finally, if you get to the case in which the weight is equal to 0.9 or even larger – and these are values

111

that are very common weights for economic time series on these lagged values with a great deal of temporal dependence – you see a lot of smoothing of this series relative to the underlying series that is being added.

Many economic time series grow over time: price levels, output, stock values, and so forth. We must deal with trending data, and I will give a brief example of how this is done. A very simple and popular way of dealing with this sort of data is to assume that the trend itself is not uncertain or random but rather a mechanical, simple function of time. What we do here is to transform a series by subtracting the trend and then look for the temporal dependence and the deviations from the trend. So, for example, if we are looking at a time series for GDP, then we might argue that there is a trending GDP but that deviations from the trend are stationary and thus do not depend on calendar time. This is a widely accepted way to deal with a trend, but it is not the only way. In another model that looks similar but has a very different feature, growth in a series is considered the sum of a constant and a disturbance, and we think of this constant as being the "drift" in the series. An important difference between this way of thinking about a trend and the first way of thinking about a trend is that in this way the forecast of a series, say, Y in this case, in the future is forever influenced by the current level of the series, and series that exhibit this property are said to have "random trends." A model with random trends has the feature that in the long run the growth rate is a constant, but the level of the series is not independent of the observed value of the series today.

Many issues that are very important in economics hinge on whether or not the best way to think about trends is to conceive of them as being either related or unrelated to current events. This was an issue in the U.S. presidential campaign of 2000 because many of the budget forecasts that Al Gore and George W. Bush relied on were forecasts that had to predict where the U.S. economy would be in eight years (and now we know). One such forecast says that wherever it will be then is unrelated to where it is now. That involves the linear trend model. The best forecast in eight years, then, would be a simple equation that does not include any information on where the economy is today. A much more optimistic view of the world, which certainly makes it easier to eliminate debt and pay for Social Security and other programs, is to allow the current state of the U.S. economy to drive your view on where the economy will be in eight years. You might think that since it is so important to get this forecast right, it is something for statisticians and economists to figure out. The good news is that statisticians and economists have spent a lot of time on this issue; the bad news is that getting the answer right is very hard and has thus far eluded us. One thing that we have learned is that even with a lot of data – say, forty years of quarterly data, which is 160 observations – we still do not have enough to distinguish effectively between these two mathematical models or these two views of the world.

What I would like to do now is to present a quick application of some of these ideas. For many macroeconomic and financial time series, it makes sense to model them as being driven by an exponential trend and to think of the series that you observe, say, GDP, as being the product of a trend term and a cycle term. If we let Y_t denote GDP at time t, we can express this as

$$Y_t = Y^{TRND}_t \cdot Y^{CYCLE}_t$$

Products are always messier than sums, and the way we handle this is to say that the trend term, in this case the one driving GDP, is an "exponential trend." This just means that the series is exhibiting exponential growth:

$$Y^{TRND}{}_t = \exp(gt)$$

Why do we pick an exponential trend? It turns out that it has a very nice property. An exponential trend has the property that the series itself, or the trend term, exhibits a constant growth rate, g. The change in the trend term is just proportional to the level of the trend term in this period. A very natural model in an economy that is growing over time is to say that the trend term is growing at a constant rate, which means that the level of the trend term itself is exhibiting exponential behavior.

So, if we say that GDP is the product of an exponential trend and a cycle, then how would we go about modeling this? If the trend is exponential and multiplicative, then the cycle is just the series divided by the trend ($Y^{CYCLE}{}_t = Y_t / Y^{TRND}{}_t$). So, we would say that the level of the cycle is the ratio of the series that we observe, say, GDP, to this exponential trend. In practice, how would we estimate a model like this one? We would try to make it a model that is linear rather than nonlinear, and what we would do in this case is to take the logarithm of the equation and just regress the (natural) logarithm of output on a time trend:

$$\log Y_t = \beta \cdot t + \varepsilon_t$$

There would then be some residual from this equation (ε_t), but we could still estimate the parameter we want to estimate, the trend growth rate, by regressing the log of output on a trend term. The justification for this would be that under the assumption of the linear trend model these errors are independent of the trend term, so that linear regression will have very desirable properties. In particular, the least squares estimate will be unbiased. The first step would be to estimate the trend by regressing the logarithm of the series on a time trend, and then the coefficient of that (β) would be our estimate of the trend growth rate (g). That would be easy to do and perfectly legitimate. The next thing we would want to do is to estimate or model the cycle. We could always plot the cycle once we have estimated the parameter g (the trend growth rate). We could then just crank out a time series for the cycle. We might want to estimate a model for the cycle. A popular model in economics is the "autoregressive" one, and a popular model for macroeconomics is an autoregressive model with a couple of lags. This essentially amounts to modeling the error term in this regression of output on the trend. In other words, the error term here is our estimate of the logarithm of the cycle. Note that we estimated the equation $\log Y_t = \beta \cdot t + \varepsilon_t$ that we obtain from taking logs to the output equation ($Y_t = Y^{TRND}{}_t \cdot Y^{CYCLE}{}_t = \exp(gt) \cdot Y^{CYCLE}{}_t$), that is, $\log Y_t = \log Y^{CYCLE}{}_t + g \cdot t$. Then $\hat{\varepsilon}_t$ provides an estimate for $\log Y^{CYCLE}{}_t$. Box 9.1 illustrates how to apply the logarithmic transforamation and the exponential trend. So, once we have our estimate of g, we can have observations on the cycle as well as on the trend. In this way of modeling the economy, when the economy is on its trend and the cycle has no influence, the variable Y^{CYCLE} is just equal to 1. So, in the multiplicative model, when output is on its trend path, the cycle is just equal to 1. Now let me give you an example of how this would actually be done. I ran a regression of the

---

Box 9.1. Application: Log Transformation and Exponential Trends

For many macroeconomic and financial time series, it makes sense to model an exponential trend and to transform the data by taking (natural) logarithms. For example, a good model of real GDP is

$$Y_t = Y^{CYCLE}{}_t \cdot Y^{TRND}{}_t.$$

We model real GDP as the *product* of a trend term and a cycle term. To see why this can make sense, assume that

$$Y^{TRND}{}_t = \exp(gt).$$

Taking the derivative of the trend term, we have

$$\partial Y^{TRND}{}_t / \partial_t = g \exp(gt) = g Y^{TRND}{}_t$$

so that the trend term exhibits a constant growth rate g. How then is the cycle defined? It is the *ratio* of GDP to the exponential trend:

$$Y_t / \exp(gt) = Y^{CYCLE}{}_t.$$

In practice, we would estimate this model by taking natural logarithms. First, we would estimate g with a linear regression:

$$\log Y_t = gt + e_t.$$

The error term is independent of the predictor variable (if our model is correct) so that the linear regression estimate is unbiased as well as consistent. We next model the cycle as

$$\log Y^{CYCLE}{}_t = b \, \log Y^{CYCLE}{}_{t-1} + d \, \log Y^{CYCLE}{}_{t-2} + \ln \varepsilon_t.$$

This amounts to modeling the error term in the trend regression, since if the model is true, $e_t = \log Y^{CYCLE}{}_t$. In this model, when the economy is on trend and the cycle has no influence, the variable $Y^{CYCLE}{}_t = 1$.

$$Y^{CYCLE}{}_t = (Y^{CYCLE}{}_{t-1})^b (Y^{CYCLE}{}_{t-2})^d \, \varepsilon_t,$$

where $\log \varepsilon_t$ is an independent draw from a distribution with 0 mean and constant variance. For example, it is often assumed that $\log \varepsilon_t$ is drawn from a normal distribution (so that ε_t said to be log normal).

---

log of U.S. GDP on a constant and a trend. These are quarterly data, so this makes sense because if you multiply this number by 4, the result is equal to roughly 2.4%. So, what this says is that between 1973 and 1999, the estimate of the trend rate of growth in the economy was roughly 2.4% per year. Now this, of course, is real GDP, so it factors out inflation. You then create the variable "LGDP" for log GDP and "TRND" for trend. You do that simply by telling the program to put the fitted values of the equation into this series so that this is just the fitted trend, and you just define the cycle, in this case the logarithm of the cycle, as the difference between the log of GDP and the log of the trend. You then might want to model the cycle,

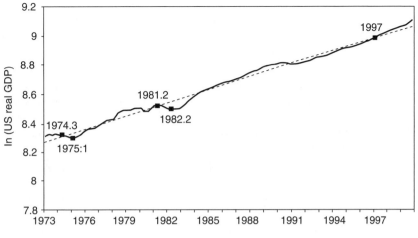

Figure 9.1. Estimating the GDP trend.

although you would not merely have to draw pictures. One possibility, which I have already shown, is to model the cycles as exhibiting a temporal dependence of this form. If you want to test the hypothesis that the cycle exhibits no temporal dependence; there is a way to do it. The one that textbooks often focus on is the "Durbin–Watson statistic." So, if you have a hypothesis that a series is just an independent draw from the same distribution and the alternative is that it is not an independent draw, then this hypothesis is easy to test. This statistic clearly indicates that this cycle term has temporal dependence, and so we model it here in this way. What we find here is a lot of temporal dependence. This indicates that if the economy was booming in the last quarter, it is likely to be booming in this quarter, but then, after two quarters, it is likely to start heading back toward the trend. We will look at some illustrations of that trend in a minute. I then applied my program, and the results are shown in Figure 9.1.

When I estimated the trend – that is, the dotted line in Figure 9.1, while the broken line is the actual log of GDP in the United States – I came to these conclusions about the time series: In periods like 1974–5 and 1981–2 the U.S. economy was in a recession. It was contracting, and output was below trend. In the late 1970s and late 1980s, the economy was booming and above trend. In 1990 there was a recession and then the economy started to grow, but then, even though it was growing, it was still operating below trend.

This brings us to the most controversial aspect of this model: According to the model, since 1997 the U.S. economy has been operating above its trend or capacity level. Of course, this has been widely discussed in the media. It is an important issue for policymakers, especially monetary policymakers, because if the economy is really working at above capacity, then we would expect higher inflation to show up as a result. However, other than some temporary blips for reasons like increased oil prices, inflation has not begun to pick up. This has led observers and central bankers to question whether or not the economy is still operating on this trend or whether there is instead a new, faster rate of economic growth.[1] The answer is that, statistically speaking, we will not know for a long time. This could be just an episode like those of 1977–8 or 1987–8, when the economy was above this trend line but then reverted back. One view is that the economy may stay above the trend line for a while but then revert back. The so-called new economy view is that the slope of this trend line is now steeper because of productivity improvements stemming from advances in information technology such as the Internet. Now if this is the trend, then what does the cycle look like? Recall that the cycle is, in percentage terms, the difference between the series and the trend. So, this is the cycle and these numbers on the vertical axis of Figure 9.1 correspond to percent deviations from the trend. Thus, another way of looking at the data is to say that big recessions occurred in 1974–5 and 1981–2 and then the economy started to grow, but for some time it was still operating below capacity. Then a recession occurred in 1990–1 followed by a recovery, and eventually, after 1997, the economy moved above the trend line.

Now let's look at the "impulse response function," which is a graph of the response of the GDP after a shock (Box 9.2).

In many circumstances, once we have either a single equation or a model of some phenomenon we are studying, say, stock prices, we want to get a historic sense of how that variable has responded dynamically over time when it has been disturbed and has moved away from its equilibrium – or, in statistical terms, from its unconditional mean. An "impulse response function" is simply a picture of the response of the series over future horizons to a given displacement from its mean. It is always useful, when you are thinking of an impulse response, to think of a series at rest, such as GDP at its mean relative to its trend, and then the disturbance of your variable by something – perhaps a change in policy, an oil shock, or an improvement in technology. What we want to recover from the data is the historic average dynamic response of a series to a displacement from its mean. We know that eventually the series has to return to its mean; if it did not, it would not be stationary. So, the question is, how do you get back to the mean level if you have moved away from it? A stationary stochastic process will revert back to its mean. A random walk process, as we saw earlier, is not a stationary process. It is not a stationary process in the sense that, if a series exhibits a random walk, shocks to that series do not die out but have permanent effects. However, we can still calculate the impulse response. A nice thing about impulse responses is that they are always relative to the mean of the series.

Let's talk about forecasting. We do forecasting all the time in economics. Some economists and political scientists have forecast who will win a presidential election based on the condition of the economy. We also forecast inflation or GDP. Wall Street forecasts earnings. Almost every application in financial economics and macroeconomics involves forecasting. What we will talk about next is how to derive some basic but important and incredibly useful properties of forecasting. Of course, forecasting is in the eye of the beholder. You may want to make your forecast by flipping a coin in a dark room, but what we want to do is describe some

---

[1] It is evident that the economy is no longer operating above the trend. This contraction is due to the global financial crisis that was spurred by the combination of various factors, such as the subprime mortgage crisis, the declinging value of the U.S. dollar, and high oil price volatility, among other economic variables.

Box 9.2. The Impulse Response Function

The Impulse Response Function

The impulse response function of a time series is simply a map of the response of the series over all future horizons to a given shock ε_t. For example, at horizon 1, the impulse response is just $\partial Y_t + 1/\partial \varepsilon_t$, while at horizon j, the impulse response is $\partial Y_t + j/\partial \varepsilon_t$. For a stationary stochastic process, the impulse response is not a function of calendar time. For example, for an AR(1) process, we have

$$\partial Y_t + j/\partial \varepsilon_t = \partial Y_t + j/\partial \varepsilon_t = \phi j$$

for all $k = \ldots, -3, -2, -1, 0, 1, 2, 3, \ldots$ and any j. Note that we do not require the process to be stationary to feature impulse responses that do not depend on calendar time. For example, the random walk process

$$Y_t = Y_{t-1} + \varepsilon_t$$

is not stationary:

$$Y_t = \varepsilon_t + \varepsilon_{t-1} + \varepsilon_{t-2} + \varepsilon_{t-3} \ldots,$$

yet it has a very simple impulse response function that satisfies

$$\partial Y_t + j/\partial \varepsilon_t = \partial Y_t + j/\partial \varepsilon_t = 1.$$

Example

The following stochastic processes have identical impulse response functions:

$$Y_t = \phi Y_{t-1} + \varepsilon_t$$

$$Y_t = \mu(1 - \phi) + \phi Y_{t-1} + \varepsilon_t$$

$$(Y_t - \eta^t) = \phi(Y_{t-1} - \eta^{(t-1)}) + \varepsilon_t.$$

---

characteristics of forecasting that have desirable or optimal qualities. In general, we refer to these as forecasts that have the property of being "rational."

"Rationality" is a loaded term with controversial implications in psychology and political science as well as economics. Here we are using it in a fairly technical way, which has the advantage that this assumption can be tested – that is, it can be proved false by actual data. Sometimes we refer to people as having "rational expectations." In this situation, we have some random variables drawn from a distribution; in particular, Y_{t+1} is a variable we want to forecast next year at period t. X is a collection of information that includes the history of Y, but it can include other variables as well. The task is to construct an optimal rule for forecasting Y_{t+1} once we observe X_t and, more importantly, once we know or someone tells us the distribution from which Y_{t+1} and X_t are drawn.

We want to derive a rule for making a forecast of one variable based upon realization of some other variables, but we want to develop this rule before we actually see these other variables. For example, suppose it is October 4, and I want to come up with a rule for making my forecast of the exchange rate in December based on information I will have in November. I make up the rule today, and then in November, when I get the information, I apply the rule to come up with my forecast for December's exchange rate. In order to come up with a forecast, we need some criteria; the most commonly used one is to try to minimize the average square error of the forecast. What I say on October 4 is, "Give me a rule that lets me process the information that will be available on November 1 so that I can make a forecast of the exchange rate on December 1. I know that sometimes my forecast will be too optimistic and sometimes it will be too pessimistic, but I want a rule that will minimize the average square of the error of the forecast, the so-called mean squared error." An optimal forecasting rule is a function of the realization of these variables that I will observe on November 1, and it is also a function of the underlying economic variable for these models. If the variable I am forecasting and the information I am going to use to forecast it are stationary random variables that are normally distributed, then the optimal forecast, the best forecast I can make (subject to minimizing the square of the error), is a simple linear function of the data that I will observe on November 1.

The most important thing to emphasize – and it is absolutely crucial for what we will do in the examples – is that if people are making optimal forecasts, then those forecasts have a particular property called the "error orthogonality property." Define the forecast error as the difference between the realization of the variable you are forecasting and the forecast itself. Recall that the forecast is a linear function of the data. A necessary and sufficient condition for the forecast to be optimal is that it satisfies this error orthogonality property, which, in other words, is that the expectation of the product of the error with each element of the information set is 0. Another and perhaps simpler way of saying this is to say that the error term is uncorrelated with each piece of information that you have.

The next thing to understand about orthogonality is that it is not only necessary but also sufficient. What I mean is the following: Give me a forecasting rule that is optimal, and it must satisfy error orthogonality. Or, to put it another way: Give me a forecast that satisfies error orthogonality, and it must be the optimal rule and uniquely define the regression coefficients. If you know the distributions that are generating the variables you are forecasting and the information that you have, and these are normally distributed, then your optimal forecast is linear in the data. The coefficients are pinned down by these complicated equations that we do not have to worry about, and the error that you make is uncorrelated with each piece of information that you have. So, for example, there can be no tendency for your errors to be large and positive when one piece of information is large or small because, if there were a tendency for the error to be positive – say, when one piece of information is big – then that systematic information should be included in the forecast, and anything left over should be unrelated to the information you had when you made the forecast. Thus, if the variable you are forecasting and the information you have are stationary random variables but they are not joint normally distributed – since, after all, the world is not generally normally distributed, even though we like to imagine that it is – then the optimal forecast will, in general, not be a linear function of the data.

However, suppose we consider a slightly different optimization problem that consists of minimizing the mean square error of the forecast, but with the restriction that the function has to be linear in X. If you want to minimize the mean square error while not enabling yourself to select across all functions of the data but only over the set of linear functions of the data, then the best linear projection is given by the same formula. This is the same expression that we would have arrived at had the data been normal. The best linear projection, then, is the function of the data that would be optimal if the data were normally distributed, but if the data are not normally distributed, then this is the best forecast that we can come up with that is linear in the data. In typical economic applications this is what we assume, and it also satisfies the error orthogonality property.

Suppose that we are trying to forecast a variable – say, the interest rate two months from now. Let's say that I work on Wall Street and this is my job: to forecast interest rates. If I want to forecast the interest rate in December, I have a lot of information available. First, I know what the interest rate is now in October. Let's denote my forecast made today as $P(R_3|R_1)$. This is the probability of the forecast rate in month 3 given the rate today in month 1. I know that next month, November, I am going to get more information on the Federal Reserve Bank's intentions for interest rates. I know that in November I may choose to change my forecast of December's interest rate. I may raise it or I may lower it based on this information. What is my forecast this month of what my forecast next month will be? Mathematically, what is my forecast today, based on the information I have today of October's interest rate, of what my forecast next month will be of the same entity, namely, December's interest rate? In both examples, the object that we are forecasting is the same thing. The difference is that, when I forecast today, I have only October's information, but when I forecast in November, I will have both October's and November's information.

There is a very important result of this discussion: If my forecast is optimal, that is, it is the minimum mean squared error forecast, then it satisfies the following property that we call the "law of iterated expectations." This law means that my forecast today of my forecast in November of December's interest rate is my forecast today of December's interest rate. My forecast of the change in my forecast next month must be 0. Why? If I am forecasting that in a month I will change my mind, then I should change my mind today since I do not know the information that I will have in a month. This is a little imprecise. I know definitely that I will change my mind next month because I know that next month's interest rate will be different from this month's interest rate. The trouble is that I do not know if it is going to be higher or lower, so I do not know whether I am going to raise or lower my forecast. This is another way of saying that holding constant the entity that I am forecasting, in this case R_3, my forecast today of the change in my forecast next month must be 0 because, if I am forecasting that I am going to change my forecast of the same entity, I am not using my information optimally. So, if I expect to alter my forecast next month of the same variable, then I am not using the information that I have today. Revisions to forecasts of a given random variable as new information becomes available must be a surprise relative to the information I have when I make the forecast. Indeed, you can write the forecast I will make in November of December's interest rate as equal to the forecast I make in October of December's interest rate plus a coefficient times the surprise in November's interest rate relative to the information that I had today.

The way to see this is to write down what my forecast in November of December's interest rate will be. It will be this linear function of R_1 and R_2, but then we can write R_2 as the projection of R_2 and of R_1 and then the difference between R_2 and that projection. When you write the equation this way, this first term is linear in R_1 and it satisfies the error orthogonality property. This is another way of stating the error orthogonality property: that the expectation of my changing my mind is 0, that is, I know I may change my mind, but I do not know whether I will change it up or down. So, on average, the expected change is 0. That is not necessarily a deep point, but it is worth remembering because you can get confused. There is a way in which this point is especially relevant for the prices of financial assets like bonds, stocks, and currencies: Especially over short periods of time, say, daily or weekly, virtually all the changes in financial data are unrelated to past information. Over longer time horizons there is some evidence that we can forecast changes, but over short periods of time our ability to forecast changes is small. Why? Well, if we could make these forecasts we could make a lot of money; thus, what happens in equilibrium is that prices adjust to incorporate that information. This adjustment is at the heart of what we call "efficient markets theory."

ROMER AND ROMER (2000): A SAMPLE APPLICATION

Now let's talk about the article by Christina and David Romer (2000). It uses in a very productive way some of the techniques that we have talked about; at this point, we have learned enough to interpret it. What is the subject of this article? The question it tries to answer is: Does the Federal Reserve has either superior information or superior forecasting abilities compared to the private sector? Why is that an interesting question to investigate? Well, it is interesting for economists because there are many economic models or theories that assert that the central bank does not have better information than the private sector – that when the central bank raises or lowers interest rates, it has the same information the private sector does and processes it in the same way. If the central bank does possess superior information, it is interesting to ask whether or not the central bank's actions – raising or lowering interest rates – reflect that information. The hypothesis also gives us occasion to think about why the central bank would have superior information. Every month the staff of the Federal Reserve Board in Washington, D.C., using their own models and drawing upon the work of the other Federal Reserve branch banks, as well as those of private forecasters, prepares their Green Book forecast. This is a confidential staff forecast that is provided to the Federal Reserve chairperson and the other Federal Reserve Board governors, which they then use in their monetary policy deliberations. Now, somewhat controversially, the Green Book forecast is confidential and is not released to the public for five years. So, ultimately, academics and the public can find out what the Fed's models were forecasting five years before, but at this point the Fed does not promptly publish the Green Book forecasts, even though they have been pressured to do so. Other countries publish their internal forecasts in a more timely fashion.

What is nice about the Romer and Romer (2000) article is that the authors have information now that the markets did not have five years ago when they were making their forecasts. They have information that is time stamped so that they know when the Fed was making its forecast with information not available to the public. To use an example, for December 1974, the authors have private sector forecasts of inflation made in that month, as well as the Fed's December 1974 forecast of inflation, but the authors know that the markets did not know in December 1974 what the Fed's forecast was. The Fed Green Book for that month was not released until December 1979.

Romer and Romer (2000) test a number of interesting hypotheses, the first of which is that private forecasts and Fed forecasts are rational or optimal in the narrow sense that they use available information in an efficient way. So, they test the hypothesis that forecasters do not make systematic mistakes, given the data that they choose or are able to process. Of course, it is quite possible that the Fed and the private sector have access to different data. The hypothesis is that the rate of inflation in the economy between period t and period $t + h(\pi_{ht})$ is equal to the private sector forecast of inflation ($\hat{\pi}_{ht}$) plus a forecast error. We are testing the hypothesis that this forecast error is uncorrelated with the forecast itself and that the coefficient on the forecast for inflation is equal to 1. You can test this hypothesis simply by regressing realized inflation in the market on the central bank's forecast of inflation ($\hat{\pi}_{ht}^F$), that is, estimating the equation $\pi_{ht} = \alpha + \beta \hat{\pi}_{ht}^F + \varepsilon_{ht}$, and using a t-test of the hypothesis that β equals 1.

We are treating the market forecast as known since it is published, and thus we do not have to infer about what the forecast was. We know what it was. It is published in readily available publications. Thus, we are not using realized inflation and making inferences about a forecast. We are using actual data on forecasts as the predictor variable. The first thing that Romer and Romer (2000) do is to regress realized inflation in the market on the central bank forecast of inflation and test the hypothesis that β is equal to 1. The error we make in forecasting inflation between periods t and $t + h$ may very well be related to future inflation. What are the samples? The samples in this article are in the range of 120 to 200 monthly observations. In this article the data are monthly, although the forecasting period is often longer than a month. The forecasting period is often three or six months or a year. When you are sampling more often than the forecast horizon, allowance has to be made in the hypothesis tests. In particular, when you have a model like this one and you estimate it with least squares, your estimate will be consistent, but the test statistics that the package prints out will not be correct unless you are looking at the special case where the sampling interval coincides with the forecast horizon. The results of Romer and Romer's (2000) investigations are shown in Table 9.1.

There are three organizations that forecast inflation and other variables: Data Resources (DRI); Blue Chip, which is an average across business economists; and another company, SPF. We have the regression of realized inflation on forecast inflation, and what we are really interested in is these βs because the intercept is usually estimated to be 0. Look at the Fed forecast, which again, we emphasize, was released with a five-year lag, though prepared contemporaneously. Romer and Romer (2000), of course, now know what the Fed was forecasting. One reason I thought this article would be a good one to teach is that it contains an interesting hypothesis that we can test in a very sensible, straightforward way using what we

Table 9.1. *Romer and Romer (2000) tests for inflation forecasts*

$$\pi_{ht} = \alpha + \beta\hat{\pi}_{ht} + \varepsilon_{ht}$$

Forecast horizon (quarters)	α	β	p-value	R^2	N
Blue Chip					
0	−0.41(0.36)	1.02(0.08)	0.082	0.76	143
1	−0.67(0.42)	1.02(0.09)	0.004	0.69	143
2	−0.71(0.75)	0.98(0.17)	0.001	0.62	143
3	−0.52(1.07)	0.90(0.23)	0.001	0.53	143
4	0.58(0.76)	0.63(0.13)	0.000	0.31	138
5	1.05(1.10)	0.48(0.19)	0.000	0.22	102
6	1.46(0.92)	0.33(0.13)	0.000	0.19	66
DRI					
0	0.26(0.27)	0.97(0.06)	0.559	0.76	219
1	0.91(0.37)	0.87(0.07)	0.052	0.56	219
2	0.80(0.46)	0.88(0.09)	0.228	0.47	219
3	1.27(0.89)	0.76(0.17)	0.342	0.35	219
4	1.88(1.25)	0.63(0.23)	0.263	0.23	219
5	2.43(1.49)	0.52(0.27)	0.202	0.15	219
6	3.16(1.87)	0.37(0.32)	0.144	0.07	219
7	3.53(1.99)	0.28(0.34)	0.089	0.04	217
SPF					
0	−0.12(0.41)	1.05(0.08)	0.569	0.71	93
1	0.42(0.50)	0.97(0.10)	0.275	0.50	93
2	0.88(0.83)	0.89(0.16)	0.442	0.33	93
3	1.76(1.06)	0.71(0.19)	0.253	0.20	93
4	2.08(1.19)	0.65(0.22)	0.217	0.16	88
Federal Reserve					
0	0.03(0.33)	1.03(0.07)	0.479	0.78	251
1	0.34(0.47)	1.00(0.11)	0.280	0.60	242
2	0.74(0.58)	0.95(0.12)	0.275	0.44	224
3	0.34(0.72)	1.03(0.13)	0.534	0.43	207
4	0.12(0.99)	1.05(0.17)	0.656	0.38	177
5	−0.16(1.15)	1.06(0.22)	0.922	0.34	118
6	−0.80(1.14)	1.09(0.28)	0.312	0.47	61
7	−1.19(1.43)	1.03(0.36)	0.000	0.53	38

Notes: π denotes inflation, and $\hat{\pi}$ denotes the inflation forecast; h and t index the horizon and date of the forecast. The sample periods are 1980:1–1991:11 for Blue Chip; 1970:7–1991:11 for DRI; 1968:11–1991:11 for SPF; and 1965:11–1991:11 for the Federal Reserve. Numbers in parentheses are robust standard errors. The p-value is for the test of the null hypothesis $\alpha = 0$, $\beta = 1$.

Source: Christina D. Romer and David H. Romer, "Federal Reserve Information and the Behavior of Interest Rates," *American Economic Review* 90 (2000): 429–57. Reprinted with permission of the authors and the publisher.

have learned, and it turns out to be a hypothesis that is confirmed by the data. These are the estimates for β for the various time horizons. The figure 0 indicates a contemporaneous estimate, and then there are data for one month, two months, and so on, up to seven months. Typically, what we want to do here is test that the coefficients are equal to 1; obviously, these would all pass that test with flying colors for the Fed.

For the private sector forecasts, at very short time horizons (for a month or a month or two), these coefficients are clustered around 1, and typically you cannot reject 1. However, as you get further out – say, six or seven months – you can in some cases statistically reject the hypothesis. Especially for the Blue Chip forecast, this is case. I guess that for DRI and SPF, statistically you cannot reject the null hypothesis. However, you can certainly see that these estimates start drifting away from 1. If anything, there is no evidence that the central bank forecasts are irrational, but there is at least some evidence that SPF and, I would argue, DRI are not using all the available information for approximately six months out.

The second thing Romer and Romer (2000) do is test the hypothesis that contemporaneous Fed forecasts, which were unavailable to the private sector when they were made, contain no additional information that would have been useful to the private sector. For example, suppose that both the Fed and the private sector have the same information, and they use the same model to process it. Then any difference between the Fed's forecast and that of the private sector would be just random noise, and we would not expect that including the Fed's forecast in a regression that includes the private sector would have a statistically significant effect on the forecast. Again, under the null hypothesis, ordinary least squares estimation is appropriate because these errors will be forecast errors that are not correlated with the predetermined variables. What happens when you do that? This is shown in Table 9.2.

Table 9.2 is a regression of realized inflation π on a commercial forecasters forecast $\hat{\pi}^C$ and on the Fed's forecast $\hat{\pi}^F$: $\pi_{ht} = \delta + \gamma_C \hat{\pi}_{ht}^C + \gamma_F \hat{\pi}_{ht}^F + v_{ht}$.

The null hypothesis is that γ_F is equal to 0, which would correspond to the Fed's not having any information that is superior to the information in the private sector. A very interesting thing happens when you include the Fed's forecast in this equation. The private sector forecasts essentially become insignificant and often enter with an unusual sign, whereas the Fed's forecasts are almost always significant. In many instances, the Fed forecast will knock out the significance of the commercial forecasts. Basically, the equation says that if you are combining the Fed's forecast and the private sector forecasts, then you essentially want to put all of your weight on the Fed's forecast and put a weight of 0 or even a negative weight on the private sector forecast. This indicates that the Fed does have some useful information that the private sector does not. A robustness check by Romer and Romer (2000) compares the private forecasts jointly, rather than comparing the Fed's forecast to each private forecast individually. The results more or less hold up and show that the weight placed on the private forecasts should be driven toward 0.

Finally, Romer and Romer (2000) compare the mean squared error of the commercial forecasts and the Fed's forecasts. Recall that the mean squared error is our criterion for evaluating forecasts, and an optimal forecast is one that

Table 9.2. *Romer and Romer (2000) tests of Federal Reserve additional information for inflation*

$$\pi_{ht} = \delta + \gamma_C \hat{\pi}_{ht}^C + \gamma_F \hat{\pi}_{ht}^F + v_{ht}$$

Forecast horizon (quarters)	δ	γC	γF	R^2	N
Blue Chip					
0	−0.06(0.40)	0.35(0.23)	0.64(0.18)	0.83	97
1	0.49(0.52)	−0.35 (0.27)	1.21(0.20)	0.81	97
2	0.56 (0.45)	−0.30 (0.25)	1.12(0.22)	0.70	97
3	0.22 (0.60)	−0.34(0.32)	1.23(0.25)	0.71	97
4	0.18(0.68)	−0.31(0.32)	1.19(0.37)	0.54	93
5	0.64(1.17)	−0.23(0.41)	0.93(0.49)	0.37	69
6	1.30(0.77)	0.55(0.18)	−0.20(0.18)	0.27	38
μ(0–4)	0.50(0.36)	−0.28(0.21)	1.11(0.21)	0.91	93
DRI					
0	−0.17(0.34)	0.39(0.16)	0.66(0.18)	0.80	170
1	0.10(0.43)	−0.03(0.21)	1.04(0.23)	0.62	170
2	0.27(0.50)	−0.19(0.20)	1.18(0.18)	0.49	168
3	−0.16(0.57)	−0.24(0.30)	1.32(0.29)	0.48	161
4	−0.51(0.65)	−0.65(0.38)	1.80(0.41)	0.46	146
5	−0.67(0.85)	−0.72(0.49)	1.87(0.53)	0.41	105
6	−0.81(1.05)	−0.33(0.43)	1.45(0.55)	0.45	60
7	−1.51(1.49)	−0.30(0.38)	1.42(0.66)	0.54	38
μ(0–4)	−0.15(0.41)	−0.53(0.36)	1.57(0.38)	0.74	146
SPF					
0	−0.00(0.38)	0.15(0.19)	088(0.18)	0.76	79
1	0.46(0.47)	−0.47(0.21)	1.45(0.21)	0.64	79
2	1.55(0.77)	−0.78(0.44)	1.57(0.38)	0.49	78
3	1.27(0.83)	−0.83(0.33)	1.70(0.32)	0.46	73
4	0.72(0.81)	−0.93(0.36)	1.89(0.34)	0.48	64
μ(0–4)	1.09(0.53)	−1.08(0.38)	1.93(0.35)	0.75	64

Notes: π denotes inflation, and $\hat{\pi}^C$ and $\hat{\pi}^F$ denote commercial and Federal reserve inflation forecasts; h and t index the horizon and date of the forecasts. The sample periods are 1980:1–1991:11 for Blue Chip; 1970–1991:11 for DRI; and 1968:11–1991:11 for SPF. Numbers in parentheses are robust standard errors. The forecast horizon $\mu(0-4)$ refers to the average of 0 to 4 quaters ahead.

Source: Christina D. Romer and David H. Romer, "Federal Reserve Information and the Behavior of Interest Rates," *American Economic Review* 90 (2000): 429–57. Reprinted with permission of the authors and the publisher.

minimizes mean squared error given the information available to the central bank. At all time horizons, the Fed's mean squared error is consistently less than that of the commercial forecasters. So, it does appear that the Fed has superior information on inflation.

One other interesting thing in the article is a test of whether the Fed has superior information when forecasting GDP growth. The basic idea here is that every month the Fed staff provides not only a forecast of inflation, but also a forecast of GDP growth. Interestingly enough, in this case, it appears that the Fed has no superior information compared to the private sector – that is, Romer and Romer again tested to see if γ_f is equal to 0. Here we find that the private sector looks more sensible. At least Blue Chip and DRI do, although the standard errors are quite high. One way to think about this is that there is again evidence here of superior information. That seems to be definite for Blue Chip at horizons of four months or so. That said, however, it is still the case that if you were comparing the Fed's forecast to that of Blue Chip at four months, you would want to put all your weight on the Fed's forecast and 0 on Blue Chip's. So, it appears again that the Fed has superior information.

Let's finish with two topics. First, do the Fed's actions provide evidence about its superior information? Another hypothesis is that the Fed signals its superior information via its interest rate policy. For example, if the Fed forecasts higher inflation, it may raise interest rates to help ward off a surge in prices. Alternatively, the superior information may be statistically significant but not valuable enough to the Fed to act in a way that would be any different from that implied by the private sector forecast. Think of a world in which the Fed's forecast is superior, but it is always in the same direction as the private sector's. Thus, the private sector may say 8 while the Fed says 9. Well, it may be that the Fed had a better forecast, but this might make no practical difference in terms of policy. Both of these forecasts might imply the same thing: higher rates. Suppose instead that the Fed was forecasting a slump and a fall in prices, but so was the private sector. Even though the Fed's forecast was more on target, the private sector's forecast might also imply a Fed rate cut, so that one could not necessarily improve on the information the private sector already had based only on observing a rate cut. What the Romer and Romer (2000) article does here is to relate the unobserved Fed forecast to the observed action the Fed took in that month – whether or not it raised or lowered interest rates. This is an attempt to see whether there is any information in the Fed's forecast that is related to the action it took over and above the information that was already embedded in the private sector forecast. To this end, Romer and Romer estimate the following equation:

$$\hat{\pi}_{ht}^F = \psi + \theta M_t + \phi \hat{\pi}_{ht}^C + \omega_{ht},$$

where $\hat{\pi}_{ht}^F$ and $\hat{\pi}_{ht}^C$ are again the Federal Reserve and the private forecasts of inflation at time $t+h$ and M_t is the Federal Reserve monetary policy action at time t. The results are shown in Table 9.3.

When θ is positive, the Fed is tightening monetary policy. That would correspond to the case where the Fed is forecasting inflation over and above the private sector's forecast, which leads it to tighten monetary policy. Here, by observing the Fed's action, one could, with enough data, make inferences about the Fed's private information. So, this is the result of that exercise. The key parameter here is θ. What does this show? The results are mixed, and certainly at shorter horizons they are not statistically significant, but at longer horizons,

Table 9.3. *Romer and Romer (2000) estimates of revelation of information about inflation*

$$\hat{\pi}_{ht}^F = \psi + \theta M_t + \phi \hat{\pi}_{ht}^C + \omega_{ht}$$

Forecast horizson (quarters)	ψ	θ	ϕ	R^2	N
A. Dummy Variable					
Blue Chip					
0	−0.71(0.71)	0.21(0.12)	1.13(0.18)	0.59	61
1	−0.45(0.47)	−0.13(0.14)	1.01(0.11)	0.60	61
2	−0.07(0.63)	0.02(0.10)	0.93(0.16)	0.54	61
3	0.55(0.90)	0.13(0.08)	0.78(0.20)	0.48	61
4	0.48(0.66)	0.16(0.05)	0.79(0.14)	0.57	61
5	0.24(0.44)	0.10(0.05)	0.84(0.09)	0.68	47
6	−0.49(0.61)	−0.10(0.07)	1.01(0.14)	0.74	27
μ(0–4)	−0.43(0.63)	0.07(0.04)	1.02(0.16)	0.76	61
DRI					
0	0.63(0.29)	0.17(0.14)	0.91(0.07)	0.85	100
1	0.86(0.33)	0.29(0.15)	0.87(0.07)	0.84	100
2	0.81(0.34)	0.29(0.12)	0.87(0.07)	0.85	100
3	1.01(0.31)	0.25(0.11)	0.82(0.08)	0.84	100
4	0.86(0.38)	0.15(0.11)	0.84(0.09)	0.81	100
5	0.67(0.29)	0.18(0.07)	0.90(0.07)	0.89	85
6	0.50(0.35)	0.08(0.12)	0.92(0.08)	0.87	52
7	1.50(0.64)	0.47(0.22)	0.66(0.18)	0.80	28
μ(0–4)	0.54(0.32)	0 19(0.13)	0.92(0.07)	0.93	100
SPF					
0	−0.57(0.41)	0.13(0.19)	1.13(0.08)	0.88	47
1	−0.52(0.38)	0.12(0.18)	1.09(0.08)	0.86	47
2	−0.42(0.44)	0.29(0.17)	1.08(0.09)	0.80	47
3	−0.47(0.40)	0.20(0.09)	1.06(0.07)	0.86	47
4	0.36(0.36)	0.27(0.09)	0.92(0.08)	0.81	46
μ(0–4)	−0.49(0.26)	0.22(0.10)	1.09(0.05)	0.94	46
B. Change in Funds-Rate Target					
Blue Chip					
0	−0.69(0.72)	0.31(0.20)	1.11(0.18)	0.57	62
1	−0.48(045)	−0.29(0.22)	1.02(0.11)	0.60	62
2	−0.02(0.59)	0.18(0.16)	0.92(0.14)	0.55	62
3	0.54(0.82)	0.33(0.09)	0.78(0.19)	0.49	62
4	0.48(0.62)	0.44(0.09)	0.79(0.13)	0.60	62
5	0.36(0.46)	0.34(0.11)	0.81(0.09)	0.69	47

Forecast horizson (quarters)	ψ	θ	ϕ	R^2	N
6	−0.39(0.60)	−0.02(0.17)	0.98(0.13)	0.73	27
$\mu(0–4)$	−0.41(0.60)	0.17(0.06)	1.01(0.15)	0.76	62
DRI					
0	0.55(0.27)	0.05(0.32)	0.93(0.07)	0.85	101
1	0.72(0.30)	0.54(0.22)	0.90(0.06)	0.83	101
2	0.68(0.29)	0.60(0.21)	0.90(0.06)	0.85	101
3	0.88(0.29)	0.42(0.22)	0.85(0.07)	0.84	101
4	0.77(0.38)	0.16(0.17)	0.86(0.10)	0.80	101
5	0.60(0.27)	0.36(0.10)	0.92(0.06)	0.90	86
6	0.47(0.27)	0.32(0.19)	0.92(0.07)	0.87	52
7	1.11(0.67)	0.71(0.47)	0.74(0.19)	0.77	28
$\mu(0–4)$	0.44(0.28)	0.35(0.18)	0.95(0.07)	0.92	101
SPF					
0	−0.61(0.38)	0 04(0.30)	1.13(0.08)	0.88	47
1	−0.56(0.36)	0.05(0.30)	1.10(0.08)	0.86	47
2	−0.62(0.40)	0.53(0.32)	1.12(0.09)	0.80	47
3	−0.59(0.39)	0.29(0.17)	1.08(0.07)	0.85	47
4	0.22(0.37)	0.21(0.10)	0.95(0.08)	0.79	46
$\mu(0–4)$	−0.62(0.23)	0.32(0.12)	1.11(0.05)	0.93	46

Notes: $\hat{\pi}^F$ and $\hat{\pi}^C$ denote Federal Reserve and commercial inflation forecasts; h and t index the horizon and date of the forecasts. M is the indicator of monetary-policy actions. The sample periods are 1984:2–1991:11 for Blue Chip; and 1974:8–1979:8 and 1984:2–1991:11 for DRI and SPF. Numbers in parentheses are robust standard errors. The forecast horizon $\mu(0–4)$ refers to the average of 0 to 4 quarters ahead.
Source: Christina D. Romer and David H. Romer, "Federal Reserve Information and the Behavior of Interest Rates," *American Economic Review* 90 (2000): 429–57. Reprinted with permission of the authors and the publisher.

especially for DRI and Blue Chip, there is evidence that θ is positive and statistically significant. For example, if you look at the forecasts four or five months out for Blue Chip, when the Fed tightens policy by 1%, this means that the Fed's inflation forecast is half a percentage point higher than would be inferred from the private sector's forecast alone, and that is statistically significant.

I want to use this example as a springboard for a general discussion of the informational implications of successful forecasting. Romer and Romer (2000) took advantage of a dataset to test some hypotheses that you could not test without those data. That's typical in social science research: Interesting conclusions often come from gathering new data, or putting data sources together in a new way, rather than simply taking another crack at an existing dataset. Romer and Romer used some fairly simple methods, and they wanted to answer the following question: When considering contemporaneous forecasts made by the Fed and by the private sector, did the Fed's forecasts show access to more information or process information in a more efficient way than did the private sector? The first thing the authors did was to analyze whether or not the forecasts made by the Fed and by the commercial forecasters were rational in the sense that they were unbiased. That test was done by running a regression of the rate of inflation between period t and period $t + h$ on a constant and on the rate of inflation that was forecast at time t over the next h periods either by the Fed or by the commercial forecasters. Of course, we need to add some error term to this equation, and if the forecast uses its information in a sensible way, we should find that the constant in that regression is not statistically different from 0 and that the estimate of the coefficient on the forecasted rate of inflation is not statistically different from 1. The authors found that for the central bank's forecasts one could not reject this hypothesis, and for many time horizons one could not reject the hypothesis for the commercial forecasters either. The more interesting part of the article was an exploration of whether or not the central bank had either more information than the private forecasters or used it more efficiently. Here we would be testing the hypothesis that the coefficient on the Fed's forecast is 0, once we allow for the information contained in the private sector forecast. In fact, the authors found that this hypothesis was decisively rejected, so it does appear that the Fed has superior information when making its forecast of inflation. In fact, over many time horizons and for many private sector forecasters, the authors could not reject the hypothesis that the value of the private sector forecasts was essentially 0 and that the best way to forecast inflation was to put a weight of 0 on the private sector forecasts and all of the weight on the Fed's forecasts.

This is similar to an analysis that statisticians have done for a silly example: predicting professional sports outcomes. For example, if you run a regression and try to predict the outcome of a football game given the Las Vegas point spread (which is, effectively, the forecast of the game outcome coming from the "market" of bettors) and other predictors, such as the teams' won-lost records, you will find that the point spread has a coefficient of 1 (well, it's statistically indistinguishable from 1) and the other predictors have coefficients that are statistically indistinguishable from 0. The other predictors do not matter, because their predictive power is all incorporated into the point spread. Given the spread, the other information is irrelevant to the goal of forecasting.

Romer and Romer (2000) also explored the extent to which the Fed's forecasts were superior. This is presented in Table 9.4, which compares the mean squared error of the private sector and of the Fed's forecast at various horizons; it shows that the Fed's forecasts have a smaller mean squared error. Recall that the minimization of the mean squared error is the criterion that we use in selecting among the various ways of making a forecast. The last thing to consider before interpreting the results is that, even though the private sector cannot observe the Fed's forecast, it can observe the Fed's monetary policy actions. Romer and Romer (2000) test whether there is any information in the Fed's monetary actions that would be useful in allowing the private sector to make an inference of the Fed's inflation forecast.

The article discusses the timing conventions involved here. We will not go into that topic, but the basic idea is to regress the next commercial forecast on the change in the Federal Reserve forecast, an indicator of Federal Reserve actions

Table 9.4. *Romer and Romer (2000) on overall accuracy of inflation forecasts*

| Forecast horizon (quarters) | Mean squared error | | | |
	Commercial forecaster	Federal Reserve	*p*-value	*N*
	(Percentage points)			
Blue Chip				
0	1.46	1.23	0.321	97
1	2.15	1.37	0.000	97
2	2.64	1.72	0.005	97
3	3.12	1.68	0.006	97
4	3.69	1.99	0.003	93
5	5.09	2.81	0.010	69
6	4.89	2.69	0.002	38
μ(0–4)	1.22	0.50	0.011	93
DRI				
0	1.93	1.71	0.390	170
1	3.98	3.13	0.034	170
2	4.91	4.03	0.001	168
3	5.44	4.37	0.061	161
4	6.34	4.65	0.033	146
5	7.51	5.50	0.077	105
6	5.91	4.06	0.118	60
7	6.59	4.06	0.145	38
μ(0–4)	2.28	1.61	0.015	146
SPF				
0	2.33	1.75	0.025	79
1	4.06	2.95	0.000	79
2	5.73	4.39	0.012	78
3	6.24	4.63	0.000	73
4	7.01	5.01	0.002	64
μ(0–4)	2.51	1.70	0.001	64

Notes: The mean squared error is calculated as the average squared difference between forecasted and actual inflation. The sample periods are 1980:1–1991:11 for Blue Chip; 1970:7–1991:11 for DRI; and 1968:11–1991:11 for SPF. The *p*-value is for the test of the null hypothesis that the Federal Reserve and commercial mean squared errors are equal. The forecast horizon μ(0–4) refers to the average of 0 to 4 quarters ahead. *Source:* Christina D. Romer and David H. Romer, "Federal Reserve Information and the Behavior of Interest Rates," *American Economic Review* 90 (2000): 429–57. Reprinted with permission of the authors and the publisher.

and the last commercial forecast before that action. The results are reported in Table 9.5. Focus here on the lower panel. A positive coefficient θ indicates that, given private sector information that the Fed is tightening monetary policy, the Fed's inflation forecast is high, and if the Fed is easing monetary policy, the Fed's

Table 9.5. *Romer and Romer (2000) estimates of response of inflation forecast to monetary-policy action*

$$\hat{\pi}^C_{h,\,t+1} = \eta + \lambda M_t + \kappa\hat{\pi}^C_{ht} + \rho(\hat{\pi}^F_{h,\,t+1} - \hat{\pi}^F_{ht}) + \upsilon_{h,\,t+1}$$

Forecast horizon (quarters)	η	λ	κ	ρ	R^2	N
		A. Dummy Variable				
Blue Chip						
0	−0.12(0.16)	0.14(0.06)	1.01(0.05)	0.11(0.07)	0.87	31
1	0.15(0.35)	0.05(0.03)	0.95(0.09)	0.17(0.09)	0.87	31
2	0.11(0.20)	0.03(0.03)	0.96(0.05)	0.10(0.10)	0.93	31
3	0.14(0.19)	0.05(0.02)	0.96(0.04)	0.17(0.07)	0.95	31
4	0.19(0.13)	0.07(0.02)	0.95(0.03)	0.07(0.06)	0.97	31
5	0.11(0.12)	0.04(0.03)	0.96(0.03)	0.10(0.06)	0.97	27
μ(0–4)	0.09(0.18)	0.05(0.03)	0.97(0.04)	0.39(0.12)	0.94	31
DRI						
0	1.24(0.23)	0.31(0.12)	0.65(0.07)	0.14(0.15)	0.68	27
1	0.19(0.16)	0.12(0.07)	0.95(0 04)	−0.14(0.13)	0.94	50
2	−0.05(0.32)	−0.01(0.12)	1.01(0.08)	−0.03(0.28)	0.86	50
3	0.33(0.24)	0.02(0.11)	0.92(0.06)	0.07(0.14)	0.88	50
4	0.57(0.24)	0.15(0.14)	0.85(0.06)	−0.31(0.37)	0.82	50
5	0.55(0.17)	0.22(0.07)	0.89(0.03)	0.14(0.18)	0.94	48
6	0.56(0.35)	0.17(0.14)	0.88(0.09)	0.96(0.52)	0.88	28
μ(0–4)	0.41(0.16)	0.03(0.04)	0.87(0.05)	0.33(0.21)	0.92	27
SPF						
1	−0.01(0.46)	0.23(0.19)	1.00(0.10)	0.35(0.14)	0.87	40
2	−0.58(0.44)	0.08(0.19)	1.11(0.09)	−0.10(0.11)	0.85	40
3	−0.22(0.27)	0.16(0.11)	1.04(0.05)	0.02(0.12)	0.90	40
4	1.13(0.27)	0.33(0.13)	0.80(0.05)	0.23(0.19)	0.83	39
μ(1–4)	0.08(0.28)	0.30(0.13)	0.99(0.06)	0.03(0.17)	0.92	39
		B. Change in Funds-Rate Target				
Blue Chip						
0	−0.06(0.18)	0.30(0.15)	0.99(0.05)	0.10(0.07)	0.86	31
1	0.19(0.35)	0.15(0.09)	0.94(0.09)	0.16(0.10)	0.87	31
2	0.16(0.22)	0.09(0.08)	0.95(0.05)	0.10(0.10)	0.93	31
3	0.22(0.17)	0.16(0.05)	0.94(0.04)	0.16(0.07)	0.95	31
4	0.27(0.13)	0.19(0.05)	0.93(0.03)	0.05(0.06)	0.97	31
5	0.14(0.11)	0.13(0.06)	0.96(0.02)	0.10(0.06)	0.97	27
μ(0–4)	0.14(0.20)	0.13(0.09)	0.95(0.05)	0.37(0.13)	0 94	31

Forecast horizon (quarters)	η	λ	κ	ρ	R^2	N
DRI						
0	1.27(0.24)	0.80(0.26)	0.63(0.06)	0.11(0.14)	0.69	27
1	0.14(0.17)	0.17(0.17)	0.96(0.04)	−0.13(0.14)	0.94	50
2	0.01(0.25)	0.27(0.43)	0.99(0.06)	0.05(0.21)	0.87	50
3	0.32(0.24)	−0.20(0.31)	0.92(0.06)	0.09(0.14)	0.88	50
4	0.47(0.23)	−0.16(0.30)	0.87(0.06)	−0.26(0.36)	0.81	50
5	0.43(0.16)	0.40(0.09)	0.92(0.03)	0.18(0.19)	0.94	48
6	0.40(0.27)	0.20(0.26)	0.91(0.07)	1.04(0.55)	0.88	28
μ(0–4)	0.37(0.16)	0.01(009)	0.88(0.05)	0.36(0.22)	0.92	27
SPF						
1	−0.03(0.45)	0.11(0.34)	1.00(0.10)	0.36(0.13)	0.86	40
2	−0.62(0.36)	0.09(0.45)	1.12(0.07)	−0.09(0.13)	0.85	40
3	−0.29(0.24)	0.19(0.28)	1.05(0.05)	0.02(0.15)	0.90	40
4	1.05(0.31)	0.23(0.36)	0.81(0.06)	0.31(0.18)	0.80	39
μ(1–4)	−0.06(0.27)	0.40(0.33)	1.01(0.06)	0.04(0.22)	0.91	39

Notes: $\hat{\pi}^C$ and $\hat{\pi}^F$ denote commercial and Federal Reserve inflation forecasts; h and t index the horizon and date of the forecasts. M is the indicator of monetary-policy actions. Because the time within the month that the forecasts are made varies across forecasters, the actual time and horizon subscripts for the inflation forecasts and the monetary-policy variable also vary across forecasters; see text for details. The sample periods are 1984:2–1991:11 for Blue Chip; and 1974:8–1979:8 and 1984:2–1991:11 for DRI and SPF. Numbers in parentheses are robust standard errors. The forecast horizons μ(0–4) and μ(1–4) refer to the averages of 0 to 4 quarters ahead and 1 to 4 quarters ahead, respectively.
Source: Christina D. Romer and David H. Romer, "Federal Reserve Information and the Behavior of Interest Rates," *American Economic Review* 90 (2000): 429–57. Reprinted with permission of the authors and the publisher.

inflation forecast is low. Virtually all of these coefficients are positive, and many of them are statistically significant.

One thing I thought about as I read the Romer and Romer (2000) article – and I could not see a good reason for not doing it this way – was that if I had had the dataset, I would have considered running it differently: I would have subtracted from the Fed's inflation forecast the commercial forecast and run that on a constant and on the monetary policy action. The idea here is that a positive θ coefficient would indicate that the Fed's inflation forecast was larger than the private sector's, and a negative coefficient would indicate that it was smaller. Nonetheless, this is not the way that the authors did it. Interestingly enough, essentially, that is what the equation reduces to. Basically, the coefficients are equal to 1, so you could not reject the hypothesis that they are equal to 1. The equation, in effect, estimates and then cannot reject the hypothesis. It is the difference between the

Fed forecast and the private sector forecasts that is explained by the monetary policy instrument.

As far as interpretation goes, I differ slightly from that of Romer and Romer. The cleanest way to interpret their article is actually in a way that the authors do not endorse. In my professorial mode, the cleanest way to link this article to what we did earlier is to say that this article supports the hypothesis that the Fed does indeed have superior information, which I take to mean more detailed information than the private sector. Romer and Romer do make a good point: It is hard to imagine the Fed having access to secret or confidential information. However, in the real world, acquiring and processing information is not costless. Indeed, it is expensive. You have to hire people to collect it and process it. Those costs have fallen with the advent of the Internet, but they are still not zero. The Fed does process and include in its forecasts much more regionally specific data than private sector forecasters do. So, I think the cleanest way to interpret these data is to say that both the private sector and the Fed efficiently use the information they have but that the Fed has more information that they can use to make a better forecast. This is not secret information, but the Fed has access to inflation trends in much more detail from around the country. Even though private forecasters could in theory access these data, they simply do not have the resources that the Fed does to monitor and improve those forecasts. Literally hundreds of statisticians and economists work for the Fed. In addition, each of the twelve regional Federal Reserve Banks has hundreds of statisticians and economists. Even a big commercial bank like Citibank might have a professional forecasting staff of five or six. Obviously, the Fed's greater resources would allow for more detailed use of existing information. At the margin, having those additional people and resources does appear to deliver better forecasts. At any rate, that is my interpretation of the Romer and Romer (2000) article.

Another possible explanation of why the Fed's forecasts seem more accurate might have something to do with the rewards system for private forecasters. If you have twenty or thirty forecasts and they are all grouped around a consensus number, it might pay for some forecasters to bet against the consensus and make an extreme forecast. You always find outliers when you look at many of these private forecasts. Why would someone want to buck the consensus? Well, if he or she is wrong, everyone will quickly forget it, and the forecaster certainly will not publicize it. But if the forecaster turns out to be right, he or she will look like a sage, and can emphasize that he or she went against the herd and was right. This is a way for a forecaster to stand out from the crowd, so there is definitely an incentive to make an extreme forecast. People working for the Fed would not have this incentive.

In economics, a reward system that favors insincere or counterproductive behavior is said to create a "moral hazard." In practice, it can be challenging to design payment systems that properly reward behavior that is socially beneficial. A related term that is sometimes used is "unforeseen consequences": An individual business decision or government policy might seem reasonable, but by implicitly rewarding certain counterproductive behavior, it can end up making things worse off. For example, suppose an industrial company decides to encourage higher quality by giving a bonus to factory managers whose production lines have zero defects while punishing those who produce defective products. Such a policy can have the unforeseen effect of encouraging managers to falsify data or to evaluate workers based on day-to-day fluctuations rather than long-term performance. The whole field of quality control is based on problems like this one. Another example involves evaluation of hospitals: If you rank hospitals based on the proportion of their patients who are released quickly, then you're setting up an incentive structure that encourages hospitals to avoid taking in difficult patients with serious diseases.

10. Two Studies of Interest Rates and Monetary Policy

In this chapter, I return to economic time series with two examples in detail. First, we'll look at an article by Cumby and Mishkin (1986), "The International Linkage of Real Interest Rates: The European–U.S. Connection." It makes some very important points and uses some of the methods we have talked about. What is the motivation for this article? There is a very important variable in the economics of the financial markets that our theories indicate should have great influence on the economy, but it is a variable that we cannot directly observe. The variable is the expected or ex-ante real rate of interest (denoted hereafter by rr_{th}, that is, the expectation at time t of what the real rate of return to holding an h-period bond from time t to time $t + h$ will be). Economists have shown that the rate of interest that is most relevant for borrowing and lending decisions is the expected real rate of interest on the loan. What is the expected real rate of interest? Basically, it is the cost of borrowing money once we take into account the rate of inflation that will prevail over the life of the loan. Inflation is just the percentage rise in the money price of goods and services while the funds are out on loan. In many loans, the stated or nominal rate of interest is known up front. For example, if the federal government wants to borrow money for one year, it auctions securities, and it knows the nominal or dollar rate of interest it will have to pay on the loan. If a bank makes a loan to a customer, it sometimes will make the loan at a fixed rate of interest. What is not known, however, is the rate of inflation that will prevail over the life of the loan. π_{th} will denote the realized rate of inflation between times t and $t+h$. We refer to the ex-post real interest rate ($eprr_{th}$) as the difference between the stated nominal interest rate on the loan (i_{th}) and the realized rate of inflation over the holding period of the loan (h):

$$eprr_{th} = i_{th} - \pi_{th}$$

Although we can observe the ex-post interest rate of the loan because we can always observe the nominal interest rate, and although we can observe realized inflation, we cannot directly observe the ex-ante real interest rate. The ex-ante interest rate, or real interest rate, is the difference between the nominal interest rate and the expected rate of inflation $(\pi^e{}_{th})$ that will prevail over the life of the loan (h periods, from time t to time $t+h$):

$$rr_{th} = i_{th} - \pi^e{}_{th}$$

Why do we care about the expected interest rate even though we cannot observe it? Think of a firm that is borrowing money to build a new factory or to buy or build a new machine. This firm will estimate the cash flows and revenues that will be generated by that investment compared to the cost of borrowing the funds. The firm knows how many dollars it will take to pay off the loan, but the firm also cares about the rate of inflation. Holding constant the nominal price of borrowing money, high inflation is good for borrowers and bad for lenders. High inflation is good for borrowers because it allows the firm to generate more dollars so that it can pay off the loan. If the stated dollars at the end of the loan period are fixed and are not a function of inflation, then high inflation after the fact and certainly high expected inflation will encourage people to borrow. The situation is just the opposite for lenders. Holding constant the nominal payment on the loan, high inflation discourages lenders from lending money because it lowers the real return to that loan. It lowers the real increase in goods and services that the lender can expect in exchange for foregoing goods and services today. At the point that a loan is made, we agree on a nominal interest rate, but we also have to form expectations of inflation. Once we agree on the nominal interest rate, higher expected inflation will encourage borrowers and discourage lenders. Thus, the equilibrium in the capital market will be an equilibrium for the expected real interest rate.

How would we go about estimating the ex-ante interest rate and testing hypotheses about it? We started by expressing the realized rate of inflation between period t and period $t+h$ as being equal to the expected rate of inflation plus a forecast error:

$$\pi_{th} = \pi^e_{th} + \varepsilon_{th}$$

If the market is efficiently using the information that it has, then ε_{th} is a rational forecast error that will satisfy the property that the expected product of the forecast error and any information that the market has when it makes the forecast is 0. This is simply the error orthogonality property that we talked about in Chapter 9. Thus, we can write the ex-post real interest rate, realized between periods t and $t+h$, as the difference between the expected real interest rate and the forecast error so that the variable that we can observe, the ex-post real interest rate, is the combination of two variables that we cannot observe, namely, the expected real interest rate and the inflation forecast error.

Even though this does not take us where we want to go, it is helpful. It tells us that what we want to observe is the sum of two variables that we cannot observe. However, one of these variables is not only uncorrelated with the expected real interest rate, it is also uncorrelated with any variable that is observed at time t. We will see in a minute how we make use of the orthogonality property. Now, suppose that we could observe the expected real interest rate, and suppose that what we wanted to do was to run a regression of the expected real interest rate on some collection of variables X that are known to the researcher at time t so that they will also be known to individuals at time t when they are making their forecasts. But this set of variables X is only a subset of the information that the market has. In this study X includes the nominal interest rate i_{th} and lagged values of inflation over the past year. The market, when it is making its forecast, knows both the nominal interest rate and its history of inflation.

We can imagine running a regression of the expected real interest rate on this collection of variables; there would be an error term in this regression that would be interpreted as a projection error.

$$rr_{th} = X_t \beta + u_{th}$$

In particular, we would not assume that u_{th} is equal to ε_{th} in the previous equation. That would be the case only when the expected real interest rate is exactly related to these variables. In general, there would be some divergence because the market has more information than just the variables in X_t.

Now we finally admit the truth. We cannot run this regression, even though it may be an interesting one to run, because we do not observe the predictor variable, but we can write the expected real interest rate as the sum of the ex-post rate and inflation. We then subtract the inflation forecast error, and this equation relates the observed real interest rate to this collection of macro variables so that now there are two sources of error in this equation:

$$rr_{th} = eprr_{th} + (\pi_{th} - \pi^e_{th}) = eprr_{th} + \varepsilon_{th}.$$
$$eprr_{th} = rr_{th} - \varepsilon_{th} = X_t \beta + u_{th} - \varepsilon_{th}.$$

There is the error that we get in projecting the expected real interest rate on its small set of variables, and then there is the error we would get in forecasting inflation based on a potentially even larger set of information. These error terms, by the assumption of rational expectations and by the construction of this equation, imply that the predictor variables of this equation, the X_t variables, are predetermined. They are certainly not independent of the error term, and they are certainly not exogenous in the sense in which we used the term in Chapter 8, but they are predetermined so that u_{th} and ε_{th} are unrelated to the history contained in X_t. Why is this useful? These variables X_t are in the information set of agents, so the forecast error will be unrelated to them. Least squares will provide a consistent estimate of the fitted value from a regression of the expected real interest rate on these variables, even if we substitute out for the expected real interest rate and use the after-the-fact or ex-post real interest rate. So, the nice insight is that even though we cannot observe the expected real interest rate, with a large enough sample we can estimate accurately the regression of the expected real interest rate on a set of variables. That gives us one estimate of the movements in the expected real interest rate that are relevant to individuals.

CUMBY AND MISHKIN (1986): AN APPLICATION

Cumby and Mishkin (1986) present some charts that show these estimates. These charts are based on a regression on a constant, the nominal interest rate at the

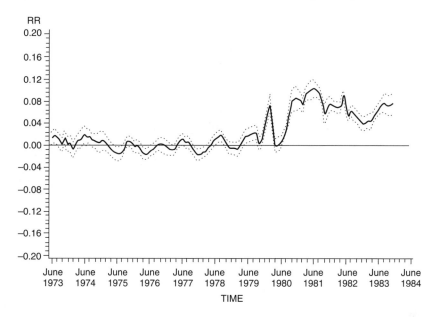

Figure 10.1. Ex ante real rates for the United States. Reprinted from the *Journal of International Money and Finance* 5, no. 1, Robert E. Cumby and Frederic S. Mishkin, "The International Linkage of Real Interest Rates: The European–U.S. Connection," 5–23, copyright 1986, with permission from Elsevier.

beginning of the period, and the history of inflation. These are estimates (Figure 10.1) of real interest rates in the United States from the 1970s to the mid-1980s, when the article was written.

The dotted lines on the graph give an indication of how uncertain we are about these estimates. Basically, you can divide these eleven years into two intervals. During the 1970s, the real rate of interest in the United States averaged zero. That is important because it indicates that not only were there periods in which realized inflation was higher than nominal interest rates, so that ex post or after the fact interest rates were negative, but it also indicates that there were periods when the real expected return to investment was negative as well. However, these boundaries, which are essentially to be thought of as standard errors, include zero. Thus, you certainly could not exclude the hypothesis that the expected real cost of borrowing money short term was zero. But, as you see, around 1979 or 1980, these real rates of interest became positive – in fact, significantly positive. If we extended this trend to the subsequent fifteen years, to the mid-1990s, the numbers would look very similar to this. The past fifteen years have been a period when the real cost of borrowing money has been high relative to what it was in the 1970s, and it is comparable to, if not somewhat higher than, the real cost of borrowing in the 1960s. The rest of these charts show the estimates or fitted values from the estimates for the different countries in this study. They are displayed in Figure 10.2.

You see a broadly similar pattern in Canada, with roughly zero expected real rates in the 1970s and significant positive real rates in the 1980s. The results for

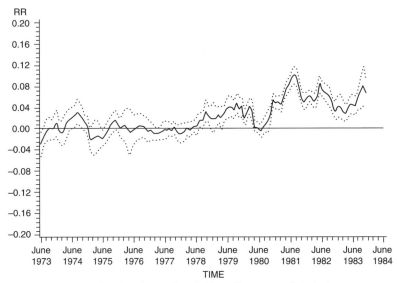

Ex ante real rates: Canada (domestic money market rates)

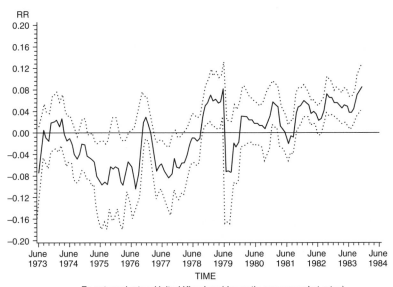

Ex ante real rates: United Kingdom (domestic money market rates)

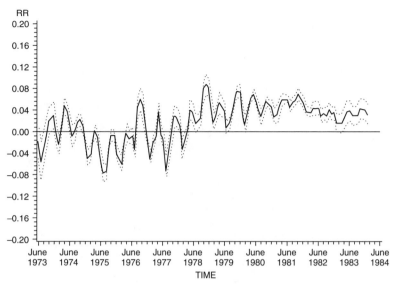

Ex ante real rates: Netherlands (domestic money market rates)

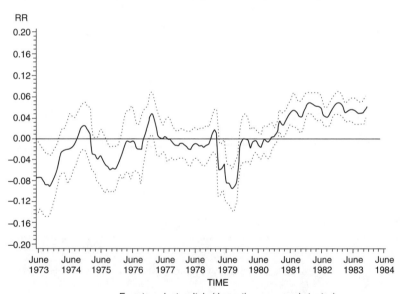

Ex ante real rates: Italy (domestic money market rates)

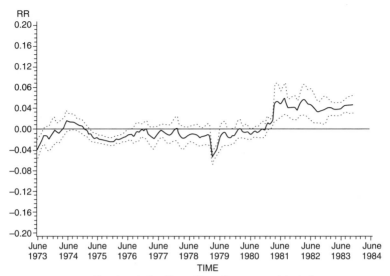

Ex ante real rates: France (domestic money market rates)

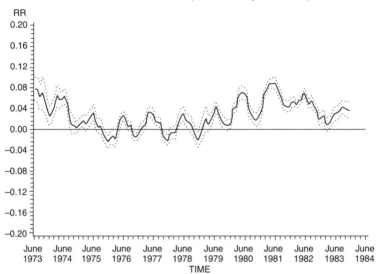

Ex ante real rates: West Germany (domestic money market rates)

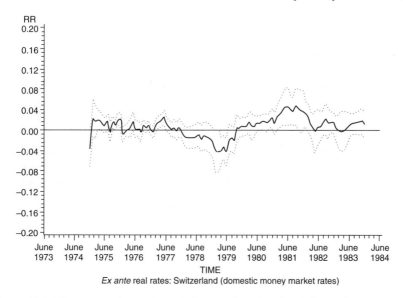

Figure 10.2. Ex ante real rates: several countries. Reprinted from the *Journal of International Money and Finance* 5, no. 1, Robert E. Cumby and Frederic S. Mishkin, "The International Linkage of Real Interest Rates: The European–*U.S. Connection*," 5–23, *copyright 1986, with permission from Elsevier.*

the United Kingdom are much more volatile, and there is a less marked pattern. The patterns for Italy and France are similar to the U.S. pattern, but again, they are more volatile. The pattern for West Germany is a little different in that the average level of real rates in the 1970s appears a bit higher than in the United States, though it certainly became higher still in the 1980s and 1990s. The basic thing that these results tell us, and that has been confirmed in many other studies, is that the real cost of borrowing money has been much higher in the past fifteen years than it was in the preceding fifteen years. The past fifteen years have also been a period of booming investment and booming economy. We often think of high real interest rates as putting a damper on investment spending. That is true to some extent, but one can interpret the existence of high borrowing costs, a surging stock market, and a booming economy as being evidence of a rise in productivity. We often hear about the "new economy," and one piece of evidence in support of this concept is that we have been able to have both high real interest rates and rapid economic growth with high investment, whereas if the high real interest rates reflected only the adjustments of monetary policy, then we would not expect to see a booming economy and high stock prices. There is ample evidence from the history of other periods of rapid growth and advancement of productivity and investment that were also periods of high borrowing costs.

The main point of the Cumby and Mishkin (1986) article is not merely to provide estimates of these real interest rate movements, but also to test an interesting hypothesis, namely, that there is such close linkage of international capital markets today that even though nominal interest rates across countries are not equalized, real interest rates are. To take a snapshot: In the summer of 2008, short-term interest rates in the United States were around 2%, while in Japan they were less than 1% and in Europe they were around 5%. So, nominal interest rates differed, but it can still be the case that real interest rates were equalized, so that one might argue that the reason European interest rates were higher than Japanese and U.S. rates is that Europe, on average, had higher inflation, and the higher interest rates were merely compensating for more inflation, leaving the real cost of borrowing equal.

Now let's talk about how we could test the hypothesis that real interest rates were equalized across countries. Also, let's consider how we would interpret rejections of that hypothesis. Again, suppose that we could observe ex-ante real interest rates, and suppose that we decided to run a regression of the expected real interest rate in country M on a constant and on the expected real interest rate in the United States, and that we could treat the error term as a true regression error:

$$rr_{th} = \alpha^M + \gamma^M rr^{US}_{th} + \omega^M_{th}.$$

We would have a simple model, and an interesting special case would be the one in which γ^M is equal to 1, and ω is equal to 0, and α is equal to 0. This model would say that expected real interest rates are equalized. We cannot estimate this equation directly because we do not have observations of expected real interest rates, but we can substitute in ex-post real interest rates for expected real rates.

$$eprr^M_{th} = \alpha^M + \gamma^M eprr^{US}_{th} + \omega^M_{th} - \varepsilon^M_{th} + \gamma^M \varepsilon^{US}_{th}.$$

That introduces new terms in the obvious places. It also introduces some additional error terms in the equation since we have now used realizations of real interest rates rather than their expectation, and this means that the error terms now include the inflation forecast error (ε's).

In this case, you can no longer assume that the predictor variable in this equation, the ex-post real interest rate in the United States, is predetermined in this equation. It is certainly not exogenous, but it is not even predetermined here because the predictor variables include the shock to U.S. inflation, and that clearly will be negatively correlated with the ex-post real interest rate in the United States. So, least squares would not be an appropriate way to estimate this equation, but there are many variables available that are valid "instruments" for the ex-post real interest rate.

A variable will be a valid instrument for the predictor if it helps explain that predictor but is not related to the error term in the equation. The ε's represent the forecast error, so they are uncorrelated with anything that is known at time t. If we also make that assumption about ω, which the Cumby and Mishkin (1986) article does, then essentially any variable at time t that is related to the real interest rate is a valid instrument. Thus, we can use the so-called two-stage least squares procedure, which starts by running a regression of the predictor on the

The Link with U.S. Real Interest Rates. Consumer Prices (June 1973–December 1983)

A. Three-month Eurocurrency deposit rates

Country	α	γ	Test of equality of real rates[b] $(\alpha = 0, \gamma = 1)$
Canada	−0.0013 (0.0010)	0.8585 (0.0984)	13.50
United Kingdom	−0.0035 (0.0042)	0.5544 (0.2865)	22.28
Netherlands	0.0001 (0.0010)	0.5275 (0.0435)	375.53
Italy	0.0024 (0.0027)	0.5416 (0.1923)	8.72
France	0.0009 (0.0013)	0.7541 (0.1159)	4.53
West Germany	0.0020 (0.0010)	0.4281 (0.0773)	86.18
Switzerland	0.0026 (0.0012)	0.0703 (0.1024)	123.46

B. Domestic money market interest rates

Country	α	α	Test of equality of real rates[b] $(\alpha = 0, \gamma = 1)$
Canada	0.0005 (0.0008)	0.9128 (0.0674)	1.67
United Kingdom	−0.0063 (0.0033)	0.7673 (0.2853)	22.01
Netherlands	0.0010 (0.0009)	0.5175 (0.0434)	241.36
Italy	−0.0032 (0.0022)	0.6370 (0.1477)	89.85
France	−0.0028 (0.0007)	0.5814 (0.0940)	55.41
West Germany	0.0037 (0.0010)	0.4373 (0.0915)	38.51
Switzerland	0.0023 (0.0009)	0.1635 (0.1043)	73.97

[a] The regressions begin in January 1976 for the Swiss money market interest rates. Standard errors are in parentheses. The instruments used in all cases were a constant, the nominal interest rate in the United States, three lagged values of inflation in the United States, and a time trend. These variables are also included multiplied by a dummy variable that is set equal to zero prior to October 1979 and one thereafter.
[b] Distributed as $\chi^2(2)$ under the null hypothesis. The critical value at the 5 per cent level is 5.99 and at the 1 per cent level is 9.21.

The Link Among European Real Interest Rates. Consumer Prices (June 1973–December 1983)

A. Three-month Eurocurrency deposit rates

Country	α	γ	Test of equality of real rates[b] $(\alpha = 0, \gamma = 1)$
France	0.0032 (0.0018)	0.5668 (0.3035)	56.09
Switzerland	0.0003 (0.0014)	0.1288 (0.1146)	213.34
Netherlands	0.0021 (0.0007)	0.4968 (0.1014)	26.88
Italy	0.0052 (0.0019)	0.3531 (0.1778)	13.30
United Kingdom	0.0021 (0.0035)	0.1538 (0.2762)	15.44

B. Domestic money market interest rates

Country	α	γ	Test of equality of real rates[b] $(\alpha = 0, \gamma = 1)$
France	−0.0013 (0.0014)	0.2395 (0.1460)	56.09
Switzerland	−0.0004 (0.0005)	0.1254 (0.0419)	758.12
Netherlands	0.0025 (0.0011)	0.3776 (0.1408)	32.73
Italy	−0.0063 (0.0016)	0.7919 (0.1594)	39.94
United Kingdom	−0.0011 (0.0033)	0.1210 (0.2431)	29.41

[a] The regressions begin in January 1976 for the Swiss money market interest rates. Standard errors are in parentheses. The instruments used in all cases were a constant, three lagged values of inflation in West Germany, the nominal interest rate in West Germany, and a time trend. These variables are also included multiplied by a dummy variable that is set equal to zero prior to April 1979 and one thereafter.
[b] Distributed as $\chi^2(2)$ under the null hypothesis. The critical value at the 5 per cent level is 5.99 and at the 1 per cent level is 9.21.

Figure 10.3. Explaining ex post rates in country M by U.S. ex post rates (instrumenting). Reprinted from the *Journal of International Money and Finance* 5, no. 1, Robert E. Cumby and Frederic S. Mishkin, "The International Linkage of Real Interest Rates: The European–U.S. Connection," 5–23, copyright 1986, with permission from Elsevier.

instruments. The second stage is to take the fitted value from the first regression and run a regression of the ex-post real interest rate on the fitted value from the first-stage regression. That will give us a useful estimate of this parameter γ^M. So long as we recognize that the first-stage regression is giving us the fitted value, we can do statistical tests of the hypothesis that γ is equal to 1. That would be the hypothesis that the expected real interest rates in country M relative to the United States, for example, are moving one to one with real interest rates in the United States. We could also test the even tighter hypothesis that the intercept term is 0. This says that expected real interest rates are equalized even if nominal interest rates are not.

What happened when Cumby and Mishkin (1986) did these regressions? We display their results in Figure 10.3. This is a regression of the ex-post real rate in country M on a constant and the ex-post real rate in the United States, but the predictor $(eprr_{th}^{US})$ is instrumented with lagged interest rates and inflation. Thus, if you look at panel A on the left, these are the bilateral regressions of all of these countries (Canada, the United Kingdom, the Netherlands, Italy, France, West Germany, and Switzerland). Each of these regressions has the predictor variable, which is the ex-post real interest rate in the United States.

What do we find? We find some interesting things. The bad news is that we must reject the simple hypothesis that capital markets are so integrated that interest rates are equalized. The point estimates are always positive, and many are significantly different from 0. In fact, I think that the only ones that are not significantly different from 0 are those from Switzerland. For Canada, the United Kingdom, Italy, the Netherlands, France and West Germany, there is a positive comovement in the data between the U.S. expected real interest rate and the interest rates in the other countries. For example, the results for Canada indicate that, over this period, for any increase in U.S. real interest rates, Canadian real rates went up by 85% of those figures. For the United Kingdom, the Netherlands, Italy, and West Germany, the results are similar. Their real rates went up about 0.5% for every 1% increase in the United States. Following is a similar analysis, but it is now limited to real interest rates within Europe and uses Germany as the center country. Thus, it tries to show how responsive real interest rates in, say, the Netherlands are to movements in real interest rates in Germany. Again here we can reject the hypothesis that real interest rates are equalized, but we do see positive comovement in Europe. During these years, there was less comovement of real interest rates when these countries are compared with Germany than there was when they are compared with the United States. This, situation, of course, subsequently changed. Today, if you were to use data on Europe from more recent times, you would get γ coefficients that were near 1. Europe has become much more integrated, since some of these countries have now become part of a monetary union. The euro, the common currency, by removing currency risk and uncertainty, links interest rates very tightly.

CLARIDA ET AL. (1998): A SAMPLE APPLICATION

The last thing we want to talk about is another application of these ideas. This application is close to my interests and to something that Gali, Gertler, and I have been working on: "Monetary Policy Rules in Practice: Some International Evidence" (1998). It is about monetary policy, as in Romer and Romer's (2000) article, and it's also about real interest rates and forecasting inflation. It will likewise use some of the statistical concepts you have been learning. The basic idea here is to formulate and test a hypothesis about the way that central banks conduct monetary policy. For example, Romer and Romer considered what would happen if the central bank tightened policy and whether that action would give us some information about the central bank's inflation forecast. In my work, which was done with some coauthors at New York University, we went one step further than Romer and Romer by writing down a specific hypothesis about the way that central banks conduct monetary policy. What we wanted to do is to propose, estimate, and test models of the way that central banks conduct policy. Then we applied this to the recent behavior of monetary policy in the United States, Germany, and Japan. We also tried to provide an interpretation of some of the events in Europe the past few years.

We hypothesized that the respective central banks have a desired or referenced rate of interest – if you will, a benchmark for thinking about policy. This benchmark is a function of the central bank's forecast of inflation, and possibly also of its forecast for output, so that x is some measure of the gap between actual output and potential output, that is, a measure of where you are in the cycle of the economy. Expected inflation is represented by π. This equation is called a "forward-looking Taylor rule." It is forward-looking because we say that the benchmark policy is a function of expected inflation and possibly of expected output. It is called a Taylor rule because John Taylor, who is a professor at Stanford, several years ago wrote a very influential paper, "Discretion versus Policy Rules in Practice" (1993), that, in effect, said, "I am not chairman of the Fed, but, if I were, I would set policy based on such and such guidelines." The only difference that we made is that whereas Taylor based policy (r^*, the central bank target for the nominal short-term interest rate) on realized inflation and realized output, we based policy on expected inflation (π^e) and expected output (y^e).

$$r_t^* = a + \beta\pi_{th}^e + \gamma y_{th}^e$$

We essentially augmented Taylor's guidelines by making them depend on the forecasts for inflation and production. That might look like a modest extension, and in some ways it is, but it has a very important implication. It implies that a central bank that is setting policy in that fashion will be a central bank for which the data have a correlation between its interest rate and a broad collection of macroeconomic variables. The basic idea is that when the central bank is doing its inflation forecast, it will be looking at the whole economy. In fact, as shown in the Romer and Romer (2000) article, the central bank is probably looking at a broader selection of variables than any private sector forecaster. If we think of the relationship between the interest rate and these macro variables, such as lagged inflation, oil prices, unemployment, and the like, then we can interpret that relationship according to this hypothesis: Interest rates in the data appear to react to movements in oil prices, exchange rates, or unemployment not because the central bank is necessarily targeting oil prices, exchange rate, or unemployment, but because those variables are useful for forecasting inflation. That actually provides a good, testable hypothesis that we will consider. Apropos of our earlier discussion of the real interest rate, if the central bank is following this benchmark, then in the data the interest rate will rise in tandem with inflation. When inflation is high, the central bank will push up interest rates in order to slow down the economy, but when inflation is low or the economy is weak, the central bank will lower interest rates. This is not inconsistent with the finding in the Romer and Romer article that when the Fed is tightening policy, its forecast of inflation is high relative to the private sector forecast.

How do you actually estimate this? Again, the problem is that we do not observe expected inflation and expected output, but we do observe realized inflation and realized output. We have instruments for these variables and, just as before, we ran two first-stage regressions, realized inflation on the instruments and realized output on the instruments. Then, in the second stage, we substituted those fitted values, which gave us estimates of β and γ. Technically speaking, we did

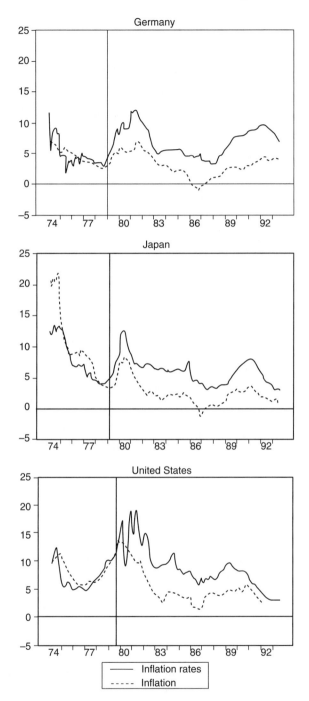

Figure 10.4. G-3 interest rates: target versus actual. Reprinted from *European Economic Review* 42, no. 6, Richard Clarida, Jordi Gali, and Mark Gertler, "Monetary Policy Rules in Practice: Some International Evidence,"1033–67, copyright 1998, with permission from Elsevier.

not use two-stage least squares, but rather a more general version of it that allowed us to have monthly data from a twelve-month forecast. Basically, this is very similar to the approach that I have presented. Our approach does not require that we specify the central bank's information set.

Including the exchange rate does have significance, though it does not change these estimated coefficients. Thus, during this period, the Bank of Japan also appeared to be trying to stabilize the exchange rate.

Finally, we have the estimates for the Fed, and here I will focus on the results after 1982 for some institutional reasons. After 1982 the estimated equation is a coefficient of 1.8 on inflation and 0.5 on output, and that is actually quite close to the benchmark policy rule that John Taylor recommended to the Fed. Figure 10.4 shows a plot of how these elements fit.

The solid line on each graph represents the actual interest rate in a country, and the dotted line is the fitted value from our estimated policy rule. What you see here is that the policy rule tracks the movements in the actual interest rate fairly closely. We were not unhappy to find that, if anything, the policy rule seemed to be a leading indicator of the actual movement in interest rates. In this period, when inflation in the United States, Japan, and Germany was high, our policy rules indicated a rise in rates, which occurred, and, when the economy started to go into the tank and inflation started to fall, our policy rules called for falling interest rates somewhat before rates actually did fall. In this period when inflation again picked up, our policy rules predicted a rise in rates a few months before it actually occurred.

In the United States, the disinflation episode after 1982 is one in which our policy rule indicated that a more aggressive easing of policy would be called for, but this is a result that became obvious only with the benefit of hindsight. Certainly, at the time, the Fed had good reason to be concerned about a resurgence of inflation. After 1985 the rule fits the U.S. data fairly well.

The final application that I want to consider is the events that have occurred recently. In January 1999, there was implemented in Europe an historic agreement to move to a single unified currency. The common currency for eleven[1] member states of the European Union became the euro, which is issued by the European Central Bank. Now, an important implication of a common currency is that securities denominated in that currency by different borrowers have to earn the same rate of return if they have the same default characteristics. Before the monetary union in Europe, the French borrowed in francs, the Italians in lira, and the Germans in deutschmarks. Interest rates could and did diverge significantly because of the exchange rate risk involved in borrowing in a foreign currency. With a common currency, of course, there is no exchange rate and therefore no exchange rate risk. If you look at a plot of European interest rates after 1987, you can see that in the late 1980s and early 1990s, interest rates diverged significantly. For example, interest rates in the late 1980s in Germany were around 3%, while in

[1] Initially, eleven EU member states adopted the euro on January 1, 1999. Two years later, Greece was admitted, followed by Slovenia in 2007 and Cyprus and Malta in 2008. Currentyl there are fifteen state, with nine states and territories using the Euro as their only currency.

Italy they were around 12%. They did begin to converge in the early 1990s but then diverged again. However, around 1998 they began to converge markedly. There are quarterly data, but if we had monthly data you would see that by late December 1998, interest rates for all eleven countries had converged to the same point, because the monetary union was to come into existence on January 4, 1999. On that date, the exchange rate between these eleven currencies was locked into place permanently.

The open question was not about convergence since, of course, there had to be convergence conditional on monetary union. The question was, to what level would interest rates converge? I would like to close by considering this question. We know that rates converged to about 3%, but what determined that? If we fit a shadow Taylor rule for Europe using euro-wide aggregates for inflation and output over this 1987 to 1998 period, we will find that the interest rate convergence that occurred in 1998 was to the level implied by the Taylor rule. We would therefore argue that Europe got off to the right start with respect to monetary policy, given the European-wide aggregates. Since that time and up to to recent years, however, monetary policy has been challenged in Europe. Because of the weakness of the euro at that time, many have argued that monetary policy for the initial eleven countries started off too loose. The statistical analysis is relevant to policy, but it certainly does not answer the question of what determined the level of interest rate convergence.

FURTHER READING FOR PART III

In Chapters 8 to 10, we reviewed some basic definitions and applications of time series econometrics. This is one area in economics where statistical and regression analyses are basic tools. And, as we have seen, the statistical estimates and hypothesis tests tie in directly with modeling assumptions from economic theory. A helpful reference to learn more on the econometrics of time series is Harvey (1993). More complete coverage of this topic can be found in Hamilton (1994). Greene (2007) is a general but thorough text on econometrics.

For a basic introduction to economics as a whole, you can start with Mankiw's (2003) introductory text. If you want an economist's version of the way things work, read Harford (2006).

A classic textbook on economic growth is Barro and Sala-i-Martin (2004). For a historical perspective and an alternative explanation for lack of growth, Easterly (2002) is an excellent read. For a recent discussion on growth and convergence, see Sala-i-Martin (2006).

EXERCISES FOR PART III

Exercises 1

1. Provide brief but complete answers to the following questions:
   a. How is economics like a science?
   b. Why is economics a "social" science?

    c. Why do economists sometimes offer conflicting advice to policymakers?

    d. Should an economic model describe reality exactly?

2. Discuss the following statement from the standpoints of equity and efficiency: "An even more progressive tax subsidy system should be implemented in the United States so that the government can better redistribute income from the richer to the poorer."

3. Classify each of the following statements as positive or normative. Explain.

    a. In a competitive market, when quantity supplied exceeds quantity demanded, price tends to fall.

    b. The economy faces a short-run trade-off between inflation and unemployment.

    c. When determining tax rates, the government should take into account the income needs of individuals.

    d. Lower tax rates encourage more saving. Based on this argument, the government should decrease taxes in order to promote economic growth.

4. Classify the following topics as relating to microeconomics or macroeconomics.

    a. The relation between the inflation rate and the unemployment rate

    b. The impact of higher investment on economic growth

    c. A monopolist's decision about how many units to sell

    d. A family's decision about how much income to spend in housing

    e. The effect of government regulations on public transportation usage

5. Stata exercise: After reading the article by Gwartney and Haworth (1974), use the file Baseball.dta (available at http://www.stat.columbia.edu/~gelman/qmssbook/) to do the following:

    a. Create summary statistics for the three variables Black47, Black52, and Won.

    b. Create a graph with Won on the vertical axis and Black47 on the horizontal axis.

    c. Run a simple regression with Won as the outcome variable and Black47 as the predictor variable.

        i. What percent of the total variation in the variable Won is explained by Black47?

        ii. What is the impact of an additional black player year on the percentage of games won?

        iii. Test the null hypothesis that Black47 has a zero effect on the percentage of games won using a 5% level of significance.

    d. Add the predicted regression line to the graph you drew earlier.

Exercises 2

1. Using an Internet mapping page, create a map of your hometown and answer the following questions:

    a. How is the map like a model?

    b. Could you use this map to determine the distance from one place to another? The traffic speed? What do your answers suggest about (i) which

elements to consider when using a map or a model and (ii) the limitations of a particular map?
2. Would you expect differences among economists' opinions to be completely eliminated as time goes on? Why or why not?
3. Provide brief but complete answers to the following questions:
   a. What is the basic problem of economics?
   b. What three problems must any economic system solve?
   c. How does capitalism solve these three problems?
   d. How does Soviet-style socialism solve these three problems?
4. Why do most economists oppose trade restrictions?
5. Stata exercise:
   a. Go to the website of the Federal Reserve Bank of St. Louis and look for the FRED database (www.stls.frb.org). Download the series of the most recent quarterly data for *U.S. Real Gross Domestic Product in Chained 2000 Dollars*.
   b. Plot the series against time.
   c. Compute the series of the natural log of GDP and do a time plot for it. Compare this graph to the previous one.
   d. Decompose the GDP series into a trend and a cycle using a linear deterministic trend model by fitting the regression, $y_t = \alpha + \beta t + \varepsilon_t$. Now use your estimates and fitted values to find the trend and the cycle of the original series. (Note: define the trend as the fitted values of the preceding regression $(a + bt)$, where a and b are the estimates for α and β, and define the cycle as y_t minus the trend.)
   e. Plot in the same graph the trend (predicted values) and the original data against time.
   f. Plot the cycle against time. What can you say about the stationarity of the cycle (detrended) series

Exercises 3

1. Provide brief but complete answers to the following questions:
   a. What is a competitive market? Briefly describe the types of markets other than perfectly competitive markets.
   b. What is the demand curve? Why does it slope downward?
   c. Define the equilibrium of a market. Describe the forces that move a market toward its equilibrium.
   d. Describe the role of prices in market economies.
2. Suppose that a technological advance reduced the cost of computer chips. How do you think this would affect the market for computers? For computer software? For typewriters?
3. Stata exercise: To do this exercise, you should have read the article by Romer and Romer (2000).
   a. Download the data file inflation.dta.

b. Plot both inflation series against time. That is, make two plots: first, graph expected inflation against time; second, graph actual inflation against time.

c. Test the hypothesis that the survey data for inflation expectations are rational. In order to do this, follow these steps:

   i. Run the following linear regression:

$$\pi_t = \alpha + \beta \pi^e_t + \varepsilon_t,$$

where π_t stands for actual inflation and π^e_t stands for the survey expected inflation.

   ii. Test the hypothesis that $\alpha = 0$.

   iii. Test the hypothesis that $\beta = 1$.

   iv. If you reject the preceding hypothesis, you can conclude (in a rough sense) that the survey is not rational. What do you conclude from your tests?

4. Stata exercise: To do this exercise, you should read the article by Cumby and Mishkin (1986).

a. Find interest rates (nominal) and inflation data for the United States and a second country, X.

b. Find the ex-post real interest rate series for the United States. In other words, find $eprr^{US} = i^{US} - \pi^{US}$, where i^{US} stands for the nominal interest rate in the United States, π^{US} stands for the inflation rate in the United States, and $eprr^{US}$ stands for the ex-post real interest rate in the United States. Once you have the series, plot it, together with the inflation series, in a graph against time.

c. Find the ex-post real interest rate series for the second country, X. In other words, find $eprr^X = i^X - \pi^X$, where i^X stands for the nominal interest rate, π^X stands for the inflation rate, and $eprr^X$ stands for the ex-post real interest rate. Once you get the series, plot it together with Country X's inflation series in a graph against time.

d. Find U.S. inflation data for the three previous years. Regress the U.S. ex-post interest rate ($eprr^{US}$) on

   i. the U.S. nominal interest rate (i_t^{US})

   ii. a time trend (t)

   iii. the three lagged inflation variables: USinfl_1, Usinfl_2, Usinfl_3.

   In other words, run the following linear regression:

$$eprr_t{}^{US} = \alpha + \beta i_t{}^{US} + \delta t + \varphi 1\pi_{t-1}{}^{US} + \varphi 2\pi_{t-2}{}^{US} + \varphi 3\pi_{t-3}{}^{US} + \varepsilon t$$

Show the estimates and standard errors for each coefficient.

e. Find the fitted values from the previous regression (part d) and call the predicted values *prrUS*.

f. Regress the Country X ex-post real interest rates ($eprr^G$) on *prrUS* and a constant; that is, run the following regression:

$$eprr^X = \upsilon + \gamma \, prrUS + \varepsilon$$

g. Test the null hypothesis that $\nu = 0$ (from regression estimates in part f).
h. Test the null hypothesis that $\gamma = 1$ (from regression estimates in part f).
   i. Testing for $\nu = 0$ and $\gamma = 1$ is equivalent to testing for the equalization of real rates in the United States and Country X. Would you conclude, from your preceding results, that they are equalized

PART IV. SOCIOLOGY

Seymour Spilerman and Emanuele Gerratana*

* Emanuele Gerratana assisted with the preparation of this section from Seymour Spilerman's lecture notes. Stylistically, first-person singular is used in the text to maintain the lecture format and because many of the items discussed are the writings of the first author.

11. Models and Theories in Sociology

Chapter 11, the first chapter in this part, explores some of the kinds of explanations and structures of explanations that are common in sociology. I will be referring to a classic monograph by Arthur Stinchcombe (1968), especially to the division "Complex Causal Structures: Demographic, Functional and Historicist Explanations of Social Phenomena." In Chapter 12, I'll provide examples of the construction and testing of explanations from some work of mine on racial disturbances. Chapters 13 and 14 cover two additional examples of empirical analysis: a study of the construction of a time series for lynchings events in the American South and an investigation of career advancement within a large corporation.

We'll start by discussing explanatory structures at a meta-level. How do sociologists go about formulating theories, and what are the structures of those theories? First, there is the issue of deductive versus inductive explanations. Should one start with a particular theory from which implications are derived? Or should one begin with the data and look for empirical regularities, essentially generalizations from observed patterns, leading to the formulation of low-level theoretical statements? Sociologists use both kinds of reasoning, as do other social scientists. Sociologists, however, tend to do more inductive work than, for example, economists. Economists have developed a robust theoretical apparatus from which hypotheses are derived and that are then tested with data. Economists usually operate under a framework of utility maximization by actors, subject to a constraint set. You rarely see this type of formulation in the work of sociologists. Sociologists do develop and test theories, and we'll look at several examples in the course of these chapters, but you'll see that these theories start at some low level of hypothesizing from the data. More elaborate theoretical structures are developed as the initial formulations are reexamined in different institutional contexts – whether work organizations, political parties, religious associations, or countries – leading to refinements and to a better understanding of the conditions under which the formulation is applicable. So, my first point is that sociologists do more inductive work than economists, though, in our use of data, we tend to be more deductive than historians.

HISTORICAL AND FUNCTIONAL EXPLANATIONS

I want to distinguish among three kinds of explanatory strategies. First is the "historical" type of explanation.[1] This is an explanation of an event or a social institution from the point of view of the factors that brought it into being. It is a straightforward causal explanation. For example, one can say that the Soviet Union had a communist form of economic system during much of the twentieth century because of certain events that took place in 1917. This is an explanation of the institution of interest from the point of view of the causes that brought it about. However, one might argue, alternatively, that a communist system existed in the Soviet Union because this economic structure solved certain critical problems facing the society. This is an entirely different sort of explanation from the historical kind, and it is called a "functional" explanation.

Whereas the historical explanation accounts for a social institution in terms of its origins, the functional explanation emphasizes the services that are performed by the institution. Since functional accounts will be new to many of you, I'll go into some detail about the formalism of this kind of explanation. As an example from physiology, to say that people have lungs so that they can breathe is a functional explanation. It is not an explanation of the presence of lungs from the point of view of how this organ came into existence; it's an account from the perspective of the service performed by the structure. Bronislaw Malinowski (1936: 132–3), a distinguished anthropologist and a major contributor to functional theory, wrote, "[t]he functional view of culture insists therefore upon the principle that . . . every custom, material object, idea and belief fulfills some vital function [in society]." Thus, social institutions such as schools, political systems, and ceremonial activities such as ritual and magic, exist because they make critical contributions to the social system. While often utilized in the social and biological sciences, and while enlightening about the interrelations among structural elements, this type of explanation does not address how the particular institution (or bodily organ) came into being or why this is the solution to the problem at hand. One can imagine, for example, other solutions besides lungs to the problem of bringing oxygen into the bloodstream. Why a solution based on lungs has developed for much of the animal kingdom is an issue that cannot easily be explored within the functional framework.

A more formal specification of the structure of a functional explanation begins with the notion of regulating a problematic *recurrent* event, such as criminal behavior or the death of a family member, and recognizes the societal interest in these matters. In the first case, the societal interest is to keep the crime rate low, which is effected through a menu of legal punishments, while recognizing that it would be prohibitively expensive to pursue a zero rate for most types of crimes. In the second case, the societal interest is to encourage the bereaved to reassume his or her social and economic responsibilities after a brief interval; religious rules that prescribe the details of the funeral ceremony and the mourning activities serve this purpose (Radcliffe-Brown 1952: 179–80). The key notion in these examples is one of "maintaining" social functioning within certain parameters.

---

[1] Not to be confused with a "historicist" explanation, as discussed in Stinchcombe (1968: chap. 3).

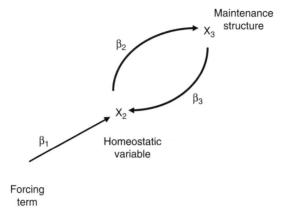

Figure 11.1. Structural representation of a functional explanation. The functional explanation requires the product $\beta_2\beta_3$ to be negative.

What do I mean by this? In the typical functional explanation there is a forcing variable that causally affects a "homeostatic" variable. The latter would normally respond to changes in the forcing variable. Calling it homeostatic means that, in the functionalist scheme, it is somehow maintained with limited variation, despite shifts in the forcing term. Once the homeostatic variable begins to change in response to the forcing term, it elicits activity by a "maintenance structure" that has a negative feedback effect, with the result that variations in the (homeostatic) variable are limited. This is a bit abstract, but we can depict the essential structure of a functional explanation graphically.

In Figure 11.1, x_1 is the forcing variable, x_2 is the homeostatic variable, and x_3 is the maintenance structure, represented here as a single variable. For simplicity, let's assume that the effects of these variables are linear, represented by the β's. We can therefore write

$$x_2 = \beta_1 x_1 + \beta_3 x_3 = \beta_1 x_1 + \beta_2\beta_3 x_2, \tag{1}$$

where the second expression results from substituting $x_3 = \beta_2 x_2$ into the prior term. Solving for x_2, we obtain

$$x_2 = \frac{\beta_1}{1 - \beta_2\beta_3} x_1 \tag{2}$$

Referring to Figure 11.1, let's assume that an increase in x_1 has a positive effect on x_2, (i.e., $\beta_1 > 0$). This would increase the level of x_2, which, in turn, stimulates activity by x_3 (i.e., $\beta_2 > 0$). But increased activity by x_3 has a negative impact on x_2 (i.e., $\beta_3 < 0$). Given these values of β_2 and β_3, it is the case that $(1 - \beta_2\beta_3) > 1$. Consequently,

$$\frac{[\beta_1]}{1 - \beta_2\beta_3} < \beta_1 \tag{3}$$

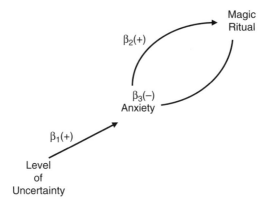

Figure 11.2. Functional explanation of the effect of magic ritual on anxiety level.

This depiction shows how a functionalist structure operates to limit the variation in x_2. Without the presence of x_3, the response to a unit change in x_1 would be β_1, but in the presence of this structure the response is reduced by the extent to which the denominator of the first term of equation (3) exceeds the value 1. Stinchcombe (1968: 130–48) discusses the technical details of some more complex functionalist models, but the preceding is the prototypical structure of a functional explanation.

Let's consider some examples. The first is from human physiology, where functional explanations are rather common. Digestive activity in the stomach causes an increase in the blood's sugar level (glucose), but the sugar level must be kept within narrow bounds for a human to remain healthy. The increase in blood sugar stimulates the storage activity of the liver, which then absorbs sugar. Thus, the sugar level in the blood (homeostatic variable) is kept within narrow bounds, and the structure maintaining this variable (the liver) achieves this end not by acting on the disturbing or forcing variable (digestion), but by acting directly on the homeostatic variable (Stinchcombe 1968: 59).

Now an example from anthropology. The Trobriand Islanders use magic rituals when they go fishing in the open sea but rarely when they fish in the bay. When they fish in the bay the likelihood of being caught in a storm is low, but in the open sea they are at great risk. When the fishermen want to go out to the sea, their anxiety rises to a level that would inhibit work unless it is controlled. According to Malinowski (1948), the fishermen manage the anxiety by performing magic rituals. This doesn't decrease the uncertainty and danger of the open ocean, of course; they can't control the weather. But the ritual does reduce their anxiety level, permitting the men to carry on with their fishing activities (Figure 11.2).

Here's another example, concerning the persistence of poverty. How do we explain the lesser academic attainments of children from poor families? You may have a school system with teachers who are dedicated to raising academic achievement, but the reality is that even when school budgets are generous, the attainments of poor children remain low. A functional explanation for the lack of response might go as follows: Academic attainment does not respond to teachers' efforts and school expenditures because there are feedback processes that maintain it. There's a social structure called a "peer group," to which many children are responsive, that has its own values and norms and allocates status and other rewards to conforming members. In poor neighborhoods the peer group often accords high rewards to success in sports like basketball or football and disvalues academic achievement. Peer group members who invest much time in their studies may lose esteem within the group. Since schoolwork is negatively reinforced by the group, there is likely to be less of it. Thus, well-intended attempts to promote academic achievement may run up against a value system that discourages schoolwork. This functionalist explanation shows how academic attainment, the homeostatic variable, can be maintained at a low level despite countervailing efforts by educators.

If you believe that this explanation is correct, it has certain policy implications: To increase academic achievement, we might decide to disassemble the peer group by assigning the children to different schools. Let's get them out of poor neighborhoods, where the prevalent values of adolescents are counterproductive with respect to educational attainment. Let's bus the children to schools in middle-class neighborhoods, where the peer groups hold values that are more conducive to educational attainment. Variants of this strategy have been tried, such as magnet schools, which seek to attract students from the wider community, with some success. The writings of James Coleman (1961, 1993) have been particularly influential on these matters. Coleman has argued that peer group culture is critical for understanding how children allocate their time and effort. His recommendation for addressing the problem of low attainment is twofold. He has advocated building large schools – of sufficient size to accommodate diverse specialty areas – that could sustain a variety of peer groups, some of which would likely support academic values. Coleman's second approach is to compete with existing peer groups in a school. Following the model of sports teams, a school might set up debating tournaments, or chess or math competitions, and reward success in these activities with recognition and prizes. The intention, then, would be to broaden the range of activities in which students can receive prestige and esteem from excelling.

Many of you no doubt are familiar with the term "culture of poverty." This label is associated with an account of the reasons that some poor families remain economically depressed, despite the presence of opportunity for upward mobility. The culture of poverty thesis suggests that poor families may be embedded in a culture that disvalues middle-class norms and aspirations, especially ones associated with stable work, an occupational career, and long-term goals (Lewis 1966). The culture of poverty thesis can be formulated as a functional explanation, with the homeostatic variable being conformity to the norms of the neighborhood culture (Spilerman and Elesh 1971). Attempts to work hard at a job may be met with disapproval from friends and neighbors; in ghetto neighborhoods one might be ridiculed for "acting white." Such comments are examples of negative feedback intended to maintain conformity to the local values. Policy proposals for helping poor families to emerge from welfare and dependence, and sustain themselves in the labor market, can be difficult to implement when they rely on strategies for promoting behaviors that are at variance with neighborhood norms.

I've provided several examples of functional explanations. I've spent more space on this kind of explanation than on historical (causal) accounts because

I assume that the latter are familiar to you. We are accustomed to explaining an institutional arrangement in terms of prior conditions and causal forces, but the functional type of explanation is less common. As noted, its weakness is that it doesn't address how the institutional structure came about – only what end it serves. In our physiological example, the functional explanation tells us nothing about how the liver came into existence, only why it is important. Did the liver come into existence to perform the function of regulating the blood glucose level? Possibly yes, but possibly no. It may have started out by serving an entirely different end and evolved over time in some complex manner. Thus, a functional explanation has both strengths and weaknesses. It gives insight into the contribution made by a variable or a structure to the maintenance of some system, but not into its origins. Functional explanations of social processes are generally conservative in a political sense: They provide an account of the status quo, of how a social institution operates and why it is important, but they are not attuned to explaining social change. To speak of change is to bring in a causal type of explanation. This does not mean that functional explanations are irrelevant to the analysis of change. They can be useful, for instance, in the study of revolution, war, stock market collapse, physical illness, even emotional depression – in short, in attempts to understand processes of system breakdowns, especially the conditions under which a maintenance structure is not able to sustain the homeostatic variable within its customary bounds.

DEMOGRAPHIC EXPLANATIONS

A third type of explanatory paradigm is what Stinchcombe (1968: 69–79) calls a "demographic explanation " and others call a "compositional explanation." It is based on a description of an event frequency at a macro level and takes the form

$$\text{Number of events} = f(\text{number of generating units}, \lambda), \qquad (4)$$

where λ is a parameter of the system and $f(.)$ describes the functional form. For example, the number of births in a population in a year can be written as a function of the number of women times the birth rate. A more precise formulation would specify this as the sum of the number of women in age group i times the birth rate of women in this age group, with the sum ranging over the age groups; that is,

$$\text{Number of births} = \sum N_i \lambda_i, \qquad (5)$$

where $N_i =$ the number of women in age group i, $\lambda_i =$ the age-specific birth rate, and i ranges over the women's ages. The sum of these products yields the total number of births. This is not a causal explanation. It's a decomposition of the process, but it is often a first step toward building a causal explanation of the determinants of the number of births.

The next step might be to examine N_i as a function of other variables. The number of women of a given age might depend on whether there had been a major war in the generation of the parents. Had a war occurred, the presumption is that fewer children would have been born and there would now be fewer women of childbearing age. There could be other variables that you would choose to include in accounting for N_i, such as the immigration rate in past years, which could affect the number of women who are now in age group i. You might also build an explanatory model of the λ_i term. For example, the birth rate of women in age group i might be a function of their educational attainment. As education increases, the birth rate generally declines. You might also want to look at urban versus rural residence, with the presumption that the birth rate is lower in urban populations. Thus, one might attempt to account for the value of λ_i using a formulation such as

$$\lambda_{ic} = g(\text{education level}_{ic}, \text{urban/rural residence}_{ic}, \text{other variables}_{ic}), \qquad (6)$$

where λ_{ic} is the number of births in a year to woman c of age group i, the terms on the right side of equation (6) refer to presumed determinants of this variable, and λ_{ic} is related to equation (5) in that the age-specific birth rate can be written as $\lambda_i = \Sigma \lambda_{ic}/N_i$, where the summation is over index c. Keep in mind that we are working at two different levels: λ_{ic} is a variable at the level of the individual woman in age group i, whereas λ_i is a statistic of the age group.

In employing a demographic explanation, one therefore starts by decomposing the variable of interest in terms of a set of other terms that are its primary components. You do this because the causal factors of importance tend to act on one or another of the constituent terms. By decomposing the variable of interest, it is possible to build an explanatory model of each component with reference to its unique determinants. In the previous example, you would formulate N_i or λ_i (or both) as a function of other variables. This is the typical structure of a demographic explanation. The words "demographic" and "compositional" refer to the first stage. In the second, a multivariate formulation such as a regression model would be used to investigate the determinants of the components. The compositional framework, then, allows for the separate examination of factors that combine in a known way, such as in the example of equation (5), to produce the ultimate variable of interest.

The compositional approach can be particularly illuminating for understanding the causes of change. Suppose that the birth rate in a population is going up and, at the same time, the proportion of women at the prime childbearing age is also increasing. Then the birth rate story would not be much of a surprise. However, if the birth rate is going up, but without a change in the age distribution of women, then there is evidence of real structural change (a shift in the values of λ_i), and it may be of interest to search for an explanation. This sort of decomposition is useful in many policy fields where the variables of interest are specified at an aggregate level (e.g., the unemployment rate in a country), while explanations for change must be sought in the behavior of the constituent units (e.g., the shifting demand for labor in different industries).

FURTHER READING

To pursue these issues I suggest, in addition to Stinchcombe's (1968) seminal volume, a text by Ernest Nagel (1961) that provides an overview of the structure of explanations in different scientific disciplines, and a set of readings in the philosophy of the social sciences (Martin and McIntyre 1994), especially part V. Another classic monograph is Thomas Kuhn's (1962) *The Structure of Scientific Revolutions*. Kuhn examines how broad explanatory formulations in the sciences, which he terms "paradigms," have succeeded one another over time. A paradigm can be thought of as a research agenda combined with a methodology for carrying out the relevant studies. A paradigm constitutes a simplification of a research field in the sense that some issues are highlighted as critical, requiring immediate attention, while others are downplayed. A paradigm, therefore, provides guidance to a researcher in choosing research problems. With time, as research findings are accumulated, most of the questions for which the paradigm is well suited come to be explored. The paradigm becomes played out and is eventually succeeded by another, possibly reflecting a deeper view of the field. Kuhn considers the intervals between paradigms, when researchers are groping for a new guiding framework, as periods of potentially great creativity. Work carried out under established paradigms is termed "normal science" by Kuhn; important new knowledge is generated efficiently from within the formulation, but in a somewhat routine way. In the interstices between paradigms, in comparison, there is great variance in the importance of research findings. A lot of work leads to dead ends, but some novel ways of framing problems also emerge, eventually generating the succeeding paradigm. Stephen Cole (2001: 37–60) has recently applied Kuhn's formulation to an assessment of the state of theory development in sociology.

For examples of causal and functional theories in the social sciences, I suggest the classic writings of Radcliffe-Brown (1952) and Malinowski (1936, 1948), who have examined the role of ritual and magic in primitive societies. Lewis (1966), Spilerman and Elesh (1971), and Liebow (1967) have applied functional explanations to the study of social class and poverty. Liebow, incidentally, provides a counterargument to cultural/functional explanations of poverty. Other applications of functional theory can be found in the writings of psychoanalysts, such as Freud (1912) and Shapiro (1965). Indeed, in psychoanalytic theory and practice, much of the difficulty with effecting change in a patient's view of the world and in his or her neurotic behavior is explained in terms of the function that is served by the neurosis. The elimination of a problematic neurosis may even require the building of an alternative, and healthier, structure that fulfils the same function.

Many of the preceding titles are classics and well worth reading. For more recent literature on social theory with an emphasis on model construction, I suggest Hedstrom and Swedberg (1998), Blossfeld and Prein (1998), and Goldthorpe (2000). Also, Reynolds (2006) presents a lucid introduction to strategies in theory construction.

EXERCISES

1. Construct a functional explanation to account for the relative stability of the inflation rate in the economy. What are the sources of disturbance in the inflation rate? What structures function to dampen the disturbances?
2. Stinchcombe (1968: 101–30) speaks of "historicist" causal imagery. Read this material to understand the way that Stinchcombe has extended the formalism

of the functionalist model. Describe a social phenomenon that can be well accounted for by this kind of explanation

3. The concept of effect decomposition can be used to understand variations in outcomes. Thus, it is the case that median household income in the United States increased only slightly, in real terms, in the final decades of the twentieth century. But the median can be viewed as an average of the trends in different household income deciles. Seek out publications of income trends in the United States – this can easily be researched using the Internet – and report what the trends have been for households that were in low and high income deciles in 1980. What might this suggest about changes in the determinants of living standards in the United States?

12. Explanations of the Racial Disturbances of the 1960s

I'd like to turn to some specific studies that illustrate the kinds of explanations I outlined in Chapter 11. I'll start with an example of the demographic type of explanation as developed in a paper of mine from 1970, "The Causes of Racial Disturbances: A Comparison of Alternative Explanations." The 1960s was a period of great social turmoil in the United States. This decade witnessed the assassinations of John F. Kennedy and Martin Luther King, the riots precipitated by the Vietnam War, and a great many racial disorders. Some years ago, I undertook a study of the reasons for the racial outbreaks. As a first step, I sought to ascertain the broad assumptions that had to be part of an adequate explanation of the racial disturbances. Thus, in the first section of the article, various models, reflecting different kinds of assumptions, were examined in an attempt to understand the general features of the process that "generated" the disorders. In the second section, I attempted to account for the disorders by estimating the parameters of the model structure deduced in the first section. It's the initial section of the article that I want to discuss now.

What do we mean when we say that we want to "explain" the racial disturbances? There are actually a number of subquestions involved. First, there is the matter of why the outbreaks occurred *where* they did. Second, there is the issue of explaining *when* they took place; why, in particular, during the 1960s? Third, there is the matter of addressing differences in severity among the riots. Finally, one needs to account for why some individuals participated in the disorders, while others didn't. These are distinct questions, each relating to the goal of explaining the racial disturbances. To pursue this objective, I undertook a series of articles that dealt with two of the questions: accounting for their distribution among cities (why they occurred where they did) and for their severity. I also thought about the question of the timing of the disorders but decided that that question was not answerable. I'll explain later my reason for this odd claim.

Let's first consider why the racial disorders occurred where they did. Why did some cities experience rioting, while others didn't? But first, how do we define a riot? What, in fact, is the phenomenon that we are addressing? The racial outbreaks of the 1960s had a distinct character. They were not instances of interracial fighting between blacks and whites, as had occurred at earlier times in American history. Rather, the violence was carried out by blacks, often in ghetto neighborhoods, and had the character of black protests, even rebellions. I removed the small number of events that didn't conform to this type of disorder since those

Table 12.1. *Distribution of racial disorders, 1961–8, and predicted distributions from Poisson and negative binomial models*[a]

1	2	3	4
(k) Number of disorders	(n_k) Number of cities with k disorders	($\hat{n}_k$) Expected number of cities with k disorders (calculated from Poisson, $\Lambda = 0.507$)	($\hat{n}_k$) Expected number of cities with k disorders (calculated from negative binomial, $\alpha = 0.255$, $\beta = 0.502$)
0	504	405	509
1	93	206	87
2	36	52	36
3	19	9	18
4	10	1	10
5	4	0	6
6	2	0	3
7	1	0	2
8	0	0	1
9	1	0	1
10	2	0	0
11	1	0	0
12 or more	0	0	0
Total no. cities	673	673	673

[a] Includes only instances of black aggression, spontaneous origin.
Source: Spilerman (1970, Tables 2, 4).

events may have had a different causal etiology from the wider class of riots. As a second matter, at what point do we decide that violence in a community has risen to such a level that it can be considered a riot? In short, we need a threshold level for an incident; I arbitrarily set a minimum of thirty participants.

The data for the study were collected from newspaper articles about violence in ghetto neighborhoods, as collated by the Lemberg Center of Brandeis University. The Lemberg accounts give a sense of the magnitude of a disturbance, permitting a decision of whether or not my criteria were met. In general, few outbreaks that received newspaper coverage had a small number of participants. Next, it is necessary to specify the relevant population of analytic units. In the 1960s, U.S. governmental publications reported detailed data for 673 cities with populations larger than 25,000, and I used these locales as the universe of cities for the study. During 1961–8, the period of large-scale rioting in the United States, there were 341 disorders in these cities that satisfied my definition of a riot. The distribution of the disturbances among the cities is reported in Table 12.1.

The first column of the table indexes the number of disorders, k, and the second gives the distribution from the empirical data – namely, the number of cities that experienced k disorders. Thus, 504 cities did not experience even one disturbance during the eight-year interval, 93 had exactly one disorder, and so on. As you can see, the maximum was eleven disorders, recorded in one city. These data provide the starting point for an investigation of the necessary ingredients for an adequate explanation of the distribution of the incidents. What sorts of assumptions, then, do we need to make in order to account for the observed distribution?

MODEL 1: THE POISSON PROCESS

Let's first assume that the disturbances were random events that could have equally impacted any locale in our universe of cities. The fact that some cities experienced more disorders than others is consistent with randomness. Such a finding doesn't necessarily mean that those cities were more riot-prone. Think of throwing a dart at a list of city names, with each having the same probability of being hit, and doing this multiple times. If you have a list of 673 cities and you throw a dart at the list 341 times (the number of disorders), many cities will always be missed. There'll be a bunch that you'll hit once. Some cities will be hit two, three, or four times. Thus, even though the resulting distribution will have arisen from chance alone, some cities will have higher numbers of hits even though they are no different from the others in any essential way. A common formulation for stating this mathematically is the "Poisson process," which we now outline.

Take a time interval $(0,t)$ and break it into many smaller units, each of size Δt. Now, for each city, we make the following assumptions, where "event" denotes "racial disturbance" in the current application:

1. At most one event can occur in any Δt; the time interval is too small for there to be more than one. (We therefore assume that multiple disorders do not break out in the same instant.)
2. The probability of an event in Δt is $\lambda \Delta t$. The probability of no event is $(1 - \lambda \Delta t)$. By assumption (i) these are the only kinds of occurrences in Δt.
3. The time intervals are independent of one another. This assumption would mean that the occurrence of a riot has no impact on the likelihood of a subsequent outbreak.

The Poisson process is derived from this simple set of assumptions. We write $P_n(t + \Delta t)$, the probability of n events in the time interval $(t + \Delta t)$, as

$$P_n(t + \Delta t) = P_n(t)P_0(\Delta t) + P_{n-1}(t)P_1(\Delta t). \tag{1}$$

Thus, we have divided $P_n(t + \Delta t)$ into two possibilities; either n events occur in time $(0, t)$ followed by no event in the subsequent period Δt or $n - 1$ events take place in time $(0, t)$ followed by one event in period Δt. Each route will yield the outcome of n events in the interval $(t + \Delta t)$. By assumption (1) there can be no other way to obtain exactly n events in the time interval. Note, incidentally, why we can multiply the probabilities in the computation of each outcome route: this is because of assumption (3) – what has transpired in the interval $(0,t)$ has no consequence for an event occurrence in the succeeding Δt. Last, using assumption (2), we substitute for $P_0(\Delta t)$ and $P_1(\Delta t)$, yielding

$$P_n(t+\Delta t) = P_n(t)[1-\lambda\Delta t] + P_{n-1}(t)\lambda\Delta t. \tag{2}$$

Now subtract $P_n(t)$ from both sides and divide by Δt:

$$\frac{P_n(t+\Delta t) - P_n(t)}{\Delta t} = -\lambda P_n(t) + \lambda P_{n+1}(t) \tag{3}$$

Taking the limit as $\Delta t \to 0$, we obtain the system of differential equations:

$$\begin{cases} \frac{dP_n(t)}{dt} = -\lambda P_n(t) + \lambda P_{n-1}(t) & \text{for } n \geq 1 \\ \frac{dP_0(t)}{dt} = -\lambda P_0(t) & \text{for } n = 0 \,. \end{cases} \tag{4}$$

This system can be solved, either recursively beginning with the equation for $P_0(t)$ and substituting the solution into the equation for $P_1(t)$, or by using generating functions to collapse the system into a single partial differential equation (see Chiang 1968: 47–8 for details).

Either way, one will have derived the Poisson distribution,

$$P_n(t) = \frac{(\lambda t)^n e^{-\lambda t}}{n!}, \quad n = 0, 1, 2, \ldots \tag{5}$$

where the symbol $n!$ denotes the product $n(n-1)(n-2) \ldots (2)(1)$ and λ is the parameter of the process, governing the frequency of events, which is estimated from the data. In the case of the racial disturbances, for simplicity we have aggregated the events from different years – essentially treating the disturbances of the 1960s as if they took place in one year; thus, we drop t and write the previous formula as[1] $P_n = (\lambda^n e^{-\lambda})/n!$. This gives the probability that a city has experienced 0, 1, 2, 3, . . . , n racial disturbances over the indicated time period.

If we assume that all the cities have the same riot proneness value, λ, and that the outbreaks are independent of one another, the aggregate process would also be Poisson with proneness value $\Lambda = N\lambda$, since it would be the sum of N independent, identically distributed Poisson variables (Ross 1985: 55). Consequently, NP_n, where $N = 673$ – the number of cities in our study, yields the expected number of locales that have incurred n disorders.

To recapitulate, this model makes several assumptions:

1. The disorder outbreaks were random events.
2. The disturbances occurred independently of one another.
3. All cities can be characterized by the same riot-proneness value, λ.

Now, these are strong assumptions, and we have reason to suspect that at least some are not correct with regard to the racial disturbances in the 1960s. Thus, contrary to assumption 2, a riot in one city might have inspired sympathetic outbreaks elsewhere (or, conversely, encouraged more effective police training, thereby depressing the likelihood of a subsequent riot, either in the impacted city

---

[1] The justification for this step is presented in Spilerman (1970: 632).

or in other locales). Likewise, assumption 3 ignores major differences between the cities in work opportunities, in poverty rates, and in discrimination against blacks, factors that might well have influenced a city's propensity to incur rioting.

Nonetheless, we'll try to fit the Poisson model. Given that it doesn't seem to mimic the riot process, why are we doing this? The short answer is that it's easy, so we might as well give it a try. A more considered response is that even though the model seems questionable, the Poisson is a standard default model for count data and provides a convenient starting point from which to modify the assumptions and, hopefully, build a more realistic model. But keep in mind that even if the Poisson model happens to fit the riot data, this doesn't prove that the model assumptions provide a correct description of the riot process; it only tells us that the observed data are indistinguishable from estimates generated by this particular random process. A very different set of assumptions might fit the data equally well.[2]

So, what actually happened? The third column of Table 12.1 shows the results from fitting the Poisson distribution to the riot data, with Λ estimated to be 341/673 = 0.507). How do the Poisson estimates compare with the observed distribution of disorders (column 2)? Clearly, they are very different; the Poisson assumptions are not consistent with the observed process. What do we do now? Well, I like the idea of thinking of riots as random events; they are hardly the sorts of incidents whose occurrence can be predicted from one month to the next. But perhaps it's asking too much to expect every city to have the same propensity for disorder, since living conditions varied considerably across cities in the 1960s. The cities differed in employment opportunities, in standard of living, and in the intensity of discrimination experienced by blacks. Perhaps, then, we should modify the model by allowing riot outbreaks to follow a Poisson process, but with each city having its own riot-proneness value.

MODEL 2: THE NEGATIVE BINOMIAL

This brings us to consider a demographic-type model to account for the distribution of riot outbreaks – essentially a mixture of Poisson processes. The only change we make is to relax assumption 3. We now adopt the more reasonable specification that the conditions that spurred blacks to riot in the 1960s differed from city to city in intensity, so that each had its own λ value. Another way of describing the new formulation is to note that it permits heterogeneity among cities in riot-proneness values. Mathematically, the revised model is specified as follows: Let P_n equal the probability of observing n riots in the universe of cities. For simplicity, you can think of P_n as the proportion of cities with n disorders, where $n = 0, 1, 2,$ and so on. We write P_n as

$$P_n = \int_0^\infty P_n(\lambda)f(\lambda)d\lambda \qquad (6)$$

where $P_n(\lambda)$ denotes the probability that a city with riot-proneness value λ experienced n riots and $f(\lambda)$ describes the distribution of λ values over the cities.

[2] For example, the Poisson distribution can be derived as an approximation to the binomial distribution.

Equation (6) suggests that we think of P_n as composed of the sum of products of the probability that cities with riot-proneness value $\lambda = \lambda_0$ incurred exactly n disorders times the proportion of cities in the population with proneness value λ_0 – namely, $f(\lambda_0)$.

Building on the prior formulation, we specify $P_n(\lambda) = (\lambda^n e^{-\lambda})/n!$; that is, each city follows a Poisson distribution with its unique proneness value λ. We still have to specify the form of $f(\lambda)$, that is, the shape of the distribution of λ values in the population of cities. Here, there is no theoretical reason to expect a particular distributional form; the shape would reflect the distribution among cities of the structural factors that affect riot proneness. We therefore choose the gamma distribution,

$$f(\lambda) = \frac{\beta^\alpha \lambda^{\alpha-1} e^{-\beta\lambda}}{\Gamma(\alpha)}, \quad \lambda > 0,\ \alpha > 0,\ \beta > 0, \tag{7}$$

where $\Gamma(\alpha)$ is the gamma function (Ross 1985: 34). The gamma distribution is a flexible family of curves that can fit a range of unimodal distributions, including the exponential as a special case ($\alpha = 1$).[3] Another reason to choose the gamma is that equation (6) is easy to integrate with this specification for $f(\lambda)$. Doing so, we obtain

$$P_n = \left[\begin{smallmatrix} \alpha + (n-1) \\ n \end{smallmatrix}\right] \left[\tfrac{1}{\beta+1}\right]^n \left[\frac{\beta}{\beta+1}\right]^\alpha \tag{8}$$

which is a negative binomial distribution with parameters α and $\beta / (\beta + 1)$ that are estimated from the data.[4] From the riot data we obtain $\alpha = 0.255$ and $\beta = 0.502$. With these estimates we can fit the disturbance data to the negative binomial distribution, which was derived under the assumption of Poisson events in a heterogeneous population. The results are reported in the fourth column of Table 12.1. This time, as you can see, the fit is rather good, and a chi-square test does not lead to a rejection of the model.

Where are we at this point? Have we proven that the riots were generated by the postulated process? In short, can we claim that the disturbances were random events, with each city having its own propensity value? In fact, we have only demonstrated that the data could have arisen from this generative process. Indeed, I can formulate a very different generative process that will also give rise to a negative binomial distribution and that fits the data equally well. In the stochastic process literature it's called an "immigration-linear birth model"; from the point of view of the riot example, we'll call it a "reinforcement model."

MODEL 3: A DIFFERENT DERIVATION OF THE NEGATIVE BINOMIAL

The imagery underlying this process goes as follows: Assume initially that no riot has taken place in any city. The first disorder occurs according to a Poisson

---

[3] When $\alpha = 1$, it is the case that $\Gamma(1) = 1$; hence, $f(\lambda) = \beta e^{-\beta\lambda}$.

[4] The first term in the product, $\left(\begin{smallmatrix} \alpha + \\ n \end{smallmatrix}{}^{n-1}\right)$, is the binomial coefficient and is defined to equal $(\alpha + n - 1)$ $(\alpha + n - 2) \ldots (\alpha + 1)\alpha/n!$ for any real number α. For details on the integration leading to equation (8), consult Chiang (1968: 49).

process, with all cities characterized by an identical proneness value, δ. But once the riot ensues, it provokes social and organizational changes in the impacted city. There has been destruction and injury. The residents are angry; polarization increases between the racial groups, with the result that a subsequent riot in the city becomes more likely. If the city has experienced one riot, the model says that its riot-proneness value is increased by a factor of μ; it is now $(\delta + \mu)$. Perhaps a second riot takes place in the city, further exacerbating racial tensions. Now that the city has undergone two disturbances, its proneness value is $(\delta + 2\mu)$. This process of polarization continues, reinforced by each outbreak of violence. The result is one of growing differentiation among the cities in riot propensity. Some have the value λ, others $(\delta + \mu)$, still others $(\delta + n\mu)$, where n is the number of prior outbreaks in the city. Thus, heterogeneity has been introduced into the model, though it's a different sort of heterogeneity than before. This process can be represented by the system of differential equations, which also gives rise to a negative binomial distribution (Spilerman 1970: 635).

$$\begin{cases} \dfrac{dP_n(t)}{dt} = -(\delta + n\mu)\,P_n(t) \ + \ (\delta + [n-1]\mu)P_{n-1}(t) & \text{for } n \geq 1 \\[2mm] \dfrac{dP_0(t)}{dt} = -\delta P_0(t) & \text{for } n = 0. \end{cases} \tag{9}$$

The heterogeneity in our prior model was assumed to be due to stable structural differences between the cities: Some have greater poverty; others have a less responsive municipal government. Race relations may be more tense in some places for any number of historical or cultural reasons. In contrast, the current model assumes no such structural differences between the cities (or assumes that whatever differences exist, they are not associated with riot proneness); rather, the city differences in proneness are the *result* of prior outbreaks. In short, the heterogeneity among cities is endogenous, a consequence of the riot outbreaks. So, we have two competing explanations; each generates a negative binomial distribution, and both are consistent with the observed data: One is a story of stable heterogeneity based on structural differences among cities; the other is based on reinforcement. Which explanation is correct? I will not go into the details here; you'll have to read the article, where I describe why this second explanation makes less sense as an account of the riot outbreaks in the 1960s. I also eliminate some other possible explanations for the distribution of the disorders. Thus, the conclusion from the first part of the study is that the riots can be viewed as random events in each city, with the cities differing in riot proneness and the proneness values reflecting stable structural characteristics.

APPLYING THE MODEL ASSUMPTIONS

This is where the first part of the study ended. We do not yet have an explanation of why the disorders occurred where they did, but we do know that we need to look for our explanation in the characteristics of cities. In essence, we want to investigate the determinants of λ in terms of city characteristics. The λ-value of a city is unobserved, but we can proxy it by the number of riots that occurred in the city between 1961 and 1968. Granted, this is a fallible estimate; from column 3 of Table 12.1, we know that even if all cities were to have the same proneness value, some will experience more disturbances than others. Nonetheless, this produces is a reasonable estimate of λ and permits us to proceed to the next step.

We now employ standard multivariate techniques and carry out a regression analysis with the number of riots in a city as the outcome variable and various city characteristics (black population size, unemployment rate, measures of political structure, poverty level, educational attainment, income, etc.) as the explanatory variables. Remember that we are justified in turning to stable structural characteristics of cities as determinants of riot proneness because of our earlier assessment; had we concluded instead that a reinforcement model was the appropriate explanatory structure, we would not be undertaking this particular second-stage analysis.

You may be surprised to learn which structural characteristics of cities were found to be related to riot proneness. Was it a high poverty rate? High unemployment? A municipal government that was unresponsive to its residents? A large disparity in income between whites and blacks? My conclusion was that only the numerical size of the black population in a city had explanatory value! Net of this term, no other city characteristic had much import. Now, it is hardly profound to discover that disorder outbreaks were more frequent in cities with large black populations – especially because the events of the 1960s had the character of black rebellions – but it is noteworthy that no other structural characteristic affected riot proneness, even in light of the large disparities among cities in the living conditions and work opportunities of black residents.

Based on these findings, I suggested that the riots of the 1960s were a response not to local conditions, however disagreeable in some cities, but to national events. For instance, a huge number of outbreaks were precipitated by the assassination of Martin Luther King; these, clearly, were not responses to local conditions. Similarly, a great many disorders followed the Detroit riot of 1967. Events like the Detroit disorder received considerable television coverage, and the rioters, when interviewed by reporters, articulated the difficulties of their lives, their frustration from not being able to get decent jobs, provide for their children, and so on. These comments resonated with black residents in other cities, who felt that they were confronting similar problems. Throughout the United States, blacks found themselves empathizing with the rioters and chose to express their anger in a similar manner. In short, the impetus for most of the riots did not arise from local conditions. City characteristics had little impact on riot proneness because the outbreaks reflected a process of identification that transcended community. What we witnessed in the 1960s was a *national-level* phenomenon. The size of the black population, however, was a powerful determinant of riot proneness because it was a measure of potentially available recruits for a disorder.

So, this is the basic thrust of the analysis and findings: First, using a mathematical formulation, we established the sorts of assumptions that would need to be made in order to construct an adequate explanation of the distribution of the disorders. At this stage, we ruled out the possibility that each city was equally likely to incur rioting. Also ruled out was the possibility that the observed distribution arose from a reinforcement process, with a riot raising the prospect of a subsequent disturbance in the same city. Even though the reinforcement model also gives rise to a negative binomial distribution, for reasons discussed in Spilerman (1970) we concluded that the correct type of explanation was one based on structural differences among the cities. In the second stage, a regression analysis was undertaken to investigate the determinants of the λ values, with the conclusion that only black population size had an impact on the disorder locations because the rioting arose from discontent that was more or less felt universally by blacks irrespective of where they resided.

THE BROADER PHENOMENON OF RIOTING

Recall that we segmented the initial question about the causes of the racial disturbances into several component issues: explanations of the incident locations, event severity, placement in time, and participation. Each of these issues requires a separate analysis. The only question we've addressed so far is the first, but I hope that from its consideration you're starting to get an idea of how sociologists go about doing their work. In general, we seek to go beyond psychological dispositions and instead relate individual behavior to aspects of social structures that inhibit or encourage a particular course of activity, whether it is voting for a particular candidate, going to college, or participating in a riot.

Regarding the other component issues, there is an article on riot severity (Spilerman 1976), which I will not discuss here; also, there is a Kerner Commission report about the riot participants (Rossi et al. 1968) that you can read. However, I do want to discuss a part of my research that was unsuccessful. In particular, I was not able to arrive at an adequate explanation of the timing of the disorders – why the outbreaks occurred *when* they did. Why, for example, did they take place in the 1960s rather than later or earlier in time? After all, black Americans have experienced many provocations in other decades of the twentiethth century.

If you look at Table 12.2, you will see that the incidence of rioting increased throughout much of the 1960s. There were a few outbreaks during 1961–5 and then an upsurge beginning in 1966. The number of disorders peaked in 1968 and then declined rapidly over the next couple of years to near zero.[5] If you looked at a time series of the number of riots over a long time period, such as from 1900 to 2000 – and remember, we are speaking about instances of black aggression – you would find that this kind of disturbance rarely occurred outside the 1960s.[6] Thus, we have a time series of events that is rather simple in shape: Little happens until the 1960s, then a rapid increase until 1968, then an even more rapid decline, followed by few disorders in subsequent decades. The problem with trying to explain the timing of the outbreaks from such data is that the time series is insufficiently complicated! Its simplicity allows it to be consistent with multiple explanations. The difficulty is not with building an explanation of the outbreaks in time, but with selecting one from among the potential alternatives.

---

[5] Table 12.2 does not show the decline since my data collection ended with 1968; however, the abrupt fall-off is evident from Figure 1 of Olzak, Shanahan, and McEneaney (1996), who have collected similar data for the period 1960 through 1993.

[6] There were other race riots before the 1960s, often involving whites attacking blacks, but they were few in number and probably had a different etiology or causal structure, so we would not want to group them with the instances of black-initiated disorders.

Table 12.2. *Distribution of racial disorders, 1961–8[a]*

(k) Number of disorders	(n_k) Number of cities with k disorders, by year				
	1961–4	1965	1966	1967	1968
0	658	665	645	566	569
1	10	8	23	85	78
2	3		4	18	18
3	2		0	3	6
4			0	1	1
5			1		1
Total	22	8	36	134	141

[a] Includes only instances of black aggression, spontaneous origin.
Source: Spilerman (1970, Table 3).

Let's look at some plausible explanations that are consistent with the time series. First, the outbreaks occurred at the time of the Vietnam War. The Americans fighting and dying in Vietnam were disproportionately black. This may have generated feelings of exploitation and hostility toward the government that came to be expressed as black rage and rebellion. Now, while this account is consistent with the growth in rioting in the early and mid-1960s, let me give you another explanation. The civil rights movement was at the forefront of national consciousness during the 1960s, with Presidents John Kennedy and Lyndon Johnson both promising massive change that would improve the lives of black Americans. This may have raised expectations to a level that exceeded what the actual pace of change could deliver, causing frustration and anger that were then expressed as rage and rebellion. So, we have two plausible, but different, explanations for why rioting occurred in the 1960s. Which is correct? Perhaps both were factors in the rioting but with different causal impacts. Unfortunately, from the very simple time series, it is impossible to assign weights to their relative importance.

The fall-off in the number of disturbances at the end of the 1960s is likewise open to competing explanations. After several years of responding to rioting, perhaps the police learned better ways of controlling incipient disturbances, preventing them from escalating into full-fledged disorders. Alternatively, the election of Richard Nixon in 1968 might have dampened black expectations of improvement, with the perverse effect of lessening feelings of frustration and rage; this might have had a pacifying effect on black ghettoes. Again, judging the relative merits of these and other explanations is impossible in the context of a simple time series.[7] It's often easier to account for a time series that has many ups

---

[7] Disaggregating the data to look at processes specific to individual cities, as a strategy to increase the number of observations, will also do us no good, assuming we accept the validity of the prior analysis about the rioting in the 1960s having been a national-level phenomenon.

and downs and unusual features. The likelihood of finding multiple explanations that are consistent with a complex time series is small, unlike one's prospects of arriving at a unique explanation for a simple time series.

So, the result is that I can't tell you why the rioting occurred in the 1960s. It's not that I can't give you plausible explanations. The problem is that I can construct too many plausible accounts, each consistent with the data. The events unfolded in such a way that they put the social scientist at a disadvantage. In this sort of situation – in which arriving at a unique explanation exceeds the capability of the data – people sometimes fall back on ideology to explain the phenomenon, choosing the explanation that best fits with their personal view of the world. Social science research can provide little help when events have unfolded in this particular way.

In the next chapter, we'll look at another time series that I turned to after my failure to explain the timing of the riot outbreaks. This is a time series of lynching events. The lynching of blacks has had a long and disturbing history in the United States, and the time series displays much more complexity than that of our riot example. I was interested in pursuing explanations for the occurrence of collective violence in time and this couldn't be done with the riot data, so I decided to look at the lynching time series. I'm still at a fairly early stage in the analysis of the lynching events, but there are several matters that are of interest from both a conceptual and a technical point of view in regard to how sociologists go about their work, so I will discuss this material.

FURTHER READING

To pursue the substantive issues, I suggest several books and papers. Racial disturbances are an instance of what sociologists call "collective behavior." A good overview of this wider field is provided in Smelser (1963). The articles from my study that were referred to in the chapter are Spilerman (1970, 1971, 1976); the last is an attempt to explain the severity of the disorders, which differed among the cities and from riot to riot. Olzak and Shanahan (1996) report a reanalysis of some of the issues raised in the Spilerman articles. The Kerner Commission (1968) produced a comprehensive report on the riots of the 1960s, and Rossi et al. (1968) prepared an analysis of the riot participants for the Commission. Also, for an investigation of a related phenomenon (terrorism) in a different country (Israel), I would recommend Stecklov and Goldstein (2004).

Regarding the technical side of this chapter, a good introduction to probability and stochastic processes is provided by Ross (1985). Chiang (1968) is also a readable text but is somewhat more advanced.

Exercises

1. The assumptions underlying the Poisson process are often used in the specification of "random events." In what sense were the racial disturbances in a city random? See Nagel (1961: 332) and Spilerman (1971: 433) for further discussions of the concept of randomness.

2. Find a dataset of event occurrences for which the Poisson assumptions provide a reasonable account of the generative process and estimate the Poisson parameter for this process. Compare the estimated distribution of outcomes with the observed distribution. How well does the Poisson model do?

3. Using the dataset from problem 2, estimate the negative binomial distribution to the data and compare the fit with the observed distribution. What assumptions have you made in fitting the negative binomial?

4. Equation (4) in this chapter specifies the system of differential equations for the Poisson process. Derive the Poisson distribution (equation 5) using both a recursive approach to solving the system of equations and the generating functions approach. See Chiang (1968: chap. 2) regarding the method of generating functions.

13. The Time Series of Lynchings
in the American South

My studies of the riots left me wanting to investigate fluctuations over time in the rate of collective violence. As noted in Chapter 12, this could not be done with the riot data; I therefore chose to examine an altogether different kind of collective violence, one that occurred at the turn of the twentieth century: lynchings of black Americans. The phenomenon of lynching speaks to the brutal dark side of American southern culture; some 5,000 persons were murdered in this manner. The data on lynchings have a rich history in social science research, in large part because they provide a long time series of a rather infamous nature. There are published records covering the period 1882 to 1966. Moreover, when we look at the time series, we see that it is much more complicated than the one for the riots of the 1960s. This complexity makes it easier to choose among competing explanations of the lynching rate. With these data, our focus is not on the idiosyncratic causes of particular lynchings, but on accounts of the varying rate over time. If we're willing to work with explanations that are likely to hold over a lengthy interval, then our time-series study might yield findings of value. To put it another way, with data covering a long period of time, there should be few plausible explanations that are consistent with the complexity of the time series.

I want to tell you about the construction of the lynching dataset that I eventually put together. I started with published datasets that other researchers have used. There are three: The Tuskegee Institute has an event listing that covers the period from 1882 to 1966. The National Association for the Advancement of Colored People (NAACP) has one for 1889 to 1936. The third dataset comes from the *Chicago Tribune*, and it runs from 1882 to 1918. The NAACP was established in 1909, so how did it get an event series beginning some twenty years before its founding? It turns out that the NAACP relied on the Tuskegee and *Tribune* files for the period before 1909, so the NAACP data for these early years are an amalgam of the other collections. After its establishment, the NAACP gathered its own data, but there was much cross-checking with Tuskegee about particular events; consequently, these two time series hardly reflect independent data collections.

The Tuskegee event list is the one that has been used by most researchers. However, the data collection was unusual, and it is problematic as well. The data collection can be divided into two periods – before and after 1904, the year when

Dr. Monroe Work came to the Institute and began compiling lynching records. For coverage of incidents during the period 1882 to 1904, the data file appears to have been constructed from a retrospective examination of newspaper accounts, supplemented by the *Chicago Tribune*'s compilation.

Beginning around 1905 and continuing for the next sixty years, the Tuskegee data were collected contemporaneously by Dr. Work and his associates. Thus, in 1905, various newspapers were read and lynching information was collected for that year. The same occurred for 1906 and later years. This data collection is problematic because the funds available to Dr. Work differed from year to year. In some years, he was able to hire perhaps three researchers; in other years, possibly one. There might even have been months in which, for lack of resources, no one collected data. The result is that some of the ups and downs in the Tuskegee time series may reflect little more than the varying quality of the data collection. We do not know how severe this problem is because the data were gathered many decades ago and the procedural records at Tuskegee are poor, but with the data collection spanning a very long period, one cannot expect similar procedures to have been used over the full interval.

CONSTRUCTION OF THE NEW TIME SERIES

This is a considerable problem if the goal of the research is to relate fluctuations in the lynching rate to changes in the economic circumstance of the nation or of southern counties. This appeared to me to be a daunting obstacle. But, several years ago, I decided to use personal research funds to collect lynching data myself, bypassing the Tuskegee listing. I thought it would be a small operation. However, it turned out to be a considerable undertaking that ran for many years. I wanted to use systematic procedures that would be identical over all the years. I decided to choose a major southern daily, like the *Atlanta Constitution*, and have students read several decades of the paper, noting every instances of a lynching. After looking at the results I realized that, especially in the early years, the Atlanta paper was a fairly comprehensive record of events in the state of Georgia but had little information about other states. We think of the *Atlanta Constitution* as a major newspaper, but 120 years ago, its news coverage was generally local and didn't extend much beyond Georgia and its environs. However, I wanted coverage of the entire South.[1] Eventually, I settled on four newspapers: the *Atlanta Constitution*, the *New Orleans Times-Picayune*, the *Charleston News and Courier*, and the *Memphis Appeal*. Together, these papers pretty much spanned the South. Each was read by several students on a daily basis covering the period 1874 to 1920. I assumed that the NAACP data were probably reliable for the years after 1920, a period when newspapers had more resources and their coverage was more comprehensive. All the old newspaper material, incidentally, is available on microfilm.

---

[1] There are a number of definitions of the American South. Our specification includes all states in the Confederacy except Texas and Missouri. The latter states were omitted because many of their lynchings were western-type executions with a different causal structure from the southern type. Western lynchings reflected struggles over cattle and farmland rather than racial transgressions.

I soon ran into an organizational problem. It turned out that my students weren't equally good as readers, and many, after having read two or three years of a newspaper, decided that they had had enough of staring at microfilm or, inconsiderately, chose to graduate from college and move on. I kept losing coders, and even when I kept them, their quality of work frequently deteriorated after a few months of reading films. To compensate for coder idiosyncrasies, I had each newspaper read four times by different students. This greatly improved the quality of the data.

The next problem – actually, the first I faced – was to define a lynching event. From reading accounts of lynchings, I settled on four necessary features:

1. The victim was killed.
2. The violence was collective: The killing was carried out by a mob of five or more persons.
3. The victim was in the custody of the mob at the time he or she was killed. Thus, an ambush is not a lynching because the victim was not held by the mob when dispatched. Similarly, if someone is killed by a posse while trying to elude capture, this is not a lynching. But if the victim had surrendered and is then killed, this is a lynching.
4. The killing was not incidental to another activity. Killings during a robbery, in fights between cattlemen and farmers, and Indian massacres are not lynchings.

In essence, then, a lynching event had the character of an execution. However, there are many borderline cases, and practical problems exist in coding from newspapers. A typical article might read, "The body of a Negro was found this morning hanging from a tree." That might be the only information. Was it a lynching? Or the account might read, "A Negro was found this morning riddled with bullets." Should we include such a case? Many of the events in the Tuskegee and NAACP listings appear to be based on little more than a news article like one of those just described. Sometimes we have a one-line account such as "John Smith was lynched this morning." But how do we know what the reporter's definition was of a lynching, that is, whether it corresponds to our formulation? Further, what should we do with an article that concludes with the sentence "Last seen, he was taken into the woods by a mob"? Tuskegee and the NAACP typically included such events in their dataset. Should we? Tuskegee didn't have the resources to send someone to investigate the events that its staff had read about in newspapers, and even if it had the resources, this would have been rather dangerous.

I think you now have an idea of the problems that must be faced in order to assemble quality data. Let me give yet another example of the kind of ambiguity we have to deal with. What do you make of an article that reads, "The Negro brute who violated fair young Daisy May, daughter of the plantation owner, was caught today and got his just deserts"? You can probably infer that he was killed. Still, inferences can be dangerous; indeed, the source materials make it clear that even the term "lynching" is not always synonymous with "killing." You might read that John Smith was lynched yesterday, and in the next day's paper he might be reported as walking around, black and blue from his lynching. Here lynching seems to take on a broader meaning that encompasses punishment short of killing.

Also, there are neologisms like "ku-kluxed." An article might state that someone was caught and ku-kluxed. It appears that this sometimes meant that the man was killed and at other times not. Possibly he was only tarred and feathered. The definition of ku-kluxed might also vary from county to county. At the other extreme, sometimes an article goes into considerable and gruesome detail in describing what was done to a lynch victim. Of course, when there's a lot of material it's much easier to decide whether the case fits our definition of a lynching, and as time went on, lynchings were covered more thoroughly in the press.

STRATEGIES AND FURTHER ISSUES

Presented with these difficulties, I decided to create various categories of lynching events relating to the certainty of classification. Some events definitely fit our definition because there was enough detail to decide. Other events, with less news coverage, were accorded a lower degree of certitude that the criteria were met, so that, in the end, we had categories of lynchings ranging from certain events to marginal cases. This approach permits a researcher to undertake a sensitivity analysis and ascertain whether the marginal cases have the same causal structure as the more evident incidents. This is one way of dealing with data that are highly differentiated in quality. This cannot be done with the incidents in the Tuskegee or NAACP listings because these sources provide only a date, a name, and the ostensible reason why the person was lynched.

In looking for hypotheses that address the fluctuations in number of lynchings – both over time and across locales – a good place to start is with the "frustration-aggression" model, since this was the thesis examined in the early studies of lynchings (e.g., Hovland and Sears 1940; Mintz 1946). This form of explanation is a "safety valve" type of theory and holds that the likelihood of violence is greater where frustration is high; aggression then provides a release for the pent-up frustration. In applications to lynchings, we can inquire whether southern whites acted out their frustrations due to poor economic conditions by attacking black residents – whether, for example, lynchings were more frequent when the price of cotton was low. But even this initial probing into the causes of lynchings returns us to issues of conceptualization and measurement.

If we want to explore a frustration-aggression explanation or a similar thesis, perhaps the phenomenon we should be examining is the lynching *attempt* rather than the successful lynching. If a person was taken out to be lynched but the sheriff intervened and stopped it, does not the incident still express the emotional disposition of the attackers? The prevention of a lynching should be irrelevant to an analysis of the impact of economic conditions on the social mood. So, in theory, the universe of events we should be considering encompasses aborted lynchings as well as completed ones. In practice, however, we run into the problem that attempted lynchings were less newsworthy and were rarely reported in the newspapers.

There is a similar issue with respect to "legal lynchings." The context for a legal lynching usually begins with a violent crime that is especially heinous, perhaps a rape or murder. The alleged perpetrator is caught, jailed, and awaits trial. A mob gathers and insists on an immediate trial, and this is agreed to by the sheriff, possibly to prevent the storming of the jail. A trial is held – perhaps in a saloon, as depicted in Hollywood movies. The alleged offender is quickly convicted and dispatched to his fate that very day, with little in the way of substantive due process. Thus, the forms of justice may be followed, but what has transpired is little more than a formality in service to mob passion.

This kind of event is problematic for our study since it is not clear whether or not it should be considered a lynching. Formally, it's not a mob killing since the execution was sanctioned by the authorities. However, the mob pressure for this outcome can be considerable, and if we are trying to assess the impact of factors that drive frustration, such as the economic climate, it's difficult to dismiss this sort of event as irrelevant to the study. We must also take into account the effectiveness of law enforcement in different southern counties. In some, an alleged offender might be quickly caught and (properly) tried, reducing the need for residents to take justice into their own hands. In other counties, where law enforcement might be lax, the community might turn to vigilantism and mob justice, in which case the event would satisfy our definition of lynching. Thus, county differences in the effectiveness of the legal system are pertinent to understanding variations in the lynching rate across locales. Regrettably, this sort of information is not available for years in the distant past. In working with data on completed lynchings, a researcher must therefore assume that these events are representative of the larger universe of relevant incidents, which includes attempted lynchings and possibly legal lynchings.

PRIOR FINDINGS AND FORMULATIONS

Before we look at the data, let me say a bit more about findings from prior research, some of which are suggestive of initial conceptualizations that will be used in the analysis. Saturday was the most common day of the week for a lynching, presumably because people were available for mob participation on that day, neither at work nor in church. For the same reason, lynchings were more frequent on holidays. Indeed, if you aggregate lynchings from all the years and look at the numbers for the period December 23–7, you obtain the sequence fourteen, thirteen, twenty, thirteen, fifteen, with the largest figure relating to Christmas Day. Some lynchings were characterized by a carnival atmosphere; in a gruesome way, these killings provided entertainment to a community – not unlike the feeding of Christians to the lions in ancient Rome. In the later years of the time series, a killing was more likely to take place in town, during the day, and with law officers present; in short, it was a community-sanctioned event.

Lynching served as a form of social control, and it has been noted that these murders were more frequent during the planting and harvesting seasons (Southern Commission 1931: 12). If a landowner felt pressed to get in the harvest, he might choose to encourage diligent work by making an example of a few troublemakers. It has also been suggested that the lynching rate may be correlated with the type of tenancy that was prevalent in a county. There were two types in wide use: cash cropping and sharecropping (Perlo 1953). In cash cropping the landlord rented out land in return for a fixed monetary sum. As long as the rent was paid, there was little reason for him to be interested in the work habits of his tenants. Thus, in counties where cash cropping was the dominant form of tenancy, the landlord had little reason to intimidate his workers. Sharecropping, on the other hand, gave the landlord an incentive to take an active interest in the work habits of his tenants since the produce, or income from its sale, would be divided between them. In this form of tenancy, it was to the landlord's benefit to motivate his workers. At the point where the marginal return to the tenant from additional labor did not warrant the effort, the tenant's work would still be productive for the landlord. Thus, the interests of the landlord departed from those of his tenant, and a bit of terrorizing could make economic sense.

Some years ago, Cantril (1941: chap. 4) classified lynchings into two categories on the basis of "orderliness" and called them "proletarian" and "Bourbon" events. The first type tended to be disorganized and chaotic affairs, and were common in southern towns where there was labor market competition between the races. Blacks might be viewed as a source of cheap labor or as potential strikebreakers, responsible for low wages in the community or for the underemployment of white workers. One way to eliminate the competition would be to threaten the black laborers, and lynching was sometimes used for this purpose by lower-class whites. This is a social control type of argument, but the viciousness of many of the killings suggests a frustration-aggression component to the violence as well.

Bourbon-type lynchings, in comparison, were comparatively orderly affairs, sometimes encouraged by leading citizens of a community and sanctioned by law enforcement officers (Cantril 1941: 94). The intent of these lynchings was to ensure white supremacy and maintain the racial norms of the community – to "keep the Negro in his place" and make it clear what was considered unacceptable behavior. The alleged offense was sometimes sexual, such as the rape or attempted rape of a white woman; on occasion, even an insulting remark or another act of disrespect to a white person could provoke a lynching. Cantril (94) suggests that Bourbon lynchings were more common in areas with dense black populations because these locales had more rigidly defined racial boundaries.

This brief overview gives you an idea of the substantive issues that can be addressed with the lynching data. Much more, of course, can be studied: whether occupational segregation by race reduced the lynching rate (since there would be less job competition between black and white workers), whether the lynching rate was lower in counties with high average education (the civilizing effect of education), whether threats to the nation such as from war, or to the county from storms and other natural disasters, served to reduce the lynching rate (because of heightened solidarity), and so forth. In this chapter, however, I have limited our discussion to matters of data quality and potential biases from the omission of certain types of killings, because these elementary considerations turn out to be critical to our ability to assess accurately the determinants of lynchings. But, now, let's turn to an examination of the dataset that I constructed, along with a consideration of the several published time series of lynching events.

ASSESSING THE QUALITY OF THE NEW DATASET

A twenty-year interval from the lynching record is presented in Table 13.1 covering the period 1881–1900. The first four columns report the number of incidents found in each of the four southern papers that I examined. The next ten columns show how the final estimates were built up from the newspaper records. Thus, the number of events found in all combinations of pairs of papers is reported in columns 5 through 10, and the number as calculated from combinations of the papers taken three at a time is noted in columns 11 through 14. Column 15 is a count of the events found in any of the four papers; this is our best estimate of the event total. For comparison, the number of lynchings in each of the published sources – the *Chicago Tribune*, Tuskegee, the NAACP – is presented in columns 16 through 18.[2] Let's now evaluate these estimates, starting with the individual newspapers.

The first observation is that very different numbers of events were reported by the papers in some years. The years 1890, 1892, and 1896 all show disparities of twenty or more events. In terms of incident totals (last row), Charleston's count is the lowest ($N = 994$), while New Orleans reports the highest number ($N = 1,275$). A perusal of the several time series makes clear the danger of relying on a single newspaper listing to make statements about the South: The year-to-year variations based on reports in the different papers might support quite disparate accounts of lynching causation.

With the papers taken in pairs (columns 5–10), we get some indication of overlapping and complementary coverage: Atlanta combined with New Orleans produces the largest number of incidents, Atlanta plus Charleston the smallest number. Even thought more lynchings are reported in the Memphis paper than in the Atlanta one (last row, columns 3 and 4), it appears that many of the Memphis events were covered in the New Orleans paper, whereas Atlanta tended to contribute new incidents. Possibly this is because New Orleans is closer geographically to Memphis than to Atlanta, with the consequence of greater overlap in news coverage. Taken three at a time, the time series become more stable; the maximum difference in event totals is now 119, versus 240 in the pairwise totals. More important, we obtain much the same pattern of variation over time in columns 11–14, and our final estimates in column 15 are not very different, suggesting that we have converged to a stable time series. Before turning to a comparison of our estimates with the published records, I want to say a bit more about the degree of confidence we can have in the new dataset.

Can we conclude that we have constructed a time series that accurately reflects the year-to-year change in the number of lynchings in the American South, at least to the extent that the events were reported in southern papers? How much would be gained by adding an additional newspaper or two to the data collection? Some insight into these questions can be obtained by examining the contribution made to the event count from each added paper.

The calculations relevant to this assessment are reported in Table 13.2. Panel A shows the number of events from 1881 to 1900 found in each paper; these are the same figures noted in the total row of columns 1–4 of Table 13.1. Thus, the *Charleston News and Courier* reported 994 lynching events, the *New Orleans Times-Picayune* 1,275, and so on. In panel B, the top box shows the *average*

---

[2] All estimates refer to lynching events, not to the number of persons who were killed. In many of the lynchings there was more than one victim.

Table 13.1. *Lynching time series for the South – combinations of four newspapers and new series; Chicago Tribune, Tuskegee and NAACP lists*

YEAR	(1) Char.	(2) N.O.	(3) Atl.	(4) Mem.	(5) C or N	(6) C or A	(7) C or M	(8) N or A	(9) N or M	(10) A or M	(11) C, N, A	(12) C, N, M	(13) C, A, M	(14) N, A, M	(15) At Least 1 Paper	(16) Chicago Tribune	(17) Tuskegee List	(18) NAACP List
1881	45	49	49	46	58	55	59	61	62	61	65	67	63	68	69	0	0	0
1882	40	40	42	38	48	51	55	52	50	56	55	56	60	57	60	38	36	0
1883	39	46	39	46	55	46	54	56	55	55	60	60	58	62	64	42	36	0
1884	39	54	43	38	65	53	52	66	63	58	72	68	63	71	75	38	46	0
1885	48	67	63	55	75	68	68	79	76	73	81	83	77	84	86	61	52	0
1886	38	59	53	44	68	57	57	71	69	63	74	73	66	75	77	53	47	0
1887	30	46	46	35	56	50	48	64	56	58	66	63	60	70	71	56	52	0
1888	39	56	63	46	75	69	64	84	77	76	87	83	80	91	93	65	56	0
1889	41	54	46	42	66	53	59	67	68	61	71	73	67	74	78	75	74	74
1890	30	51	43	38	57	50	48	66	61	56	68	64	60	71	73	74	58	56
1891	59	86	72	81	99	82	93	108	104	99	113	111	105	116	121	104	100	100
1892	66	94	74	86	107	91	102	113	109	105	120	119	114	123	129	117	116	118
1893	89	92	97	84	113	114	108	121	109	111	128	119	122	124	130	106	76	78
1894	76	80	73	84	106	97	106	103	113	106	116	125	116	124	130	102	97	97
1895	52	70	56	71	83	67	81	82	81	78	88	88	84	87	91	75	73	73
1896	43	68	50	62	77	60	76	79	81	75	88	87	80	87	90	79	76	77
1897	55	68	57	73	77	70	78	79	79	79	82	81	83	83	85	82	79	80
1898	50	63	59	67	75	71	74	76	81	79	83	84	84	88	91	67	63	63
1899	49	62	61	63	67	66	67	76	71	73	77	73	75	79	80	59	57	58
1900	66	70	71	77	84	84	85	91	88	89	96	92	93	95	98	79	78	69
Total	994	1275	1157	1176	1511	1354	1434	1594	1553	1422	1684	1669	1610	1729	1791	1372	1272	943

C: *Charleston News and Courier*; N: *New Orleans Times-Picayune*; A: *Atlanta Constitution*; M: *Memphis Appeal.*

number of events in the four papers. Now, if you take all combinations of two papers and compute the mean, you get 1,478. Thus, on average, a second newspaper adds 328 new incidents. If we add a third paper, the total goes to 1,673 events, with 195 new incidents. Going to a fourth paper adds 118 events, yielding a total of 1,791 – our final estimate of the number of lynchings in the twenty-year interval. If we focus on the proportion of new events that were added at each stage, we go from 28.5% for a second paper, to 13.5% for a third, to 7.1% in moving to four papers. What, then, can we expect from a fifth paper – assuming there was a fifth southern daily of equivalent quality for the years under study? Well, given that each paper adds, on average, about half the percentage of new events contributed at the prior step, a reasonable assumption is that a fifth paper would yield some 3–4% in new incidents. This computation suggests that there probably wouldn't be enough of a payoff to justify the effort of incorporating a fifth paper.

Now let's compare our lynching series with those constructed from the published records. Remember, we have undertaken the considerable effort of constructing our own time series because of doubts about the quality of the existing datasets. Initially, let's compare the three published series with one another (the last three columns of Table 13.1). Note, first, that none reports any events for 1881; this is because both Tuskegee and the *Chicago Tribune* begin compiling lynching incidents in 1882 and the NAACP in 1889. For the years that the NAACP and Tuskegee both report data, an examination of the two series suggests that they are very similar. The Chicago data, in comparison, are quite different in some years – note 1890 and 1893 – suggesting independent data collections, but the event totals are very similar in other years, for example 1895–1900.

From these numbers alone, it's difficult to make a strong judgment about the quality of the published lynching records. Are the Tuskegee and NAACP data so similar because each institution did a careful search for incidents and reached similar conclusions? Or are they similar because of copying and cross-checking between the two institutions, which would suggest that we should not look at these time series as independent estimates? From our earlier discussion, we know that the latter was the case. With respect to the *Chicago Tribune*, the record of correspondence with the other institutions is murky, but a reasonable assumption would be that each, in trying to produce an accurate listing, made use of all available resources including the records of the other institutions.

But the real issue concerns how the new time series stacks up against the others. We have already said much about the data collection and the building of our own series: four papers read on a daily basis, each by three coders using similar procedures for all years of the series; moreover, there is a fall-off in the number of new events found with the addition of each paper, so that a fifth can be expected to yield few new incidents. Further, in the case of our series, we know what definition of a lynching incident was used and what sorts of events were excluded; these matters are unknown with respect to the published listings. But how do our estimates compare with the other time series?

A simple approach would be to examine differences among the series in year-to-year variations. It is, after all, the fluctuations in the time series that we will eventually seek to explain, so a comparison of this sort between our series and the

Table 13.2. *Construction of the lynching time series for the South, 1881–1900*

(a) Number of events, 1881–1900, by newspaper:

Charleston	New Orleans	Atlanta	Memphis
994	1,275	1,157	1,176

(b) Average number of added events, by level of aggregation:

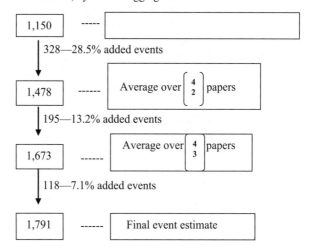

(c) Number of events added by a fourth newspaper:

Omitted paper; number of events in the three remaining papers

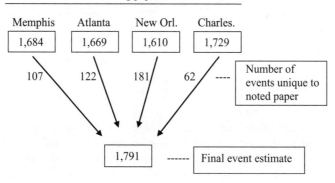

published ones is of great interest. First, though, how many reversals appear among the published series – instances of one showing an increase across years with another reporting a decline? In the twelve years covered by both Tuskegee and NAACP there are no reversals, which is not surprising since, as noted, the NAACP relied upon the Tuskegee list. A comparison of Tuskegee with Chicago yields three reversals in the nineteen years of overlapping coverage, the most notable being the change from 1893 to 1894 – Chicago reports a decline of four events, Tuskegee an increase of twenty-one. But how do the Tuskegee and Chicago lists relate to our new time series? A comparison with Chicago yields eight reversals; an examination of Tuskegee also produces eight. Some of the discrepancies are large: Between 1888 and 1889 Tuskegee reports an increase of eighteen events, whereas our new series shows a decline of fifteen; similarly, from 1892 to 1893 there is a decline of thirty events in Tuskegee, in contrast with an increase of one in the new series.

With our new series, we are in a position to carry the comparison one step further; we can restrict the categories to events for which we have a particular degree of certainty that our lynching definition was met. The preceding estimates used an inclusive definition: All incidents labeled as a lynching by one of the newspapers were included, irrespective of the amount of detail in the account. If we restrict the series to those events for which the detail is sufficient to conclude that our definition was indeed met (not shown) and compare the resulting series, we find six reversals with the *Chicago Tribune* and five with Tuskegee over the nineteen-year period. This is still a sizable disparity, and it provides further evidence that the differences between our series and the published ones are not simply a result of Tuskegee and Chicago having used a conservative definition of a lynching incident.

Because the disparities are considerable, it is quite possible that a researcher will reach different conclusions about the causation of lynching, depending on the time series that is analyzed. We won't go into the results of our study – the research is ongoing at this writing – but we do want to convey the criticalness of the data preparation stage and the variety of decisions that have to be made. The bottom line is that the results from an analysis can be no better than the quality of the data used. Unfortunately, in many published social science reports, one has little information about how the dataset was constructed or how the conclusions might depend on subtle coding decisions.

A COGNITIVE MAP OF THE SOUTH

There is a final exploration that I want to undertake with the newspaper data because it gives some insight into the coverage areas of the four papers and into the way that the coverage by the individual papers comes together to span the South. I call this the construction of a "cognitive map" because we will be generating a two-dimensional representation of the South based on the sensitivities of the four papers to events in the different states. We do this by using a data reduction technique called "multidimensional scaling" (Kruskal and Wish 1978).

We want to build a map of the South based on the way that lynching events across the region were covered in the newspapers. To build our map, we need a measure of distance between each pair of states, akin to mileage between cities, but our distance measure will tap information flows. Remember that we are talking about newspapers in the last decades of the nineteenth century, a period before radio or telephone, a time when news coverage and the flow of information tended to decline with physical distance, as well as being limited by the interests of the readers in events in various other locales. The latter would reflect social and organizational links across state borders, paths of migration, and the like. All these considerations affect newspaper coverage and will be factored into the structure of our cognitive map.

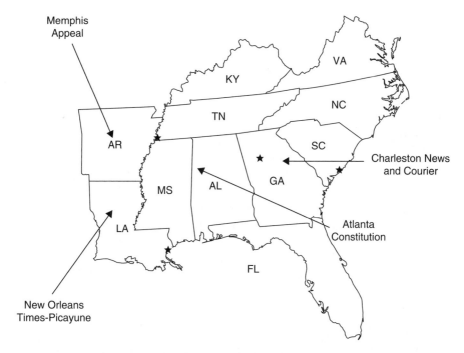

Figure 13.1. Locations of the four southern newspapers.

Indeed, it was the very assumption about the fall-off in coverage with physical distance that underlay our choice of newspapers, with the intended goal of obtaining a comprehensive account of lynching events throughout the South. In Figure 13.1, I have marked the locations of the four newspapers; you can see that no section of this region is very distant from at least one of the papers. Indeed, it is precisely the differential coverage by the papers of events in the various states that permits us to build the cognitive map.

To construct a measure of distance between states, I retabulated the newspaper reports of lynchings for the twenty-year period that is presented in columns 1–4 of Table 13.1. Instead of enumerating the events by year, I sorted them by state. Thus, for each state, we have the total number of lynchings as noted in each of the papers. For the state of Arkansas, for example, there are 71 lynchings in the Charleston paper, 127 in the New Orleans paper, 76 in Atlanta, and 138 in Memphis. In comparison, the respective numbers for Virginia are 55, 42, 49, and 49. The first thing to do is standardize these event counts by the state totals to adjust for the tendency of some locales to have had many more events than others; we don't want the state totals to influence our estimates of cognitive distance. For Arkansas the standardization yields the percentages 17.2, 30.8, 18.4, and 33.4 for the four papers; for Virginia the respective values are 28.2, 21.5, 25.1, and 25.1. This calculation was done for each state.

I then used the Euclidian distance metric to model the dissimilarity, or distance, between states in the newspaper coverage they received. Thus, the distance d_{ij} between states i and j is defined to be

$$d_{ij} = \sqrt{\sum \left(x_{ia} - x_{ja}\right)^2}, \tag{1}$$

Table 13.3. *Distances between states, calculated from the four newspapers,*
Euclidean metric

State	VA	ARK	FLA	GA	LA	NC
Virginia	0.0					
Arkansas	17.9	0.0				
Florida	7.5	17.7	0.0			
Georgia	13.1	23.7	13.9	0.0		
Louisiana	22.8	15.8	17.0	24.9	0.0	
N. Carolina	7.7	20.4	9.5	5.4	22.8	0.0

where x_{ia} specifies the percentage for newspaper a in state i, the sum is over the papers a, and the calculation of d_{ij} is carried out for all pairs of states. The distance between Virginia and Arkansas, for example, is computed as the square root of $(17.2 - 28.2)^2 + (30.8 - 21.5)^2 + (18.4 - 25.1)^2 + (33.4 - 25.1)^2$, which equals 17.9. To illustrate the results, I show in Table 13.3 the calculated distance values for six of the southern states.

Note, first, that we have a triangular matrix. It is triangular because the distance between pairs of points (states) is symmetric. Also, the zero entries in the main diagonal reflect the distance of a point to itself. The nonzero entries indicate the distances between states based on the newspaper coverage of lynching events. Our assumption is that the disparity in coverage will be small for adjacent states or for states that are a small distance apart, but if the states are geographically distant, they are likely to have received quite different press coverage in the various papers and the disparity measure will be large. Indeed, if we look over the entries in Table 13.3, it appears that the estimates are consistent with this argument: States near one another, such as North Carolina and Virginia or North Carolina and Georgia, have small disparity scores; states that are geographically far apart, such as Arkansas and Virginia or Louisiana and North Carolina, tend to have large values. Some entries, however, don't appear consistent with physical distance alone, such as the small disparity between Virginia and Florida.

We can't just plot these disparities or cognitive distances on a two-dimensional surface, as you can with airline distances, because a precise fit will require several dimensions. What multidimensional scaling does is generate a best fit to the matrix of disparity scores that is consistent with either a two- or three-dimensional surface. Since we are interested in constructing a map, I chose the two-dimensional solution. The other attractive feature of many of the scaling programs is that you can select a measurement level that is appropriate to your data; in the case of the disparity scores based on newspaper coverage, both ordinal and interval measurement seem appropriate and the results are not very sensitive to the choice.[3] I won't go into further details about the scaling technique (see Kruskal and Wish 1978 for this), but I do want to show you the results, which are displayed in Figure 13.2.

---

[3] The software program used was ALSCAL, as implemented in the SPSS 11.0 statistical package. The variables are standardized by the program somewhat differently than described in the text.

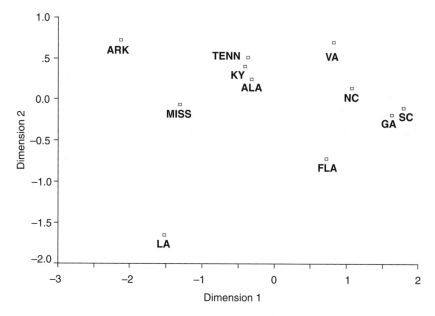

Figure 13.2. Representation of state locations based on disparities in reports of lynching events, four newspapers, 1881–1900. The ALSCAL program was used for scaling, with an ordinal level of measurement.

We have in this figure a map of the state locations based on reports of lynching events in the four papers. For reasons I have described, I call this a cognitive map. But how does it compare with a geographic map of the South, such as Figure 13.1? Well, the similarities are remarkable. The placement of almost every state is correct, though there are evident distortions – Georgia and South Carolina are too far to the right, Florida is too high (or perhaps Louisiana is too low). Nonetheless, the state locations in this cognitive map generally follow their placement on the geographic map. The only clear reversal is between Kentucky and Tennessee, but these states are quite close, both on this cognitive map and geographically. So, to conclude our account of the construction of the new lynching file, we find that our newspaper choices have done rather well in spanning the South, suggesting that the dataset is fairly representative of events in the region.

FURTHER READING

To acquire an understanding of the phenomenon of lynching in American history as well as some insight into the theoretical formulations that have been utilized, I recommend two old but classic publications – Raper (1933) and Cantril (1941) – along with a more recent edited volume, Brundage (1997). One of the best quantitative studies of lynchings is by Tolnay and Beck (1995). It should be noted that they relied on the published lists of lynching events, which I have criticized. However, the data problems were partially addressed by the authors through a review of newspaper accounts of all the incidents, with the result that many were discarded – see their Appendix A. While this recoding does not ameliorate the problem of underreporting, since only events that appeared on one or more of the lists were examined, many of Tolnay and Beck's analyses are cross-sectional, with the lynching rate investigated in terms of county characteristics. Such studies are less sensitive to the defects of data collection that have been emphasized in this chapter since year-to-year variations in the quality of data collection would be unlikely to introduce bias into our estimates of incident locations. Also relevant to the issues of this chapter are general studies of event coding from newspaper articles. A good entry point to this literature is Snyder and Kelly (1977).

Exercises

1. Lynching in the American South was intimately tied to issues of race and dominance. Many lynchings also took place in the West during the second half of the nineteenth century. From what you know about these lynching, perhaps from cowboy movies, construct an explanation of the causes of these killings. Possible factors for consideration: cattlemen, sheep herders, farmers, and effectiveness of law enforcement in an area.
2. Multidimensional scaling is a powerful technique for examining proximities among actors or objects. If you have access to a scaling program such as ALSCAL in SPSS, cmdscale in R (this package is part of the MASS library), or mdsmat in Stata, input the driving times among ten cities such as can be found on an AAA map, run the multidimensional scaling routine, and request a two-dimensional solution. Compare the map based on driving times with an areal map. Explain the differences.
3. You have now read chapters on rioting and lynchings. Terrorism, a phenomenon of the present century, is a related type of event. In what ways is terrorism similar to riots and lynchings? In what ways is it a different phenomenon? From what we have discussed about the formulation of studies of riots and lynchings, how would you go about examining terrorist incidents in, say, the country of Israel, where many attacks have occurred?

14. Attainment Processes in a Large Organization

I want now to turn to a very different sort of issue. To this point, we have considered the behavior of individuals in social settings that are not constrained by formal rules. That is, there are no established rules about how one should behave in a riot or as part of a lynching party. Sociologists, however, spend much of their time examining the structures of formal organizations – schools, churches, workplaces, and the like – and studying the behavior of individuals in these settings. In this chapter I discuss such an investigation, one that examined the structural features of a large corporation and tried to assess how its structural arrangements have differentially influenced the advancement prospects and attainments of male and female employees. The data come from an American insurance company that, a few years ago, gave me access to the records of its employees, which numbered around 16,000 at any point in time. These data cover an eight-year period during the 1970s. Because of employee turnover, I have career history information for some 25,000 workers.

We need, first, to define what we mean by advancement. It could mean a salary increase. That's certainly one measure of getting ahead. It could also mean promotion or a combination of promotion and salary increase. I decided to focus on promotion since I was interested in questions of organizational structure, and promotion is a concept that is linked to movement across structural units. But we still have to specify what constitutes a promotion. Is it getting a better job title? Greater responsibility and more people working for you? Moving up on the organizational chart? These are the usual ways that promotion is defined by researchers, but when I looked at the rules of the insurance company, I found that they used a quite different definition. The insurance company constructed a set of job lines (which they called "job foci"), with several "grade levels," essentially salary ranges, assigned to each line (see Table 14.1). Promotion, in turn, was defined as a change of grade level, which frequently took place within a job focus. Thus, for example, there are seven grades of secretary. Movement to a higher secretarial grade is a promotion, though there might be no change in responsibilities or duties as a consequence of the move.

Why this unusual definition? In the more common specification of promotion, an increase in responsibility is associated with advancement; essentially, there is a change in the job task performed. This means, however, that there must be a "vacancy" for a promotion to take place; for example, the manager of

Table 14.1. *Distribution of employees in the insurance company by grade level and job focus category, 1977*[a]

Grade level	(1) Machine operator	(2) Secretary/ steno	(3) Typist	(4) Figure clerk	(5) Misc. clerical	(6) Claims/ contract	(7) Math/ program.	(8) Sales support	(9) Underwriting/ investment	(10) Admin. – focus not assigned	(11) Misc. admin.
1	11	141	113	202							
2	139	256	212	108	426						
3	245	491	295	353	434						
4	131	555	214	109	642	264					
5	99	412	123	70	572	77				196	29
6	32	301	12	11	163	184	76	115	88	129	223
7	32	114			23	99	73	139	112	153	201
8	27				17	61	75	100	85	144	155
9	48					52	113	67	42	160	100
10						47	103	46	102	216	126
11						18	78	33	82	189	52
12							71	76	92	227	85
13										324	
14										368	
15										267	
16										271	
17										188	
18										154	
19										100	
20										69	

[a] Entries are number of employees on January 1, 1977. For readability, a few scattered entries with $n < 9$ have been suppressed. Foci (1)–(5) are classified by the company as "clerical"; foci (6)–(11) are termed "administrative."

Source: Reprinted from *Social Science Research* 28, Seymour Spilerman and Trond Petersen, "Organizational Structure, Determinants of Promotion, and Gender Differences in Attainment," 203–27, copyright 1999, with permission from Elsevier.

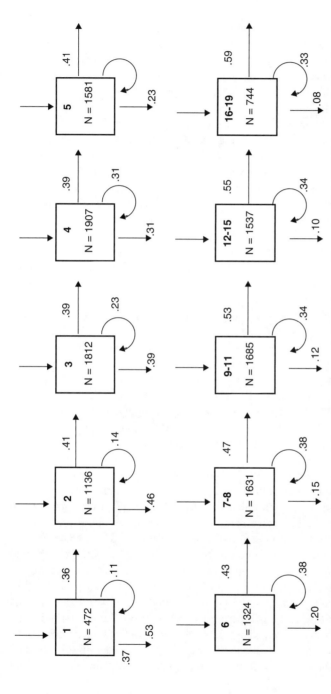

Figure 14.1. Personnel flows in the insurance company between $t_0 =$ January 1, 1977, and $t_1 =$ December 31, 1979. N's are the number of employees in the grade at time t_0. Entries on arrows are proportions of employees who had been in the grade at time t_0. Higher-level grades are grouped because of small N's.

department X has retired and a replacement is needed or the company has expanded and additional supervisors are required. Now, promotion is used by a firm not only to fill upper-level positions but also as a motivating device, a reward for superior performance. Indeed, capable and ambitious employees expect to have reasonable prospects for upward mobility. But how, then, does a company offer career advancement if it is not growing or if there is little turnover? Morale can suffer if the possibilities for promotion are choked off by a lack of vacancies; the firm might even lose its more able workers to competing companies.

To overcome this "tyranny of demography," the fact that promotion in the usual specification is tied to the presence of vacancies, over which a firm might have little control, many large companies have adopted a human resource struc-ture in which status rank is divorced from occupational task. A new structural dimension is created – the grade level hierarchy – and promotion is defined as upward movement in this hierarchy. Since the grades are status ranks, not tied to functional tasks, this reward structure does not require a vacancy for promotion to take place; employees can be advanced whenever they merit the recognition. When a change in functional task does occur, such as a shift from foreman to manager, this will likely be accompanied by a grade increase (promotion), but employees can now also move upward in the firm without a corresponding change in job responsibilities. Of course, there are limits to this flexibility; it would not do for an able secretary to be promoted to a higher grade than the manager to whom she (or he) reports. Nonetheless, this organizational innovation gives a firm great flexibility in motivating its employees.

The grade level structure provides a useful framework within which to study personnel flows. There are twenty grades in the insurance company; many of the personnel flows during the period $t_0 =$ January 1, 1977, to $t_1 =$ December 31, 1979, are shown in Figure 14.1. New hires can enter any grade, though the majority begin employment in grades 1–6. The flows between grades provide the material from which to study promotions; downward mobility (demotion) is not shown in the figure because it is rare in American companies. Instead, the more common penalty for unsatisfactory performance is either cessation of advancement or dismissal. Departures from the firm can also be studied using this framework. However, whether it is promotions or departures that one wishes to examine, this formulation sensitizes a researcher to the possibility that the determinants of the outcome may be *grade dependent*; that is, the factors influencing promotion or departure decisions may be quite different for employees in grade 15 than for those in grade 5.

The entries in Figure 14.1 compare the status of employees at time t_1 with their grade locations at t_0. For example, looking at the 472 workers who were in grade 1 at the initial time point, by t_1 some 36% had reached a higher grade,[1] 53% had left the company, and 11% remained in grade 1. If we look over the grades, some interesting patterns emerge. Departures from the company decline monotonically with grade level, from 53% in grade 1 to 8% in grades 16–19. Promotions, however, show a tendency to increase, from a low of 36% in grade 1 to 59% in the highest grades. However, one cannot facilely draw a conclusion

[1] A few employees were promoted more than once between the time points. For simplicity, they are treated as if they advanced one grade.

about how the promotion rate varies with grade level because these figures are influenced by the departure flows; in particular, many of the departers might have been promoted before they left the company.[2] Now, we could compute estimates of the promotion rates differently, such as by ignoring departers and restricting our calculation to employees who remained in the company at t_1. However, this calculation assumes that none of the departers had been promoted before leaving, which would also be in error. In fact, any calculation that does not take into account what occurred in the interval between t_0 and t_1 will produce a biased estimate of the true promotion rate.

A SURVIVAL ANALYSIS APPROACH

Fortunately, there is an analytic formulation that avoids this problem. It is called "survival analysis" and involves a type of regression in which the "risk" of an event (e.g., promotion) is modeled from longitudinal data. Survival analysis makes use of the notion of a "risk set"; in the present example, a person in grade i is "at risk" for promotion as long as he or she remains in this grade. Thus, both termination of employment and promotion mean removal from the risk set. Survival analysis involves the construction of a "hazard rate" – a duration-specific rate of the event occurrence. In the present context, "duration-specific" refers to the possibility that the promotion rate may vary with time in the grade. A new entrant into grade i is unlikely to be advanced during the initial months in rank; after all, the person has just begun in the grade. With the passage of time, the likelihood of promotion will increase. But if the duration exceeds a few years, the employee has probably been judged unfit for further advancement and his or her promotion prospects will decline.

Survival analysis also incorporates information from "censored observations" of the parameter estimation. In the example of the insurance company, if a person departs the risk set for a reason other than promotion, the observation is "censored" in the sense that we do not know what the waiting time to promotion would have been. However, we do know that the waiting time exceeds the period spent in grade by the employee, and this information is taken into account in the estimation.

Formally, if T is a positive random variable denoting the time to an event, $f(t)$ is its density function, and $F(t)$ is the cumulative distribution function, that is,

$$F(t) = \int_0^t f(u)du = \Pr(T \leq t), \tag{1}$$

then the hazard rate, $h(t)$, is defined as

$$h(t) = \lim_{\Delta t \to 0} \frac{\Pr(t + \Delta t > T > t \backslash T > t)}{\Delta t} = \frac{f(t)}{1 - F(t)}. \tag{2}$$

---

[2] There is a similar problem with drawing conclusions about the departure rate in that the entries do not take into account promotions before leaving the company.

$Pr(.)$ in equation (2) denotes the probability of an event in the interval $(t, t+\Delta t)$ conditional on no event before or at time t, and the limiting operation makes it clear that we are speaking about an instantaneous rate.

I'm not going to delve into the details of this formulation, as there are many excellent texts on survival analysis (e.g., Box-Steffensmeir and Jones 2004; Kleinbaum 1996), except to emphasize that the estimation of the regression parameters involves finding the vector **b** that maximizes a likelihood function of the form

$$L\{\mathbf{b}|(t_i, \mathbf{x}_i)\} = \prod_{i=1}^{n} \{f(t_i|\mathbf{x}_i, \mathbf{b})\}^{d_i}\{1 - F(t_i|\mathbf{x}_i, \mathbf{b})\}^{1-d_i}, \tag{3}$$

where t_i refers to the time at which the event (promotion) or censoring occurred for observation i, $d_i = 1$ if observation i ended with the event (completed spell), $d_i = 0$ for a censored spell, x_i is a vector of characteristics of individual i, and the product is taken over all observations in the dataset. The first term in the product is the density of waiting times for completed spells, and the second refers to spells for which the waiting time exceeds t_i – which is the information we have for censored observations. It is by means of the latter term that censored spells are taken into account. And it is through the specification of the density, $f(.)$, that a particular hazard regression model is selected.

The model we estimated in the study of promotions is based on a partial maximum likelihood approach (Box-Steffensmeir and Jones 2004: chap. 4), a variant of the preceding one, and takes the form

$$h_{i,i+1}(t|\mathbf{x}_i) = h_0(t) \exp (\beta_1 \mathbf{x}_{i1} + \beta_2 \mathbf{x}_{i2} + \cdots + \beta_n \mathbf{x}_{in}), \tag{4}$$

where $h_{i,i+1}(t|\mathbf{x}_i)$ is the hazard of promotion from grade i to $i+1$, $h_0(t)$ is a "nuisance function," of little importance in the present discussion, and "exp" denotes exponentiation. While equation (4) is of a form that will be new to many of you, by taking the logarithms, it can be rewritten as

$$\ln\{h_{i,i+1}(t|\mathbf{x}_i)\} = \ln\{h_0(t)\} + \beta_1 \mathbf{x}_{i1} + \beta_2 \mathbf{x}_{i2} + \cdots + \beta_n \mathbf{x}_{in} \tag{5}$$

and can now be understood to be little more than a linear regression model except that the outcome variable is the logarithm of the hazard. It's the β's, however, that will concern us, and they can be interpreted as unstandardized regression coefficients, such as those you are familiar with from least squares regression.

Now that we have a powerful formulation from which to study the determinants of promotion, let's return to the insurance company data and inquire how the promotion rate was influenced by its organizational features, especially the grade level structure, and by characteristics of its employees. Results from this analysis are reported in Table 14.2, where the coefficients are the β's from a model of the form of equation (5). We focus on the effects of grade level on the promotion rate. First, regression (1) in the table shows the grade level effects relative to the reference category, grades 1–3. It is evident that there is a fall-of in promotions in grades 4–5 and 6–7 and a small improvement in grades 8–10, followed by a second decline in the senior grades. In regression (2), characteristics of the employees have been added. Not surprisingly, they show that more educated workers have better promotion prospects; however, black employees do less well

Table 14.2. *Effects of grade level terms and employee characteristics on the promotion rate*

Variable[b]	Equation[a]		
	(1)	(2)	(3)
Black		−.096*	−.098*
Oriental		.046	.044
Hispanic		−.101*	−.097*
Female		−.104*	−.094*
Education (years)		.061*	.054*
Age (years)		−.044*	−.045*
Age^2		.00025*	.00027*
Seniority (years)		−.036*	−.036*
Seniority^2		.00060*	.00050*
GL4–5	−.380*	−.223*	.059
GL6–7	−.350*	−.109*	.010
GL8–10	−.161*	.081**	.106*
GL11–14	−.208*	.091**	.126*
GL15–20	−.375*	−.016	.027
Cleric x GL4–5			−.306*
Cleric x GL6–7			−.395*
x^2	4,114	6,337	6,428
N (spells)	33,468	33,468	33,468
Pct. Completed	.510	.510	.510

[a] Entires are unstandardized regression coefficients from a survival model. Each equation also contains seven dummy terms which convey the effect of duration in grade.

[b] "White" is the omitted category among the racial terms; "GL1–3" is the omitted category among the grade level terms. "Cleric" is a dummy variable, coded one for job foci 1–5 and zero otherwise. Interactions with GL dummies were estimated only for grades having both clerical and administrative employees.

** $p < .05$.

* $p < .01$.

Source: Reprinted from *Social Science Research* 28, Seymour Spilerman and Trond Petersen, "Organizational Structure, Determinants of Promotion, and Gender Differences in Attainment," 203–27, copyright 1999, with permission from Elsevier.

than whites (the reference category for race), and women do less well than men (the reference category for gender). For further details on the education and race effects, I refer you to Spilerman and Lunde (1991); here we shall examine only the gender effects.

GENDER DIFFERENCES IN ATTAINMENT

What does organizational structure have to do with women's attainments? In American corporations, as many of you know, the occupational success of women falls well short of that of men and few women occupy the upper rungs of the corporate ladder. The insurance company is no different in this regard, and the substantial negative coefficient for women in column (2) is consistent with the wider observation. One common explanation for the lower attainments of women emphasizes discrimination by employers. This surely is part of the story and was even more of a factor in past decades, such as the 1970s, to which our data pertain. But there are other considerations that are relevant to understanding the gender gap in achievement; in this regard, the conflicting obligations of employed married women, to work and to family, is often mentioned (e.g., Finch 1983; Pleck 1977).

In the majority of American households, women take primary responsibility for childrearing. This means that women who are in a dual-career marriage must juggle family and work tasks, especially when there are young children at home. While this can also be a problem for husbands, it is normative in America for women to take primary responsibility for family chores and for men to focus their efforts on work and income. Moreover, it is more common for men to have stay-at-home wives than the reverse; in short, women more frequently find themselves in dual-career unions. As a consequence, when decisions have to be made that can affect employment and career prospects – who will stay home with a sick child or take time off from work to assist an ailing parent, or whether the family will relocate to take advantage of a job offer to one spouse – it is likely that the wife's career will be compromised. In light of this assessment of decision making in American households, I wanted to examine how these processes might play out in corporate settings.

Let me tell you about a couple of studies that motivated the present investigation. Spilerman and Schrank (1991) show that when workers terminate employment, women typically state reasons related to family responsibilities; men cite factors that stress career development – leaving for a better job or a higher salary. Also, when there are young children in the household, women far more frequently than men take unplanned days off from work, presumably in response to an immediate need by a child. And, using a dataset from a different company, Hoffman and Reed (1981) report that women often turn down offers of promotion on the grounds that the time required by the higher-level job would intrude upon their family responsibilities.

I wanted, then, to explore how the organizational structure of the insurance company may have influenced the attainments of women, and it is these results, from Spilerman and Petersen (1999), that I shall describe in some detail. As a starting point, let's turn back to Table 14.1. How are female employees distributed among the job foci? The first five foci are clerical lines; the remainder are administrative lines. From what we know about women's occupational affiliations, we would expect them to be concentrated in the clerical lines; indeed, while 72% of employees in the company are women, they comprise 90% of the clerical workers but only 44% of the administrative staff. After examining hiring records, I can say that this disparity does not appear to be due to the steering of women into clerical lines; rather, it is a result of self-selection by women into secretarial and clerical jobs. Possibly this is because these positions demand less time and effort, which can be in scarce supply for married women.

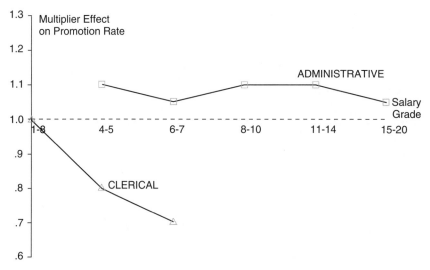

Figure 14.2. Summary of a fitted model of promotion processes.

What is evident from Table 14.1 is the very different grade distributions associated with the various job foci and the fact that while each focus provides opportunity for several promotions within the job line, the clerical foci have low ceiling grades. The company does facilitate lateral transfers across foci, and some employees avail themselves of the opportunity to move to a job line with a higher ceiling grade. Yet, such shifts can require a change of work group – and even of residence location since an insurance company has offices in several cities – and many employees choose to forgo the possibility of further advancement rather than accept such dislocations. A reasonable hypothesis, then, is that the ceiling grades serve as structural barriers to advancement, lowering the promotion rates in the top ranks of a job line.[3]

Model (3) of Table 14.2 speaks to this possibility. We have introduced interaction terms for clerical focus by grades 4–5 and 6–7; these terms permit an assessment of whether the promotion rates from these ranks differ between the clerical foci (where they constitute ceiling grades) and the administrative foci (where they are not ceiling grades). The interaction terms show strong negative effects, indicating lower promotion rates in the top grades of the clerical lines. The model (3) findings can be effectively summarized in a graph; see Figure 14.2. It is clear from this figure that while the administrative foci show little variation over rank in the promotion rate, the clerical lines exhibit a sharp fall-off as the ceiling grade is approached.

So, despite efforts by the company to facilitate upward mobility via changes in job focus, there is clear evidence of promotion blockage. How does this play out with respect to the advancement prospects of women? Table 14.3 reports results

[3] Grade 12 appears to be a ceiling for many of the administrative lines. This, however, is not the case. For its own reasons, the insurance company automatically reclassifies all employees in grades higher than 12 as "administrative – focus not assigned."

Table 14.3. *Summary of gender differences in the promotion rate, by grade level*

		Regression coeff.	Female advantage[a]
Variable	(1) Percent female	(2)[b] Δ(F–M)	(3) $\exp(\Delta) - 1$
Average Effect (No GL terms)[c]	72	–.170	.84
Average Effect (GL terms present)[d]	72	–.106	.90
Gender Effect, by Grade Level			
GL1–3	91	–.114	.89
GL4–5	88	–.298	.74
GL6–7	72	–.296	.74
GL8–9	49	.048	1.05
GL10–12	30	.029	1.03
GL13–15	17	.165	1.18
GL16–20	11	.360	1.43

[a] Female promotion rate as a proportion of the male rate.
[b] Difference between female and male regression effects, calculated from the hazard model.
[c] Terms included for the employee characteristics listed in Table 7.
[d] Terms present for grade level and for employee characteristics.
Source: Reprinted from *Social Science Research* 28, Seymour Spilerman and Trond Petersen, "Organizational Structure, Determinants of Promotion, and Gender Differences in Attainment," 203–27, copyright 1999, with permission from Elsevier.

from another survival regression, one carried out with interaction terms present between gender and grade level, which permits the "female advantage" in the promotion rate to be calculated for each grade – see Spilerman and Petersen (1999) for methodological details; here, I focus on the findings. Column (2) of Table 14.3 shows the coefficients of the gender difference from three regressions of the promotion rate on grade level and characteristics of the employees (row 1, row 2, and the remainder of the table). But it is the column (3) entries that are easiest to understand. They are the exponentiated values of the column (2) figures and have an interesting interpretation. Look back at equation (4) and note that the exponentiated term can be rewritten as

$$\exp(\beta_1 x_{i1} + \beta_2 x_{i2} + \cdots + \beta_n x_{in}) = e^{b_1 x_{i1}} e^{b_2 x_{i2}} \cdots e^{b_n x_{in}}. \qquad (6)$$

From the second expression, it should be clear that a unit increase in any variable x_j ($j = 1, \ldots, n$) will have a *multiplicative effect* on the promotion hazard of size e^{bj}. In particular, exponentiating the coefficients in column (2) of Table 14.3 gives a measure of the "female advantage" in promotion rate as a proportion of the male rate.

These entries tell the following story: If we control for employee characteristics but not grade level, the promotion rate of women is 84% of the male rate (row 1); in short, women in the insurance company do notably less well than men, but not to an extent that differentiates this company from many others in America, especially in the late 1970s. If additive terms for grade level are introduced, which permits the differential promotion rates in the grades to be taken into account, the disparity is reduced from 16% to 10% (row 2). But if we estimate the gender difference in promotion rate separately for each grade, we find a most interesting pattern, one that was obscured in the prior regressions. The female *dis*advantage is 11% in grades 1–3 and increases to 26% in grades 4–5 and 6–7, but then reverses.

The fall-off in the promotion rate of women in grades 4–5 and 6–7 is what is often called the "glass ceiling" effect, which intimates that that there is a limit to the upward mobility possibilities of women in American companies. What is added by our analysis is an understanding of how the glass ceiling effect comes about. It's not due to a management decision to slow the advance of women beyond a certain rank, but rather to a structural impediment to mobility from the way that the job ladders are formulated. Moreover, it is the case that above grade 7 there is a clear tendency for women to have *higher* promotion rates than men! Indeed, in the most senior grades, the female advantage is some 43% over the male rate. This striking finding is not unique to the insurance company; it has been supported by the work of other researchers, especially DiPrete and Soule (1986, 1988), who studied a very different corporation.

How can we explain this last result? How can it be that women in the senior grades have a higher promotion rate than men, in light of all that has been written about the limited career opportunities of women? Let's first note that the number of employees in grades 13 and higher, where women enjoy an advantage, is only 13% of the workforce; thus, few women reach levels at which they can benefit from this favorable treatment. But, still, why is there a higher promotion rate than for men? In the absence of discrimination, we would expect to find that the genders have equal rates – unless we believe that the women are smarter, more effective, or more ambitious than their male colleagues. In fact, there is reason to suspect that these women may be particularly capable. Some of them would have entered the company in the clerical foci and shown great agility in avoiding the ceiling grade blockages. Many of the women would have proven efficient in managing the competing demands of home and work, while others might have chosen to forgo marriage and family and invest instead in career attainments.

Yet, there are other explanations that are consistent with the high promotion rates of women in the senior grades. The 1970s was a time of government oversight in the areas of race and gender discrimination, a time of lawsuits filed by aggrieved employees and by federal and state agencies. One defense against a charge of "disparate impact" in the operation of a firm's reward structure would be to show that the gender differences in the senior ranks were not large and that whatever disparities did exist could be explained in terms of "business necessity." But if we look at the percentage of women in grades 13 and higher (column 1 of Table 14.3), we see that it was very low. Quite possibly, the insurance company sought to reduce its exposure to lawsuits by instituting affirmative action promotions into the senior grades and into the vice-presidential ranks, which comprise the organizational levels above grade 20.

What should we think about all this? Who is responsible for the lesser attainments of women in American companies, and what should be done to improve their career prospects? Well, first, there is decision making in the household between husband and wife, but it is most difficult to intrude into such affairs. As to employers, the great majority are acutely aware of the severe legal penalties associated with discrimination, and they seek also to avoid organizational arrangements that will have an adverse effect on women's attainments. The latter fall under the legal specification of disparate impact, which is permitted only if a business necessity can be successfully argued. And what about the government? What interest should it take in these matters, aside from ensuring that there is no discrimination of either the differential treatment or disparate impact varieties.

A lot of this comes down to our moral sense of what we believe the obligations of different institutional actors should be, but social science research can shed some light on the possibilities. For one thing, we know that the critical point with respect to pressure on women's careers comes at the time of childbearing and childrearing, because the demands of children cannot easily be put off to a time that is convenient for parents. Some European countries, like the United Kingdom and the Scandinavian countries, address this problem by encouraging large firms to add a child care facility to the workplace; this makes it possible for women to bring very young children to work and even take time during the day to breast-feed a child. Other countries, such as France, Sweden, and Canada, generously subsidize a system of stand-alone child care facilities. In America we do neither, with a consequent high price in the career opportunities for women.

FURTHER READING

Several articles related to the study of the insurance company are Spilerman and Lunde (1991), Spilerman and Schrank (1991), and Spilerman and Petersen (1999). The first examines the different effects of educational attainment on promotion prospects by grade level; the latter two look at aspects of women's careers. Hoffman and Reed (1981) describe survey results from an airline company, in which they find that women make career decisions primarily to minimize conflict between work and home responsibilities rather than solely for career advancement. The Spilerman and Schrank study comes to much the same conclusion, but an essential difference is that Hoffman and Read report the expressed preferences of men and women, while Spilerman and Schrank largely infer the impact of family obligations from aspects of the work behaviors of men and women. DiPrete and Soule (1986, 1988) report a study of a different company, along the lines of the Spilerman and Petersen (1999) article, and Rosenfeld (1992) provides a review of many articles and books on career processes. Last, for an in-depth study of a variety of aspects of men's and women's careers in corporate settings, I refer you to Rosabeth Kanter's (1977) classic monograph, *Men and Women of the Corporation.*

In this chapter, I have also made use of techniques that will be new to many of you, especially the methods of survival analysis, also known as "event history analysis." These are techniques for the study of discrete events in time, as distinct from time series methods, which are appropriate for the study of continuous variables. Some excellent introductory textbooks on the subject are Box-Steffensmeir and Jones (2004) and Kleinbaum (1996).

EXERCISES

1. I have said little about the choice of the $f(t)$ density in equation (2). This choice describes the general way we believe that the event rate varies with the waiting time – whether, for example, the promotion rate rises, peaks, and then declines with time in grade or perhaps behaves differently. The first four chapters of Steffensmeir and Jones (2004) provide a good overview of the principal procedures of survival analysis. Read these chapters and pay particular attention to the different functional forms that can be used in the specification of $f(t)$. Note also the Cox model, which takes a different approach to the issue of the distributional form.

2. As you have seen, this empirical investigation has brought us to issues of policy and law in regard to what is permissible in corporate decision making. I have used terms such as differential treatment, disparate impact, and business necessity. These terms have legal meanings. To better understand the issues involved, I encourage you to look over some of the basic federal legislation in regard to employment discrimination: Title VII of the Civil Rights Act of 1964 and the Equal Pay Act of 1963. You can easily find discussions of this legislation on the Internet.

3. Much of the federal legislation in the area of employment discrimination is concerned with "equal pay for equal work," that is, the principle that women should be paid the same wages as men if they perform the same work. However, as we have seen in this chapter, women often do different jobs from men, which raises the issue of how women's jobs should be priced. A controversial literature called "comparable worth" addresses this question (England 1992). Look over the England volume, as well as other references you will find on the Internet. Most companies are opposed to this approach in setting the wages of women's jobs. Why do you think this is so?

PART V. POLITICAL SCIENCE

Charles Cameron

15. What Is Political Science?

Politics is part of virtually any social interaction involving cooperation or conflict, thus including interactions within private organizations ("office politics") along with larger political conflicts. Given the potentially huge domain of politics, it's perfectly possible to talk about "the politics of X," where X can be anything ranging from table manners to animal "societies." But although all of these are studied by political scientists to some extent, in the American academy "political science" generally means the study of a rather circumscribed range of social phenomena falling within four distinct and professionalized fields: American politics, comparative politics, international relations, and political theory (that is, political philosophy).

AMERICAN POLITICS

Broadly speaking, the academic field of American politics is exactly what one would expect: public opinion, voting, elections, legislatures, courts, and so on.

What's new and interesting here? Well, something very peculiar and quite disturbing has happened in American politics (the real thing). Every day in the halls of Congress and every night on political talk shows, partisans from the right and left fight a culture war with the intensity and viciousness of scorpions locked in a bottle. But for the most part, the public doesn't notice, isn't listening, and doesn't care. In short, political elites have polarized ideologically but, on average, ordinary citizens have not. Perhaps the most interesting recent work in American politics (the field) documents this strange development, explores why it has occurred, and investigates its consequences.

How do we know that the split between elites and masses has occurred? The evidence on the nonpolarized public comes from public opinion polls. Two excellent references are DiMaggio, Evans, and Bryson (1996) and Fiorina, Abrams, and Pope (2005). Basically, the evidence shows that most Americans tend to be centrists, and their opinions are no more extreme or polarized today than they were several decades ago (with one notable exception, opinions about abortion).

Figure 15.1 gives a sense of the general evidence on polarization. The data come from the National Election Study, a survey conducted every two or four

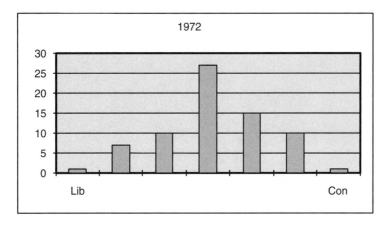

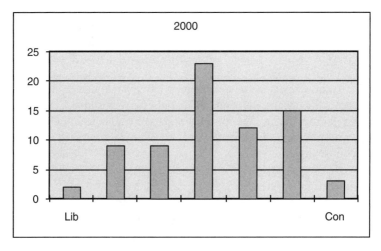

Figure 15.1. Americans' self-placement on the National Election Study's 7-point political ideology scale, from survey data in the presidential election years from 1972 to 2000.

years by political scientists in connection with national elections. The survey asks the respondents to place themselves on a 7-point scale, with "1" being extremely liberal and "7" being extremely conservative. Compare an early distribution of self-placements – say, from 1972 – with a later one – say, from 2000. If you didn't know which distribution corresponded to 1972 and which one to 2000, would you be able to guess? There is a little more polarization (more people place themselves at the extremes, fewer in the middle category) in more recent years, but not as much as you might expect from the discussion of "culture wars" in the media.

What about political elites? Measuring the ideology of elites is trickier, but one way to get at the question is to infer the ideology of congressmembers – critical elites, such as presidents, Supreme Court justices, governors, and state legislators – through their roll call voting. At one level, this exercise can be straightforward: Many interest groups give congressmembers a score based on

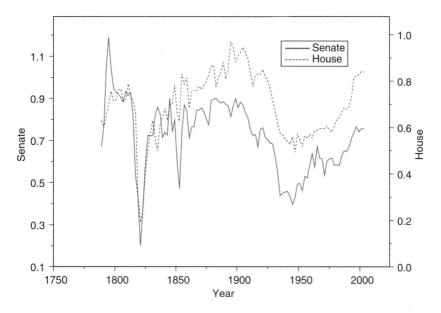

Figure 15.2. Ideological polarization in the House and Senate, 1790–2000. Adapted from Poole and Rosenthal (1997).

how frequently they vote the "right" way, according to the group. So, a senator who receives a score of 80 from the liberal Americans for Democratic Action is more liberal than one who receives a score of 20.

Political scientists have extended this simple idea by using multidimensional scaling techniques to study roll call votes in the House and Senate. The estimated ideology scales can be tied down across congresses and between the House and Senate by taking advantage of the fact that some congressmembers serve for multiple terms and some move from the House to the Senate. Then, given scores for individual congressmembers, one can calculate the score of the average Republican and the average Democrat (or whatever the major parties were at the time). The distance between the two average party members offers a simple and intuitive measure of polarization across the parties.

If one calculates this score, what does it show? To see, glance at Figure 15.2. It displays this measure of cross-party polarization, using the most widely employed ideology scores, Poole and Rosenthal's NOMINATE scores. One could use the figure to structure a political history of the United States. But focus on the second half of the series. You will see that polarization was relatively high at the time of the Civil War and subsequently peaked during the 1880 or 1890s, a period of huge social change and social strife in the United States. From about 1900 to about 1950, polarization steadily declined and remained low throughout the 1950s and 1960s. But then cross-party polarization began to tick up and continued to do so steadily for the next three decades. At present, polarization in Congress is at about the same levels as before the Civil War.

This is all quite interesting and extremely consequential for American politics. But rather than pursue the question, for the moment let me also point out the

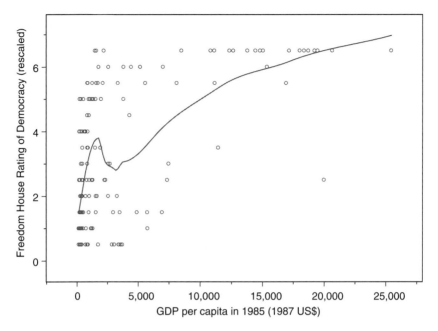

Figure 15.3. Democracy and per capita GDP for countries around the world. Line shows a fitted, locally weighted regression (lowess) curve.

staggering amount of effort behind Figures 15.1 and 15.2: Thousands of people were interviewed with an identical question, using statistically representative samples, over decades, and hundreds of thousands of roll call votes were tabulated and analyzed using sophisticated statistical techniques. Both of these graphs represent an enormous investment in social science by the American government and by many scholars.

COMPARATIVE POLITICS

Specialists in comparative politics in the United States study the politics of countries other than the United States. An example of a topic in this area is the study of democratic transitions: What causes countries to become, and stay, democracies? A long-standing answer has relied on the apparent link between wealth and democracy: If a country becomes rich enough, it becomes a democracy. Figure 15.3 shows the positive correlation between gross domestic product (GDP) per capita (adjusted for inflation, by pegging to the 1987 dollar) and democracy scores from Freedom House.[1]

A graph like this raises more questions than it answers. Does growth cause democracy or democracy growth? (Or, to put it more precisely, to what extent does growth affect democracy, and to what extent does democracy affect growth? There is no reason that causality has to go in one direction or the other.) If there is

---

[1] We flipped the Freedom House scores, so a high value means a robust democracy and a low value means a nondemocracy. This sort of simple transformation can be extremely helpful in data analysis.

some relationship between wealth and democracy, why should this be? And are the forces that encourage transitions to democracy the same ones that prevent transitions out of democracy?

At least on the last score there has been something of a debate. After examining democratic regimes in 135 countries from 1959 to 1990, Przeworski and Limongi (1997) insist that economic development does not necessarily trigger transitions to democracy. Rather, they suggest, affluence helps sustain democratic regimes once they come into existence. We thus see an apparent relationship like that in Figure 15.3, but it is simply because wealthy countries tend to remain democratic if they ever become democratic.

Boix and Stokes (2003) dispute this claim. Their empirical strategy is to extend the data to include observations from the mid-nineteenth century through World War II. These authors insist that economic growth does trigger democracy. They show that in more recent decades, some countries that developed but remained dictatorships would be expected to democratize very quickly.

The relationship between economic development and democracy remains a topic of active investigation. Clearly, the results have important implications for the future.

INTERNATIONAL RELATIONS

The field of international relations focuses on political relations between countries. The archetypal examples are war and trade. Recently, international human rights and international law have been actively studied. But surely the most interesting and potentially consequential development has been the idea of the so-called democratic peace.

The basic idea is that democracies are much less likely to fight wars against one another than against other types of states (autocracies, dictatorships, monarchies).[2] So, a world of democracies would be a world at peace – the fulfillment of one of humanity's eternal dreams. By implication, a prime goal for the foreign policy of democracies like the United States should (perhaps) be to support fragile democracies and encourage dictatorships to become democracies. Doing so makes the world safe for democracy.

The idea of a democratic peace is extremely contentious within the field of international relations. One reason relates to theory. Within international relations, one of the most influential theoretical frameworks has been "realism," the model in which the competitive pressure for survival is so strong at the international level that the domestic structures of countries don't matter – democracies, autocracies, and monarchies must all behave more or less the same way or they go under. The idea of the democratic peace thus flies in the face of a fundamental assumption held by many of the field's leading authorities.

Given the subject's intrinsic interest, relevance for foreign policy, and theoretical bite, you will hardly be surprised to learn that the literature on the democratic peace is huge. A handy review article is Ray (1998). At the heart of the

---

[2] There are a number of related empirical claims – for example, that democracies are more successful at warfare than nondemocracies, suffer fewer casualties, and fight shorter wars.

literature are two questions. The first is empirical: Is it true that democracies are more peaceful than nondemocracies, especially with respect each other? The second is theoretical: If it is true, why?

You might think it is easy to tell if democracies are less warlike than non-democracies: Just tally the wars by regime type and perform a simple statistical test, say a t-test. But if you think about it for even a little while, you'll see that what seems so simple at first must be rather difficult in practice.

First, what do we mean by "war"? Should we include civil wars? How many battle deaths does it take before we call something a war (a frequently used definition requires 1,000 battle deaths)? What time period should we use (often 1816 on)? The simple logistics of tabulating the data will be formidable.

Second, what do we mean by "democracy"? How extensive must the franchise be before we call a country a democracy? Was nineteenth-century Britain a democracy? If a society allows slavery, is it a democracy? Was Periclean Athens a democracy? If we conceive of democracy as a continuum, at what level of democratic-ness do we score a country as a democracy for purpose of the democratic peace?

A third problem involves statistical methods and the idea of country-year "dyads." War involves a relationship between two states. In any given year there is a certain number of countries in the world, and each may interact (engage in war) with another. In particular, if there are n states, there are $\frac{n!}{2!(n-2)!} = \frac{n(n-1)}{2}$ possible dyads (pairs of countries). With a sizable number of countries, the number of dyads can be immense: Many of the empirical studies in this area examine something on the order of a quarter of a million dyads. Of course, most dyads are nonsensical as real war-pairs: Mongolia versus Uruguay, Tibet versus Zambia, and so on. What is a reasonable way to compare the war rate between democracy dyads versus nondemocracy dyads, taking into account the rarity of war and the absurd quality of most dyads?

By the time people argue themselves into exhaustion over these questions, there may not be anything left as an empirical finding. In fact, though, most analysts agree that the incidence of war among democracies is low, and it is much lower than that among nondemocracies and between democracies and non-democracies. This is a striking empirical finding.

Of course, the finding could be spurious. For example, as argued by Farber and Gowa (1995), it may just be an artifact of the Cold War (others disagree). It might be that peace causes democracy rather than democracy causing peace. It might be that some other factor causes both peace and democracy (like economic prosperity). Getting serious about the endogeneity of regimes leads in the direction of instrumental variable studies, similar to Acemoglu, Johnson, and Robinson's (2002) study of democracy and economic growth.

Still, if the finding is real, the question remains: why? Are democracies just nicer than nondemocracies, or at least tend to share similar values (the "norm" argument)? Are the costs of warfare higher for democratically elected officials, making them more reluctant to engage in it (the "political survival" hypothesis)? Are democracies more economically interdependent and thus more reluctant to blow up profitable trading partners? Are democratic governments more transparent so that war (due to incomplete information) becomes less likely? All these ideas have a degree of plausibility and have been (and are) under investigation.

POLITICAL THEORY

The fourth subfield of political science, political theory, examines the normative dimensions of politics – for example, what is the best type of government (and what do we mean by "best" anyway?)? I won't spend much time on this normatively oriented subfield. However, a useful introduction to recent approaches is Shapiro (2003).

CONNECTIONS TO OTHER SOCIAL SCIENCES

Topics of interest to political scientists often overlap with other fields. An example is the study of racist attitudes in the United States. First, if you ask people on surveys questions about race, their answers sound a lot less racist than they once did (Page and Shapiro 1992). There are some long-running survey questions that make it appear, if you take the data at face value, that there has been a transformation in American racial attitudes. Second, if you look at voting scores in Congress during the twentieth century using dimensional analysis, for the most part you need two dimensions: the economic dimension and the racial dimension. Archetypically, you would find southern Democrats who were liberal on economic issues but very conservative on racial issues. Those two dimensions have more or less collapsed into one. One way to look at this finding is to say that race has become unimportant and it's all economics. Another way to look at it is to say that race and economics have become so intertwined as to become one. It will typically be the case that economic conservatives will oppose affirmative action while many liberals will support it, the result being a sort of ideological polarization of racial attitudes.

So, on the one hand, there is a group of political psychologists who say that Americans are still fundamentally racist but that they cloak their racism in economic doctrine, and that the conservatives are in fact racists but they try to avoid that label by recourse to economic arguments. When someone says, "I'm opposed to affirmative action because I'm in favor or equality of opportunity," that's not really a statement of a liberal attitude but just a cover for racism. From the other perspective, you could say, "This is nonsense. There's no clandestine racism here, and the arguments in favor of equal opportunity based on merit are sincere." This second school of thought sees a principled objection and argues that people have become less racist. Political psychologists become very heated about this. The difficulty here is, of course, that it would probably be impossible ever to prove the sincerity or disingenuousness of these arguments about affirmative action. For this reason, the argument usually degenerates into an ideological battle between true believers.

The question still remains: Are Americans really becoming less racist or are they just cloaking their racism under new guises? There are obviously normative considerations here, and it's tough to decide who has the better argument. By "normative considerations," I simply mean the values by which one might assess practice.

There has also been some interesting experimental work with media in this area using specially prepared videotapes of television news stories (Iyengar and Kinder 1987). The videos show the same stories but vary the race of the actors. The subjects of the experiment are asked questions before and after to get their response to the video. The finding is a sort of priming of race on certain issues. This experimental method appears promising and may be able to answer some of the questions about how Americans feel about race. There have also been some surveys that were cleverly designed to get people to tell the experimenter things they normally don't want to say. By designing the questionnaires properly, the experimenter can get estimates in the aggregate of the percentage of respondents who are not being candid. So, there have been innovations in survey research that have been quite interesting.

ROLE OF QUANTITATIVE METHODS

Quantitative data and methods have become central to the study of American politics, comparative politics, and international relations. My three previous examples, which all involve quantitative methods and data, are fairly representative of a great deal of work in political science. Quantitative methods are relevant even to political theory, because political philosophers are increasingly interested in evaluating real politics rather than debating about imaginary worlds that could never exist. (Sometimes this style of political philosophy is called "empirical democratic theory.") I don't want to exaggerate, though: In most political theory, the only numbers you'll find are on the corners of the pages. But today, one can't be a serious student of American politics, comparative politics, and international relations without a degree of facility in quantitative methods. The importance of quantitative methods often comes as a shock to first-year graduate students, who discover that their undergraduate courses did a poor job of conveying what the discipline is really like. On the other hand, for a student in a neighboring area such as psychology, sociology, or economics, the sort of political science that is necessary might use game theory (see Chapter 3), which is quantitative in its own way but different from statistical modeling and data analysis.

There is a good reason why quantitative data and methods are so important in professional political science: Evidence matters. When it comes to politics, you are entitled to your own opinion but not your own facts. And if you care about facts, you naturally gravitate to quantitative data. Given a number, you can argue whether it really measures what you're interested in. If not, you can work to improve the measure and show other people why the new measure is better. Given a group of numbers, you can deploy amazingly powerful methods for finding reliable patterns, methods developed over hundreds of years by some of the brightest people who've ever lived. It takes a Picasso to paint a Picasso and it took the Wright Brothers to build an airplane, but even an average person can, with sufficient training, fly a plane or, more to the point, use statistical tools – and use them pretty well. Then other people can check your findings for themselves and see whether you've made a mistake, exaggerated what you've discovered, or missed something important. Perhaps because politics is so contentious, methods of argumentation with high transparency and easy verifiability are extremely attractive.

I don't mean to suggest that quantitative evidence is the only kind of evidence about politics or even, in some circumstances, the best kind of evidence. A refreshing aspect of contemporary academic political science is its openness to many different kinds of evidence: qualitative, historical, ethnographic, and introspective as well as numeric. And this is surely a good thing. Still, political scientists have invested enormous effort in building public databases on many of the subjects central to the discipline, such as public opinion, elections and voting, legislative roll call votes, types of governments around the world and throughout history, the frequency and severity of wars, and many, many other topics. If you have a computer connected to the Web, you can access much of this data instantaneously at zero marginal cost. In addition, collecting new data has never been cheaper – although, in some cases, it is not so easy anymore, for example in sample surveys, where response rates have steadily declined over the decades as Americans have become saturated with surveys of all sorts.

In addition, political scientists are increasingly sensitive to the value of non-traditional data, for example from laboratory and field experiments. As the accessibility of old data has grown, the cost of collecting new data fallen, and the openness to nontraditional data increased, the reach of quantitative political science has expanded tremendously. In truth, we are living in the golden age of quantitative political science.

Is there anything distinctive about the quantitative tools political scientists use or the way they use them? Basically, no. Quantitative data and techniques are central to contemporary political science, but the methods we use are also applicable to – and are often derived from – other fields. Examples include regression analysis, propensity score matching (used by statisticians), instrumental variables and models for selection bias (used by economists), network models (used by sociologists), and measurement and scaling models (used by psychologists). The applications of these methods to political science problems are often innovative, but the basic structure of the models is similar across the social sciences.

On the other hand, I do think that political scientists deserve great credit for their openness to techniques invented elsewhere. In this sense, political scientists are the magpies of the social sciences: always on the lookout for methodological developments elsewhere and quick to steal them for their own purposes. This openness to new methods has a cost: a sometimes embarrassing amateurishness or naiveté about new methods. It also creates somewhat silly cults and fads in methods. But it does have the great virtue of injecting perpetual freshness, excitement, and growth into quantitative political science. The perpetually moving frontier means that whole new fields of inquiry suddenly become accessible. If you enjoy learning new skills and applying them in novel ways, you'll find quantitative political science tremendous fun.

ORGANIZATION OF CHAPTERS 15 TO 17

Before getting to the detailed examples, I will briefly discuss the relationship between theory and evidence in political science. I feel pedagogically obliged to present this material, but I'm not going to belabor it unduly.

Then, in the following two chapters, we will examine in detail an analysis of an empirical puzzle I pursued for several years, concerning the politics of Supreme Court nominations. Ultimately, the puzzle involves the strategic use of scandals and other bad news to sink nominees. I'll take you through this research roughly the way it actually unfolded. We use least squares regression, locally weighted regression, logit analysis, kernel density smoothing, Poisson regression, quasi–maximum likelihood estimation, and negative binomial regression, as well as some interesting techniques for analyzing data visually using conditional plots. The data used in these sections are publicly available, so you can download them and explore them more on your own if you want to.

HOW POLITICAL SCIENCE WORKS

Political science has been called "slow journalism." There is a way in which this quip captures something important about the field. But there is also a way in which it wildly misrepresents it. Let's start with the way in which political science really is slow journalism and then look at of the some ways it isn't.

Facts, Bounds, and Causal Mechanisms

A big part of political science is establishing facts by collecting systematic evidence and using the facts to put bounds on the size of social relations. Learning the facts is important because it rules out ridiculous claims based on "what everybody knows" but isn't actually true, freakish anecdotes, and other types of junk evidence. Making incorrect or exaggerated claims based on crappy evidence is a ubiquitous practice in political debate. (You may have noticed this.) So, simply discovering the facts, or putting some bounds on what you can claim with a straight face, is a very valuable endeavor. In this drive to get at the facts, political science (like all social science) does resemble journalism. But because we emphasize systematic evidence, which often takes time to collect, it is slow journalism.

But establishing facts and bounds is just the beginning. Once you have some grasp of what you're dealing with, there is a natural drive to go beyond mere facts to ask "why" questions. The emphasis shifts from "just the facts" to explaining the facts in terms of causal mechanisms.

I appreciate that "causal mechanism" has the clunky sound of social science jargon. But I have to say that this is a piece of jargon I like. The idea that the phrase tries to convey is: We are interested in something less than natural laws, because there aren't any natural laws in social science – just people making decisions and trying to live their lives. But even if there aren't any natural laws, things are not completely random. There is a logic to campaigning for office, voting in legislatures, directing bureaucracies, offering and accepting bribes, making revolutions and initiating wars, and so on. Nothing is deterministic but things often happen for a reason, at least on average. The causal mechanisms are the little engines driving the empirical regularities.

It's thinking in terms of causal mechanisms that distinguishes political scientists from political journalists, at least in my opinion. Thus, it's not the statistics

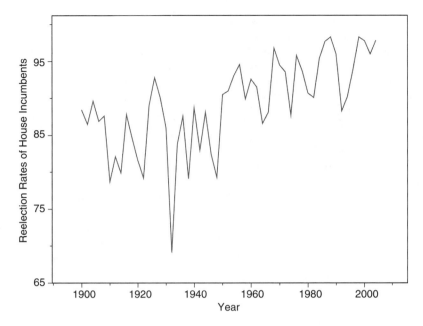

Figure 15.4. Reelection percentage (among those running for reelection in each year) in the U.S. House of Representatives, 1900–2000.

and game theory per se – these are just aids for finding systematic patterns, on the one hand, and thinking clearly about them, on the other. Rather, it's the habit of looking beneath the surface to try to understand the logic of what's happening that's key. On this account, De Tocqueville and Madison were great political scientists, which seems right to me.

I have been emphasizing the so-called positive side of the endeavor – facts, bounds, and causal mechanisms. But it's important to recognize the normative or evaluative side as well. Over time, one sees the community of political scientists obsessing over different questions. A question catches on and a seemingly endless stream of articles flows out, many dealing with apparently small, technical, or even trivial parts of the question. Is this just faddish behavior? Not really, because almost invariably the questions that really grab people have a big normative component. All the obsessive concern over measurement or just the right statistical technique, then, comes from a desire to get it right – because the answer matters for a burning normative question.

Let me illustrate the facts-bounds-mechanism trajectory. From 1980 to 2000, what percentage of incumbent congressmembers running for reelection won their races? Now, I could give you any number from, say, 25% to 98%, and you might believe me. The actual answer is 86% for senators and 95% for representatives. These numbers appear quite high. Certainly a world in which most congressmembers regularly win reelection is a different world from one in which most lose reelection.

Let's look more closely at the congressional reelection data. Figure 15.4 shows that reelection rates in the House of Representatives really are high and always have been, at least for the past century. So, if we hear the claim that American democracy is falling apart because congressmembers don't have to worry about reelection, we know that we should be skeptical because, if this is true, American democracy has been falling apart for 100 years or more.

Let's think a little harder about that high rate. House members must get reelected every two years. For a congressmember to last for a decade – which doesn't seem to be an unreasonable ambition for someone who aspires to a career in politics – he or she has to win five elections in a row. Suppose the chance of winning in each case is 90%. Then the chance of making it to a decade is $0.9^5 = 0.59$ – in other words, better than 50–50 but not hugely so. From this perspective, a congressmember who wants a reasonable chance of holding on to his or her seat for an appreciable length of time absolutely needs what appears to be an astronomical reelection rate. This is an example of what I meant by bounding a social phenomenon. (This analysis is only an approximation, though, because actual elections are not independent events: Some congressmembers have essentially a 100% probability of reelection, while for others the probability is closer to 50% – and congressmembers in these districts typically do not have long careers.)

Now let's look at Figure 15.4 again. Note the big dip in about 1930. What went on there? The obvious explanation involves the stock market crash and the Great Depression. Could there be a systematic relationship between congressional reelection rates and economic performance? That would be interesting if true, because it suggests that congressmembers might have an incentive not to wreck the economy.

Second, note the way the time series appears to have two halves, one before about 1950 and one after. Reelection rates appear to jump from about 85% to about 95%. To confirm this intuition, let's do a little time series analysis.

Time series analysts have devised "structural break" tests exactly for situations like this (Hansen 2001). The basic idea is to estimate time series models before and after a hypothesized break and then compare the estimated parameters to see if the difference is more than could be explained by chance. Recent advances allow you to detect breaks without specifying their location beforehand. Performing such a test (the Zivot and Andrews [1992] structural break test, which is available in Stata), we find strong evidence of a permanent shift in the time series (statistically significant at the 1% level) in 1950. So, the pattern we see by eyeballing the data seems likely to exist.

Why should there be a structural break after the Second World War, with higher reelection rates after the war? Maybe part of the answer involves better management of the economy – perhaps the rates went up because the government understood better how to avoid economic busts. But that might not be the entire story.

Another obvious difference before and after World War II is the growth of government. Between the Great Depression and World War II, the federal government got much, much larger. This has led some scholars to suggest that congressmembers use the opportunities created by a burgeoning bureaucracy to perform ombudsmen services for their constituents – activities like finding lost Social Security checks, dealing with problems involving immigration, the Internal Revenue Service, and so on. In turn, such services create a personal connection between some voters and their congressmember, a so-called personal vote.

This story has a degree of plausibility if you have had any experience working for a congressmember or hanging out in his or her office. Moreover, it has a nicely ironic touch because it suggests that congressmembers had it coming and going – that is, congressmembers got reelected by giving voters the big government they wanted, then did even better by helping voters with the problems created by big government.

If you want to pursue these ideas, you might check out Jacobson (2003), Fiorina and Noll (1978), and Cain, Ferejohn, and Fiorina (1990). But my point here is not to analyze congressional reelection rates per se. Rather, it is to show the movement from (1) acquiring a factoid (quick journalism), to (2) reviewing systematic evidence and establishing bounds (slow journalism), to (3) asking "why" questions, trying to tease out what causes what, and thinking in terms of causal mechanisms (social science).

One can – and I would argue, should – take this example even further. Suppose we could get some good ideas about why congressional reelection rates look the way they do. We can now ask: Would making elections more competitive actually increase democratic accountability? If the reelection rates are so high because congressmembers work frantically to give people what they want, boosting competition might not increase accountability very much. But if legislators use high rates to pursue extremist policies or pander to interest groups, greater electoral competition might well boost accountability. And if so, how can we make elections more competitive? In other words, we can start to ask normatively oriented "so what" questions.

I find data like this endlessly fascinating, but some people of my acquaintance find them a bit boring, at least when the data come from the United States. For some reason, they insist on examples from countries across the big water. So, let me just refer to another example. Let's start with a factoid question: What percentage of votes cast in national elections in Germany's Weimar period were cast in favor of the Nazis or other antidemocratic parties? The answer is: 33% for the Nazi Party and 17% for the Communist Party of Germany in the eighth German Federal Election on November 21, 1932, and 44% for the Nazi Party and 12% for the Communist Party of Germany in the ninth German Federal Election on March 5, 1933. In other words, a large portion of the electorate did *not* support antidemocratic parties.

This factoid suggests a very different world from one in which an overwhelming majority of the German public voted for the Nazis. Knowing this factoid might lead us to ask a question requiring systematic data: When democracies perish, how much support for the antidemocratic forces is there in the public at large? This question has a real normative punch, because it is another way of asking whether mass electorates can be trusted with democracy. And then: If mass electorates can be trusted and the problem is antidemocratic elites, how can we protect democracy from its elite enemies? If you find these questions interesting, you can learn more in Bermeo (2003).

An interesting related question, perhaps falling closer to psychology or history than political science, is why it is such a common belief that the Nazis won in a democratic election. Perhaps this (false) belief is popular because it leads to an interesting story and a "paradox" of democracy – What should be done if an antidemocratic party wins in a democratic election? – or perhaps it simply arose from a misunderstanding of historical writings.

Theory

Perhaps you've already discerned the structure I tried to set up in my description of research trajectories: on the one side the facts, on the other side normative evaluation and possibly prescriptive design, and in the middle causal mechanisms or theory. Thus: facts to theory to normative evaluation/prescription. In this framework, the careful elaboration of causal mechanisms – the theory – is the key component connecting data to practical recommendations. This emphasis on theory, and the willingness to concede it primacy, makes political science quite different from slow journalism.

Theory is not an end in itself, or at least no more than barefoot empiricism is. One wants theory because one wants to make sense of a mountain of brute facts (on the one hand) and to guide normative evaluations and policy or design prescriptions (on the other). From this perspective, nothing is more practical than a good theory.

But what's a good theory? I used that phrase as if it were obvious what makes a theory good. Unfortunately, it isn't. As silly as it may sound to non–social scientists, the proper standard for evaluating theories frays tempers in many departments. In fact, a few years ago, hundreds of political scientists attending the big national convention went around wearing little colored buttons to show their allegiance to one side or the other in the "theory wars," sort of like the Ghebbellines and Guelphs in the Middle Ages – or, perhaps I should say, like kids in the color wars at a summer camp. One could get a laugh out of grown people behaving this way if professional advancement and status weren't so tied up in it. Which, of course, is why things get so heated.

This is not the time or place to provide a detailed exegesis of political science's theory wars. Also, I am hardly a neutral party. But people love controversy, so let me just sketch the basic contours.

I have suggested that, in the realm of quantitative techniques, political scientists are the magpies of the social sciences. This is true for theory as well. If you look at classic works of political science from the 1950s and 1960s, you find that their authors borrowed heavily from sociology and social psychology. More recently, political scientists have borrowed heavily from the theories of economics and cognitive psychology. Some of this shift just involves keeping up with developments in other fields. But many political scientists see compelling reasons to move from a vague, ad hoc style that I associate with sociology to a more theory-based approach that I associate more with economics. Basically, these political scientists want their work to have strong microfoundations, they want the logic of their arguments to be as tight as possible, and they want the evidence they use to be closely tied to theory (which, in turn, demands clear theory).

This sounds fine in the abstract, but if you push really hard on strong microfoundations, tight logic, and clear theory, you can end up in some surprising places. One place is "rational choice theory," which isn't a theory at all but a set of theoretical impulses (or bets) plus a formidable toolbox. The theoretical impulse is that many people approach politics instrumentally, that is, they have something they want from politics and they go about getting it in a fairly sensible way. The theory is silent about what people want from politics – you can fill in that blank any way you want (including "feeling good about yourself" or "meeting your civic obligations"). The toolbox includes decision theory, standard noncooperative game theory, evolutionary game theory, agent-based modeling, and so on: lots of math-based tools.

It is quite incorrect to see rational choice theory as hegemonic in political science, in the way it truly is in economics. But it is the single most cohesive theoretical movement and is well represented in all four fields, especially American politics. Not surprisingly, it has provoked a backlash (and did so from its first appearance in the early 1960s).

The backlash takes two forms. The first comes from people who are not opposed to theory in theory, just in practice. These critics are typically very fact-oriented, skeptical about the empirical reach of any theoretical framework, and hostile to pure theory as a waste of time. Sometimes they also dislike quantitative work, because they are suspicious of generalization in any form. (This tends to be the case in comparative politics and international relations.) Thus, these critics tend to favor work that is historical or semianthropological in style. But sometimes the "hostile in practice" critics are very quantitatively oriented, but in an exclusively inductive fashion. This tends to be the case in American politics, for example. Members of the latter group typically favor the older social psychological mode of work.

The second group of critics are not just opposed to rational choice theory in practice; they are opposed in theory. To see where they are coming from, recall that old quip about the difference between economics and sociology: "Economics is about how people make choices; sociology is about how they have no choices to make." If you think about this, you can see that both points of view have validity. On the one hand, people are constantly making choices, including ones they see as important. Understanding what they are doing, as they perceive it, seems worthwhile. On the other hand, our lives are severely constrained by our economic situation, our understanding of the world, how we see ourselves (our identity), and how other people perceive us. From this perspective, the room for individual choices is relatively uninteresting; the interesting part is where the constraints come from and how they change.

You can take any of these positions – rational choice, inductive/historical, or sociological/constructivist – and argue for or against it in the abstract and make a seemingly convincing case. Well, of course! Otherwise, bright people wouldn't hold to them. In this sense, the theory wars strongly resemble arguments in theology or literary criticism, a fact that has not gone unnoticed. But social science isn't theology or lit crit, or at least I don't think it should be. To me, the test of a methodological position is: Does it deliver the goods? In other words, can you use the ideas to produce really compelling social science, what they call "killer apps" in Silicon Valley? If you can, I'm willing to listen. If you can't, then the sound of angels dancing on pins becomes deafening.

In the examples we'll pursue, I will employ the rational choice approach because I will ask: Why are people doing this? And the answers I come up with typically have the form: They had a reason, that is, they were trying to get something, and this appeared to be a good way to do it. You can decide for yourself whether this approach seems methodologically suspect in these cases.

Exercises

1. *American Politics.* "The Democrats will win elections if they stand for something. They should forget moderates and concentrate on getting out their base." "The Republicans have lost their way because they have abandoned their conservative principles." Perhaps you have heard one or both of these claims. Design a research strategy that would provide hard quantitative evidence on whether the claims are true or false.

2. *American Politics.* In his book *What's the Matter with Kansas?* (2004), journalist Thomas Frank claims that the Republican Party has forged a dominant political coalition by convincing lower-middle-class Americans to vote against their own economic interests in an effort to defend traditional cultural values against radical bicoastal elites. Have lower-middle-class whites abandoned the Democratic Party due to a conflict over values? Is this argument correct or incorrect? How could you tell? Describe the data and the statistical methods you would need to evaluate the argument. Hint: After you have thought about this for a while, look at Bartels (2006) and the accompanying discussion in the *Quarterly Journal of Political Science*.

3. *Comparative Politics.* Do good political institutions cause prosperity or does prosperity bring good political institutions? Consider this question from the perspective of instrumental variables. You may need to reread this section in your statistics textbook. After you have thought about it for a while, read Acemoglu, Johnson, and Robinson (2002). How does their article alter your thinking?

4. *International Relations.* Does peace cause democracy or does democracy cause peace? Again, discuss this question from an instrumental variable's perspective and in light of Acemoglu et al. (2002).

16. The Politics of Supreme Court Nominations: The Critical Role of the Media Environment

In this chapter and the next, we'll work through an extended empirical political analysis involving the politics of Supreme Court nominations. I'll present this material in approximately the way the analysis took place, rather than in the cleaned-up and artificially neat way one presents it in a seminar or paper. I'll begin by reviewing an earlier study on how senators vote on Supreme Court nominations. The voting analysis raises a puzzle, apparently concerning the choices presidents make when they select nominees. But, as we shall see, the puzzle isn't really about presidents at all. Rather, the puzzle involves how the news media portray nominees and (ultimately) how hostile members of the Judiciary Committee manipulate the media environment in order to damage nominees. Or so I claim.

The point of these chapters is to show how a real analysis unfolds, which takes place in a way that is quite different from what one might think after reading journal articles or scholarly books. So, as we go, I'll discuss some personal background, the places where I was stumped, how luck entered in, where the ideas came from, and how I dealt with measurement issues. I'll also make comments about various statistical techniques and choices. The following chapter will consider the interplay of theory and data as well.

THE SPATIAL MODEL OF VOTING

We start with the basic model that political scientists use to describe voting based on issue positions. This so-called spatial model is commonly used to characterize voters in an election, but here we will use it to describe U.S. senators deciding whether to vote to confirm nominees for the Supreme Court. The central idea comes out of mathematical psychology. (Remember when I said that political scientists often use methods developed in other social sciences? This is a case in point.) The original psychological question was: How can you tell if two objects, like a ball and a bat, are similar or different? Well, define some dimensions on which to measure the objects – weight, color, shape, and so on. The Cartesian product of these dimensions defines a space, and the characteristics of the ball and bat then yield two vectors in the hyperspace.

To put it another way: Suppose there are three continuous dimensions, which you can think of as the three dimensions of the room you're in: length, breadth, and height. A specific item measured on these dimensions (length, breadth, and height) then becomes a point (a vector) in this three-dimensional space. Another item with somewhat different characteristics then becomes another point in the space. For example, you could have one object at (.25, .25, .5) and another at (.75, .75, .75). The triple (x, y, z) indicates the position of the items in terms of length, breadth, and height.

Now define a distance metric in the space, in other words, a yardstick for measuring the distance between the two points. One such measure is the Euclidean distance based on the Pythagorean formula you studied in school. In this case, the distance between object 1 and object 2 is

$$d_{12} = \sqrt{(x_1 - x_2)^2 + (y_1 - y_2)^2 + (z_1 - z_2)^2}.$$

In our example, this would be

$d_{12} = \sqrt{(.25 - .75)^2 + (.25 - .75)^2 + (.5 - .75)^2} = .75$. In the psychological setup, you can use this metric to see how closely two items resemble each other.

You can play with the distance metric in various ways. For example, you can add weights to each dimension to indicate which ones are more important or less important (these are called "saliency weights" by political scientists). You can replace the squares with absolute values and dispense with the square root. You can dispense with the square root and just used the squared distance. And so on. You get the basic idea.

Political scientists stole this shiny piece of technology for their own purposes. Suppose the dimensions in the figure represent political dimensions of some sort. For example, we can represent a candidate's general domestic policy liberalism as a location on one dimension, her general foreign policy position on another, and her position on some issue I particularly care about on the third. A point in the space then represents a candidate. And suppose I have preferences about policies – in particular, suppose I have a favorite policy point or location in the space, my "ideal point." Then I can say which of two candidates is closer to my ideal position. If I am choosing between them, say in an election, I can vote for the closer of the two if I wish.

In fact, you can use the distance from the ideal point as a measure of the "utility" of one candidate or alternative. Then we imagine voters choosing the alternative with the greater utility, which is equivalent to saying that they choose the closer of two alternatives in the space.[1]

This set of tools has proven incredibly useful in political science, so much so that representing policies, laws, and candidates in spatial terms has become ubiquitous. For example, as an empirical matter, congressmembers appear to act as if they have a stable ideal point in a one-dimensional space, bills come with a location in the space (a number), and congressmembers vote for the closer bill

---

[1] In some circumstances, it might be better to vote for a more distant alternative rather than the closest one – for example, if you know that voting for the closest alternative is just "throwing your vote away," while voting for a somewhat more distant choice can head off a really bad outcome. Any textbook on game theory and politics will explain situations like this in detail if you are interested (Ordeshook 1968). For more on spatial theory, see Enelow and Hinich (1984).

when they can (Poole and Rosenthal 1997). This policy space looks like a generic "liberal–conservative" dimension. At times during history, Congress appears more two-dimensional, with the second dimension typically related to race or geographically specific issues. But those times are relatively rare, and at present Congress looks very one-dimensional.

VOTING ON SUPREME COURT NOMINEES

Define two variables: q_j, the "perceived qualifications" of nominee j, and d_{ij}, the ideological distance between senator i and nominee j.[2] We measured these using newspaper editorials: We had research assistants gather and code hundreds of editorials from liberal and conservative newspapers. To get q_j, we had them code the percentage of editorials that said that the nominee was "qualified" to be on the Court. To get the ideological position of the nominee, we coded the percentage of editorials that said that the nominee was "liberal." (The variable was actually measured on a scale from -1 to 1.)

Coding of this sort is called "content analysis," which is an almost absurdly fancy term for reading newspaper stories carefully. What separates content analysis from just perusing the newspaper is how systematic you are. We tried to be very systematic. For example, we wrote down rules for what counted as statements in the editorials. We employed several different coders and, using random samples, made sure that there was a high degree of intercoder reliability among them.[3] If you used the same rules and practiced a little, and then read and coded the stories yourself, I am confident that your results would strongly resemble ours – at least for ideology. The coders had some trouble getting consistent results on "quality" – they tended to pick up editorial endorsements and the general tone of the editorials. With practice, however, they seemed to get better at coding whether the editorialists said that the nominee was qualified to serve on the Supreme Court.

We wanted a measure of d_{ij}, the ideological distance between senator i and nominee j, so we also needed a measure of each senator's ideology. To get that, we used ratings from the liberal interest group Americans for Democratic Action (ADA). Today, I would use the professional standard, the Poole-Rosenthal NOMINATE scores, which I mentioned in Chapter 15. You will recall that these are derived from scaling every roll call vote ever taken in Congress. The NOMINATE scores come in slightly different flavors, but the better ones to use here would be those that are comparable over time. The ADA scores fail in this regard, but I'll pass over that point here. It turns out that, for our analysis, if we had used the NOMINATE scores, the substantive results would have been unchanged.

---

[2] Because every senator presumably finds better qualifications more attractive, perceived qualifications is a "valence dimension," in the jargon of spatial theory. There is an interesting literature on valence dimensions in politics, but we don't need to go into all the details.

[3] If you want to learn more about how social scientists use content analysis, you can read Weber (1990).

A tricky issue is that our measure of nominee ideology and our measure of senator ideology weren't measured on the same scale. You can think of the two scales as being something like Fahrenheit and Celsius scales for temperature. You can easily look up a formula for converting Fahrenheit into Celsius, but we had no such formula for these ideological measures. However, we needed one so that we could calculate distances between senators and nominees. We solved this problem with brute force.[4] That is, we assumed that the conversion formula between the two was linear (of the form $y = ax + b$), calculated many such conversions, and ran the analysis over and over to see what conversion weights seemed to work best. A lot of subsequent work has gone into trying to find a common scale for congressmembers, presidents, and Supreme Court justices, and different methods have different strengths and weaknesses. Fortunately, these voting data are so strongly structured that the results are fairly insensitive to which method you use.

What did we find? To a surprising degree, senators appeared to vote as if they were using the following distance metric:

$$d_{ij} = b_1 + b_2(1 - q_j) + b_3 \left(x_j - x_i\right)^2 + b_4(1 - q_j)\left(x_j - i\right)^2 \qquad (1)$$

Then senators would vote "yes" if d_{ij} was below a critical threshold and "no" if it was above.

Let me explain equation (1) a little more. The first term is just a constant. The second term measures perceived lack of qualifications, since perceived qualifications are on a 0–1 scale. The coefficient b_2 indicates the weight for lack of qualifications; this is a parameter you estimate from the data. The third term is the ideological distance between the senator and the nominee, with x_j being the measure for the nominee and x_i being the measure for the senator. I've explained how we measured those. The coefficient b_3 is the weight on this term, again estimated from the data. The fourth term is an "interaction" between lack of quality and distance: For highly qualified nominees or very close candidates, the term is small. But for poorly qualified, distant ones, it is large. The coefficient b_4 measures the importance of this term.

It turns out that this model provides an elegant and powerful description of senators' voting behavior on Supreme Court nominees, at least from 1937 to 1994. I emphasize description, since it's important to remember that all regression equations like this one are just summary descriptions of patterns in data. By themselves, they don't explain anything; supplying interpretation – in terms of causal mechanisms – is up to you. Anyway, I now know that the equation misses a few things; for example, after the *Brown v. Board of Eduction* Supreme Court decision, southern Democrats voted against a sequence of nominees they saw as racial liberals. This pattern ended shortly after the enactment of the Voting Rights Act. Then the equation kicked in again for southern Democrats. But improvements in the equation are not what I want to discuss.

Rather, I want to get back to the question, What does the equation mean substantively? Superficially, the equation says that a senator will vote in favor of a nominee if the senator likes the nominee enough – that is, if the senator sees the

---

[4] In the next chapter, I'll describe a method Jee-Kwang Park and I derived that I think is much better.

nominee as qualified and ideologically proximate. But in fact, the estimated weights in the equation say something much more intriguing than this. Consider the "quality" variable, q_j. Pick a high number, such as .8, so that the nominee is perceived as being of high quality. Then all the senators will vote for the nominee, regardless of their ideology. In other words, the nomination is consensual, and this is true even for ideologically extreme nominees. Now pick a low number for q_j, like .3. Senators who are close to the nominee lie on high contours, but those who are more distant from the nominee lie on low contours. So, the nominee's ideological soul mates vote for the nominee even if he or she is a "turkey," but those farther away vote against the nominee. The nomination becomes conflictual and ideologically polarized. This can happen only if the nominee is of low quality.

If you think about this for a moment, it should strike you as rather weird. It says that an extreme liberal like Ted Kennedy will vote for an extreme conservative, like Antonin Scalia, if Scalia is perceived as being of high quality by the editorialists (this actually happened, by the way). And an extreme conservative will vote for an extremely liberal nominee if she is perceived as being of high quality. In effect this occurred with the nomination of Arthur Goldberg and the initial nomination of Abe Fortas, in which conservatives acquiesced to a voice vote. But we haven't had a situation like this in a while.

Now you can see the first puzzle raised by the empirical results, which is: Why do senators behave this way? Why (as a senator) can you vote against someone you hate ideologically only if he or she is also a turkey on quality grounds? This is good puzzle indeed, but it's not one we will consider right now. So, let me continue laying out essentially the same results in a different way. This will help you see the magnitude of the effects we're talking about.

Let's switch from individual roll call votes to aggregate Yes–No votes for nonwithdrawn nominees between 1937 and 2005 (through the Roberts nomination). The data on individual votes allow us to connect senators' behavior to some well-developed theory, but if you are interested in the politics of Supreme Court nominations – especially outcomes – it's aggregate votes you really care about.

Figure 16.1 shows the distribution of Yeas and Nays in votes on Supreme Court nominations between 1937 and 2005. When there was a roll call vote on a nomination, I use the split in the actual roll call vote; for cases with a voice vote, I count the nomination as a unanimous Yes vote. So, the figure shows you the number of nominations with percent Yes votes in various ranges.

The key point to gain from Figure 16.1 is that most nominations are consensual, with all or almost all senators voting Yes. But there are quite a few nominations that are not consensual – there are substantial numbers of No votes. Incidentally, if we looked at all the data from Reconstruction period on, the pattern would be almost exactly the same.

If you put the logics of equation (1) and Figure 16.1 together, you can make a pretty sharp guess on which nominations are consensual and which are conflictual – in other words, where the No votes come from: No votes tend to occur when the nominee is perceived by the editorialists as of poor quality. Moreover, if you suspect that Democratic presidents typically nominate rather liberal justices

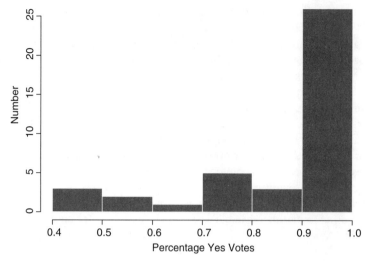

Figure 16.1. Distribution of the proportion of Yes votes in the Senate for all nonwithdrawn Supreme Court nominations, 1937–2005.

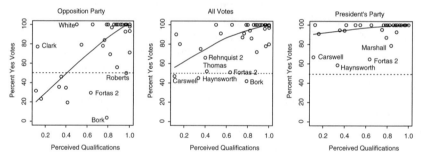

Figure 16.2 Percentage of Yes votes in the Senate as a function of perceived qualifications for Supreme Court nominations, 1937–2005.

and Republicans rather conservative ones (which is exactly what happens), then from equation (1) you might suspect that low qualifications provoke more No votes from members of the opposition party than from members of the president's party.

Figure 16.2 confirms these conjectures. What is shown is the percentage of Yes votes as a function of the nominee's perceived qualifications for each nomination from 1937 to 2005 (through Roberts) that went to the floor. (In other words, the data exclude the three nominations in that period that were withdrawn before a vote was taken: Homer Thornberry, Douglas Ginsburg, and Harriet Miers.) The middle panel displays votes from both parties; the panel on the left shows the relationship for members of the opposition party, while the panel on the right shows it for members of the president's party. The lines in the panels are the fits from highly flexible, nonparametric regression models, locally weighted regressions, so-called lowess lines (Cleveland 1979).[5] I love using lowess regressions when exploring data. They let you see the main patterns in the data very clearly, including essential nonlinearities.

Let's start with the middle figure, which presents the overall relationship across both parties. As shown, the relationship seems clear and pretty strong. Particularly interesting, though, are those nominations that are unusually low. So, I've indicated which nominations those are. The percentages of Yes votes in the nominations of G. Harrold Carswell and William Rehnquist to be chief justice are low but seem in line with the overall pattern. However, the percentages of Yes votes in the nominations of Clement Haynsworth, Clarence Thomas, Abe Fortas for chief justice, and especially Robert Bork appear unusually low.

Now consider the left and right panels. One immediately perceives a dramatic difference in the behavior of members of the opposition party and the president's party. In the opposition party, support for the nominee plummets if his or her perceived qualifications are low. But support remains quite strong in the president's party, even for nominees whose qualifications are said to be poor in the newspaper editorials.[6] One can see in the figures that opposition Republicans displayed unusual mobilization against Abe Fortas (for chief justice), as did the Democrats against Robert Bork. In-party Republicans displayed unusually low support for Carswell and Haynsworth, and in-party Democrats showed unusually low support for Thurgood Marshall and Abe Fortas for chief justice. The Marshall defections reflect the opposition of southern Democrats to the first African American nominated to the Supreme Court.

Among the "safe" or consensual nominations, only 16% of the nominees were scored with low qualifications. Among the failed nominations, 100% received low qualifications ratings from the editorialists. Among the polarized nominations, two-thirds received low qualifications ratings from the editorialists.

PROBABILITY OF CONFIRMATION

To look at the situation in one more way, consider the probability that nominees are confirmed simply as a function of their perceived qualifications. Essentially, if the president nominates someone with a perceived qualifications score above .8, the chance of approval is very high. But if he nominates someone whose score is below about .6, the chance of approval falls dramatically. Unsurprisingly, a simple logistic regression finds perceived qualifications to be a statistically significant predictor of approval.

The conclusion is clear: If the president nominates someone whom the editorialists score as highly qualified, the nomination will probably be consensual. Even if it isn't, it will probably avoid serious trouble. Conversely, if the

---

[5] If one runs simple linear regressions, the coefficients on perceived qualifications are highly statistically significant in all three cases, with intercepts and slopes (respectively) of 26 and 69 (opposition party), 58 and 39 (all votes), and 81 and 19 (president's party). I will present some regressions like this one shortly.

[6] At this level of aggregation, one cannot say whether the difference across the parties is due entirely to ideological distance or to some particular "party" factor, though regressions at the individual level suggest that any such party factor is small relative to ideological distance.

president nominates someone the editorialists perceive as low in quality, the nomination may fail. Even if it succeeds, there may well be a serious struggle in the Senate.

THE PUZZLE ... OR IS IT?

The puzzle should now be clear: If presidents can get whatever they want ideologically just by nominating the sort of person newspaper editorialists like, why do presidents ever nominate someone the editorialists see as a turkey?

I certainly didn't believe that presidents would deliberately choose poorly qualified nominees. (This analysis preceded Harriet Miers's nomination, which is hard to explain using any theory of rational presidential choice.) It was obvious that something big was going on with nominations beyond the narrow bounds of our spatial model. But what?

I didn't know, and that's where things sat for several years, until I joined the faculty at Columbia and (of course) had to teach several courses each year. The department at Columbia prided itself on offering small, intense, research-oriented seminars to seniors majoring in political science, and there was always a need for such courses. I didn't have a lot of big lecture-type courses ready, so I volunteered to teach a senior seminar on the politics of Supreme Court nominations. The course proved to be fairly popular, so I taught it for several years.

I had the good fortune to have a string of terrific students in the course. These students had little sense of modern social science research – perhaps this book will be a help here – but they were extremely bright and extraordinarily hard-working, and they needed topics for their seminar papers. So I dreamed up a series of questions that someone who didn't know any statistics or game theory would have a fair chance of answering through hard work alone. Most of these involved rather intense data collection, such as counting every question asked a nominee during the Judiciary Committee hearings or finding all the occasions when presidents "went public" on behalf of nominees.

Most of the students seemed to enjoy doing these papers. The idea that you can ask a clear social scientific question, collect systematic data, and then actually nail the question seemed to be a revelation to most of them. I was delighted that some graduated with honors as a result of their papers. One student even went on to graduate school in political science and now has a successful academic career (I claim no credit for her success).

A paper I wasn't enthusiastic about was one several students proposed, on scandals and Supreme Court nominations. The subject seemed rather frivolous. But once I got the students to formulate a clear research design (which – surprise – involved systematically collecting and coding newspaper stories), I was willing to let them try it.

ENTER SCANDALS

The students worked hard, and after several months they brought back the data in Table 16.1. In retrospect, they didn't get things quite right but they came pretty close.

Table 16.1. *Scandals and results of Senate confirmations for*
U.S. Supreme Court nominations, 1937–1994

	No Scandal	Scandal	
Confirmed	27	6	33
	1	4	5
Not Confirmed	28	10	38

A table like this ought to send shivers up the spine of any social scientist who likes data. It certainly did mine! What does it say? In 96% of nominations without scandals, the nominee was confirmed. In nominations with scandals, this figure was only 60%. Wow! But hold on. Perhaps this apparently striking difference is due to the smaller number of nominations with scandals – the supposed difference could be due to chance, given the smaller numbers. So, let's check with a chi-square test (easy to do with my handy computer). I calculate the chi square as 5.7 with 1 degree of freedom, which is statistically significant, indicating a lack of independence. In short, it is highly unlikely that the apparent difference in the confirmation rates between scandalous and nonscandalous nominations is due to chance alone.

Well, then, case solved! Presidents don't nominate turkeys. Rather, presidents nominate apparently good candidates. Some then turn out to be turkeys. Being a turkey tanks your perceived qualification score and provokes a conflictual vote, a withdrawal, or even a turn-down.

This may be true, but we haven't shown it yet. And (I will argue) this simple understanding may be a little naive about scandals. But let's take things one at a time.

WHAT DRIVES "PERCEIVED QUALIFICATIONS"?

I am going to cheat a little at this point. What actually happened was that I got excited about scandals and went back and coded the newspapers extremely carefully for a much longer range of time (starting with the Reconstruction period that followed the Civil War). Then I started thinking about the strategic role of scandals in nominations. It was only later that I collected the data we are going to look at now. We'll take up strategy and scandals in the next chapter.

Next, I want to consider the question of what seems to drive the evaluations of the editorialists. What is being captured by our "perceived qualifications" measure? To answer the question, I am going to introduce three new variables:

Objective qualifications: A scale from 0 to 3, on which a nominee receives 1 point each if he or she has (1) served as a judge at either the state or federal level, (2) held a responsible position in the executive branch as a lawyer (for example, solicitor general or deputy attorney general), or (3) been a professor in a law school. This variable has a mean of 1.7, and half of the observations fall between 1 and 2.

Negative tone of media coverage ("*tone*"): The percentage of stories in *The New York Times* about the nominee that report "bad news," including improper behavior, poor qualifications, protests by groups and mobilization against the nominee, or extreme ideological positions. The mean for this variable is 22%, and half of the observations lie between 7% and 33%.[7]

Ideological extremity: Since ideology was measured on a −1 to 1 scale, extremity is just the absolute value of ideology. It has a mean of .59, and half of the observations fall between .40 and .81.

The connections between these variables and perceived qualifications, as indicated in editorials, are obvious. The variable "tone" provides a measure of overall media coverage, while "objective qualifications," "scandal," and "extremity" provide more detailed looks at the likely content of the media coverage.

Before undertaking any statistical analysis, it's always a good idea simply to look at the data. You'll be surprised how often you find data entry mistakes and miscodes or see a relationship you hadn't thought about. One useful device is a scatterplot matrix, which most statistical packages will produce. In doing this, we found perceived qualifications to be strongly (negatively) related to negative media tone, somewhat correlated with objective qualifications and scandals, and not particularly related to extremism.

Now let's do the thing most political scientists would find natural, which is to start running linear regressions. Let me warn you, though: The models I am going to show you next are terrible models of the data. They fundamentally misrepresent what's actually happening in the data. So, let's see if you can find out why, just from the results as they come out of the computer.

The estimated coefficients and standard errors for several different models are shown in Table 16.2. As you can see, they actually look pretty good – many of the coefficients are more than two standard errors away from zero, indicating statistical significance at the usual 5% level – except perhaps that objective qualifications don't seem to have any impact and extremism has the wrong sign. But you can easily rationalize the latter finding: It might be that presidents who want to nominate ideologically extreme nominees pick particularly attractive people to offset their extremity.

I've already suggested that we shouldn't be content with these results. The most important things to check in a linear regression model are nonlinearity and interactions. Basically, you have to worry about assuming that a variable comes in linearly when it doesn't.

In the example here, a key issue is interactions. How can you check quickly and easily for interactions? One approach is to use conditioning plots, so-called co-plots. Co-plots are an extremely elegant and extraordinarily powerful visual device for detecting interactions. Surprisingly, they are not widely used by political scientists. I suppose this is because they were invented fairly recently by

[7] To identify the stories, I first searched the digital *New York Times* via Proquest, using the name of the nominee, from the time she was nominated until the date the nomination ended. Then I eliminated all stories that were not centrally about the nominee rather than a peripheral mention; these central stories are the denominator (but the statistical results don't change much if you just use the raw count of stories mentioning the nominee). Then I coded the central stories for "bad news" as defined previously.

Table 16.2. *Estimated coefficients (and standard errors) for coefficients in regression models predicting Supreme Court nominees' perceived qualifications*

	Model 1	Model 2	Model 3	Model 4
Intercept	.96 (.05)	97 (.05)	.89 (.09)	.82 (.09)
Tone	−.90 (.18)	−.67 (.20)	−.62 (.20)	−.76 (.20)
Scandal	—	−.19 (.08)	−.20 (.08)	−.19 (.08)
Objective qualifications	—	—	.04 (.04)	.02 (.04)
Extremism	—	—	—	.23 (.11)
Degrees of freedom	39	38	37	36
R^2	.38	.47	.48	.54

Note: Cases are all nominations from 1937 to 2005. It would be better to display these estimates and uncertainties graphically (thus making comparisons clearer), but we show them as a table here to illustrate the common practice in social science research.

a statistician and don't appear in econometrics textbooks, which is where most political scientists learn statistics.[8] You can learn more about co-plots in Cleveland (1993), a wonderful book that I recommend highly to anyone who likes to interrogate numbers.

The basic idea in a co-plot is to look at a series of bivariate scatterplots (with lowess lines, of course) as you vary a third variable. If the fit in the bivariate scatterplot simply shifts upward or downward as the third variable moves from low to moderate to high, this is evidence of an additive effect from the third variable. But if the slope of the fit in the bivariate scatterplot changes in a major way, this is evidence of an interaction between the third variable and the x-axis variable. (You can vary a fourth variable simultaneously as well.) If an interaction is at all sizable, you will easily see it in a co-plot. In fact, the major danger when using powerful tools like co-plots is not missing something; it's overfitting the data.

So, let's take a look at the relationship between perceived qualifications and tone as we vary scandal. Since scandal only takes the value 0 or 1, this is about as simple a co-plot as you can get. It is shown in Figure 16.3, where the left panel shows the relationship between perceived qualifications and tone for the nominees without a scandal and the right panel shows the relationship for those with a scandal.

Figure 16.3 screams interaction. As you can see, if the nomination process failed to uncover a scandal, perceived qualifications were unrelated to negative media tone. In fact, media tone was mostly positive (less than .3) and perceived qualifications were favorable (above .8).[9] But if there was a scandal, perceived

[8] Sometimes political scientists call their statistics "econometrics" even though their work involves no economic theory. It's because they learned their statistics from econometrics books.
[9] The two obvious outliers are Sherman Minton and Harriet Miers, both of whom had low objective qualifications and had engaged in partisan political activity.

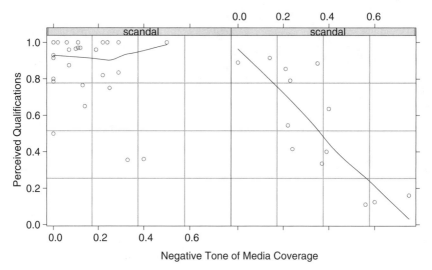

Figure 16.3 Conditioning plot of perceived qualifications, negative tone of media coverage, and scandal for Supreme Court nominations, 1937–2005.

qualifications were very strongly related to media tone. Here, most observations were greater than .3 for tone (that is, more negative in tone) and less than .8 for perceived qualifications.

Table 16.3 displays some simple linear regression fits exploring the interaction. The first two columns show models run separately for nominations with and without scandal. These strongly confirm the pattern in Figure 16.3. (Additional variables add little to these models, so I do not show them.) The third column shows the obvious model for all nominations: tone and scandal as main effects, plus the interaction between tone and scandal. The model suggests that only the interaction is doing any work. The final model forces the main effects to zero to focus on the interaction. Some analysts strongly object to dropping main effects in models with interactions, but little changes from the model with the direct effects.

What does this all tell us? One plausible interpretation is that negative media tone picks up a variety of information about the nominees, all sorts of bad news and possibly good news too. But a scandal is particularly bad news and it has a kind of double whammy on the editorialists, especially if it's a bad scandal.

Let's check this possibility by running some regressions on media tone and qualifications versus the content variables (scandal, objective qualifications, and extremism). These are shown in Table 16.4.

As you can see, the regressions suggest that perceived qualifications are largely driven by scandal: The presence of a scandal drops perceived qualifications by about 33 points. You will recall that a drop like this is usually enough to shift a nomination from consensual to conflictual. The coefficient for "Objective qualifications" has a plausible sign (although not statistically significant, being less than two standard errors from zero), so one might count this result as suggestive. "Extremism" seems to have the wrong sign, but its effect (if any) is measured very imprecisely.

Table 16.3. *Estimated coefficients (and standard errors) for coefficients in more regression models predicting Supreme Court nominees' perceived qualifications*

	Nominations without scandal	Nominations with scandal	All nominations (Model 1)	All nominations (Model 2)
Intercept	.90(.05)	.96(.10)	.90(.05)	.87(.03)
Tone	−.21(.24)	−1.23(.26)	−.21(.24)	—
Scandal	—	—	0.07(0.12)	—
Tone x Scandal	—	—	−1.01(.36)	−1.03(.15)
Deg of freedom	26	11	37	39
R^2	.03	.66	.56	.54

Table 16.4. *Estimated coefficients (and standard errors) for coefficients in more regression models predicting two different outcomes regarding Supreme Court nominees*

	Perceived qualifications	Negative tone of media	Negative tone – model dropping one case (Clark)
Intercept	.70(.10)	.16(.07)	0.11(.07)
Scandal	−.33(.08)	.18(.05)	0.14(.05)
Objective qualifications	.065(.05)	−.06(.03)	−0.05(.03)
Extremism	.10(.12)	.17(.08)	0.24(.08)
Deg of freedom	37	37	36
R^2	.36	.34	.36

Note: The regression attempts to estimate the effect of good and bad news on perceived qualifications and media tone.

In contrast, the second model suggests that negative media tone responds quite sensibly to good news and bad news about the nominee: Scandal raises negative media tone about 18 percentage points, as does extremism. Better objective qualifications are associated with a reduction in negative media tone, about 5 percentage points for every 1-point difference in qualifications. This is about the same magnitude uncovered in the previous regression, but it is estimated more precisely.

Examination of the residuals from the tone model uncovers little, except one moderately influential outlier (Clark again). The issue is that opposition support for Clark was unusually high, given the media tone. It might be worthwhile to recheck the Clark data to make sure that the coding was correct. However, if we drop the Clark observation and run the analysis again, the substantive results are very similar. So that you can see what I regard as little substantive change, I show this as the third model in the table. If the effects had been large and the data continued to look fine, I might consider using robust methods to down weigh the observation without dropping it altogether. Fortunately, it doesn't appear to be very consequential. And this time, examination of co-plots finds little evidence of important interactions. Thus, a simple additive model seems to represent the structure in the tone data pretty well.

VOTES RECONSIDERED

We now see that the variable perceived qualifications, coded from newspaper editorials, is largely a proxy for bad news in the form of scandals, as reported in news reports. So, suppose we go back to the original model that we devised for individual roll call votes and substitute the variable scandal for the variable perceived qualifications. What do you think happens? I leave this as an exercise for you to do. But perhaps you will believe me when I suggest that you will get substantively similar results.

FITTING THE MODEL

Estimating parametric models for the data is not straightforward since the possibilities are numerous, once one admits the possibility of interactions and nonlinearities – and that's considering just three input variables! There is a tension between wanting to keep the models simple to avoid overfitting and wanting to capture evident patterns in the data. And many models will fit the data essentially equally well. But the different models will often have different substantive interpretations.

So, what should you do? In the absence of a theory strong enough to specify which variables to include and what functional form to employ – in other words, almost all the time in political science – we are well into "art." Different people have different philosophies about this. In my view, you need to get to know the data well. This means using visualization aggressively and running a great many models but being extremely skeptical about each one. After a while, if you think hard about what you find, you will get a feel for robust patterns in the data. By "robust," I mean patterns that almost certainly exist and that don't hinge on tweaking the specification in just the right way or including or dropping a critical outlier. In my view, you should report the models that highlight only these robust patterns, rather than the models with the best R^2 or most impressive t-statistics. Then you can feel confident about the results, and you don't have to worry about everything falling apart the next time you get a new observation.

I should note a corollary to this "get to know the data" philosophy: It becomes almost impossible to really know the data once the number of predictor variables becomes large. The possible specifications proliferate beyond anyone's capacity to grasp. Political methodologist Chris Achen has formulated a "Rule of Three": Don't believe regression results that include more than about three predictor variables. Because, almost certainly, the analyst doesn't really understand what's going on in the data (Achen 2002).[10]

---

[10] Here we are referring to predictors that you use to explain the outcome causally. It's certainly okay to include many predictors as control variables: for example, predictors such as age, sex, education, and ethnicity, which can capture some of the variability in a model of individual-level survey data.

To return to our example, let me suggest a few models for the aggregate voting data that satisfy Achen's Rule. (I urge you to try fitting some models yourself.) First, let's begin by fitting the opposition and copartisans separately, using tone and scandal. In other words, let's fit the top and bottom halves of Figure 16.4 separately. This will allow the intercepts and slopes to float freely, at the cost of smaller numbers of observations. Let's try the simplest additive model, and then include an interaction between tone and scandal. (I checked for nonlinearities in tone using a quadratic specification, but I won't show you the results since they don't suggest robust nonlinearities even in the lower right panel in Figure 16.3.)

These models are shown in Table 16.5. What are the take-away points? First, the intercepts in all four models look about the same, just as we saw in Figure 16.3. Second, in both populations, the main effects have the correct signs, seem to have plausible magnitudes (given what we know from Figure 16.4), and appear to differ across the two populations in the way we expect. They also are statistically significantly different from zero, except when the "Tone × Scandal" interaction is included, in which case little is statistically significant. This is not unusual if the main effects and interaction display a high degree of multicollinearity. Especially in models with relatively small numbers of observations, it becomes difficult to measure effects precisely.

An obvious way to get more precise estimates is to pool the two populations while allowing some flexibility to capture important differences. An obvious strategy here is to force the same intercept across the two populations, estimate common main effects across the populations, and then estimate "add-on" main effects between the populations. This allows us to test whether the main effects actually do differ across the populations and to see how big the differences are. Because Figure 16.3 so strongly suggests an interaction, we can add the interaction to the basic additive model. But in the interest of avoiding overfitting, we can force the interaction to be constant across the populations. This is a middle path between overfitting and underfitting.

The results are shown in the rightmost two columns of Table 16.5. What are the main take-away points here? The tactic of pooling has increased the precision of the estimates without substantially changing their magnitudes from the earlier estimates. The coefficients on "Tone" and "Scandal" in Model 1 are essentially the same as those in Model 1a in Table 16.5. The coefficient on "Tone × Copartisan" added to the "Tone" coefficient mimics that coefficient on "Tone" in Model 2a in Table 16.5, and similarly for the "Scandal" coefficients. As you can see, the magnitudes are about the same. We can test the difference between the two populations, captured by "Tone × Copartisan" and "Scandal × Copartisan." As you can see, the differences appear to be real. The "Tone × Scandal" interaction has the right sign and a plausible magnitude but is not statistically significant at the 95% level (the estimate is less than two standard errors from zero).

Are we done yet? No, because we need to examine residuals (always) and check for influential outliers. Doing so uncovers what one might expect: The two outliers we discussed in the lower right quadrant of Figure 16.3 are large and exert considerable leverage on the results. If we drop either or both of these

Table 16.5. *Estimated coefficients (and standard errors) for coefficients in two regression models predicting total Senate votes (with the opposition party and the president's party considered separately, then pooled), given information on scandal and the tone of the media during the confirmation process*

	Opposition		Copartisans	
	Model 1a	Model 1b	Model 2a	Model 2b
Intercept	100(5)	98(6)	101(2)	100(2)
Tone	−58(21)	−39(29)	−17(9)	−8(12)
Scandal	−27(8)	−18(13)	−7(3)	−2(6)
Tone x Scandal	—	−40(42)	—	−18(18)
Deg of freedom	37	36	37	36
R^2	.50	.51	.28	.30

Table 16.6. *The change in percentage of Yes votes in the Senate for Supreme Court nominees, comparing cases with and without negative media tone*

	Copartisans		Opposition	
	No Scandal	Scandal	No Scandal	Scandal
Estimated separately, no interaction	−17	−17	−58	−58
Estimated jointly, no interaction	−16	−16	−60	−60
Estimated separately, with interaction	−8	−26	−39	−79
Estimated jointly, with interaction	−5	−34	−45	−74

observations, the size of the coefficients in Model 2b in Table 16.5 remain about the same (the shift effect of scandal becomes smaller and the "Scandal × Tone" interaction becomes somewhat larger). But the "Scandal × Tone" interaction becomes strongly statistically significant. A robust regression retaining the two outliers yields coefficients that differ little from those of Model 2b in Table 16.5.

I conclude that Model 2 is a pretty good representation of the aggregate voting data. In my opinion, we shouldn't be overly concerned about the lack of precision in the estimate of the Tone × Scandal interaction because the two outliers misleadingly raise the standard errors on this variable. Analysts who adopt a slavish attitude to *t*-tests would object and insist on the simple additive model. But if you have a good feel for the data, you'll believe that the simple additive model somewhat distorts what is the most likely pattern in the data.

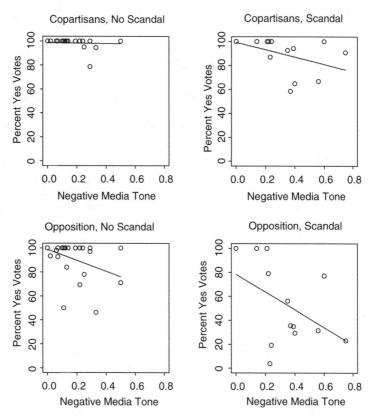

Figure 16.4 Predicting aggregate votes: the fit from the model in Table 16.5.

INTERPRETING THE RESULTS

We still aren't done because we need to understand the substantive size of the estimated effects. This is somewhat complicated in the models with interactions. So, we'll do this in two different ways, first numerically, then visually.

Table 16.6 shows the marginal impact of tone on aggregate votes in the models we estimated in Table 16.5. To get these figures, I just took the partial derivative of aggregate votes with respect to tone. Equivalently, you can set the values of the indicators (scandal, copartisan) to 0 or 1 and add up the coefficients involving tone to get the corresponding marginal effects. This method will work in linear models like this.

As Table 16.6 shows, the effects of negative media tone appear to be substantial. Interestingly, the marginal effect of tone in the simple additive models is approximately an average of the separate "Scandal" and "No scandal" marginal effects in the models with the interaction.

Now consider a nomination without a scandal but with a terrible media tone. The estimated effects suggest that on average the nomination will nonetheless succeed, even when the opposition holds most of the seats in the Senate. But the nomination could be in serious trouble. On average, though, the size of the coefficients suggests that it takes a scandal with adverse media tone to sink a nominee.

Before accepting these results about scandal at face value, though, we should add a condition. Accusations of financial improprieties, racism, or sexual misconduct mobilize the opposition and degrade support among the president's copartisans, especially when the accusations poison the coverage of the nominee in the media. That is the lesson from historical experience, as captured in the data and the models. But accusations of scandal are not the only thing that can mobilize the opposition. Some figures are so polarizing that the opposition behaves as if the nomination itself is a scandal. You can see this in the Bork nomination and also in that of L.Q.C. Lamar, the first southerner nominated to the Court after the Civil War. In both of these cases, the opposition acted as if it were in "scandal mode" despite the lack of any real evidence of misconduct by the nominee.[11] Nominating such figures can be problematic, at least during divided party government when the opposition holds a majority of seats in the Senate.

CONCLUSION

Let me review what we have done so far. We started by reviewing earlier work on voting on Supreme Court nominees by individual senators. That work identified a key variable, perceived qualifications of the nominees, as indicated by newspaper editorialists. We then looked at aggregate voting patterns and found that, generally speaking, nominees get in trouble only when their perceived qualifications score is low. However, this happens surprisingly often.

We then took a closer look at the perceived qualification scores. We found that when the nominee is tarred by a scandal, his or her perceived qualifications score largely mirrors the tone of press coverage. Otherwise, the perceived qualification score is generally high. So, broadly speaking, the perceived qualifications score is mostly a proxy for scandal.

We then examined the tone of press coverage and found that it responds in a very sensible way to features of the nominee. In particular, better qualifications result in a more positive tone, accusations of scandal makes the tone of coverage more negative, and ideological extremism makes press coverage more negative. We finished by showing that the tone of press coverage, in tandem with accusations of scandal, works quite well in predicting aggregate voting on the nominees.

Where does this leave us? Again, what does it mean? The story that emerges emphasizes the media environment: This environment is critical for the success or failure of a nomination. If the environment is positive – composed mostly of good news – the nominee breezes through the Senate and receives a unanimous or near-unanimous vote. That's true regardless of the ideology of the nominee. But if the media environment turns nasty, the opposition party is likely to mobilize against the nominee. Support in the president's own party will weaken somewhat.

---

[11] That is, assuming one doesn't see as misconduct behavior like firing the Watergate special prosecutor, expressing a judicial philosophy far from the mainstream, or serving in the Confederate army. My point is, in both cases opposition senators acted as if they did consider such behavior scandalous.

If the opposition is sufficiently numerous, the nominee can be in big trouble. The president may have to pull the nominee or risk defeat.

We used systematic data to paint a picture of what typically happens during Supreme Court nominations, but we haven't said much the calculations of political actors. However, our picture has strong implications for political strategy. In particular, management of the media environment is critical. If the president can craft a positive media environment, he can almost guarantee his nominee a seat on the Supreme Court. Conversely, if opponents of the nominee can poison the media environment, they have a real chance to derail the nomination.

How do you go about manipulating the media environment? This is what we will take up in the next chapter.

Exercises

1. Devise a model predicting which nominees will have scandals.
2. Redo Figure 16.1, adding a kernel density smoother to the figure. Use a quantile-quantile plot to examine the distribution.
3. Download the updated roll call voting data from Lee Epstein's web page (http//epstein.law.northwestern.edu) and reestimate the original Cameron–Segal voting model. Can you improve it?

17. Modeling Strategy in Congressional Hearings

In the previous chapter, we concluded that manipulating the media environment is a central concern for strategic players in the "game" of Supreme Court nominations. From this perspective, the president and his allies must try to establish a favorable media environment for the nominee. Individuals opposed to the nominee and the president must do the reverse: establish a hostile environment. Of course, a favorable environment may include flying under the radar – no attention in the media, or very little.

How can strategic actors manipulate the information environment? A useful distinction is between direct and indirect manipulation. By "direct manipulation," I mean, for example, the president going public (making speeches) on behalf of the nominee, interest groups staging protests and demonstrations, and members of the Judiciary Committee shaking their finger at the nominee and asking "gotcha" questions about judicial doctrine. These are direct manipulations because the media may deem them newsworthy and broadcast them or report on them.

Indirect manipulation is somewhat more subtle. The idea is that you engage in actions that make direct manipulations (your own or others) more or less effective, or encourage reporters to write the right kinds of stories on their own. Consider, for example, the president's choice of a moderate versus an extreme nominee or a highly qualified one versus a marginally qualified one. These choices are indirect manipulations of the media because they affect how the media portray the nominee. These choices also make the president's statements about the nominee more or less credible (at least arguably). As we have seen, selection of a moderate, able nominee will encourage favorable press reports, while selection of an extremist hack will tend to generate negative publicity. As another example of indirect manipulation, an interest group compiles incriminating statements – for example, "The Book of Bork" assembled by anti-Bork activists – and turns them over to the press. Thus, the interest group does the work of investigating the nominee for the press, which leads to increased press coverage of the kind the group wants.

What about the Judiciary Committee? How can the chairman or the majority party of the committee indirectly manipulate the press? Suppose the chair is hostile to the nominee. Then an obvious way to indirectly manipulate the media is to do a thorough investigation and uncover some really damaging evidence of improper behavior. (We saw in the previous chapter the huge impact of scandals on media coverage.) Then, during the hearing itself, the chair and like-minded members of the committee can beat the nominee over the head with his or her transgressions. Thus, the indirect manipulation – searching for a scandal – enhances the direct manipulation, the public hearings.

One might suppose that a friendly chair should do the same: investigate thoroughly to reveal how clean the nominee is, then publicize it during the hearings. But, as we saw, when it comes to Supreme Court nominations, no news is good news: Absent a scandal and a broadly hostile Senate, a nominee is practically sure to be confirmed. So, a better bet for a friendly chair is to move the nominee through the process so as to avoid accusations of scandal. In practice, this means, hustling the nominee through as fast as possible.

In this chapter, I explore these ideas in more detail. We'll take a close look at the duration and intensity of public hearings during Supreme Court nominations. I'll try to convince you that the public hearings are longer and more intense when (1) the chair of the Judiciary Committee is hostile to the nominee, (2) the chair has some red meat to work with, that is, when the prior search or good luck uncovered a scandal or other bad conduct, and (3) staff resources are more abundant, so prolonged hearings are less costly of effort to senators. We'll also find some evidence suggesting that hearings became longer and more intense beginning in the late 1960s in the wake of the controversial Warren Court.

You may be willing to believe all this already, without looking at any data or models. So, at some level, the findings may not be terribly surprising. But my point isn't to unfold a shocking revelation about American politics, though I do want to explore this material carefully. Instead, I want to return to a theme I introduced in Chapter 15: the interplay of theory and data. I will show you, in a simple way, how this works.

The analysis proceeds in six steps. First, we'll probe the logic of the situation. To do so, we'll develop a simple formal – that is, mathematical – model of the chair's behavior. (I claim that the model is a more general representation of congressional investigations of the executive.) We'll interrogate the model deductively to generate specific empirical predictions. Thus, we'll know in a very precise way how a set of theoretical assumptions maps onto empirical hypotheses.

Second, we'll try to measure the key variables indicated by the theory. This will involve a fair amount of work (all too common, I'm afraid). Third, we'll search the data for structure, looking for the predicted patterns but also for unexpected ones. As before, we'll rely on artful visualizations and highly flexible, nonparametric modeling.

Fourth, we'll fit parametric models to the data, testing the formal model's predictions. We'll use models appropriate for count data and briefly discuss some issues that arise there. Fifth, we'll ask what could go wrong with the analysis – how much should I believe the theory?

Finally, we'll address some normative questions. Given what we've found, how should we evaluate the kind of partisan behavior emphasized by the theory?

A NEW THEORY OF CONGRESSIONAL HEARINGS

What do political scientists know about the length and intensity of congressional hearings? Is there a standard model for the process? In fact, there is an empirical

literature that examines how frequently Congress holds hearings and what the
hearings are about (Aberbach 1991, 2002; Baumgartner and Jones 2002). There is
a small theoretical literature that treats hearings as signals from a congressional
committee to an agency about the committee's interest in a matter (Cameron and
Rosendorff 1993; Ferejohn and Shipan 1989) or as a signal from a committee to
floor members of Congress about the committee's knowledge of an issue (Dier-
meirer and Feddersen 2000). None of the theoretical works focus on hearings as
an opportunity for congressmembers to gain publicity or to damage the investigation target. So, let's build a new model of public hearings from scratch, bearing
in mind the case of Supreme Court nominees. Our theory will be based on the idea
of publicity-seeking partisans who use hearings to generate news stories.

We'll begin by assuming that (1) public hearings generate negative messages
about a nominee, (2) negative messages bring a reward to the chair of the committee, at least when he or she is ideologically estranged from the nominee, and
(3) public hearings are costly to the chair to conduct (time and effort costs and
forgone leisure). We will assume that the objective of the chair is to maximize his
or her net rewards, that is, maximize rewards less effort costs. The pieces of our
model are negative messages, a production function for creating negative messages, a reward function from generating negative messages, and a cost function
for producing negative messages. We'll think a little harder about each of these
pieces, then put them all together and consider the chair's behavior in the model.

Let's denote the number of negative messages as n and the negative message
production function as $n = f(x;\theta)$, where x indicates the duration of the hearing
and θ the stock of "bad stuff" known about the nominee. We'll take θ as fixed; it
reflects the prior work by the committee staff and interest groups in digging up
dirt on the nominee. The chair builds negative messages by extending the public
hearings. So, negative messages increase with the length of the hearings. A
seemingly sensible assumption is declining marginal productivity; longer hearings
mean more bad messages, but at a declining rate from each additional day of
hearings. Another sensible assumption is that the more ammunition the chair has
to use against the nominee (the bigger is θ, the greater the number of bad messages for the same level of effort. In addition – and this is critical – we assume
"increasing differences" in duration and dirt. A figure is useful at this point,
especially to explain increasing differences.

Examine Figure 17.1, which illustrates the type of production function I have
in mind. The lower curve shows the effect of longer hearings (x) at a lower level
of dirt (θ), the higher curve the effect at a higher level. You can see the declining
marginal effect of hearing duration with each curve, in that they tend to flatten
out. You can also see increasing differences at work: As duration increases, the
difference between the high-dirt curve and the low-dirt curve increases. At any
duration, the marginal effect of duration is greater when θ is greater.[1] An example
of a function like this is $n = \theta\log(x)$, which is the parametric form of the curves in
the graph.

---

[1] If the production functions are differentiable, the increasing differences assumption is just
$\frac{\partial^2}{\partial x \partial \theta}f(x,\theta) > 0$: More dirt raises the marginal increase in negative messages from longer hearings.

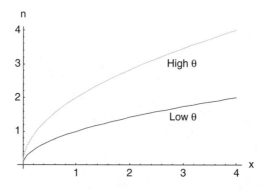

Figure 17.1. Hypothesized production functions for negative messages.

Now let's consider the return to the chair from the production of negative messages. We'll assume that the chair's return is a function of negative messages – and that the effect of negative messages depends on the ideological distance between the chair and the nominee. Let's call this ideological distance δ. Then we can denote the return to the chair from negative messages as $r(n;\delta)$. How do we imagine this return function works? If the chair is close enough to the nominee, he or she doesn't want any negative messages about the nominee: $r(n;\delta)$ is negative for positive n if δ is small enough. But beyond a certain degree of ideological estrangement, $r(n;\delta)$ will be positive for positive n. Plausibly, the greater the ideological distance between the chair and the nominee, δ, the more the value to the chair of negative messages.

Again, it may be helpful to look at a picture, so examine Figure 17.2, which illustrates a return function. The lower curve is the return from negative messages to a chair who is ideologically proximate to the nominee. As shown, the return to the chair is negative, so he or she wants no negative messages about the nominee. The middle line is the return function to a chair who is somewhat estranged from the nominee, say, a moderate Democrat facing a somewhat conservative Republican nominee. The top curve is the return function for a very liberal chair who faces a very conservative nominee. An example of a return function like this is $r(n;\delta) = (\delta - \bar{\delta})n$, where $\bar{\delta}$ represents the critical distance at which the return function switches from negative to positive.

Our third building block is the cost of holding public hearings. Here we'll assume a cost function $c(x;\kappa)$ in which costs rise with the duration of the hearing but decline with, say, the abundance of staff resources κ. Presumably as well, the cost of zero hearings is zero, that is, $c(0) = 0$. An example of such a function is x/κ.

We now have our building blocks. Let's assemble them to describe the chair's objective. Pursuing the idea that the chair is interested in the net returns from hearings, we have

$$\Pi(x, \theta, \delta, \kappa) = r(f(x, \theta), \delta) - c(x, \kappa). \qquad (1)$$

This is just the return function minus the cost function. We imagine that the chair wishes to maximize this function by choosing a hearing duration x. In Figure 17.3, I've used the component equations I mentioned previously to construct a specific net

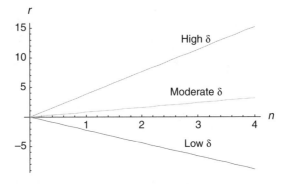

Figure 17.2. Hypothesized return functions from negative messages.

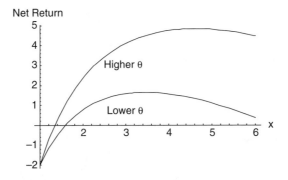

Figure 17.3. Hypothesized net returns from hearing lengths at high and low levels of dirt.

return function at two different levels of θ. As you can see, at least in this example, there is a clear optimal length for each level of dirt. Call this length x^*.

An obvious question is, when will equation (1) have a well-defined maximum? This is not a trivial matter and has been the subject of much thought by mathematicians. You can probably see that if the net return function is continuous and the allowable hearing duration is a continuous closed interval, like 0–6, the net return function must have a maximum value in the interval. In such a case, if the net return function is differentiable, you can find the (or at least a) maximum using simple calculus. Things can get more complicated, though, if, for example, the net return function has jumps or the allowed duration of hearings takes only integer values, and so on.

At this point, we could go off on a long digression on the theory of optimization, but instead, let's keep our eye on the theory–empirics link. To do so, we need to think harder about the optimal hearing duration x^*. Presumably x^* is the length of public hearings the chair will choose; at least, that's our assumption. We can observe hearing lengths across different nominations, which will become the outcome variable of interest. Now the optimal hearing length will be a function of the exogenous variables in equation (1), specifically, the amount of dirt θ, the ideological distance δ between the chair and the nominee, and the size of staff resources κ. In other words, optimal length is itself a function $x^*(\theta, \delta, \kappa)$. Over a series of nominations, we may be able to observe the values of these variables, which will become our predictor variables. So, if we can coax our theoretical model into making predictions about the behavior of the function $x^*(\theta, \delta, \kappa)$ as θ, δ, and κ change, we will have some testable predictions relating our outcome and predictor variables.

Let me introduce some jargon. Assuming that $x^*(\theta, \delta, \kappa)$ is differentiable (which we don't actually have to assume), the predictions we want concern $\frac{\partial x^*}{\partial \theta}$ (the change in x^* as θ increases), $\frac{\partial x^*}{\partial \delta}$ (the change in x^* as δ increases), and $\frac{\partial x^*}{\partial \kappa}$ (the change in x^* as κ increases). These three partial derivatives are called "comparative static multipliers," which is probably not completely transparent terminology. But the terminology is too well established to change, so let's go ahead and use it.

From a theoretical point of view, the comparative static multipliers summarize the model's empirical content – for most practical purposes, they are its empirical content. Rebecca Morton, in her useful book *Methods and Models* (1999), discusses some other ways to test theoretical models in the social sciences. But in general, comparative statics is the starting point for empirical understanding of formal mathematical models in political science.

So, our problem is to derive the comparative static multipliers for our model. I should note that, typically, we will not be able to establish exact numerical values for the comparative static multipliers. For example, we will not be able to say, "The theory predicts that if the stock of bad news about a nominee goes up by one unit, the hearing duration will increase by five hours." Predictions like this demand too much from theory. But we may be able to get predictions about the sign of the multipliers – for example, whether x^* gets larger or smaller or stays the same (or we can't tell) as the stock of bad news about a nominee increases.

How do we derive the comparative static multipliers in our model? Basically, there are three ways to do it. The first is to derive a closed-form solution. This is the easiest method to understand. The idea is to assume specific functional forms for the production function, return function, and cost function and then solve for the function $x^*(\theta, \delta, \kappa)$. If we are careful about specifying the underlying functions, this may be possible. Then, given an explicit $x^*(\theta, \delta, \kappa)$ function, we can see how x^* changes as the exogenous variables change, either through inspection, calculus techniques, or direct calculation.

I will work out a closed-form solution next, but the obvious difficulty with this approach is that the results are hostage to the specific equations we assume. Consequently, there may be little or no generality to the results. Perhaps if you used a somewhat different but equally plausible return function (for instance), you might get completely different predictions. And any test of the model based on a closed-form solution will actually be a test of the full set of assumptions – not just the general equation (1) but all the specific forms for each of the components.

A second method is to use some powerful results in the theory of robust comparative statics. In recent years, economic theorists have worked out general results concerning the behavior of equations like (1).[2] If you feel comfortable

---

[2] For example, see Milgrom and Shannon (1994). An accessible introduction written for political scientists is Ashworth and Bueno de Mesquita (2006); also see Athey, Milgrom, and Roberts (1998) for the perspective from economics.

making some rather broad assumptions about the components of equation (1) – the kinds of assumptions we made earlier, like "increases in x and θ with increasing differences between x and θ" – you can apply powerful theorems directly to the problem and immediately get the comparative static results. I was careful to make the right kinds of assumptions as we went along, so we can do this. I won't go into too much detail about this, but a nice implication of this approach is that, because we know that the results are perfectly general so long as we maintain the underlying assumptions about the component equations, we can use any tractable functional forms we want and derive closed-form solutions whose behavior is (in a qualitative sense) perfectly general. These solutions, in turn, can supply specific estimating equations. (You may want to think about the logic of this for a minute.) So, combining the two methods is very attractive when taking theory to data.

A third method is somewhat intermediate between the specificity of the first approach and the generality of the second. Here you make some general assumptions about the shapes of the component equations but not their specific form, and also some strong assumptions about their smoothness and continuity. Then you can use calculus-based methods to work out the comparative statics. This approach typically involves quite a bit of algebra, so we won't do any more with it.

Let's assume the specific functional forms I used earlier, since we know that the results we'll find in this case are actually quite general. Thus, equation (1) becomes

$$(\delta - \bar{\delta})\theta \log(x) - x/\kappa. \tag{2}$$

This function is what is shown in Figure 17.3 for the values $\delta = 3$, $\bar{\delta} = .7$, $\kappa = 1/2$, $\theta = 3$, and $\theta = 4$. (I picked these values through trial and error to get pretty shapes for the curves.) As you can see, there is a clear optimal hearing length, the point at which the net return is highest. This optimum length increases as the amount of available dirt increases. Make sure that you understand this point: The optimal length (the point where the curve is highest) shifts to the right as θ increases. Simply from inspection of the curves, we can see our first comparative static in action.

I could redo the picture, varying each of the parameters in equation (2) to give a pictorial version of the comparative statics. Instead, let's derive an expression for the optimum length. Using a little algebra,[3] I find this to be

$$x^*(\delta, \bar{\delta}, \theta, \kappa) = (\delta - \bar{\delta})\kappa\theta \tag{3}$$

This is actually pretty neat. The optimal length is simply the product of the three relevant parameters (counting $(\delta - \bar{\delta})$ as a single parameter).

A point that jumps out of equation (3) is that if the chair is close enough to the nominee (if $\delta \leq \bar{\delta}$), the chair will not want to hold any hearings at all: x^* is zero (obviously, hearing length can't be negative). Or, if zero hearings aren't feasible, the chair will hold the shortest feasible hearings. Before the late 1940s or so, the

---

[3] Take the first derivative of (2) with respect to x and set this equal to zero (i.e., assume an interior maximum), then solve for x at the interior maximum.

Senate Judiciary Committee sometimes allowed Supreme Court nominations to go to floor votes without holding public hearings. After the late 1940s, the committee stopped doing this; apparently, having no public hearings at all seemed unacceptably cavalier. But even then, some hearings were very brief, pro forma affairs. We'll look at some data on this shortly.

Using equation (3), we can get our comparative static predictions directly.[4] When $\delta > \bar{\delta}$ and $\theta, \kappa > 0$:

$$\frac{\partial}{\partial\delta}x^*(.) = \kappa\theta > 0$$

$$\frac{\partial}{\partial\theta}x^*(.) = (\delta - \bar{\delta})\kappa > 0 \qquad (4)$$

$$\frac{\partial}{\partial\kappa}x^*(.) = (\delta - \bar{\delta})\theta > 0.$$

In words, when the chair and the nominee are estranged ideologically, hearing duration lengthens as the degree of estrangement deepens, the stock of dirt increases, and the committee staff swells. If we just used the robust approach, we would get similar results, except that in general, each of the equalities would be weak (greater than or zero rather than greater than). Note that if $\delta \leq \bar{\delta}$ (the nominee is close to the chair), these equalities all become (weakly) negative, implying a minimal hearing length.

We'll take the model to data, proceeding in several steps. First, we'll visualize the relationships nonparametrically, using extremely flexible functional forms. This is a good way to listen to the data – we'll let the data talk to us without forcing them into any procrustean beds. This approach fits neatly with the robust comparative statics philosophy: We eschew specific functional forms and look for the broad patterns. But we'll also estimate parametric equations inspired by our closed-form solution. This is attractive since equation (3) is so simple, and the parametrics allow us to do standard diagnostics on this regression – for example, making sure that the results are robust to influential outliers, and so on.

To summarize our progress so far: We have developed a new theory of congressional hearings, with an eye toward Supreme Court nominations. Our theory is based on the idea that congressmembers are ideological partisans. According to the theory, the chair of the Judiciary Committee drags out the hearings in order to publicize nasty bits of information about an ideological enemy. In contrast, the chair hustles an ideological soul mate through the hearings in order to limit any damage to him or her. Thus, public hearings on Supreme Court nominees are not a seminar in a philosophy class or law school. Rather, they are a kind of political warfare, at least when the chair and the nominee are ideologically estranged. Our key predictor is the ideological distance between the chair and the nominee. Also important is the availability of dirt on the nominee. Under some reasonable and fairly general assumptions, we worked out the empirical implications of our theory. Because we did this mathematically, we can be sure that our logic is tight.

Now let's turn to the data.

---

[4] Just take the partial derivative of (3) with respect to the parameter of interest.

DATA: DEFINITIONS AND OVERVIEW

The data come from all nominations from Hugo Black (1937) through Samuel
Alito (2005). Two variables, length of the hearing (duration in days) and size of
the hearing report (length in pages), represent the intensity of hearings and are our
outcomes. Our theory suggests three predictor variables: (1) a measure of ideological distance between the nominee and the chair of the Judiciary Committee,
(2) an indicator for scandal, measuring the dirt or bad news about the nominee at
the time of the hearing, and (3) the number of Judiciary Committee staff. In
addition, a little knowledge of history suggests a fourth: an indicator for senatorial
courtesy (explained shortly).

Length of the Hearing

The first measure of intensity of public hearings is the number of days of hearings
for each Supreme Court nominee, as reported in Rutkus and Bearden (2005). This
measure is the actual number of days on which public hearings were held. For
example, in the Powell nomination, the public hearing started on November 3,
1971, and ended on November 10, 1971, a total of eight days. However, hearings
were not held on November 5, 6, and 7. Thus, the recorded number of hearing
days is five rather than eight.

Using this measure, the mean duration of hearings was 3.3 days and the
median was 2 days. The minimum length was zero days, the maximum 12 days
(the Bork nomination), and the variance was a little over 10 days.

Volume of the Hearing Report

The Senate Judiciary Committee publishes an official report on each hearing. The
report contains transcripts of the witnesses' testimony, senators' questions, and the
nominee's answers, plus various items the senators want to put on the record. It
seems natural to view the volume of the report as proportional to the intensity of
the public hearing.

The average number of pages in the committee reports is 454, with a median
of 128. The minimum length is zero and the maximum is 3,350 (again, the Bork
nomination). The variance is huge.

Figure 17.4 shows the distribution of the number of pages in the reports, on the
original and the log scale. At this point, it should be no surprise that the raw data
do not follow a normal (bell-shaped) distribution. Taking the logarithm com-
presses the long right tail and hints that there may be two distinct populations.

Ideological Distance

The theory indicates that the more distant the nominee's ideology is from that of
the Judiciary Committee chair, the longer the hearing will be (with all else
unchanged). To estimate the distance from the nominee's ideology to the chair, we
need to measure the ideologies of the chair and the nominee and put them on the
same scale. This takes some work!

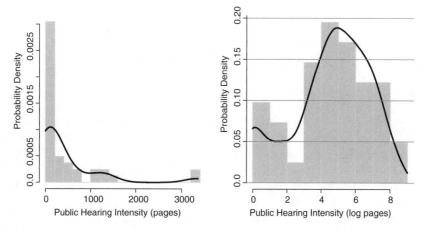

Figure 17.4. Distribution of intensity of public hearings for Senate nominees, as measured by number of pages in committee reports and shown on the log scale. Histograms show the data, and curves show density estimates. The histograms give a clearer picture of the data. The histograms would be improved by showing actual counts on the y-axes so that the reader could get a sense of the amount of data in each histogram bar.

Assigning a score to the Judiciary Committee chair is quite straightforward. We first identified the Judiciary Committee chairs at the time of each nomination and then located their DW-NOMINATE scores in Rosenthal and Poole's dataset.[5] I mentioned these scores in Chapter 15. Poole and Rosenthal's DW-NOMINATE scores, based on all recorded roll call votes in Congress, are widely used by political scientists as measures of congressmembers' ideologies and are generally considered highly reliable.

The process is much more complicated for the nominees and requires a little explaining. First, given our use of a roll call–based measure for senators, it might seem natural to do the same thing for Supreme Court justices. Then, given something like a DW-NOMINATE score for a justice, we could try to put the nominee measure and the senator measure in synch somehow. In fact, several scholars have tried to do this (Bailey and Chang 2001; Epstein et al. 2007).

I believe that voting scores for Supreme Court justices have their uses, but they are not well suited for studying nomination politics. First, there are no voting scores for failed nominees since they never made it to the Court (obviously). That creates a problem immediately. Second, even for the successful nominees, we are more interested in the way they were perceived at the time of the hearings than in how they actually voted later on the Court. The two are surely related, but they are not the same thing. Finally, there are good theoretical and historical reasons to believe that the voting behavior of Supreme Court justices may not be a simple expression of their preferences. For one thing, their votes surely reflect the changing docket of cases, which they themselves choose.

---

[5] Available at www.voteview.com.

To see why this is a problem, consider the voting of an ideologically moderate justice when a conservative majority controls the docket. This justice, who will often split from the conservative majority and vote with liberals on the Court, is apt to look rather liberal. But if a bloc of liberals controlled the docket, this same moderate justice would often vote with conservatives, thus making him or her look rather conservative. So, the result is an artificial extremism that fluctuates with the docket. But this is hardly the only problem with voting scores.

In addition to docket effects, the voting behavior of justices may reflect the political environment facing the Court. History suggests that the justices often moderate in the face of political opposition from the other branches (Rosenberg 1992). In my opinion, given a largely or completely endogenous docket and the possibility of strategic voting by the justices, it takes a lot of faith to see the justices' voting scores as a pure measure of their ideologies. In fairness, similar criticisms have been directed at the congressional DW-NOMINATE scores, but despite some rather intense work on the subject, no one has been able to show that docket effects or strategic behavior contaminate those scores in a profound way.

The bottom line is, for the nominees we need something other than their subsequent voting scores as a measure of their ideology, and we want this measure to be scaled like DW-NOMINATE scores. What to do?

Here is our solution. For the nominees who served in Congress, we start with their DW-NOMINATE scores. More specifically, five nominees (Black, Byrnes, Burton, Vinson, and Minton) served as legislators before they were nominated, so we can directly use their DW-NOMINATE scores as a measure of their ideology.[6] For those who did not, we start with the NOMINATE score of the president who nominated them.[7] This is hardly perfect, but it seems reasonable to believe that the ideology of the nominating president contains valuable information about the nominee. To complement this measure, we also employ the nominee ideology scores calculated by Jeffrey Segal and Albert Cover (1989), mentioned in the previous chapter. These scores are based on contemporaneous editorial evaluations in four major newspapers (two liberal, two conservative): *The New York Times*, the *Washington Post*, the *Chicago Tribune*, and the *Los Angeles Times*. Roughly speaking, they indicate the percentage of editorial evaluations that score the nominee as a liberal.

We believe that both sets of scores tap into the nominee's true ideology, though probably with error. To recover the posited common factor underlying the two measures, we performed a principal component analysis (PCA) on the two measures. Then, to put the PCA scores into the DW-NOMINATE space, we simply regressed them on the DW-NOMINATE measure associated with each nominee (their score or the president's score). Using the estimated coefficient, we then converted each PCA score into a DW-NOMINATE score. Essentially, we took a DW-NOMINATE score for each nominee (either his or her own or that of the nominating president) and then adjusted it based on contemporaneous perceptions of the nominee.

---

[6] Aficionados of ideology scores will note that we converted all of the scores into the Senate space.

[7] Because presidents announce their position on many bills, they have been scaled just like senators or House members.

Table 17.1. *Supreme Court nominees with scandals*

Nominees with hearings			
Scandal before hearing	Scandal during hearing	Scandal after hearing	No hearing
Haynsworth, Carswell, Rehnquist, 1 Bork, Kennedy, Breyer	Clark (last day), Fortas, 2 Rehnquist 2 (last day), Thomas	Jackson, Warren	Black

The recovered DW-NOMINATE scores have a great deal of face validity; that is, justices we know were liberals show up that way, and so do conservatives and moderates. These scores also do a pretty good job of predicting the future voting behavior of the nominees who make it onto the Court.

Finally, given the chair's score and the imputed score of the nominee, we calculate the simple distance between them (the absolute value). Given the range of observed DW-NOMINATE scores, the distances range between 0 and 1. The mean distance is .34 and the median is .31. The minimum distance is virtually 0 and the maximum is almost 1. The standard deviation is .2.

Scandal

The theory indicates the importance of some dirt for the chair to work with. We will use the presence of a scandal as our measure of the stock of dirt. According to our data, coded from stories in *The New York Times*, thirteen nominees experienced some sort of scandal or scandals. Since we are interested in the effect of scandal on the length of hearing and the volume of the hearing report, the actual timing of the scandal is critical. We classified the nominees with scandal into three categories according to this timing; see Table 17.1.

We did not score late-breaking scandals – those that happened after the public hearings had concluded – since, for our purposes, we sought a measure of dirt existing at the time of the hearings. We did count the scandal involving Black, as it emerged between the time Roosevelt nominated him but before he was confirmed, which occurred without a hearing. A trickier case involves scandals that emerged during hearings. If one suspects that the chair engineered their emergence, or that they had an effect on the subsequent duration or intensity of the hearings, one should count them as dirt. But if one views them as nonengineered and not liable to affect the choreography of the hearings, one might not count them. So, one might count all four of the "hearing scandals" as scandals, or none of them, or just the two that occurred prior to the last day (indicated in Table 17.1). In our data analysis we opted for the first of these choices, but we reran all the results using the other coding choices, and it didn't make much difference to the results.

Staff Size

For the size of the Senate Judiciary committee staff, we began with Keith W. Smith's compilation of data on congressional committee staff

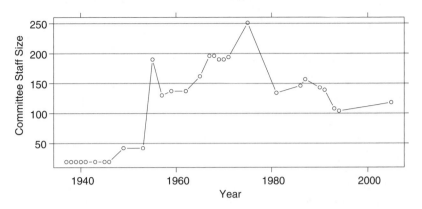

Figure 17.5. Size of the Senate Judiciary Committee staff at the time of Supreme Court nominations, 1937–2005.

(1947–98).[8] Smith compiled the data from standard sources. We have updated and checked these figures, using staff directories published by *Congressional Quarterly*. For pre-1947 nominations, for which we've had trouble locating exact numbers, we use the number for 1947. Figure 17.5 displays the data over time. As you can see, the size of the committee staff has varied greatly over time. Basically, staff increased steadily until the Stevens nomination in 1975 and then fell to a moderate and fairly stable level. So, this is not a story of simple growth.

Senate Courtesy

Supreme Court nominations are usually referred to the Senate Judiciary Committee, which typically schedules a public hearing on the nominee. However, by unanimous consent, the Senate can directly consider and confirm a nomination without referral to the Judiciary Committee. This fast-track nomination process, called "Senate courtesy," has been invoked for a few nominees, invariably former or current senators. For example, Byrnes skipped the hearing due to Senate courtesy. Of course, Senate courtesy is hardly an inviolable rule (we find it hard to imagine that it would be invoked today). In fact, some former or current senators were nonetheless sent to the Judiciary Committee for hearings. However, in these cases, the nominee usually had a nominal hearing and the nomination was quickly sent to the full Senate for a vote. We identify Black, Byrnes, Burton, Vinson, and Minton as filling the historic requirements of Senate courtesy.

VISUALIZING THE DATA

As we've emphasized repeatedly, visualizing your data is an essential part of any analysis and a cornerstone of modern applied statistics (Cleveland 1985, 1993). This is still true when you are testing a formal model, because you want to be fair

---

[8] Available on his personal Web site, http://trc.ucdavis.edu/kwsmith.

Basic Public Hearing Data

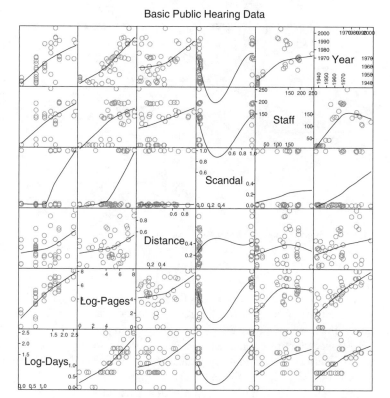

Figure 17.6. Scatterplot matrix of the data from the public hearings of Supreme Court nominees. Each dot represents a different nomination.

with the data. By this we mean that you want to be confident that the predicted patterns really exist. In addition, you want to know if the data contain interesting patterns that the theory doesn't predict. Surprises are great, because they are food for thought. They may even stimulate you to create a new theory. And there's nothing like clever visualizations for uncovering surprising patterns (and for finding coding errors or other mistakes, which happen all the time).

So, where do we start? I like a scatterplot matrix with nonparametric smoothers imposed on each panel: simple to do but often effective. This is shown in Figure 17.6.

Each row of Figure 17.6 has the indicated variable on the y-axis and each of the other variables on the x-axis. For example, look at the bottom row in the figure. The y-variable here is days of hearings (logged). Log-days is arrayed against each of the other variables in turn. It's nice to see log-days and log-pages track each other pretty closely, suggesting that both tap into the same thing, presumably hearing intensity. In fact, each of the key predictors (taken singly) appears to have a strong impact on the duration of the hearings and, in the next to bottom row, on log-pages. In the next to bottom row, you can see what looks like a threshold effect from staff on log-pages. Looking again at the bottom row, you may see something similar for duration, now that you look harder. In other words,

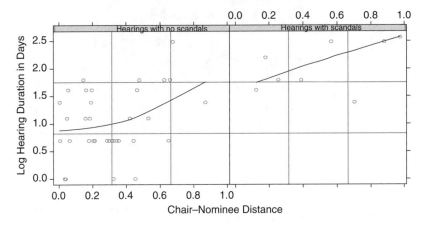

Figure 17.7. Hearing duration and ideological distance between the chair of the Senate Judiciary Committee and the Supreme Court nominee. The left and right halves of the graph show nominations without and with scandals.

once you get beyond a certain level of staff (130 or so), additional staff doesn't seem to have much effect. Now that we're a little sensitized to threshold effects, look again at the relation between distance and days and pages. This is interesting since the distance–duration relationship is central to the theory. Again, it looks like a threshold effect. This is gratifying, because our theoretical model predicted it (remember minimal hearings for proximate nominees?).

Examining the last column, you can see that most of the variables increase over time, though staff turns down again (we saw that earlier). This comovement over time is a little worrisome because it suggests that we may have trouble untangling all the relationships. I will return to this point later. Skimming the matrix for other strong relationships, I see that staff increases with the distance between the chair and the nominee. This suggests that the Judiciary Committee has more staff when it is estranged from the executive. It might be worth thinking harder about potential endogeneity, but we won't spend more time on this here.

So, despite a few worrisome issues, our initial cut at the data looks promising. What would be a potentially illuminating visualization, given our theory? Personally, I want to see the relationship between duration and ideological distance, for scandal-ridden nominees versus nonscandalous ones, and for staff-poor versus staff-rich nominations.

Figure 17.7 shows log-days as a function of the ideological distance between the chair and the nominee. The left panel shows the relationship for nominations in which no scandal emerged before or during the hearings. As shown, when the chair and the nominee are ideological soul mates (ideological distances under about .3 or .4 in DW-NOMINATE units), hearing durations are usually very short. Nor, in these circumstances, are durations particularly responsive to distance. But when the chair and the nominee are estranged (ideological distances greater than .4 or so), the durations get noticeably longer as ideological distance increases.

The right panel of Figure 17.7 shows data from nominations with scandals, and there the situation is even more dramatic. The hearing duration is much longer

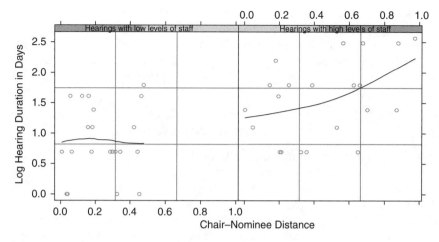

Figure 17.8. Hearing duration and ideological distance between the chair of the Senate Judiciary Committee and the Supreme Court nominee. The left and right halves of the graph show nominations with low and high levels of staffing.

even for ideological soul mates and goes up from there. In fact, the duration is longer for the closest scandal-ridden nominee than it is for the more distant scandal-free ones. Beyond the .4 mark, the slopes of the two lines don't really look that different, suggesting a merely additive effect of scandal rather than an interaction. One caveat worth noting: As the panels show, most of the scandal-free nominations involve ideologically proximate nominees. The scandal-ridden nominations span the ideological spectrum.

Now let's check out the effect of staff, as shown in Figure 17.8. Again, the figure shows the duration–distance relationship, but now the left-hand panel shows nominations in which the committee staffing was relatively skimpy (below 133, with a minimum value of 27). The right-hand panel shows the relationship for nominations in which staffing was relatively abundant (above 133, with a maximum of 251). The left half of the figure reveals that all the ideological distances are small. So, the figure says: When distances are small and staffing is tight, durations are typically short. It is tempting to add: "and they don't vary with distance." But we have to careful here because of the limited range of the data. For really big distances the durations might tick up, but we can't tell since we have no observations in that range.[9] The right half of the figure has observations spanning the ideological spectrum. We see both an upward shift in the curve and a notably positive slope. Again, all this looks quite consistent with our theory.

---

[9] It is easy to be sloppy about projecting relationships outside the range of their data. Relying exclusively on tables of regression coefficients encourages this often risky practice. The defaults in the "trellis graphics" package I'm using won't project the smoothers outside the data, which is nice. More generally, when showing the fit from a regression, it is also a good idea to show the actual data points if possible or, barring that, a "rug" at the bottom of the figure with a dash for each data point, so that the reader can see the distribution of the data. Simple practices like this would contribute to more honesty (and self-awareness) in quantitative political analysis.

An obvious question now is: What happens if we vary staffing and scandal at the same time? If we had enough observations, we could use conditioning plots to examine both relationships simultaneously. Unfortunately, we don't have enough scandal-ridden nominations to do much with. However, we can take a closer look at the scandal-free nominations, and the patterns do not appear to change compared to the analysis of the full data.

FITTING PARAMETRIC MODELS

We've learned a lot about the data just from plotting them in artful ways. So, let's go ahead and fit some parametric models. However, before we do so, we should ask ourselves: What class of models should we fit? There are at least three possibilities.

First, based on equation (3), we could fit log-days or log-pages using ordinary least squares. This is certainly the simplest option and, in light of what we saw earlier, we know it is likely to work well (there might still be heteroskedasticity with the pages data, though). However, there are several problems here. First, we have to decide what to do with the zero-duration nominations, since log(0) is undefined. One choice is to use $\log(\text{days}+1)$, but this is arbitrary and has no theoretical justification. Also, it is inconvenient to constantly have to convert back from log-days to days.

The second option is to treat the data as count data and model them appropriately. This means fitting the data with Poisson or perhaps negative binomial regressions. This approach automatically takes care of the zero-duration nominations, and we won't have to worry about converting back from log-days to days. Running count models is simple, so this is an attractive choice.

Third, some people view the hearing data as duration data. Accordingly, they would want to estimate survival curves and hazard rates. This is a perfectly sensible choice. But note that the theory does not say that the chair holds a hearing for a day, decides whether to stop or continue, depending on the realization of some random variable, holds it for another day if he or she continues, decides to stop or not, and so on. That would truly suggest a survival analysis. Rather, the theory says that the chair determines the length of the hearings ex ante, based on the information he or she has in hand. This suggests a count model[10] in which the expected values of the data are modeled on the log scale, with a probability distribution used to model the outcome, which can be 0, 1, 2, and so on.

To illustrate, let's cheat a bit and look ahead to Model 1 in Table 17.2, which shows the estimated coefficients (and standard errors) in a simple regression model. The mean values of "Ideological distance" and "Staff size" are 0.34 and 114, respectively. If we set those variables as their mean values and set scandal to

[10] The data are not quite durations in that the outcome is a count of "hearing days" on which the hearing was actually conducted. If we were to pursue the idea of a duration model, we would want a measure of the onset of each spell of hearings, noting each day a spell was in the risk set of termination. Be that as it may, we checked the statistical results of the Poisson and negative binomial regressions with a duration analysis, a Weibull parametric regression. The results of the Weibull analysis are essentially the same as those of the count models.

Table 17.2. *Two simple models of hearing duration and volume*

	Hearing duration (days)		Volume of documents (pages)	
	Model 1	Model 2	Model 3	Model 4
Ideological distance	1.1(.3)	1.1(.3)	1.6(.8)	1.7(.7)
Scandal	.6(.2)	.6(.2)	1.3(.5)	1.2(.4)
Staff size	.005(.002)	.005(.002)	.011(.004)	.007(.004)
Senate courtesy	–	−1.4(.8)	–	3.0(.7)
Constant	−.4(.3)	−.0(.3)	3.3(.5)	3.8(.5)
N	42	42	41	41
Pseudo R^2	.18	.21	.04	.06
Log likelihood	−78.8	−76.1	−260.3	−254.0

Note: These models are overdispersed Poisson (i.e., negative-binomial) regressions with a logarithmic link so that coefficients can be interpreted on the log scale. For example, from Model 1, cases with and without scandals (with all other predictors unchanged) differ, on average, by .6 in their log duration. To put it another way, having a scandal corresponds to a duration that is, on average, $\exp(.6) = 1.8$ times longer.

zero, we calculate $E[y|\bar{\Delta}, \theta = 0, \bar{\kappa}] = e^{-.36+1.14(.34)+.61(0)+.01(114)} = 3.2$ days. This is the predicted duration of a scandal-free nomination, when "Staff size" and "Ideological distance" take their mean values. A similar calculation shows that the equivalent value for a scandal-wracked nomination is 5.9 days. You can see that the switch from no scandal to scandal increases the duration by $(5.9 - 3.2)/3.2 = .84$ – in other words, an 84% increase. An approximation that is often used is that, roughly, the percentage change in $E[y|x_1, \dots x_n] = 100$ times the coefficient times the size of the change. So, for example, if ideological distance increases from 0 to 1, duration will go up 114%, that is, more than double (using the coefficients in Model 1). This approximation suggests about a 60% increase with the switch from no-scandal to scandal.

This all implicitly assumes a causal interpretation for the regression coefficients. To be more scrupulous, we would say something like "Comparing two nominations that differ in ideological distance but are identical in all other aspects, we would expect the nomination with ideological distance equal to 1 to have a duration 114% of that of the nomination of ideological distance 0." This is not the same as what would happen if the ideological distance of a particular case were to be changed (whatever that means). It is common to describe regression coefficients causally, but for observational data (which is almost always what we have in political science), all these coefficients actually tell us only about descriptive comparisons.

What would be a reasonable first-cut model, in light of the theory and our knowledge of the data's structure? The most straightforward answer is to model hearing length (days) and intensity (pages) as an additive function of ideological distance, scandal, and staff size. In addition, we should investigate senatorial courtesy. Finally, it would be a good idea to look at interactions among the important predictors (as discussed in the previous chapter).

Table 17.3. *Estimated coefficients and standard errors (all on the logarithmic scale) for overdispersed Poisson regressions of hearing durations (in days), with a distance threshold and a mid-1960s break*

	Model 2	Model 5	Model 6
Ideological distance	1.1(.3)	1.7(.4)	1.4(.4)
Scandal	.6(.2)	.6(.2)	.5(.2)
Staff size	.005(.002)	.005(.002)	.002(.002)
Senate courtesy	−1.4(.8)	−1.4(.7)	−1.3(.8)
Pre-1967	−	−	−.7(.3)
Constant	−.0(.3)	.2(.3)	.9(.4)
N	42	42	42
Residual deviance	43.0	41.6	35.1

Note: In Models 5 and 6 ideological distance is a threshold variable. Deviances can be compared to a null value of 115.

Take a look at the models in Table 17.2 of hearing length (days) and the volume of documents in the hearing. Model 1 is a plain vanilla model of the data. It contains just the three key variables: ideological distance, scandal, and staff size. Model 2 then adds senatorial courtesy. The three predictors are statistically significant at the 5% level (that is, the estimates are more than two standard errors from zero) and have the positive coefficient predicted by the formal model's comparative statics. Senate courtesy is not quite statistically significant. Models 3 and 4 show the corresponding results for the volume of the hearing report.

ADDING A THRESHOLD

Our earlier discussion emphasized a threshold in distance as a distinctive theoretical prediction, one that received some support when we visualized the data. Let's fit a parametric model with a threshold to the days data and see how it compares to the earlier models. Here is a simple approach.[11] Let's say that we think that the threshold should be 0.4 on the distance scale. First, define an indicator variable that takes the value 0 if the distance is less than 0.4 and 1 if it is greater. Then interact this variable with (distance − 0.4). This procedure creates an elbow-shaped threshold variable: The variable takes the value of 0 at and below the threshold, then increases linearly (from 0) as distance increases above 0.4.

Let's estimate this model using the elbow version of distance and compare it with our simple model. Table 17.3 shows the results. The first column repeats Model 2 for purposes of comparison (that is, the distance measure is the simple absolute value used earlier). The second column shows the same model, but using the threshold version of distance. As you can see, the coefficients on the other variables have about the same magnitude (the intercept is different, of course).

---

[11] Another method is to estimate a so-called generalized additive model, with distance entered in a flexible way, say via smoothing splines (see Hastie and Tibshirani 1990). This gives similar results in this example.

However, the new distance measure is steeper (and more statistically significant). The overall fit of the model is modestly better. In sum, the data are equally compatible and perhaps favor the threshold version of ideological distance.

WHAT COULD GO WRONG?

At this point, we could declare victory and go home. After all, we crafted a new theory of committee hearings, which we formalized in a mathematical model; we interrogated the formal model to uncover its empirical implications; we collected appropriate data to test the empirical predictions; we explored the data for structure using nonparametric models; we fit parametric models to the data; and both the parametric and nonparametric models behaved as the formal model predicted. Given this, we can now interpret the politics of public hearings on Supreme Court nominations in a way that is both theoretically informed and historically grounded. Admittedly, understanding the duration and intensity of public hearings on Supreme Court nominations is a small question, not like world peace or ending poverty. But still, in a modest way, we might call this a good day at the office.

But wait! We should ask one more question: What could go wrong with our pretty picture? Is there some way in which we haven't been completely fair with the data, something we overlooked perhaps because it didn't mesh with the theory?

I will leave the following as an exercise for you. Fit the model again, partitioning the data into early (pre-1967) and late (1967-on) groups. Since there are no senatorial courtesy nominees in the later period, you will have to drop this variable for the latter. You will find that the model works well in the later period (though staff is no longer significant). Even the coefficients look similar. But in the earlier period, the model seems to fall apart in that only the courtesy variable remains statistically significant.

What are we to make of this? There are two obvious interpretations. One interpretation is that the relationships elaborated in the theory hold throughout the period under study, but the effect of ideological distance is muted in the early period by the low values of distance in that period. Then, in the later period, we can detect it because distance takes on a wide range of values, all the way from 0 to 1. The second interpretation is that the world suddenly changed in 1967 (or thereabouts). Prior to that, the theory simply didn't apply because ideology was unimportant. Then suddenly, ideological conflict became critical in Supreme Court nominations. So, the first interpretation is that the evidence powerfully favors the theory after 1967, and we can understand why it would be hard to detect in the earlier period even if it held (the circumscribed range of the variables). So, we should assume that the theory holds throughout. The second interpretation is that the theory holds only in the last part of the dataset due to an (unexplained) structural break.

Let's see if we can get a little leverage on the two interpretations by examining residuals. Consider the top row of Figure 17.9. It displays the residuals from Model 5 in Table 17.3, our best model so far. The left panels of Figure 17.9 show the residuals for the early observations, arrayed against the (raw) distance measure. The right panel shows the residuals for the late observations. A lowess

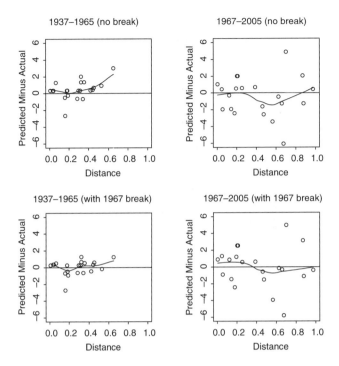

Figure 17.9. Early and late residuals for the Supreme Court model, plotted versus ideological distance, without (top row) and with (bottom row) a 1967 break

smoother shows the pattern in the data: The model tends to overestimate durations in the early period, especially if distance is greater than the threshold, 0.4. The model also tends to underestimate durations in the late nominations. This pattern indeed suggests a pre/post-1967 effect, but perhaps only a shift rather than a radical break.

So, let's fit that model. This is Model 6 in Table 17.3. There you can see that an indicator variable for whether a nomination came before 1967 is statistically significant. In this model, the staff variable is no longer statistically significant but this is not terribly surprising, given the time pattern in staffing. The bottom rows in Figure 17.9 display the residuals from this model. As you can see, the model fits the early observations much better. In the later period, the model no longer consistently underestimates the durations. However, it tends to slightly overestimate durations for nominations with small ideological distances and underestimate durations for those with large ideological distances. So, there remains some unexplained structure in the data, but Model 6 clearly outperforms the earlier ones.

The pre/post-1967 effect is completely ad hoc – it emerged from the data rather than from the theory. Of course, we can imagine some plausible reasons why 1967 might denote a watershed in the politics of Supreme Court nominations. We might point to the judicial activism of the Warren Court and the proliferation of new interest groups that occurred at that time. Controversial Supreme Court decisions coupled with burgeoning groups may have boosted the political salience of Supreme Court nominations, leading to greater publicity-seeking behavior on the Judiciary Committee, beyond the simple effect of increased ideological distance.

So, it seems that we might want to tweak the theory to account for the varying political salience of the Court. In turn, this could lead us to collect systematic data on salience so that we can unpack the pre/post-1967 effect and see if our conjecture about salience and groups holds water.

I will stop here, but I hope you are getting a feel for the interplay between theory and data, a sort of back-and-forth tennis game between deduction and induction. Both halves are fun and worthwhile, but what I enjoy most is volleying back and forth.

THE NORMATIVE ISSUES

In Chapter 15 I said that it was important to ask normative, evaluative questions once we had a solid foundation of theory and data upon which to stand. Well, we have a theory that works quite well, according to the data. What are the normative questions here? The model assumes that the chair of the Judiciary Committee tries to block ideologically distant nominees by exposing scandals. What are the implications of this model? Is this process a good thing?

Clearly, the process has some positive features. For one thing, turkeys get a good airing, at least when the nominee is ideologically far from the Judiciary Committee chair. So far as it goes, this is surely a good thing, as it lets senators know what they are voting for or against. It also makes it easier for citizens to evaluate their senators' votes and the president's performance as a chooser of nominees.

But I don't want to exaggerate. Even at the simplest level, the asymmetries in the process are disturbing. First, ideologically proximate turkeys tend to get a free pass in the Judiciary Committee, or at least a less costly passage. Hugo Black is an extreme case in point. So if you think that exposing turkeys is a good thing, then the manifest ideological bias in the process is a bad feature. If you feel this way, you might favor giving greater scope to the minority members of the Judiciary Committee, who will be inclined to be tougher on nominees the majority favors.

There is a second kind of asymmetry that many people find disturbing: the asymmetry between scandal and ideology. The model says that the real engine driving the process is ideology. But the hearings aren't forthrightly about ideology; instead, a hostile chair makes hay by publicizing the nominee's unsavory or shady behavior. Some people may see this behavior as trivializing or even misdirecting the process. The example of Black may be disturbing in this regard, as many observers believe he was an excellent justice despite his early membership in the Ku Klux Klan. But he surely would have had a tough time in hearings before a Republican-controlled Judiciary Committee and might well have been rejected by a Republican Senate. So, the emphasis on scandal may do a poor job of screening future justices.

The nasty way the hearings unfold during periods of ideological polarization may also contribute to public alienation from or disgust with government. Obviously, we haven't confirmed this conjecture with systematic data, and it might be hard to do so. But the point does suggest itself. Still, even if this is true, it is probably an inevitable consequence of ideological polarization: Historically in America, polarized politics is nasty politics.

The process clearly creates incentives for the president, who can anticipate the action in the Judiciary Committee. First, it creates an incentive for the president to vet nominees and weed out the turkeys before they enter the hearing room, especially when the Judiciary Committee is hostile. Surely this is a good thing. It would be interesting if archival evidence showed this happening. Second, because of the way scrutiny is tied to ideology, the process may create an incentive for the president to avoid ideological extremists, at least when the chair is far from the president. By doing so, the president can take some of the steam out the hearings. If so, one might see this as a good feature of the process, especially in an age when most voters are moderates and most politicians are extremists. But we would need to investigate the president's choices in depth to see if this is really true before we start lauding the process for encouraging moderation.

Ultimately, we are concerned with a much larger normative question: Does the nomination process keep the Supreme Court within the ideological mainstream of American politics, and staffed with judges of intellectual competence and high integrity? For if the Court wanders outside the mainstream, it is apt to provoke potentially disastrous assaults on judicial independence. And a judiciary filled with corrupt, venal hacks will inevitably undermine the rule of law. The theoretical and empirical work in this chapter is only a very small step toward answering the big question we really care about. But the only way to build a cathedral (as it were) is by laying one brick on top of another, one at a time.

Exercises

1. *Theory.* The formal model in Chapter 16 has implications about how many negative stories about the nominee we should see during the period of public hearings. To derive these implications, substitute equation (3) back into equation (2) and solve for the number of negative stories, n. Using this expression, derive comparative static predictions about n. Indicate what data you would need to test these predictions and what statistical methods you would use.
2. *Co-plots.* Form a conditioning plot similar to Figures 17.1–17.3 but conditioning on senatorial courtesy. Use the data shown in the scatterplot matrix to make two more conditioning plots of your choice.
3. *Senatorial courtesy.* Devise a logit or probit model that predicts when we should see senatorial courtesy. Think about the possible explanatory variables, such as ideological distance between the two parties. Do you believe your model?
4. *Analysis of the pages data.* Complete an analysis of the pages data similar to that in the chapter on the days data. In particular, fit negative-binomial and Quasi-Maximum Likelihood Estimation (QMLE) regressions after including the pre-1976 variable, and test whether a threshold version of distance is comparable with the data. (Refer to Table 17.1.)

FURTHER READING FOR PART V

1. The Scope and Content of the Social Sciences

The ambitions of the social sciences. Historic development. Current disciplinary divisions. Warring tribes and allied coalitions. Enduring tensions.

REQUIRED READINGS

Ralf Dahrendorf, "Social Science," pp. 800–2 in *The Social Science Encyclopedia* (2nd ed.). This encyclopedia has a pronounced British and decidedly sociology-centric bent. Nonetheless, it is a fairly handy one-volume compilation of definitions and brief essays. This essay, by a distinguished sociologist, has some virtues.

OPTIONAL READINGS

Jon Elster, *Nuts and Bolts for the Social Sciences* (1989). If possible, read this and the new 2007 edition.

Dorothy Ross, *The Origins of American Social Science* (1991). The best intellectual history of pre–World War II American social science. But often it is tough going because of the author's postmodernist twitches.

Alain Desrosieres, *The Politics of Large Numbers: A History of Statistical Reasoning* (1998). A wonderful and social-scientifically sophisticated history of statistics and statistical concepts. The chapter on econometrics is particularly good.

2. How to Read Social Scientific Studies

Other courses focus on the tools you will need. But a quick and dirty introduction to some basics is necessary to understand the readings in this course. Part V covers theory–operationalization–data linkages. Basics of research design. Internal versus external validity. Small n versus large n: strengths and weaknesses. How to read and criticize regression results. The rhetoric of persuasion.

OPTIONAL READINGS

Donald T. Campbell and Julian C. Stanley, *Experimental and Quasi-Experimental Designs for Research* (1963).

3. Case Study: Progress in the Social Sciences – How It Works

How, and to what extent, progress – not an unproblematic concept – is made in the social sciences. Role of evidence. Incentive structures for social scientists.

REQUIRED READINGS

Steven G. Brush, "Dynamics of Theory Change in the Social Sciences: Relative Deprivation and Collective Violence" (December 1996). The rise and fall of a social scientific theory. Pay attention to the history of what happened and to the article itself as a piece of social science.

David Hull, "The Need for a Mechanism" (1988). This is a somewhat eccentric choice, but Hull offers extremely acute comments about how science works, including such phenomena as attribution and credit claiming, citation practices, the role of mechanisms and evidence in persuading others, insiders and outsiders, cooperation, competition, personal rivalries, and scientific fraud. Can you see what he is talking about in the history of "relative deprivation"? In addition, Hull sketches a social scientific theory of scientific progress.

4. Overview of Political Science

The subject matter of political science. Subfields. Typical concerns. Important concepts. History of the discipline. The behavioral revolution. The rational choice revolution. Where the field is going.

REQUIRED READINGS

Robert Goodin and Hans-Dieter Klingemann, "Political Science: The Discipline" (1996). As your interest takes you, skim through the rest of the volume. The essays by Keohane, Barry, Weingast, Alt and Alesina, and Carmines and Huckfeldt are pretty good.

5. Case Study: Pluralism and the "Economic" Theory of Regulation

Who wins and who loses from government programs? What is the government up to, anyway? Illustrates the rational choice approach in political science. Extremely practical ideas for understanding public policy.

REQUIRED READING

George J. Stigler, "The Theory of Economic Regulation" (1988).

OPTIONAL READING

David Truman, Introduction to *The Governmental Process*: *Political Interests and Public Opinion* (1993).

6. Case Study: The Impact of TV News on Viewers' Political Behavior

How does TV news affect viewers' political beliefs and electoral behavior? Illustrates social psychological approaches, experimentation, and clever research design.

REQUIRED READING

Shanto Iyengar, "Experimental Designs for Political Communication Research: From Shopping Malls to the Internet" (1992). This article is available online and includes some of the media manipulations used in Iyengar's recent work.

Shanto Iyengar and David R. Kinder, *News That Matters* (1987). The best book on television and politics.

7. Case Study: The Activity Puzzle in Congressional Elections

Do the activities of congressmembers affect their reelection chances? It seems that they should, but the evidence says no; what's the problem here? Illustrates the kind of puzzle-solving that typifies the field of American politics. Also, the idea of selection bias: why it is pervasive and important in quasi-experimental data and one way to handle it.

REQUIRED READINGS

David Mayhew, *Congress: The Electoral Connection* (1973), a classic book on congressmembers' reelection activities.

Eric Schicler *Disjointed Pluralism: Institutional Innovation and the Development of the U.S. Congress* (2001).

Kenneth Shepsle and Barry Weingast, eds., *Positive Theories of Congressional Institutions* (1995).

PART VI. PSYCHOLOGY

E. Tory Higgins, Elke Weber, and Heidi Grant

18. Formulating and Testing Theories in Psychology

OVERVIEW

What is a good theory, and what are its characteristics? In this part of the book, we'll discuss several theories in psychology, along with methods for using and evaluating formal theories to understand experimental results. We'll be focusing in large part on the theories rather than on specific methods of data analysis. If you want to understand research methodology, you can't really succeed without first understanding what you're trying to accomplish by using these methods, and this requires an understanding of theories and how they work.

Whether the theory is implicit or explicit, as you're conducting research you have something in mind that you're trying to observe or demonstrate. In other words, you're typically trying to find a pattern in the data that you can make sense of. Your purpose, if possible, is to make some more general inferences from your specific data. So, you hope that your end result will be some general rule or description. In a way, you can think about statistics as a method for finding some order in your data, but that's not what comes first. You begin the process of conducting research by formulating a question that you want to answer, and this question will be grounded in a particular theory (either your own or someone else's). This part on psychology begins with a discussion of theory in an abstract sense. What are theories? What makes a theory good or bad? Once we know how to understand the merits and weaknesses of a theory, we'll talk about specific psychological theories as examples.

Because we're aiming to use examples that generate critical thinking and discussion, we have chosen theories that we think you'll find interesting in themselves. We've chosen some psychological theories that have had general applicability and an influence on the social sciences outside of psychology. So, while we're learning about theory, we'll also be learning about particular theories whose history is not restricted to psychology. You are strongly encouraged to consult the readings at the end of this part of the book, even if they are not assigned to you by your instructor, as we will only be able to give you a brief overview of these important theories in these chapters.

In this first chapter, we'll be discussing two highly influencial theories: *Gestalt* theory (with emphasis on the theory of cognitive dissonance, which is an example of *Gestalt*), and learning theory (with emphasis on reinforcement theory and the ideas of B. F. Skinner). The exercise at the end of the chapter involves comparing the predictions of both theories in a particular experimental situation.

WHY ARE THEORIES IMPORTANT?

Even if you intend to go into business rather than staying in academia, it would be a mistake to think that outside academia you won't be dealing with theories. There is a misconception that only a specialist in academia is a theorist. This represents a misunderstanding of what theory is. At the simplest level, a theory involves a question that you have and some idea of how to answer the question. In business there are many questions to deal with, and you must have some idea of how to go about answering them. Imagine that you are having a business meeting with other coworkers. If you present an idea of actions that you think your organization should take, you doubtless, at least implicitly, have some sort of theory in mind to justify your proposal. If someone else challenges you and comes up with another idea, he or she is also working from a theory, though it's different from yours.

We are all working with theories, whether we make them explicit or not. Theories don't necessarily have to be at the level of abstraction of $E = mc^2$. So, even though we will be dealing with theory, what we are going to say is definitely practical. It is the stuff of everyday life. Almost any time you're seeking the answer to a question, you'll first formulate a theory that will guide you to the information or data you'll need to answer your question. Everything you are learning about the gathering and analyzing of data doesn't matter very much if you start out with a bad theory in the first place. Years ago, a famous German psychologist, Kurt Lewin, said, "there is nothing as practical as a good theory." We might add as a corollary that there is nothing as prejudicial as a *bad* theory. Therefore, you need to have some idea of what a theory is, how to go about testing it, and how to compare it to alternative theories.

WHAT IS A GOOD THEORY?

Communicating Your Theory to Others

Let's start by addressing the question of what we mean by a good theory as opposed to a bad theory. First, people have to be able to *evaluate* your theory. Your theory has to be something you can express clearly to yourself and to others. It's important to understand that theories are ultimately always social products. If you can't communicate your theory to other people, it will go nowhere. And if no one accepts your theory, it will likewise go nowhere. Theories are sociological or sociopolitical products, and their success or failure has a lot to do with the ability to persuade others that they are good.

There is a mistaken belief that a good theory is obvious in itself. Often mathematics is pointed to as consisting of such obvious and indisputable theories, but anyone who tries to tell you this doesn't know the history of math. One of us plays a game with his daughter in which he proves that $2 = 1$ by using flawless algebra. The fault is not with the algebra but rather with an assumption in math that is violated, leading us astray. Without this assumption, however, math just doesn't work. Think about why you can't divide by 0. The fact is that at some point it was simply decided that certain mathematical operations won't work properly unless we all agree that you can't divide by 0.

Math, like all other sciences, is not some heavenly light shining truth down upon us; rather, it is a *social product*. So, since your theory is a social product, it is very important that it be clear and comprehensible to others. If others are not persuaded by your theory, then it is of little use. Now we say this bearing in mind that many of you will want to go into business. Obviously, if your theory is unclear, you can't persuade your colleagues of its usefulness, and your efforts will be wasted. Unfortunately, in formal philosophy of science, there is little talk of this aspect of theorizing as a social product.

Testing Your Theory

Second, a theory needs to be *testable*, and this is trickier than you might at first think. It's tricky because there can be a difference of opinion as to what counts as testable. B. F. Skinner felt, for example, that there is an inherent problem in relying too much on statistics. He pointed out that by buying into statistics, you buy into the idea that you can't really test a conclusion unless you have large enough samples. Only if your samples are large enough can you use the appropriate statistical methods. Skinner argued that statistical methods are thus problematic in at least two ways. One problem is the necessity of having so many experimental subjects. Skinner saw this as potentially wasteful and expensive. Second, you have less flexibility to change the experiment as you go along. Once an experiment is designed and many experimental subjects are engaged, it is hard to change course. The research process thus becomes too rigid.

For Skinner, the use of statistics was merely one way to show the validity of a theory. There are, he argued, other ways. Skinner himself used a single animal and repeatedly introduced or removed certain variables, ending up with a pattern of behavior that could clearly be the result only of his interventions. His method was that of the animal trainer: Given knowledge of an animal's repertoire of behaviors, if you can induce a behavior in the animal that has never occurred before, you can be pretty confident that it was because of your intervention. The point here is that while a theory needs to be testable, people can disagree on what constitutes an adequate test.

The classic meaning of "testability" is that of falsifiability, that is, that a theory can be proven to be wrong. But more importantly, a testable theory is one for which you can gather evidence that can convincingly support your conclusions. So, "testable" also means that there is evidence for your theory by which you can persuade others. It does little good to just assert your theory. You have to be able to convince others why it should be believed.

It is important to realize that even in philosophy of science, when words like "validity," "reliability," and "objectivity" are discussed, each of these words in its original meaning has to do with verification by others. But all of these words have an important social element to their meaning. Objectivity means that the facts we observe can be observed by others, too. If your evidence is something that can be observed only by you, then it is *subjective*, not objective. Reliability means that your work can be replicated by someone else. If your work is reliable, some other lab can find the same result that you did. Validity means that your theory can be understood and endorsed by others. All of these words have to do with a social process of verification.

Theory, then, has to be testable in the sense that you can find evidence that is convincing to others. We want to emphasize this point because this is probably not the way you usually think of a theory's verifiability. There's even a tendency for many psychologists to overlook this fact. Most of them think of a theory as something for which you can design an experiment to prove or disprove it and leave it at that. This is the classic way of thinking about the problem. Ideally, your experiment would be designed to have no confounding variables and no artifacts and would allow you to draw the conclusion that either would support your hypothesis or disconfirm it. The problem with stating things in this way is that it might lead you to think that the only way you can make your case convincingly is to follow this experimental method. Clinical researchers, for instance, don't consider this traditional experimental method necessary. They think that you can have a single client, and you can understand that client well enough so that he or she will provide evidence to help you comprehend what it really means to have a borderline personality. So, the right kind of careful observation of a client with a borderline personality might be very convincing to another clinician.

As you probably know, there are areas even in the physical sciences where a controlled experiment is out of the question – in astronomy, for instance. More generally, a successful theory is simply one that others find convincing. Even in business, if you're trying to persuade your colleagues to go in a certain direction, you have to come up with an argument that they find convincing. You have to have evidence that will compel belief. You're not proving the truth of some proposition grounded in absolute truth outside the social and cultural realm – a sort of Platonic absolute. You are marshalling evidence that others will find convincing.

Making Predictions from Your Theory

What else makes a theory good? How about predictability? Certainly in science, if you want to convince someone of the truth of your theory, there are few more clear-cut and exciting ways to demonstrate it than to make a prediction and have it come to pass. Although theories might be convincing even without the ability to predict, there is probably no more emphatic way to convince others of your theory's truth than to make an accurate prediction. To be able to predict the future is almost like magic and is very impressive to others.

Of course, what you predict can't be something trivial that anyone might have foreseen. Predictability in itself is not enough. You have to be able to predict something surprising and novel. A good theory has to go beyond what existing theories can tell us. Your theory must do more than make a prediction; it has to make a prediction that other theories have not made. If another theory already makes the same prediction, there is little need for yours. A big part of convincing others about your theory, then, involves showing not only that it can predict the future but that it can predict something surprising and novel, something that no other theory would have predicted. If your theory can do this, people will pay attention.

Simplicity

Another important principle is the principle of Occam's Razor, which identifies the best theories with simplicity and economy. This is a major topic in philosophy of science: the claim that a good theory is one with few variables. When you have two theories that make the same prediction, but one theory has ten variables and the other has two, you go with the simpler theory. We don't think this rule is as important as some of the others we've talked about. If you were in fact presented with two theories that did the same thing and one was much simpler than the other, of course you'd go with the simpler one. But in the real world, two theories rarely make identical predictions. Also, it could be the case that although one theory has more variables than its competitor, its variables are easier to understand. The theory with ten variables might be more comprehensible than the one with two variables.

Generalizability

Another characteristic of theories that makes them convincing is generalizability. A good theory has a *wide range of applicability*. This gets closer to what people usually mean when they talk about a great theory. Einstein's simple equation $E = mc^2$ can be applied to an extraordinary range of physical phenomena. Freud's theories also made sense out of a wide variety of psychological phenomena. We'll see later, however, that there are advantages and disadvantages to having too broad a range of applicability. Sometimes a theory pays a high price, so to speak, for great generalizability.

Explanatory Power

Let's talk about one last thing that a good theory must have: explanatory power. Explanatory power is essential, and whereas the ability to predict had to do with the future, explanatory power has to do with the past. A good theory must have the power to explain the known data. So, when a theory is presented, no one is going to be convinced unless it can explain the historical data. It's not sufficient to make predictions about the future. The new idea must fit in with facts we already know and connect past events together so that they make sense. Very often a good theory will grow out of an attempt to explain the historical data.

Distinguishing the Good from the Great: Generativity

As we mentioned earlier, perhaps the single most important thing about a theory is its generativity. Ironically, "generativity" is not a term that you'll hear much in philosophy of science. From a strictly philosophy-of-science perspective, you might conclude that good theories are ones that can be confirmed. This is nonsense. No scientist would ever say such a thing. The scientist is in the business of coming up with ideas that generate something new. All the other characteristics we've discussed are tools. If they are present, the chances that your theory will be generative are greater, but there is nothing more important than generativity. For instance, what was so impressive about Einstein's theory was that it made a multitude of predictions that were new and not at all obvious. You couldn't imagine making some of these predictions without his theory. Some of them still seem like science fiction. Some couldn't even be tested until years later, when more sophisticated tools became available. It was astounding that all of these odd predictions came true. What one does is to try to maximize a theory's generativity while never losing sight of the fact that science is a social product. These two things are critical. The theory has to be generative – that is, it has to make predictions that are novel and testable – but in addition, the evidence for the theory must be communicable and persuasive to others. Einstein's theory was persuasive even before many of its predictions could be confirmed because its explanatory power was enormous; it accounted for a great deal of data that was already known. Also, the theory was stated very clearly and concisely, and it generated a novel set of predictions.

EXAMINING SPECIFIC THEORIES: *GESTALT* THEORY AND LEARNING THEORY

Now let's talk about existing theories and evaluate them by using the character-istics of a good theory that we've been discussing. As we go forward (and when you read about and discuss the theories in the Further Reading section at the end of this part of the book), try to think about how these particular theories satisfy the criteria we've been discussing. For instance, how does the *Gestalt* theory fare in terms of economy, comprehensibility, novelty, explanatory power, or gen-erativity? We're not asking you to evaluate whether the theories are true or not. That is only one of the questions you might want to address. For example, even if you think that Freud's psychoanalytic theory is mostly false or at best untestable, you might have to admit that it's been generative. If nothing else, for better or for worse, it changed the face of the humanities. You see the influence of the theory in novels, movies, and popular culture. It certainly persuaded many people and had a tremendous impact.

Learning Theory

We begin with learning theory, sometimes called "behaviorism," "conditioning theory," or "reinforcement theory." Learning theory began as a reaction to introspectionism. Introspectionists (like William James) were people fascinated with internal events – thoughts, images, and the like. They studied psychological phenomena by reflecting or introspecting on them – by analyzing their own minds and perceptions, so to speak. Of course, this led to some very subjective assess-ments of what psychological truth was.

Behaviorists considered this approach total nonsense. In the history of science as a whole, the move away from introspectionism and toward behaviorism was part of the larger movement away from metaphysics and toward logical positivism. Behaviorism was a psychological manifestation of the general dissatisfaction with metaphysical explanations. Logical positivism looked at the sorts of pseudoproblems that metaphysics claimed to answer and insisted that just because you can formulate a question, this doesn't mean that there is an answer to that question. After all, "How many angels can dance on the head of a pin?" looks, at least grammatically, like a perfectly good question. However, a syntactically correct question might be nonsense from the point of view of science.

Behaviorism postulated that all that a scientist can know is what he or she can observe. The scientist cannot possibly know what goes on within a subject's head. As a consequence, behaviorists had no interest in studying states of mind. They argued that the scientist is confined to observing the link between certain *stimuli* in the real world and the *responses* of the subjects. We can only track the relationship between stimuli and responses. Like any good scientific theory, learning theory's purpose was to look for and predict laws and regularities in phenomena.

CLASSICAL CONDITIONING. The notion of "conditioning" has to do with some very general laws about stimulus–response relations. "Classical conditioning" refers to the finding that there are certain stimuli to which there is an "unconditional response." These are stimuli that the subject automatically responds to without conditioning. In other words, these responses don't have to be learned. The famous experiment by Pavlov is based on the unconditional response of a dog to food being put in its mouth: The dog automatically salivates. The stimulus that creates an unconditional response is called the "unconditional stimulus" (in this case, the food). Pavlov showed that if you took some arbitrary event (e.g., bell ringing) and placed it temporally prior to the unconditional stimulus (food), then the subject would eventually learn to produce the unconditional response (salivating) to the arbitrary event (bell ringing) even when the unconditional stimulus (food) was not present. Pavlov rang a bell just before giving the dog food. Eventually, the dog came to associate the ringing of the bell with food and salivated automatically, as if food was present even when there was none. Salivating in response to the ringing bell is "learned" or "conditioned behavior."

If you stop to think about it, this is a truly extraordinary result. By just ringing a bell or using some other arbitrary stimulus, Pavlov could evoke the same response in the dog as if food were actually present. His experiment is so famous, so legendary, that we are blasé about it now, but in fact, it was a bit magical. It revolutionized psychology and showed how much learning and conditioning mattered.

OPERANT CONDITIONING. What Pavlov did by associating the bell with food (and thus producing the salivating) is called classical conditioning. "Operant conditioning" or "reinforcement" has a different pattern. Here the response occurs first. An animal emits a response and is then either punished or rewarded. This method was first pioneered at Columbia University by Edward Lee Thorndike, who showed that what follows a response influences the probability that that response will occur in the future.

It can be any response. In this case, unlike in classical conditioning, it is the response that is arbitrary. You can wait for a response that almost never happens or, through the magic of reinforcement, make it happen often. Sophisticated models of reinforcement emphasize that reward value depends on the importance of the need that is being satisfied. Whatever the reward is, whether it is food, money, social approval, or some other thing, there is a hierarchy of needs to be satisfied. Reinforcement value depends on how high the need stands in this hierarchy. For an animal, obviously, the reinforcement value of food is higher if the animal is hungry than if the animal has just eaten.

Given this fact, a study has to take into account that the efficacy of, say, food as reinforcement declines in proportion to the amount the animal has already eaten. The idea is that if you control for hunger, the reward value is constant. This principle has relevance for economics, though some economic models do not take into account the state of the need in question. You can't make a general statement that the more you consume of something, the less its utility. That doesn't have to happen as long as you make sure that the state of the need remains constant. The basic idea is that as the reinforcement increases in magnitude, the motivational effect increases. A larger reinforcement should lead to a larger response. "Larger" could also mean "more intense," "faster," or "more frequent."

It's important to understand that there are other versions of reinforcement theory that aren't, strictly speaking, like Thorndike's or Skinner's. In Thorndike's and Skinner's work with animals, a response is either punished or reinforced, but the animal doesn't know beforehand. In experiments using people rather than animals, you can tell the subjects ahead of time that their behavior will be rewarded or punished so that they know before the response that a reward or punishment will follow. It's obviously easier to train a person than an animal since you can tell a person, for instance, "If you sit down, I'll give you ten dollars." Psychologists usually refer to the kind of reward that's known about beforehand as an "incentive."

For a strict behaviorist, incentive effects are not a matter for scientific study, since they refer to unobservable states of mind. But if you are willing to admit that there is something going on in the subject's mind, then all conditioning is due in some way to incentive effects. From this you might argue that classical conditioning and operant conditioning aren't as different as they might seem. They seem very different if you look just at the observables, but for many organisms, what is going on in classical conditioning and reinforcement is really the same thing. The animal is simply learning about the *relation* between certain events. It is learning about contingencies. You can talk about both classical conditioning and reinforcement in the same way. The subject can think, "When this happens, I get food" or "When I do this, I get a reward." An expectation has been created based on the observed relationship between two events. The expectation of reward becomes an incentive, which is a stimulus occurring before the response, just as in classical conditioning.

By the way, you might be interested in knowing that later studies showed that the sort of anticipatory salivation of dogs in Pavlov's experiment is not identical to the salivation of the dogs when real food is present. It's different in both quantity and chemical composition. Apparently, there is a type of salivation that is preparatory and a type that responds directly to food. So, the simple behaviorist model, which can't account for expectations and anticipation since it allows for no mental states, is inadequate.

Gestalt Theory and Dissonance

Let's turn to a very different theory – namely, the theory of cognitive dissonance as an example of *Gestalt* theory. *Gestalt* theory differs from behaviorism in that it looks not at the relationship between separate elements, such as stimulus and response, but instead considers these events as interrelated parts of a single whole. According to *Gestalt* theory, you can't even separate stimulus and response into independent things. Organization is everything. It's the classic case of the whole being more than the sum of its parts. The parts themselves aren't nearly as important as the interrelations among them.

For example, if you have a baseball team and over time the players get replaced by other players, after a while none of the current players are the same as the original players but the baseball team still exists. What makes the team, then, is not the particular players. They are just arbitrary content. It's the roles and relationships among the different positions on the team that matter. In a melody, the notes don't matter. What matters is the relation between them. The same melody exists if it is moved up to a different key, even though now none of the notes are the same. Today connectionist models in neuroscience say that it's really the pattern of activation, not the actual elements in the pattern, that produces some concept or idea. This is a *Gestalt* idea, and it's still an extremely important idea in psychology.

In *Gestalt,* not only does organization matter, but some organizations are better than others. There are *Gestalt* theories as to what makes a good organization. Similarity (i.e., like goes with like) makes a good organization, as does proximity, but not all organizations work equally well. As a matter of fact, the whole field of group dynamics (identifying successful vs. unsuccessful group structures) came out of *Gestalt* theory. Cognitive dissonance theory, proposed by psychologist Leon Festinger, is just one example of a *Gestalt* theory. Cognitive dissonance theory posits that ideas in your mind can be organized in a way that's either good or bad.

According to Festinger, when you have two ideas or more and they are consistent with each other (e.g., "America is good" and "I like America"), this is called "consonance," but when you have two ideas or more that are inconsistent with each other (e.g., "Bob stole five dollars" and "Bob is honest"), it's called "dissonance." Two ideas like "I married this guy because I loved him, and he's also very rich" are consonant. "I married this woman because she's beautiful but her mother is a beast" are dissonant ideas. The ideas can be anything. If you hate having classes at 7 A.M. but you just wrote an essay stating that it's terrific to have classes at 7 A.M., that creates dissonance. If you believe something but then behave in a manner inconsistent with your belief, that creates dissonance. Dissonance is unpleasant, and people try to find a way to get rid of it.

The magnitude of dissonance is a function of the number of dissonant elements, weighted by their importance, divided by the number of consonant elements, weighted by their importance. For example, if you're choosing between two cars and you finally choose car A, then the dissonant elements are all the things you like about car B and all the things you dislike about car A. The consonant elements are the inverse of the dissonant ones, that is, all the things you dislike about the car you didn't choose and all the things you like about the car you did choose. And obviously, each thing you like or dislike plays a bigger role, depending on its importance to you. For example, if you are told by a professor to write a paper expounding a belief contrary to your real belief, then the difference between your belief and what you write creates dissonance, but the fact that the professor asked you to write it and offered a reward or punishment creates consonance by justifying your actions.

One of the most interesting things about this theory is the predictions that it makes – its generativity. Given this theory, you would predict that every time you have a difficult choice, there will be a lot of cognitive dissonance. The theory says that in these cases you must somehow deal with the dissonance. One way to deal with the dissonance is to add new consonant elements. You might, for instance, read as much as you can about why the choice you made was good. If you chose car A, you could read an article praising car A to add to the consonant elements in your mind about car A. What you choose affects the kind of information you seek out after making your decision. If you're writing that essay expounding a belief you don't agree with, it's quite possible that, while writing the essay, you'll convince yourself that there are good elements in the ideas you had rejected. This would reduce dissonance by adding new consonant elements. Changing your attitude is one way to deal with dissonance. What you're doing is creating a new *Gestalt* organization in your mind.

As you can see, *Gestalt* and cognitive dissonance are quite different from behaviorism. The latter says that the cognitive – that is, what's going on in the subject's mind – doesn't matter, while the former considers the mental activity as *all* that matters. (This is not to say that *Gestalt* is introspectionism. Cognitive dissonance is studied experimentally using fairly objective measures.) According to *Gestalt,* your motivations about your own cognitions are what matters. The cognitions are so powerful that it really matters to you whether they fit together and make sense. Making these cognitions fit together is a very strong motivation. Confronted with dissonance, you'll take action or make changes to try to increase consonance. Studies have shown that you can get people to write essays about how grasshoppers are great to eat, and these people will then go ahead and eat grasshoppers. So, it's not just attitude that changes but behavior, too.

EXERCISE

Read the Festinger and Carlsmith (1959) article. Your assignment is to compare the predictions that learning theory/ behaviorism and cognitive dissonance theory would each make. For learning theory, you can choose either operant conditioning or classical conditioning.

Begin by stating the assumptions, axioms, and postulates of each theory relevant to making predictions for the study. For each theory, any further assumptions that you believe need to be made in order to make predictions must be clearly identified as your additional assumptions (as distinct from the theory).

Suppose that you choose Skinner's reinforcement theory. To complete the exercise, pretend that you're Skinner and that you've been given a certain set of conditions in an experiment, and you have to predict what will happen. Then repeat this exercise as if you were Festinger and make predictions based on cognitive dissonance theory. Think about how the predictions differ.

The purpose of this exercise is to find out what theories do and don't do. Many people study theory, and they just memorize the theory. They never test whether that theory allows them to do something like make predictions. Also, often people already have the data. In this case, it's easy to say, "Here are the data. Now I'll show you how the theory explains them." Explanations are much easier than predictions. What you'll find out as you do this exercise is that there will be gaps. You'll ask yourself questions like "Should I assume that the students really made an effort to write this essay?" "Should I assume that they all wrote a pretty good essay or not?" You'll have to make some assumptions, to add information that doesn't exist, in order to make the prediction. The assumptions you have to make for the two theories will be different. In part, that's the point of the exercise. What you're adding is often not even mentioned in the original statement.

It's interesting that the different theories will require different assumptions. How then, you may ask, can you design a study to test competing theories? The assumption in science is always that when you test a theory, you are testing it against some competing theory. But rarely is a study an actual test of competing theories. It's a real problem in the history and sociopolitics of theory. We want you to be sure that you don't make that mistake. If you add something, you must make it clear that you added it and that it wasn't in the original theory.

As for the length, aim for four or five typewritten, double-spaced pages: two or three pages per theory. For the predictions, you should have about one page per prediction. Use illustrations – one for your dissonance prediction and one for your conditioning prediction. In other words, write the paper as if you were writing a scientific report with tables and figures.

19. Some Theories in Cognitive and Social Psychology

Let's begin by discussing the exercise in the previous chapter. As you learned if you read the Festinger and Carlsmith (1959) article, cognitive dissonance theory more accurately predicted the results of the experiment. And you may have noticed that in order to evaluate these theories and their predictions, you had to make assumptions about the difference between *asking* the subject to do something and *requiring* him or her to do it.

WORKING WITH THE THEORY OF BEHAVIORISM

First, what does reinforcement theory say about the difference between asking and requiring? Answer: *Nothing* in reinforcement theory says anything about the difference between asking and requiring a subject to do something. You might think it's reasonable to assume that if you're asked, you'll write a higher-quality essay than if you're required to do it – that being asked provides a greater incentive. That's a reasonable assumption, though it is certainly *not* a part of reinforcement theory. Reinforcement theory just says that when a behavior is observed and then reinforced, there will be a larger effect if the reinforcement is larger, repeated, or more intense. There are different qualities of reinforcement that will increase or decrease its impact, but the theory only refers to the quality of reinforcement *given the behavior*. The difference between being asked and being required concerns the behavior itself *prior* to reinforcement. What you'd say about the behavior itself is *not* part of reinforcement theory, though it could be part of other kinds of learning theories.

This is the distinction we referred to in the previous chapter. You must always be careful to make it clear when you're adding something to what the theory actually says, even if what you may be be reasonable and justified. It may be reasonable to assume that asking will provide a greater incentive than requiring, but if you make that assumption, you are *adding* something that is not in reinforcement theory. There might be theories other than reinforcement theory that would justify the assumption you're making, but with operant conditioning you're not supposed to take into account what the subject might be thinking or feeling.

282

In addition, you may also have found that the whole logic of conditioning that associates a stimulus with a response gets muddled when it is difficult to tell what the stimulus is. The stimulus can't be what the experimenter *thinks* the stimulus is. It must be what the *subject* of the experiment thinks it is. Often in ordinary life, this is almost impossible to pin down. In laboratory situations, it was thought that it would be easier to identify. But it turns out that even in situations where the reward or punishment is as simple as food or a shock, things are not straight-forward.

WORKING WITH THE THEORY OF COGNITIVE DISSONANCE

On the other hand, the theory of cognitive dissonance has problems of its own. For example, if you're in a situation where you are required to do something and you're given a large incentive, you may feel that you're being bribed. If people feel uncomfortable when they're being pressured or paid to do something they don't want to do, then that's dissonant with being an honest person who does only what he truly believes, not what he's force or bribed to do. If that's true, you can argue that those circumstances would create a highly dissonant state. If, on the other hand, you feel that you are *not responsible* for things you are required to do, even if you are paid, then that would be consistent with doing something you otherwise wouldn't do and would create a consonant state. One of the difficulties in using cognitive dissonance theory is figuring out what the *theory itself* says about what counts as dissonant and what counts as consonant. And the truth is that the theory doesn't say anything about this.. The theory just gives the equation for calculating the total amount of dissonance. There is no separate theory that articulates the psychological principles for determining what counts as dissonant and what counts as consonant. You often end up relying on intuitions about people like "People feel bad when they say something that they don't believe."

Almost all the research based on cognitive dissonance theory makes the assumption that if you're asked to advocate a position on an issue that is the opposite of your real opinion, you feel dissonance. In other words, counter-attitudinal advocacy is assumed to cause dissonance. That sounds reasonable. It assumes that people care about the truth. But how can we be sure that that's always true? The problem is that the theory relies on the assumption that people prefer honesty, but it does not say this explicitly.

Another problem is one of resolution. The theory assumes that one of the ways you resolve dissonance is through attitude change. At least the predictions in the studies make that assumption. Is attitude change the only way to deal with dis-sonance? Might another method be to become schizophrenic? A schizophrenic might simply disavow the dissonant behavior and claim that she didn't do it. Might the subject just resolve her dissonance by thinking "This experiment stinks, I hate psychology, and I'll never participate in one of these experiments again"? This is called "derogating" the experiment or the experimenter, and it has actually been observed as a mode of resolution. Certain people who tend to derogate won't show any attitude change at all. So, you have made an assumption that attitude change will be the mode of resolution, but attitude change might not necessarily follow.

One more thing: We have always been fascinated by the dissonance equation itself. Remember that Amount of dissonance = [no. of dissonant items × importance]/[total no. of dissonant and consonant items × importance]. The funny thing about this equation is that no one has ever really questioned it. Why do you divide the dissonant elements by the consonant ones? Couldn't you make a case for an equation that subtracts the consonant elements from the dissonant ones? That's a theoretical choice. If you believe that as consonance goes up dissonance goes down, you have the choice of either dividing dissonance by consonance or subtracting consonance from dissonance. This is a choice you have to make when you construct your theory. And when you make that choice, you'd better have a reason for choosing one rather that the other.

One advantage of the equation as constructed is that by having dissonant elements divided by consonant elements, when the number of dissonant elements is zero the whole equation equals zero. We suppose this is the reason this construction was chosen, but we're not sure that we see the justification for it. The theory seems to assume that dissonance is higher in the hierarchy of motivations than consonance, so that in its absence there is no motivation to change attitudes. But couldn't achieving *even greater consonance* be motivating?

ANOTHER BIG THEORY WORTH MENTIONING: PSYCHODYNAMICS

Now, let's move on to a completely different topic. What can we say about Freud's psychodynamic theory? Is it a good theory? Is it even one theory or is it more than one? Recall our discussion in the previous chapter about the characteristics of a good theory. One controversial aspect of psychodynamic theory is its distinction between the conscious and the unconscious or preconscious. In the early version of the theory, there was a repressed unconscious. Then Freud developed the idea of the ego and the superego, which made for a very different theory. And then there are those psychosexual stages.

Evidence for Repression

People say that it's hard to know what psychodynamic theory predicts, but it depends on what part of the theory you're talking about. The part of the theory that deals with repression – the contention that people repress unwanted thoughts – has been tested. In fact, there is a fair amount of research on the extent to which people will repress thoughts. Researchers have looked at thoughts that they know are difficult for people to bear and have studied the extent to which people repress them. One way to test for repression is to give subjects words that are printed in different colors and ask them to name the colors as quickly as possible. All they're supposed to do is name the colors. The more accessible the word is to consciousness, the more difficult the task is. For example, if we hold up a sign with the word "blue" but written in the color red (e.g., blue), it is more difficult to for you to name the color (red) because you're looking at the word "blue." The word is interfering with your ability to say the name of the color the word is written in, because it is very accessible to you. If a word is less accessible (and, as a result, does not slow down color naming), psychologists conclude that the associated thought may be repressed.

For example, in the experimental situation you might have a variety of different words mixed with a variety of innocuous control words, but you might include words like "mother" or "penis" and then note how slow the subject is in naming the color. If the word is repressed, the subject will actually name the color very quickly. In this case, the subject represses the word to such an extent that it is easy to name the color. The more an idea comes to consciousness, the less it's repressed and the harder it is to name the color. This is a very clever, nonobvious way of testing for repression. So there are, in fact, parts of psychoanalytic theory that are testable and have been tested. You can, therefore, use at least parts of the theory to make predictions.

Evidence for Psychosexual Stages

A classic study done years ago that we really like is an example of what you could do with psychodynamic theory if you made the effort. (Most people just haven't made the effort.) The study we're referring to was done by a psychological anthropologist at Harvard in the late 1920s to early 1930s. He tested the psychosexual stage idea, which would seem to be one of the harder ideas of the psychodynamic theory to test. Of the alleged psychosexual stages, the first is the oral stage (during the first year or so of life), in which, according to Freud, infants get their sexual gratification through the mouth. The infant can become fixated by having too much oral stimulation or too little. There are positive fixations as a result of having too much stimulation and negative fixations as a result of having too little. Usually the theory focuses on negative fixations, and this study did, too. In the case of a negative oral fixation, it usually means that the baby didn't get enough breast-feeding.

You can go to different cultures and find out what really occurs when the child is taken off the breast. Historically, all cultures have breast-feeding, but they differ as to when the child is weaned. The time for weaning might come at one month, six months, or even a few years. There's significant variation in the acceptable time for weaning in different cultures. This anthropologist reasoned that if Freud was correct, the sooner breast-feeding ends, the more likely the baby is to develop a negative oral fixation.

The second psychosexual stage is the anal stage, and the study examined the evidence across cultures for the existence of fixations related to this stage. According to the theory, from age one to about age three, it is the anal area where sexual gratification is received. Here the main issue has to do with toilet training. Toilet training supposedly has to do with whether one becomes anal-retentive or anal-expulsive. Again, this is an area where cultures differ. Some cultures expect a child to train himself, do it correctly, and not make a mess by one year of age. Other cultures allow a child to grow to six or seven without the strict expectation of toilet training. The Harvard researcher recorded the age at which children were weaned and later toilet-trained. Based on this information, the theory should have been able to predict the prevalence of oral or anal fixations.

Separately, another set of researchers classified people according to what kind of medical knowledge they had. Freud's theory was that fixations worked their way out symbolically via sublimation. One way a culture could work out fixations symbolically would be in decisions about health care. This is obviously a very important issue across cultures, which all have some sort of accommodation for taking care of the body. The idea was to classify the cultures in terms of whether they try to deal with issues orally or anally. The prediction was that the more that the prevalence of oral or anal fixations in the culture seemed called for according to the theory, the more the medical care could be classified as either oral or anal. This would be the way the culture would compensate symbolically for the childhood fixations. This research project was carried out, and a relation was found that accorded with the theory.

Truth be told, we find the results to be a bit incredible, and the experiment has never been replicated. The point, however, is that it is unfair to say that the psychosexual stages theory doesn't make predictions that you can test. The theory does in fact make predictions that are interesting and not obvious. Clearly, without the theory, the sorts of cross-cultural predictions these experimenters made would not have been made or even thought of. One the best things about a theory is the extent to which the logic of the theory suggests looking for something that you never would have thought of looking for without the theory. Who'd have thought of comparing toilet training and weaning ages and methods without Freudian theory? We are not saying that this is a great theory, but we'll give it credit for making nonobvious predictions.

Defense Mechanisms and the Problem of Testability

The criticism of psychoanalytic theory is accurate not in its claim that the theory makes no predictions but in the claim that the theory gives itself so many degrees of freedom that it's hard to know, in some cases, what would count as a disconfirmation. The study we have just mentioned on symbolic compensation in medical practice would be an exception to this criticism. Here it is pretty clear what would count as a disconfirmation. Nonetheless, there are many other aspects of psychoanalytic theory that are very hard to disprove. A prime example is *defense mechanisms*. Even in the study just mentioned that predicted symbolic compensation in medical practices, you have to wonder what psychoanalytic psychologists would have said had the experiment gone the other way. If the results had been the opposite of what the theory predicted, what would the defenders of the theory have said? We, unfortunately, think that they would have simply dismissed the experiment as having made the wrong prediction in the first place. Adherents might say that symbolic compensation was not the thing to predict at all. They might say that, on the contrary, the theory predicts repression, which would produce the opposite of the results the experimenters predicted.

In fact, the theory is so flexible that it could be used to justify just about any outcome you want. For repression, there are many defense mechanisms that are essential for understanding the clinical aspects of psychodynamics. The theory of defense mechanisms generally allows the theory to explain away anything that seems to contradict the theory. Concepts like "projection," the claim that another person has the feelings that you yourself have, likewise can be used to explain away any inconsistencies in the data. If the data show that you have the feelings that the theory predicts, then the theory is right. If you don't have the right feelings, then you're projecting them onto someone else. The concept of "reaction formation" is also very slippery. For example, the theory predicts that there should be hatred for the father as an authority figure and a symbol of phallic aggression. In the sixties, when students were rioting and trying to wreck institutions like Columbia University, psychoanalytic adherents said, "You see, the institution is a symbol of phallic authority, so what is happening is the kind of aggression against the father figure that the theory would predict." The riots of the sixties, then, were said to serve as proof of the theory's validity.

But what if the students show love for the institution? After all, the students in general haven't tried to destroy Columbia. They might even express a certain love for the institution. Psychoanalytic theory is ready here too with an explanation, but now it's "reaction formation." They claim that the students really hate the institution, but since that is an unwanted impulse, they repress it. By the logic of reaction formation, you love the thing you hate. As you probably guess, this sort of flexibility tends to frustrate all but true believers in the theory. This is what we mean when we say that the theory has too many degrees of freedom. In fact, psychoanalytic theory is probably the best example that we have of a theory with too many degrees of freedom, but this may be why it's so powerful in other areas like literature, literary criticism, theatre, and the arts in general. The theory gives you the freedom to provide a learned and seemingly profound explanation of anything you want. It can be very inspirational in the way that any belief promising certainty can. Also, it tells you about yourself and your deep, hidden inner longings, and people like to contemplate themselves and imagine very complex inner lives. You could probably find something in the theory to confirm just about any pet peeve or grudge you've ever had. Does it appear that your mother loves you? Aha! It's just a reaction formation, and she really hates you and has caused all your problems in life. It's this kind of thing that drives the opponents of psychoanalytic theory up the wall.

NEWER THEORIES: PROSPECT THEORY AND EXPECTANCY-VALUE THEORY

Prospect Theory

Let us move on to some other theories of how people think. Prospect theory (Kahneman and Tversky 1979) argues that any choice between two options, A and B, can be influenced by whether or not you frame it as a choice between *gains* or *losses*. So, in one case you might prefer A to B, but when the same choice is framed in another way, you might prefer B to A. This is not good; in fact, it is a serious violation of the economic assumption of description invariance, that is, that it should not matter how choice alternatives are described as long the final objective outcomes are the same. For example, if you ask someone to choose between a sure gain of $250 (option A) and a 25% chance to gain $1,000 and a 75% chance of getting nothing (option B), even though the options have the same expected value, the person will probably choose A. So, it looks as if he tries to avoid the risk in option B. Now if you frame the question as one that is equivalent in terms of final outcomes but described in terms of losses, the same person will choose option B: You tell the decision maker that he has been given $1,000, but now hehas to choose between a sure loss of $750 (A) and a 75% chance of losing $1,000 and a 25% chance of losing nothing (B). The choice of option B seems to imply a preference for risk. In terms of economic logic, it makes no sense. Even though the final outcomes of the two options are equivalent under the two frames, the preferences of most people actually reverse.

The explanation for this result has to do with the way people think about gains and losses. Losses are assumed to be psychologically powerful – even small losses are unacceptable. People can't stand the sure loss of anything, and they are willing to take on risk to avoid it. Losses also hurt more than gains feel good. Therefore, people tend to alter the way they receive information based on whether the question is framed positively (as gains) or negatively (as losses). People will prefer risky options when the question is framed in terms of a loss and will be more risk averse when the question is framed in terms of a gain. Even if the expected outcome of an event is the same, they will take on risk when confronted with the alternate possibility of a sure loss, and they will avoid risking a gain even in return for a chance for more profits. These are important findings for a branch of economics called "behavioral finance."

One of the theory's more straightforward predictions is that loss is more motivating than gain. But the exercise at the end of this chapter is meant to give you an appreciation of how even a theory that seems very clear is really not straightforward. Many people consider prospect theory very clear, and in areas of decision making like marketing, management, or behavioral economics, for instance, there is probably no current theory that is used more often than prospect theory. It is often used, however, after the fact, just as reinforcement theory was formerly used.

One concern that people had about reinforcement theory was its application to human behavior. What Skinner often did was to present various examples of human behavior and then explain how reinforcement theory could account for them. People complained that Skinner always seemed to be able to explain things after he already had the results, but he could not predict those results beforehand. This is because in any experimental design that is at all complicated, it is very hard to know exactly what reinforcement theory will predict. Unfortunately, prospect theory has the same problem. It's often hard to know what to predict using it, unless you oversimplify the choices.

EXPECTANCY-VALUE THEORY

Now let's talk about expectancy-value theory. This theory, fortunately, is relatively straightforward. It argues that the strength of a behavioral intention, which could be a decision to do one thing rather than another, equals expectancy (i.e., likelihood of success) times value (i.e., how good the outcome is). The more you believe that your action will work out, that is, the higher your expectancy, the more motivated you are to take the action. So, the idea is very simple. You are much more likely to take an action if you are fairly sure that the result will be what you want. Also, you are much more likely to do something if the outcome is something you value.

The two main features of the theory are pretty straightforward, but it's their interaction that is interesting. There is an important use of the theory in economics in what are called "subjective expected utility models." There are different forms of subjective expected utility models, but what they have in common is the idea that there is a multiplicative combination of expectancy and value. The logic here is as follows: Suppose I go into the lottery, and the jackpot is $1,000,000; I'll care about the likelihood of winning or not winning. If I hear that there is only a one in a billion chance of winning rather than a one in a thousand chance, I'll care about that difference. But if the lottery is something I don't value since, for example, there is only $1 in the jackpot, who cares what the odds are? There's only $1 at stake.

From a mathematical point of view, a key aspect of the expectancy-value model is that it has two main effects plus an interaction. Expectancy as the main effect will almost always occur, and value as the main effect will almost always occur, but the interesting part of the model is the interaction. The rest is pretty pedestrian.

EXERCISE

Think about a particular question that may be relevant to your discipline and try to predict the outcome by using prospect theory and expectancy-value theory. Please be sure to indicate the predicted differences that may exist from applying both theories and the commonalities. For example, political scientists could explain how voters choose a candidate by using prospect theory and expectancy-value theory. Economists could explain how a portafolio manager picks stocks based on these theories. A historian could explain a general's decision to go into a battle by realizing the gains or loses predicted by prospect theory and by expectancy-value theory. Again, the purpose of this chapter's exercise is not necessarily to get the right answer but to think through the logic you will try to use to get this answer. With prospect theory, we think it is fair to say that the theory should be applicable to the exercise because, in fact, it has been used for very similar kinds of problems. There's a sense in which, in the case of expectancy-value theory, one has to be more careful in regard to what's fair and what's not fair for that theory.

When expectancy-value theory has been used, it is more commonly used subject by subject. So, the usual way is to give every subject each of the different frames and say, "For you, what is the value of this, and what is the likelihood of this outcome?" You'd get the actual subjective value for each subject. Then if you randomly assigned the subjects to different conditions, you'd know the values of each person, and you could make a prediction. This shows how constrained that model would be in certain circumstances. In many circumstances, you simply cannot go to every individual for whom you wish to make a prediction and get him or her to list all the values and all the expectancies for every possible condition. It's simply not practical. If that's what you have to do to use the theory, then you just have to accept it, but you can also see that this limits the usefulness of the theory.

To make it useful, it might be legitimate to say, "What might the subjects say about the expectancy values of these different conditions?" However, what you will probably want to do in the exercise we gave you is to work at a higher level of analysis rather than looking at the content. So, if you could say something about expectancy value with respect to the manipulation itself, that might be better. You might ask, "What feels more valuable?" In other words, you're imagining that anticipating the positive outcome is more valuable than anticipating the negative outcome or vice versa. You can do this regardless of content and make a general statement about it. Is it more valuable to get the positive outcome you want or escape the negative outcome you want to avoid? This is a subject that psychologists know something about.

In fact, Kahneman and Tversky (1979) have taken advantage of some of that work in prospect theory. Work that was done in animal learning and early psychology many years ago argues that the intensity of avoiding the negative is greater than the intensity of approaching the positive. Psychologists have measured this effect by such means as attaching a harness to an animal and then putting out food and measuring how hard the animal pulls to approach it. To measure the negative effect, psychologists have applied a shock to animals and measured how hard they pull on the harness to get away. We personally feel great uncertainty about this "rat-in-harness" data, if for no other reason than that you can't equate the food used in one part of the experiment with the shock used in the other. Maybe if the experimenters had used a very slight pain versus a large reward, the result would have been different; or imagine the result if they had starved the animal beforehand or if the animal was dying of thirst. In science it's always an iffy proposition to make claims about the relationship between two very different variables because you can't calibrate their manipulation. You can never argue that the manipulation of one is equivalent to the manipulation of the other. This isn't a problem in prospect theory, where you're comparing, say, the gain of five dollars with the loss of five dollars. That's very different from food versus shock.

20. Signal Detection Theory and Models for Trade-Offs in Decision Making

SIGNAL DETECTION THEORY

The first topic we will cover in this chapter is signal detection theory (SDT). Let's begin by considering an area of psychology closely associated with SDT – psychophysics. The first psychological experiments ever conducted were in psychophysics. Psychophysics describes how physical stimuli, such as light or sound waves, are translated into subjective impressions – what we see and hear. For example, we know that the wavelength of light determines the color we perceive.

But our subjective impressions do not map onto physical stimuli in a one-to-one fashion. There are several variables that can affect our subjective impression. Take the *physical environment.* Imagine that you are listening to another person at a cocktail party, and the party grows so loud that you have a difficult time hearing the person. This is an example of the physical environment interfering with your perception. The *neural structure* of the perceiver can make a difference as well; if the person has some sort of neural damage, it can interfere with or alter his or her perceptions of a physical stimulus. People who are red-green color-blind do not have the subjective impressions of green or red. Finally, the *motivation* of the perceiver can make a difference, especially when a task is difficult. Imagine that you are looking in a Where's Waldo puzzle. The probability that you will find Waldo in a specified time is a function not only of the physical stimulus, in this case the complexity of the picture, but also of the effort and attention you put into the task.

SDT is a theory of behavior in imperfect performance domains such as perception, where there is human error and much of our performance is in some sense *probabilistic.* Imagine that you are asked to perform a task in which a person standing 500 yards away from you has a flashlight, and you are asked to indicate every few seconds whether the flashlight is on or off (assume that the person is in fact turning the flashlight on and off randomly). If it is a sunny day, this will be a fairly difficult task. You will probably say that the flashlight is on when in fact it is off several times, and vice versa. How can we describe your behavior on this task? It will be a function of the difficulty of the task, your motivation to do well, and maybe your personal bias toward saying "yes" or "no" SDT is a framework

291

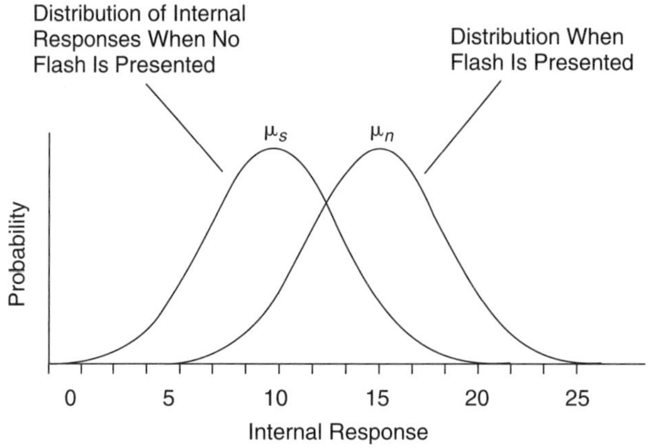

Figure 20.1. Diagram of signal and noise distributions for signal detection theory (SDT).

that combines perceptual processes and motivation and decision-making processes. It allows us to describe quantitatively the kinds of mistakes people make, as well as the likelihood of mistakes, given a particular perceptual task.

SDT begins with the "signal," a random variable whose presence one is trying to detect (in the previous example, the flashlight being on). Background physical and neural activity (such as the sunlight) creates "noise," also a random variable. The subjective intensities of signal versus noise activation have different distributions. We assume for simplicity that both distributions are normal with the same standard deviation, but with a shift in the average, or mean, level.

In Figure 20.1, we've drawn the mean for the noise distribution, μ_n, to the left of the mean for the signal distribution, μ_s, because the subjective intensity of the noise is typically lower than that of the signal. The farther the signal distribution is to the right of the noise distribution, the more distinguishable the signal will be from the noise. The regions where the two distributions overlap are the areas in which errors in perception are made – places where you think you saw the signal but you didn't (false alarms) and places where the signal was present but you didn't perceive it (misses). As the distance between μ_n and μ_s increases, this overlapping area decreases, resulting in fewer errors. For any internal response, x_i, that you generate, the height of the line from x_i to the top of the two probability distributions tells you the likelihood that the observation came from the signal distribution, $p(S|x)$, or from the noise distribution, $p(N|x)$.

How should you set your criterion C on the internal response axis, X_i, such that for values greater than C you will say that the signal was present and for values less than C you will say that it was not present? One possible decision rule would be:

If $p(S|x)/p(N|x)$ is at least 1, then say "yes," it's a signal;
If $p(S|x)/p(N|x)$ is less than 1, then say "no," there is no signal.

The decision appears to be straightforward, and as you can see from Figure 20.1, if you place your criterion C at the intersection of the two

Table 20.1. Payoff matrix for SDT

Truth Is:	Say "Yes"	Say "No"
Signal	Hit +	Miss −
Noise	False Alarm −	Correct Rejection +

probability distributions where $p(S|x)/p(N|x) = 1$, then the probability of a miss is equal to the probability of a false alarm. But, what if the two types of error are not equally costly? Here we need to introduce the concept of a "payoff matrix." When deciding whether x_i is a signal, there are four possible outcomes, and each outcome can be associated with a different level of benefit or cost Table 20.1).

In the case of sentencing a criminal to the death penalty, it is clear that the cost of a false alarm, or judging someone guilty who is in fact innocent, can be immeasurable. Or consider, for example, a radar operator whose job is to alert the military base to incoming enemy planes. The operator thinks he saw a momentary blip on the screen, and now he or she must decide if it was a true signal – an enemy plane – or just noise. What are the various costs of the two kinds of errors associated with this decision? The operator will no doubt suffer some penalty for a false alarm – putting the base on red alert when there is in fact no danger is a waste of time and effort on the part of many people. But the cost of a miss – of failing to recognize the signal of the enemy plane – is potentially far greater, and could result in the destruction of equipment and the death of personnel. The consequences of the four different outcomes can be represented by a utility value for each outcome, which will typically be positive for the hits and correct rejections and negative for the misses and false alarms.

If you know the probabilities of the four potential outcomes, you can compute the expected utility (EU) of saying "yes" ("defendant is guilty," "it's an enemy plane") and of saying "no" The average or EU of each action can be represented as follows:

$$EU(\text{"Yes"}|x) = p(S|x)U(Hit) + p(N|x)U(\text{False Alarm})$$
$$EU(\text{"No"}|x) = p(S|x)U(Miss) + p(N|x)U(\text{Correct Rejection})$$

The probabilities of the four types of events depend, of course, on where you set your criterion C for declaring x to be either a signal or noise. As you move C to the right – that is, as you become more conservative in calling something a signal – you reduce your chances of false alarms and of hits, but you also increase your chances of misses and correct rejections. A decision rule that makes sense when the two types of correct decisions and the two types of errors have different consequences is the following:

Say "yes" if and only if $EU(\text{"Yes"}|x) > EU(\text{"No"}|x)$.

if misses, for example, are far more costly than false alarms, as in our military example, you would move C to the left to reduce the chances of misses. If false alarms are far more costly than misses, as in our death penalty example, you would move C to the right to reduce the changes of false alarms. In the next section, we discuss how to compute where C should be.

As we mentioned earlier, the number of both types of error decreases as the distance between μ_n and μ_s increases, that is, as overlap decreases between the two types of distributions. The distance between μ_n and μ_s represents how difficult the task is. It is referred to as d' and is calculated by taking the difference between μ_n and μ_s and dividing by the standard deviation of the populations. If you make the simplifying assumption that the distributions are standard normal, and thus have a standard deviation of 1, then you can calculate d' simply by subtracting the z-scores for μ_n and μ_s:

$$d' = Z\mu_s - Z\mu n$$

We also discussed how a perceiver may be biased toward saying "yes" or "no" as a result of the payoff matrix. The bias parameter most often used in decision making is called C, and it is calculated in the following manner:

$$C = -.5(Z(\text{Hit Rate})) + (Z(\text{False Alarm Rate})).$$

C will be 0 when there is no bias, in other words, when

$$\text{False Alarm Rate} = \text{Miss Rate} = 1 - \text{Hit Rate, and therefore } Z(\text{FA}) = -Z(\text{Hit}).$$

MODELING DECISION MAKING

Psychologists have long been interested in decision making, particularly when decisions are complex and difficult. One interesting avenue of research has looked at the ways in which statistical models and human experts *differ* in the ways in which they use information and the kinds of decisions they make. Now we'll talk about how we can use statistical models to make predictions or decisions based on a set of data, how we can compare the output of statistical models to the judgments made by experts, what to do when building a statistical model based on outcome data is not possible, and how to build a statistical model from expert judgments.

This area of research – multiattribute decision making or multiple-cue predictions – is important in politics and economics as well as in everyday life. One can imagine studying this in different ways: From a historical perspective, it might be interesting to see what information has actually been used by decision makers. For example, political scientists have studied the following question: How much do politicians base their decisions on political polls? We hear a lot about poll-driven politics, but how often do politicians actually alter their policies based on that information? Or, from a statistical perspective, one can study the effectiveness (the "statistical properties") of various algorithms for predictions or, as in Part III of this book, compare predictions made by different individuals or institutions.

Here, we describe some research from the psychology literature on the effectiveness of various prediction methods that decision makers sometimes use. For example, assume that you are asked to predict the grade point average (GPA) of a sophomore at Columbia University. You are given the following information about the student:

first name	physical attractiveness
hair color	verbal SAT
interest in school	math SAT
high school GPA	hobbies
social skills	

How would you use this information to arrive at an estimate of the GPA? How would this differ from what a statistical or *actuarial* model would do?

You might begin by reflecting on past experience and assign weights to different factors. You might, for example, decide to weight high school GPA heavily and to assign a weight of 0 to name and hair color. An actuarial model would be based instead on actual values of both the predictor variables and the dependent measure that you are trying to predict; you would need to have a dataset that contained the values of all predictor variables and also the actual GPAs of a set of sophomores. Using linear regression, the actuarial model calculates beta weights for each variable, which tell you how *diagnostic* each variable is for the prediction of GPA. Then you can plug in the data for any individual and get an estimate of GPA.

Why does the way in which human experts use predictor variables like name and undergraduate GPA often differ from the way an actuarial model uses them? And why should we use human experts in the first place when an actuarial model can make those predictions for us?

Let's answer the second question first: Why should we use human experts to make predictions about the future instead of using an actuarial model? First of all, you often don't have the data necessary to build an actuarial model, so you need to rely on experts. Second, sometimes the prediction you are making isn't important enough to go to the trouble to get data and build a model. Another important consideration is that actuarial models are based on the *past*, and the environment in which you make a prediction could change in ways that alter the diagnosticity of your predictors. Finally, actuarial models lack common sense, or what is referred to as the human ability to pick up on "broken-leg cues." An actuarial model may predict that a certain person will win a marathon based on past performance and conditions on the day of the race, but it will be way off the mark if that runner broke his leg and the model has no broken-leg variable. A human expert, in contrast, has the real-world knowledge and ability to include any number of unforeseen variables in his or her decision making.

So, an expert has the advantages of not needing past data, speed, sensitivity to changes in the environment, and the ability to pick up on commonsense cues. What are the disadvantages of using human experts? Unfortunately, there are some serious disadvantages. Experts are *inconsistent*, to varying degrees, due to many factors – including fatigue, boredom, and distraction. Experts' strategies for making decisions can vary over time and change without their awareness. Another problem is that different experts use different strategies, and without actuarial data, it is difficult to know which strategy is the best.

Now we're going to introduce a technique called "bootstrapping," which allows us to make the implicit judgment strategies used by experts explicit, thereby allowing us to remove the inconsistency characteristic of most experts. (Please note that this is not the same as the bootstrap method used in statistics.)

To bootstrap a human judgment or prediction, you begin by regressing each of the predictor variables used by the expert onto the expert's predictions. Using the example we began with, you might end up with an equation such as

$$Y = .04 + 1.0 \text{ high school GPA} + .08 \text{ Verbal SAT} + .05 \text{ Math SAT}$$
$$+ .3 \text{ Interest in School} + \text{ residuals.}$$

This equation shows you the average weights that the expert gave to each of these factors when estimating college GPA. The regression equation also tells you which of these weights are significantly different from 0, that is, which ones influenced the estimate of college GPA.

To determine how good this expert's bootstrapped model is, you can correlate the model's predictions with the actual GPA data. To determine how consistent the expert is, you can correlate the model's output (the value predicted by the bootstrap model) with his or her actual intuitive judgments; the higher the correlation, the more consistent the expert is.

FURTHER READING FOR PART VI

If your want a good introduction to social cognition, you can read the book by by Susan Fiske and Shelly Taylor (2007), which is one of the best advanced introductory texts on the topic. If you want to know more about social science methodology, the book by John Gerring (2001) is very solid and very thorough.

On methods for psychology, see the book by John J. Shaughnessy, Eugene Zechmeister, and Jeanne Zechmeiste (2006). Finally, on decision making, the book by Reid Hastie and Robyn Dawes (2001) compares rational choice and the psychology of judgement.

For your assignment, you will be given a set of problems and will be asked to calculate the parameters d' and C.

EXERCISES

PART 1

The following data come from an experiment on face recognition, where viewers discriminate "old" (previously seen) faces from "new" ones. The task consists of saying "yes" when they think that they have seen a particular face before and "no" otherwise.

	Response	
Shown face actually is	"yes"	"no"
OLD	75	23
NEW	23	75

I. Compute d' as an estimate of viewers' memory sensitivity in this experiment. Also, compute an index of their response bias, C, and another response bias index, β.
II. The next set of data come from a replication of the same experiment, except that the investigator hypnotized her respondents this time in an effort to improve their memory.

	Response	
Shown face actually is	"yes"	"no"
OLD	99	1
NEW	69	31

Compute d', β, and C for the responses of these hypnotized viewers. Comparing these values to those of nonhypnotized viewers, did hypnosis improve viewers' memory for faces?

PART 2

Following are data for twelve people who graduated from Columbia University's Graduate School of Business in 1989. For each student, the table shows the undergraduate GPA, the number of months of previous business experience, verbal and quantitative Graduate Management Admission Test (GMAT) scores, graduate GPA, and whether she or he concentrated in finance or economics (dummy coded), as well as the category (marketing, finance, consulting, or other; also dummy coded). Your first task is to make predictions of their starting base salaries (excluding bonuses). To do so, please cover up the last column in the table, which lists the actual salaries they received. The salaries range from around $40,000 to $110,000, with a mean of about $75,000. Write down the estimates in another column on the right-hand side of the page. After you are finished, write down which predictor variables you felt were the most important when making your predictions.

Student	UGPA	BUSEXP	VGMAT	QGMAT	GGPA	FinEcon	Market	Cother	Firm	Internet	Sother	Salary
1	2.5	0	35	30	2.6	0	0	1	0	1	0	43000
2	3.2	0	36	40	3.3	0	0	1	0	0	1	63000
3	4	38	41	35	4	1	0	0	0	1	0	58000
4	3	6	33	46	3.3	0	0	1	0	0	1	69000
5	3.6	23	38	35	2.4	1	0	0	1	0	0	85000
6	3	60	32	45	3.4	0	0	1	1	0	0	108000
7	3.16	18	47	31	2.7	0	1	0	0	1	0	68000
8	3.36	0	42	37	2.8	0	1	0	1	0	0	79000
9	3.41	41	40	40	2.9	0	1	0	0	0	1	89000
10	3.5	0	41	43	3.2	0	0	1	0	1	0	47000
11	3.3	0	40	50	3.8	1	0	0	1	0	0	109000
12	2.85	18	28	37	2.9	1	0	0	0	0	1	83000

Your task is to consider three questions:

I. How well does a statistical, actuarial model predict a specific criterion based on past data?
II. Can a model of your own judgment processes outpredict your own judgments (bootstrapping)?
III. Would a combination of your predictions and those of the statistical model outpredict both you and the statistical model?

For Question I

Use the data to perform a regression (using all the predictor variables) and determine the best set of predictors. Determine the relevant regression output of this model, including R-squared and coefficients.

For Question II

Develop a linear model of your own judgments and see whether the model can outpredict you. To do this, enter your data into the computer program and run a regression of your own judgments onto various predictors. Compare you own ability to predict salaries with that of your model (using correlation as a measure of predictive performance).

   You need to regress your own predictions, $\hat{y}$ = "ownpred", onto the predictors in the database. You need to save the fitted values from this model, the $\hat{y}$ = "bootpred", and the residuals, z = "bootres". First, examine how well your model accounts for your own judgments, $R = r(\hat{y}\ \hat{y}\ ) = r$(ownpred, bootpred). Then calculate how well the model accounts for the criterion being predicted, $r = r(y\ \hat{y})$ = r(salary, bootpred). Compare this to your own subjective predictive accuracy, $r(y\ \hat{y}\ ) = r$(salary, ownpred). Does bootstrapping work?

For Question III

First, determine where your own predictions differ from those of a statistical model based on past data. To do this, regress your own predictions for the sample of twelve graduates onto the statistical model's predictions of the same (regress ownpred onto modpred) and save the residuals as "intuit".

   Second, regress the criterion for the graduates, salary, onto both the statistical model's predictions and your own, that is, modpred and ownpred. This model will give the predictive ability of model plus intuitive judgment. The validity of "intuition" can be gauged by calculating the correlation between salary and intuit.

PART 3

Ilana is a student at Columbia University who will graduate with an MBA degree this coming spring. In an effort to gauge whether the starting salary offers from companies that she and her friends are expecting to receive are at the right level, she has collected data on the starting salaries received by last year's graduating class; 153 students responded to her survey. They provided her with data on fourteen variables, including age, sex, citizenship, GMAT score, undergraduate major (technical or nontechnical, dummy coded), undergraduate and business school GPA, and length of prior business experience, to the students' concentration in Business School (in marketing or finance; dummy coded), as well as the job category (marketing, finance, consulting, other; also dummy coded). In addition, each person provided his or her starting salary.

  I.   Based on this information, what kind of model can Ilana use to help her answer her question about the appropriateness of any offer that she might receive this year? How would she proceed?
  II. Under what circumstances would this model give her a good answer? When might it fail?
  III. If last year's students had refused to provide their starting salaries (for confidentiality reasons) but had provided all the other information, is there anything Ilana could have done with that information? If so, what? What other information would she need to collect, for example, and what would any resulting model tell her? (Be creative in developing your answer!)

PART 4

Mr. Sen, who works for the New York City board of education, recently took the Quantitative Methods in the Social Sciences class and got the idea of testing the ability of the teachers in a pilot program in his district to correctly predict the academic achievements of their first graders six years later, when they move to the next school. In this pilot program, teachers predict the GPA that they expect a given student to achieve in grade 6 when he or she enters in grade 1. The prediction is based on seven predictor variables that include sex, socioeconomic status, IQ test score, parental involvement, and two measures of student motivation.

   For each teacher in this pilot program, Mr. Sen can find, on average, about 200 students for whom the teacher made a GPA prediction six years ago, which can now be checked against the actual GPA of those students in grade 6. For three teachers (let's call them A, B, and C), the correlations between predicted and actual GPA are as follows:

   Teacher A: r (predicted GPA, actual GPA) $= .45$
   Teacher B: r (predicted GPA, actual GPA) $= .31$
   Teacher C: r (predicted GPA, actual GPA) $= .57$

  I. Which of these teachers is the best judge? How good/bad is he or she?
  II. What do you think of the performance of all three judges? Could you evaluate whether their performance is a function of the difficulty of the task or is due to personal characteristics (e.g., carelessness)? If so, how would you do that? You may want to illustrate your answer by providing some hypothetical results of what you might find.

PART VII. TO TREAT OR NOT TO TREAT: CAUSAL INFERENCE IN THE SOCIAL SCIENCES

*Jeronimo Cortina**

* We thank Jennifer Hill for helpful comments.

21. The Potential-Outcomes Model of Causation

In this final part of the book I explore one of the most influential theoretical perspectives on causal inference in the social sciences. Chapter 21 outlines the model of causality, in which the effects of an experimental or observational treatment are defined in terms of the potential outcomes that could have occurred under different possible interventions. Chapter 22 provides a classic example from the causal inference literature, highlighting what we gain by thinking within the potential-outcomes perspective. Chapter 23 provides an example of the impact of migration on social solidarity using survey data from Mexico.[1]

Let's start by discussing what causal inference is. One goal of using quantitative data and techniques is to model the relationship between an outcome and a series of variables that predict and answer specific questions about a phenomenon of interest. Probably the basic purpose of quantitative research is to identify causal relationships between outcomes and their predictors.[2] A causal relationship occurs when one variable, under certain contextual conditions, increases the probability that an effect, manifested in another variable, will occur (Eells 1991; Gerring 2005). We can never be sure, though, that X caused Y (especially when we use observational rather than experimental data) because there are so many possible confounding variables that we cannot control for, every single one of which might have a direct or an indirect effect on Y. As has been discussed by philosophers, statisticians, and applied researchers, we cannot, in general, try to find the ultimate cause of any outcome, because there can always be many contributing causes and we want to avoid an endless search for an undefined true or original cause. In statistical analysis we seek to estimate the effects of causes rather than the causes of effects. The point is that although we

---

[1] The data come from the *Oportunidades* program, a social assistance program aimed at families with low incomes. For more information, see www.oportunidades.gob.mx.

[2] Not all social science research needs to be causally based. For example, in Part III of this book, Richard Clarida and Marta Noguer discuss how economists forecast a country's gross domestic product, exchange and interest rates, inflation, and so on, by taking certain predictors into account. The final objective is to extrapolate the values of these variables into the future, not to create "why" or "what if" types of questions, that is, questions that would seek to discover the possible causal mechanisms between outcomes and predictors. In this particular case, prediction is the goal and causal inference may be more or less indirectly relevant.

may never be certain that X causes Y, with a solid theory supporting our models, we can hypothesize causal mechanisms that help us understand the relation between an intervention and an outcome.

The definition of causation that I have adopted in this chapter raises another interesting issue. Given its probabilistic nature, causation can be conceptualized and materialized in many ways. Its most basic manifestation occurs when we explain a phenomenon by citing an earlier phenomenon that caused it (Elster 2007). The issue, then, is to decide whether a relation is causal or associational (Winship and Sobel 2004).

Thus far, the discussion about causality may seem to be fairly intuitive. All of us can come up with many causal descriptions. For example, if we push the gas pedal, the car will start to move; however, not many of us can fully explain why the car moves. So, what tools do we have at our disposal to construct a causal model and its causal mechanisms? In what follows, I answer this question by discussing the potential-outcomes model, which is one of the most influential statistical frameworks for studying causality. Next, I'll go through some examples in which I illustrate how to incorporate this model empirically.

THE POTENTIAL-OUTCOMES MODEL

The statistician Donald Rubin applied a set of statistical ideas mainly used in experiments in order to formalize the phenomenon of cause and effect when using observational data. Rubin's approach builds upon various preexisting methods and ideas in statistics and econometrics (Fisher 1925; Neyman 1923); related ideas have been developed in computer science (Pearl 2000), epidemiology (Robins and Greenland 1992), and economics (Heckman and Vytlacil 2005).[3] In any case, here we consider the core ideas, using the terminology proposed by Rubin in the 1970s. The model is based on a "potential-outcome" account of the causal relation of a particular treatment over a certain variable. That is, causal inference is based on assumptions or inferences about alternative realities. For example, a fact would answer a question like: What happened when Jose received the medicine? The *counterfactual*, in contrast, would answer a question such as: What *would have happened* if instead Jose had not received the medicine? The causal effect in this case would be the difference between taking the medicine and what would have happened if Jose had not taken the medicine. For our purposes, the most important concept to emphasize is the satisfaction of a conditional counterfactual statement.

It is impossible to give and not to give Jose the medicine at the same time, so how can we apply this counterfactual account? One way to think about this factual–counterfactual relation is via a thought experiment. Thought experiments help us answer "what if" questions such as: What would be the result if we had

---

[3] There is active debate on how credit should be shared for these ideas and also on how exactly they should be applied. For a good overview that is not tied to any particular school of inference, see Morgan and Winship (2007). In addition, the exchange of articles and comments by Sobel (2005) and Heckman (2005), while not resolving any debates, at least airs some of the controversies. Gelman and Hill (2007, chaps. 9 and 10) give a more nuts-and-bolts treatment, emphasizing implementation in the statistical package R.

carried out a randomized experiment? The point is not to actually design a randomized experiment; the point is that by going through the process of a thought experiment, we can learn a lot about a particular social phenomenon. So, before trying to explain why X causes Y, it is essential to make sure that this causal relationship really exists. In other words, we need to ask ourselves, "Does X really increase the probability of Y?" before asking, "Why is it so?" Moreover, going through a thought experiment allows us to contemplate alternative explanations that may validate or invalidate our own explanation.

Let us first look at an example. I was once involved in a project that studied the impact of international migration on children left behind, that is, on those children who did not migrate with their parents and stayed in their home countries with some of their relatives. When we started the project, there were no comprehensive national-level data that addressed this issue; nonetheless, there were many case studies and much anecdotal evidence suggesting that the impact of international migration was mixed. On the one hand, the migration of one or both parents appeared to increase school enrollment and improved children's access to health services. This was most evident among those households that received remittances in comparison to those that did not. On the other hand, the migration of one or both parents appeared to increase children's psychological and emotional problems. For example, children tended to be sadder, and in some cases they developed drug and alcohol addiction problems. Now, for the sake of argument, let's concentrate on the potential causal relation between international migration (the cause) and a child's emotional state (the outcome). So, if someone believes that a causal relation persists, that is, if someone believes that children left behind by their parents who migrated are more likely to be sad than children who live with their parents, then one also must consider the following potential outcomes:

PO1. Without parental international migration, children would not be ever sad.
PO2. With parental international migration children would tend to be sad.

How can we test which of these potential outcomes is true? One way would be to implement a survey with comparable populations differing only on their migratory experience and ask them directly. This approach would be costly and would require a great deal of preparation. Underlying this strategy it is a counterfactual thought experiment such as the following: What would have happened to children's emotional state (sadness/happiness) if a particular set of parents (comparable in terms of number of children, education, occupation, income, etc.) were selected from a particular country, and half were randomly chosen to migrate to a specific country, while the other half were selected to stay in their home countries?

There are many possible answers to this question, but two plausible possibilities are:

A1. Children would be equally sad whether their parents had migrated or not.
A2. Children would be sadder if their parents had migrated than if their parents had not migrated.

Answer (A_1) rejects (PO_1) and (PO_2), whereas answer (A_2) supports (PO_1) and (PO_2). The most important part of this thought experiment is that we get to compare counterfactual states for the same child or group of children. Statistically, the cleanest way to estimate these types of causal quantities is with a randomized experiment, which, more often than not, is quite complicated to create because of ethical and budgetary issues.[4] However, thought experiments enable us to create hypothetical scenarios that would help us, at least, to ensure that the differences between treated and control groups – that is, that the differences between the children whose parents migrated and those whose parents stayed – in fact exist and are not caused by confounders or variables that our theory failed to take into account. It is precisely here that the potential-outcomes model of causation is helpful. The model can be thought of as an extension of the conceptual apparatus of randomized experiments applied to the analysis of nonexperimental data (Winship and Sobel 2004: 482). In what follows, I summarize Rubin's notation and provide some examples of how it can be applied.

Let's assume that there is a finite population of units i and a set of treatments γ. Let $Y_{i\gamma}$ (drawn from the distribution of a random variable $Y_{i\gamma}$) denote the outcome or response when treatment γ is applied to unit i. We assume that this value $Y_{i\gamma}$ does not depend on the treatments to which other units were assigned (this assumption is known as the Stable Unit Treatment Value Assumption or SUTVA). In other words, the outcome of unit i depends only on its assignment to a particular treatment γ and not on the assignment of other units to another particular treatment γ. In a randomized experiment, each unit has a known and predetermined probability of receiving each particular treatment γ, and hence the assignment to treatment is independent of the units' potential outcomes. The underlying logic of SUTVA is precisely to imitate the random assignment of units i to treatments γ when using observational data.[5]

Now, let's define $Y_{i\gamma}$ as the effect for unit i under treatment γ and $Y_{i\gamma'}$ as the effect for unit i under treatment γ'. The unit effect would be given by the difference between treatment γ and treatment γ', that is, $Y_{i\gamma} - Y_{i\gamma'}$. We cannot estimate this effect because we cannot observe both outcomes ($Y_{i\gamma}$ and $Y_{i\gamma'}$) at the same time on unit i; however, we can estimate the average effect for the whole population $E(Y_{i\gamma} - Y_{i\gamma'}) = E(Y_{i\gamma}) - E(Y_{i\gamma'})$. To do so, we draw units from the population or a sample of the population and assign them a random treatment T_i, which equals γ that denotes the treatment to which unit i was assigned. Given that we can observe only one treatment per unit at a single point in time, this is like having a missing data problem (Rubin 1976), in which the state or treatment that we do not observe is the counterfactual. To estimate the treatment effect, we can use the data on the units that were assigned to treatment γ to compute $E(Y_{i\gamma})$; for example, we can use the mean response among units assigned to this treatment ($\bar{Y}_\gamma$) and use the data on

[4] Economist James Heckman (2005) argues that the randomized experiment should *not* be thought of as a gold standard for social science inquiry. Heckman makes the point that experiments typically involve conditions different from the way interventions would be implemented in general practice.
[5] This does not imply that random data are free of all impurities; we could also have violations of the stable unit treatment value assumption with randomized data if the data generation procedures are not done properly.

units assigned to treatment γ' to estimate the expected value $E(Y_{i\gamma'})$. Again, we can use the potential average outcome among units assigned to treatment γ' ($\bar{Y}_{\gamma'}$). In reality, what we are estimating is $E(\bar{Y}_{i\gamma}|T=\gamma)$ and $E(\bar{Y}_{i\gamma'}|T=\gamma')$. Under randomization, the treatment assignment is independent of the potential outcome. This, in turn, implies that $E(Y_{\gamma}|T=\gamma)=E(Y_{\gamma})$ for all γ. So, with randomization, we can use $\bar{Y}_{\gamma}-\bar{Y}_{\gamma'}$ as the estimate of the average effect of treatment γ versus treatment γ'.

In the social sciences, a unit cannot be subject to a treatment γ and a treatment γ' at the same time.[6] To make a well-supported causal argument about a particular phenomenon, in addition to having a good, solid theory, we need to assume that the potential outcomes are independent of the treatment assignment: $(Y_1, \ldots Y_y) \perp T$. This is like randomly assigning units to a treatment group and to a control group, as one would do in an experimental setting. To better illustrate the implications of this assumption, we continue with our previous example.

To recapitulate, we are interested in the impact of migration (T) on children's emotional states (Y). To test this, we need to compare the effect of migration on children's emotional states across different values of the treatment. That is, we want to estimate the potential effects on children's emotional states when households are exposed to migration (γ) versus when they are not exposed to migration (γ'). Then we want to estimate $E[Y_i(\gamma) - Y_i(\gamma')] = E[Y_i(\gamma)] - E[Y_i(\gamma')]$, but if we are not dealing with a random assignment to treatment, we cannot use $\bar{Y}_{\gamma}$ or $\bar{Y}_{\gamma'}$ to estimate the causal effect without bias.

IGNORABILITY AND PROPENSITY SCORES

If we observe *all* the confounding covariates (X) that are likely to influence the treatment (parental migration) as well as the outcome (children's emotional states), we just need to adjust for these confounding covariates in order to reduce bias such that $E[Y_i(\gamma)|X_i=x] = E[Y_i(\gamma)|T=\gamma, X_i = x]$ and $E[EY_i(\gamma')|X_i=x] = EY_i(\gamma')|X_i=x] = E[Y_i(\gamma')|T=\gamma', X_i=x]$ and use $\bar{Y}_{T=\gamma, X=x}$ and $\bar{Y}_{T=\gamma', X=x}$ to estimate $E[Y_i(\gamma)|X_i=x]$ and $E[Y_i(\gamma')|X_i=x]$, respectively. We need to assume that, given the background variables X, the treatment assignment is independent of the potential outcomes $Y_i(\gamma)$ and $Y_i(\gamma')$, that is, that the treatment assignment is ignorable. In other words, this means that two similar households on all the confounding covariates (X) are equally likely to have received the treatment.

This procedure will be valid when we have a large sample and if we believe that the potential outcomes and the treatment are independent. However, if we do not have a large sample or we do not have a good reason to believe that ignorability does hold, and if we can estimate both the probability that a household with some specific characteristics would be assigned to the treatment group,

---

[6] A setting where two treatments can be applied to the same unit, with no potential for interference, is computer experimentation – for example, simulation of a climate model under different initial conditions or evaluation of different machine learning algorithms on a single dataset. In chemistry or biology it is possible to apply different treatments to identical compounds or organisms, but then there is the possibility of the experimental conditions differing in some other way, for example from variation in the temperature of the laboratory.

$\Pr(T = \gamma | X)$, and the outcome, then the procedure just described will be valid. This equation is known as the "assignment mechanism," and $\Pr(T = \gamma | X)$ is known as the "propensity score."

The propensity score is the probability that a unit with characteristics X is assigned to the treatment group. If the treatment assignment is ignorable conditional on X, then $\Pr(T = \gamma | X = x, \gamma, \gamma') = \Pr(T = \gamma | X = x)$. The probability of being assigned to the treatment group is a function of the observable variables X and is conditionally independent of the variables Y_γ and $Y_{\gamma'}$. Under these conditions, we know that the treatment assignment is independent of $Y_i(\gamma)$ and $Y_i(\gamma')$; in other words, ignorability holds on the propensity score. This means that in order to estimate the causal effects when using observational data, rather than separately control all of those variables that determine the assignment to the treatment and outcome, we need only control for the propensity score.

The propensity score, if specified correctly, has all the information needed to create a design in which the treatment and control groups have identical distributions of X, assuming that sufficient overlap exists. Having groups that, on average, have similar distributions means that our design is balanced, which implies that we are going to compare households with similar incomes, number of siblings, education, and so on.

Now, how do we estimate the propensity score? We can estimate it using a logistic regression model (or similar) that estimates the probability of assignment to the treatment group, given all the covariates X that determine individuals' assignment to the treatment group $\Pr(X) = \Pr(T = \gamma | X) = \text{logit}^{-1}(\alpha + \beta X)$. We cannot know all the covariates (X) that are related to the treatment assignment and to the outcome, so there is often some bias introduced from unmeasured variables.

In the following chapter, we explore how the potential outcome framework helps us think about how to evaluate our causal inferences (or to decide what we should do) based on a counterfactual of the causal relationship when working with observational (nonexperimental) data.

22. Some Statistical Tools for Causal Inference with Observational Data

PROPENSITY-SCORE MATCHING

In order to apply the potential-outcome framework to get causal estimates that don't depend too strongly on untestable assumptions, we first need to make sure that the distributions of the treatment and control groups are balanced. This means, in other words, that we need to make sure that we are comparing apples with apples. To do so, we need to match those units that receive the treatment and those that do not receive the treatment, using a number of covariates (X). Going back to our example in Chapter 21, we need to find households that are identical in all possible, pre-treatment aspects (income, education, health, number of siblings, geographical region of origin, etc.) but that differ in their migratory experience. This procedure would create a smaller dataset with only the matched households. Once we accomplish this, we just need to estimate the average difference in means ($E(Y_\gamma - Y_{\gamma'}) = E(Y_\gamma) - E(Y_{\gamma'})$) to find the impact of migration on children's emotional state. The life of an applied researcher, however, is not that easy. The introduction of a significant number of covariates (X) such as income, education, health, number of siblings, geographical region, and so on, makes it very difficult to match treated and control households. For example, if we match two households on income, then we are probably going to unmatch them on another dimension, such as number of siblings. Therefore, matching on a large number of covariates creates a high-dimensionality problem (Dehejia 2004). A common solution to this problem is to create a one-number summary of all the covariates and then use this summary to match the households. One such one-number summary is the propensity score.

What are the virtues of matching on the propensity score? First of all, if ignorability holds and if sufficient overlap exists, then we will have, on average, probabilistically similar treatment and control groups. This means that matching will help ensure that we are comparing apples with apples. Another virtue of matching on the propensity score is that we do not have to make any assumptions about the functional form between the outcome and the Zs. Moreover, matching on the propensity score tends to be more efficient, given that we are using fewer parameters than we would in a regression setting, which could be very useful when we are working with relatively small samples (Winship and Sobel 2004).

Now, if ignorability on the propensity score holds, then the only thing that we need to do to estimate the treatment effect is to estimate $E(Y_\gamma - Y_{\gamma'}) = E(Y_\gamma) - E(Y_{\gamma'})$, which will be an unbiased and consistent estimate of the treatment effect. Before we go through a hypothetical example, let's summarize a set of possible steps that we need to go through in order to match using the propensity score:

1. Use a logistic regression model (or similar) to estimate the propensity score for all units.
2. Randomly list individuals in the treatment group (if the treatment group is smaller than the control group; if the opposite is true, then we need to match on the control group).
3. Select a treated case and note its propensity score.
4. Match the case selected in (3) with the closest propensity score of the control group.
5. Remove the cases and start again with (3) until we match all the treatment cases (removal is necessary only if we are doing matching without replacement).

Table 22.1 gives a hypothetical example showing how matching can work.

The first column of Table 22.1 indicates the household ID; the second column indicates which household is subject to the treatment (one or both migrant parents = 1) and which household is subject to the control (no migrant parents = 0). The third column shows in which region the household is located; if the household is located in a high-prevalence migratory region, then the value is 1, and it is 0 otherwise. Column 4 shows the average household income, while columns 5 and 6 indicate the hypothetical potential outcomes for the treatment (Y_γ) and control ($Y_{\gamma'}$) groups, respectively. Column 7 indicates the observed outcome, which depends on the treatment status of each household. Columns 8 and 9 show the propensity score derived from the logit regression. Finally, column 10 shows the matched parings.

Once we have our data ordered as in Table 22.1, we need to select a treated case and note its propensity score. Then we need to find the household in the control group with the closest propensity score and match them. For example, we match HH1 with HH6, HH2 with HH9, and so on. Assuming that ignorability holds, we just need to apply $E(Y_\gamma - Y_{\gamma'}) = E(Y_\gamma) - E(Y_{\gamma'})$ to estimate the average treatment effect.

To sum up, to estimate the treatment on the treated using propensity-score matching, we need to identify those pretreatment variables that predict the treatment and the outcome. Then we run a logistic regression (or similar) in which the outcome variable is the treatment and the predictors are all the confounding covariates. Once we obtain the propensity scores (the probability that a unit received the treatment), we find for each unit in the treatment group a unit in the control group with the closest propensity score (remember that we would need to check that the distributions of the treatment and control group have a good overlap and balance). When we are matching with no replacement, the match in the control group is removed and cannot be used again, whereas if we are matching with replacement, the control group unit can be used as many times as necessary.

Table 22.1. *Hypothetical example of matching*

Household (1)	Treatment (2)	Migratory Region (3)	Household Income (4)	$Y_\gamma(5)$	$Y_\gamma(6)$	Y(7)	PSCORE (8)	PSCORE (9)	Matched Units (10)
HH1	1	1	806	350	100	350	0.77	0.65	HH6
HH2	1	1	855	654	745	654	0.40	0.69	HH9
HH3	1	1	650	812	265	812	0.35	0.28	HH10
HH4	1	0	456	742	413	742	0.41	0.75	HH4
HH5	0	0	917	320	985	985	0.526	0.24	HH7
HH6	0	1	806	350	100	100	0.77	0.65	HH1
HH7	0	0	723	145	859	859	0.526	-0.80	HH5
HH8	0	0	456	742	413	413	0.41	0.75	HH2
HH9	0	1	855	654	745	745	0.4	0.69	HH2
HH10	0	1	650	812	265	265	0.35	0.28	HH3

A CLASSIC EXAMPLE: THE NATIONAL SUPPORTED WORK
DEMONSTRATION

In the mid-1980s, Robert Lalonde (1986) evaluated the effects of a labor training program on posttraining income levels. To accomplish this, he used data from a randomized evaluation of the National Supported Work (NSW) Demonstration. The NSW provided work experience for six to eighteen months to individuals who had economic and social problems prior to enrolling in the program. In addition, the NSW had preprogram information on the randomly selected participants such as preintervention income, marital status, education, and ethnicity. Therefore, if some individuals with similar preintervention characteristics were randomly assigned to the program and others were assigned to the control group, a difference in means, $E(Y_\gamma - Y_{\gamma\prime}) = E(Y_\gamma) - E(Y_{\gamma\prime})$, would be a consistent and unbiased estimate of the impact of the training program.

Lalonde compared the experimental results with nonexperimental estimators (regression, fixed effects, and latent variable selection models) to determine whether the latter could be used to replicate the unbiased, randomized experimental results. To compare the experimental results with the nonexperimental estimators, Lalonde constructed two comparison groups using data from the Panel Study of Income Dynamics (PSID) and Westat's Matched Current Population Survey–Social Security (CPS). After constructing these fake observational studies, Lalonde concluded that the nonexperimental estimators yielded results that were inaccurate relative to the experimental outcome or that were sensitive to the model's specification.

Many years later, Rajeev Dehejia and Sadek Wahba applied propensity-score methods to a subset of Lalonde's dataset to estimate the treatment impact of the NSW on postintervention earnings. In contrast to Lalonde's findings, Dehejia and Wahba (1999) found that propensity-score estimates of the treatment effect were much closer to the experimental results. This was because propensity-score matching improved the overlap between the treatment and control groups in terms of pretreatment variables. In other words, by matching on the propensity score, Dehejia and Wahba found individuals in the treatment and control groups who were, on average, probabilistically similar to each other in terms of the pretreatment variables and discarded individuals in the comparison group who were dissimilar to the program participants, thus mimicking, to some extent, a randomized experiment.

In addition to including Lalonde's confounders, Dehejia and Wahba included another variable, 1974 earnings. Including pretreatment earnings not only helped estimate the effect of job training programs but also reduced the bias generated from unmeasured variables.

Dehejia and Wahba applied the same estimators used by Lalonde (linear regression, fixed effects, and latent variable selection) to their subset of data with and without the 1974 earnings variable and found that Lalonde's basic conclusions remained unchanged. Table 22.2 shows Lalonde's and Dehejia and Wahba's results. Panel A reproduces Lalonde's results using the original variables and data. Panels B and C apply the same estimators to Dehejia and Wahba's subset without and with the 1974 earnings variable.

Table 22.2. *Lalonde's earnings comparisons and estimated training effects for the NSW male participants using comparison groups from the PSID and the CPS*[a]

Comparison group	A. Lalonde's original sample — NSW treatment earnings less comparison group earnings 1978 Unadjusted[b] (1)	Adjusted[c] (2)	Unrestricted differences in differences: Quasi-difference in earnings growth 1975–1978 Unadjusted[d] (3)	Adjusted[e] (4)	Controlling for all variables[f] (5)	B. RE74 subsample (results do not use RE74) — NSW treatment earnings less comparison group earnings 1978 Unadjusted[b] (1)	Adjusted[c] (2)	Unrestricted differences in differences: Quasi-difference in earnings growth 1975–1978 Unadjusted[d] (3)	Adjusted[e] (4)	Controlling for all variables[f] (5)	C. RE74 subsample (results use RE74) — NSW treatment earnings less comparison group earnings 1978 Unadjusted[b] (1)	Adjusted[c] (2)	Unrestricted differences in differences: Quasi-difference in earnings growth 1975–1978 Unadjusted[d] (3)	Adjusted[e] (4)	Controlling for all variables[f] (5)
NSW	886 (472)	798 (472)	879 (467)	802 (468)	820 (468)	1,794 (633)	1,672 (637)	1,750 (632)	1,631 (637)	1,612 (639)	1,794 (633)	1,688 (636)	1,750 (632)	1,672 (638)	1,655 (640)
PSID-1	−15,578 (913)	−8,067 (990)	−2,380 (680)	−2,119 (746)	−1,844 (762)	−15,205 (1155)	−7,741 (1175)	−582 (841)	−265 (881)	186 (901)	−15,205 (1155)	−879 (931)	−582 (841)	218 (866)	731 (886)
PSID-2	−4,020 (781)	−3,482 (935)	−1,364 (729)	−1,694 (878)	−1,876 (885)	−3,647 (960)	−2,810 (1082)	721 (886)	298 (1004)	111 (1032)	−3,647 (960)	94 (1042)	721 (886)	907 (1004)	683 (1028)
PSID-3	697 (760)	−509 (967)	629 (757)	−552 (967)	−576 (968)	1,070 (900)	35 (1101)	1,370 (897)	243 (1101)	298 (1105)	1,070 (900)	821 (1100)	1,370 (897)	822 (1101)	825 (1104)
CPS-1	−8,870 (562)	−4,416 (577)	−1,543 (426)	−1,102 (450)	−987 (452)	−8,498 (712)	−4,417 (714)	−78 (537)	525 (557)	709 (560)	−8,498 (712)	−8 (572)	−78 (537)	739 (547)	972 (550)

(*continued*)

313

Table 22.2. (continued)

	A. Lalonde's original sample					B. RE74 subsample (results do not use RE74)					C. RE74 subsample (results use RE74)				
	NSW treatment earnings less comparison group earnings 1978		Unrestricted differences in differences: Quasi-difference in earnings growth 1975–1978		Controlling for all variables[f]	NSW treatment earnings less comparison group earnings 1978		Unrestricted differences in differences: Quasi-difference in earnings growth 1975–1978		Controlling for all variables[f]	NSW treatment earnings less comparison group earnings 1978		Unrestricted differences in differences: Quasi-difference in earnings growth 1975–1978		Controlling for all variables[f]
Comparison group	Unadjustaed[b] (1)	Adjusted[c] (2)	Unadjusted[d] (3)	Adjusted[e] (4)	(5)	Unadjusted[b] (1)	Adjusted[c] (2)	Unadjusted[d] (3)	Adjusted[e] (4)	(5)	Unadjusted[b] (1)	Adjusted[c] (2)	Unadjusted[d] (3)	Adjusted[e] (4)	(5)
CPS-2	-4,195 (533)	-2,341 (620)	-1,649 (459)	-1,129 (551)	-1,149 (551)	-3,822 (671)	-2,208 (746)	-263 (574)	371 (662)	305 (666)	-3,822 (671)	615 (672)	-263 (574)	879 (654)	790 (658)
CPS-3	-1,008 (539)	-1 (681)	-1,204 (532)	-263 (677)	-234 (675)	-635 (657)	375 (821)	-91 (641)	844 (808)	875 (810)	-635 (657)	1,270 (798)	-91 (641)	1,326 (796)	1,326 (798)

Notes: Panel A replicate the sample of Lalonde (1985, table 5). The estimates for columns (1)–(4) for NSW, PSID1–3, and CPS-1 are identical to Lalonde's. CPS-2 and CPS-3 are similar but not identical, because we could not exactly recreate his subset. Column (5) differs because the data lie that we obtained did not contain all of the covariates used in column (10) of Lalonde's Table 5.

[a] Estimated effect of training on RE78. Standard errors are in parentheses. The estimate are in 1962 dollars.

[b] The estimates based on the NSW control groups are unbiased estimates of the treatment impacts for the original sample ($886) and for the RE74 sample ($1,794).

[c] The exogenous variables used in the regressions-adjusted equations are age, age squared, years of schooling, high school dropout status, and race (and RE74 in Panel C).

[d] Regresses RE78 on a treatment indicator and RE75.

[e] The same as (d), but controls for the additional variables Ested under (C).

[f] Controls for all pretreatment covariates.

Source: Rajeev H. Dehejia and Sadek Wahba, "Causal Effects in Nonexperimental Studies: Reevaluating the Evaluation of Training Programs," *Journal of the American Statistical Association,* vol. 94, no. 448 (December 1999), pp. 1053–62. Reprinted with permission from the *Journal of the American statistical Association.* Copyright 1999 by the American Statistical Association. All rights reserved.

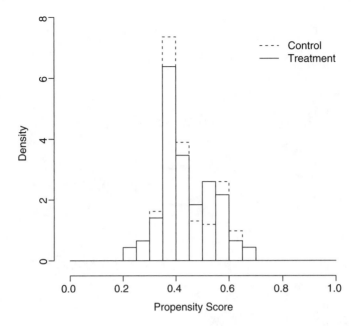

Figure 22.1. Histogram of the estimated propensity score for the NSW and PSID subset.

The first notable finding in Table 22.2 is the difference in the treatment effect resulting from the composition of the original sample versus the subset ($886 vs. $1,794), given that those who joined the program earlier or who were unemployed before they entered the program had higher treatment effects. The treatment effects depicted in Panels A and B when using the PSID and the CPS data are negative, supporting Lalonde's conclusion that nonexperimental estimators can be inconsistent estimators of the experimental treatment effect. When the 1974 earnings variable is included, the estimates somewhat improve; however, they do not alter Lalonde's basic conclusions.

So, why do we get the same results, even though Dehejia and Wahba included a new variable that reduces bias and used a more polished subset of the data? The basic explanation for these patterns is that the groups remain quite different. This is evident just by comparing the sample means of the pretreatment characteristics from the NSW and the PSID and CPS comparison groups, which differ in important ways; see Table 22.3. What Lalonde demonstrated was that linear regression is not an adequate tool to adjust for the differences between treatment and control groups.

To show how matching on the propensity score improves the overlap of the treatment and control groups in terms of their pretreatment characteristics, I used Dehejia and Wahba's data subset that includes information on 1974 earnings. The subset has 185 treated and 260 control observations, which are, on average, probabilistically similar on their pretreatment characteristics (see Table 22.3 RE74 subset).[1]

Figure 22.1 shows the distribution of the estimated propensity score for the subset of treated and control units. The figure shows a reasonable overlap of

[1] The data are available from http://www.nber.org/%7Erdehejia/nswdata.html.

Table 22.3. *Sample means of characteristics for NSW and comparison groups*

	No. of observations	Age	Education	Black	Hispanic	No degree	Married	RE74 (U.S. $)	RE75 (U.S. $)
NSW/Lalonde:[a]									
Treated	297	24.63 (.32)	10.38 (.09)	.80 (.02)	.09 (.01)	.73 (.02)	.17 (.02)		3,066 (236)
Control	425	24.45 (.32)	10.19 (.08)	.80 (.02)	.11 (.02)	.81 (.02)	.16 (.02)		3,026 (252)
RE74 subset:[b]									
Treated	185	25.81 (.35)	10.35 (.10)	.84 (.02)	.059 (.01)	.71 (.02)	.19 (.02)	2,096 (237)	1,532 (156)
Control	260	25.05 (.34)	10.09 (.08)	.83 (.02)	.10 (.02)	.83 (.02)	.15 (.02)	2,107 (276)	1,267 (151)
Comparison groups:[c]									
PSID-1	2,490	34.85 [.78]	12.11 [.23]	.25 [.03]	.032 [.01]	.31 [.04]	.87 [.03]	19,429 [991]	19,063 [1,002]
PSID-2	253	36.10 [1.00]	10.77 [.27]	.39 [.04]	.067 [.02]	.49 [.05]	.74 [.04]	11,027 [853]	7,569 [695]
PSID-3	128	38.25 [1.17]	10.30 [.29]	.45 [.05]	.18 [.03]	.51 [.05]	.70 [.05]	5,566 [686]	2,611 [499]
CPS-1	15,992	33.22 [.81]	12.02 [.21]	.07 [.02]	.07 [.02]	.29 [.03]	.71 [.03]	14,016 [705]	13,650 [682]

	No. of observations	Age	Education	Black	Hispanic	No degree	Married	RE74 (U.S. $)	RE75 (U.S. $)
CPS-2	2,369	28.25 [.87]	11.24 [.19]	.11 [.02]	.08 [.02]	.45 [.04]	.46 [.04]	8,728 [667]	7,397 [600]
CPS-3	429	28.03 [.87]	10.23 [.23]	.21 [.03]	.14 [.03]	.60 [.04]	.51 [.04]	5,619 [552]	2,467 [288]

Note: Standard errors are in parentheses. Standard error on difference in means with RE74 subset/treated is given in brackets. Age = age in years; Education = number of years of schooling; Black = 1 if black, 0 otherwise; Hispanic = 1 if Hispanic, 0 otherwise; No degree = 1 if no high school degree; 0 otherwise; Married = 1 if married, 0 otherwise; REx = earnings in calendar year 19x.

[a] NSW sample as constructed by Lalonde (1986).

[b] The subset of the Lalonde sample for which RE74 is available.

[c] Definition of comparison groups (Lalonde 1986):

PSID-1: All male household heads under age 55 who did not classify themselves as retired in 1975.

PSID-2: Selects from PSID-1 all men who were not working when surveyed in the spring of 1976.

PSID-3: Selects from PSID-2 all men who were not working in 1975.

CPS-1: All CPS males under age 55.

CPS-2: Selects from CPS-1 all males who were not working when surveyed in March 1976.

CPS-3: Selects from CPS-2 all the unemployed males in 1976 whose income in 1975 was below the poverty level.

PSID1–3 and CPS-1 are identical to those used by Lalonde. CPS2–3 are similar to those used by Lalonde, but Lalonde's original subset could not be recreated.

Source: Rajeev H. Dehejia and Sadek Wahba, "Causal Effects in Nonexperimental Studies: Reevaluating the Evaluation of Training Programs," *Journal of the American Statistical Association*, vol. 94, no. 448 (December 1999), pp. 1053–62. Reprinted with permission from the *Journal of the American statistical Association*. Copyright 1999 by the American Statistical Association. All rights reserved.

pretreatment characteristics, summarized in the propensity score, which makes it possible to compare the groups.

The matching-based estimates of Dehejia and Wahba are indeed much closer to the experimental treatment effect. For the PSID sample, the matching-based estimate was $1,690, compared to $1,790 for the randomized experiment, while the propensity score–based estimate from the CPS was $1,580. What would have happened to the treatment effect if different, or more or maybe fewer, pretreatment characteristics had been available? In other words, how sensitive is the estimate to the particular pretreatment variables that determine the assignment to the treatment group and outcome? The results are sensitive to the set of pretreatment variables used, which is probably the most significant weakness of propensity-score matching, in the sense that we may never have *all* the pretreatment covariates that determine the assignment to treatment and outcome. Nevertheless, as mentioned before, with a good theory supporting our hypotheses and controlling for all of the variables that influence the assignment, matching on the propensity score should provide us with estimates of the treatment effect close to the unbiased experimental results, just as in Dehejia and Wahba's study.

Dehejia and Wahba's study suggests to us that what is important are the pretreatment covariates, the construction of treatment and control groups, and ignorability. If we create groups that are, on average, comparable to each other in terms of pretreatment cofounders and if ignorability holds, then we can yield good estimates of the treatment effect.

Following this logic, I turn in Chapter 23 to a specific study that illustrates the kinds of explanations I have been sketching.

23. Migration and Solidarity

My work on migration, and specifically the field visits that I have done in migrant-sending countries, left me with questions about how migration may reshape prevailing social structures in those communities. One of the aspects that interested me most was how the support from or solidarity of the community with migrant households changed relative to nonmigrant households. In other words, I was interested in investigating if migrant-sending households, especially those with male migrants, received more nonmonetary help (food, clothing, or help with daily activities) from people who lived in the same or a nearby community compared to nonmigrant households in the same community. So, using data from Mexico's Oportunidades, a conditional cash transfer program of the federal government that covers more than 2 million rural families in more than 2,000 municipalities (approximately 80% of Mexico's municipalities), I decided to investigate further the impact of international migration on solidarity from non-household members to migrant and nonmigrant families who live in the same community or in nearby communities.

In order to isolate the effects of local solidarity, I did not take into account the help or solidarity that households might receive from their relatives or friends in foreign countries or from family members who live in another state since this could distort the effect of migration on local solidarity.

The literature on the impact of migration on those left behind is rich; for example, Alejandro Portes (1997, 1998), Peggy Levitt (2001), and others have found that the impact of migration is both positive and negative, depending on the characteristics of the community in which migration takes place. If migration takes place in a community in which most of the households have at least one migrant member, then migration may have a quite different impact on, say, local income inequality than in a community in which only a fraction of the families are migrant families. The material impacts of migration on migrant-sending communities have been studied in considerable detail, but the nonmaterial effects of migration have received less attention. There are various reasons for this paucity of research, including the lack of systematic data collection efforts in order to quantify some of these impacts.

Even though the data were somewhat scarce, there were some useful case studies and quantitative analyses that I used to guide my research. One thing that the data pointed out was that the impact of migration depends on the context: What happens in one migrant-sending community may not be true in another migrant-sending community with different social structures and a different migration history. To return to the statistical language of causal inference, the treatment effect could vary conditional on background variables, which would make it essential to balance treatment and control groups in any observational study and would suggest the inclusion of treatment interactions in any model.

This context dependence suggests that the impact of migration on solidarity is shaped by who migrates. For instance, if most of the immigrants from an area are young men, then their exit from their communities of origin may impact gender dynamics at home. Women left behind may have to assume some roles that traditionally were filled by men, such as being household heads or disciplining the children. So, given the migratory patterns of young men, the whole social arrangement of the community may shift from a patriarchal to a matriarchal structure, which in turn may increase solidarity from the community to migrant households in order to help those women left behind.

How can we gauge the impact of migration on solidarity? In order to answer this question, we need to compare migrant households with nonmigrant households. Why? Let's consider the impact that migration may have on solidarity between migrant and nonmigrant households. Suppose that in a given migrant community solidarity suddenly increases. Given our personal and professional experience, we believe that migration may be the underlying cause driving the increase in solidarity, but we need to make sure that this is the case.

To put it simply, in order to investigate if our hypothesis is right or wrong, we need to compare households that are probabilistically similar on a large number of dimensions but that differ in their migration status (migrant vs. nonmigrant).

Why can't we just fit a regression model with an indicator describing a household's migration status? Why is it crucial to compare similar households that differ only in their migration status? In theory and in practice, we could just run a regression with an indicator and some interactions; however, this does not ensure that we are necessarily comparing households that have similar overlapping distributions.

So, our first step is to estimate the probability that a given household has migrants, given several predictors, including a battery of the household's economic characteristics and some community-level variables such as the degree of development of the area. Once we obtain the propensity score, we match each migrant household with households in the control group – that is, nonmigrant households – that have similar propensity scores.[1] Again, the overall purpose is to create groups that are, on average, comparable to each other in the background variables that affect the outcome and the probability of receiving the treatment. As discussed, some bias is often introduced from unmeasured confounders; for now, however, let's assume that ignorability holds, with our burden being to convince skeptics that we have included enough information in our set of background variables to make ignorability a plausible assumption.

[1] The matching procedure can be done, for example, using STATA's command *psmatch2*.

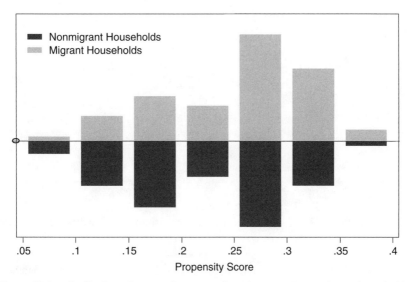

Figure 23.1. Distribution of propensity scores for migrant and nonmigrant households.

Our next step is to plot the distribution of propensity scores in treated and control groups, that is, in migrant and nonmigrant households to verify if our model has achieved good balance and overlap. Displays such as Figure 23.1 can help reveal problems with the comparison between treatment and control groups. What we want, ideally, is to have enough treated and control households that share similar characteristics summarized by the propensity score differing only in their migration status.

Figure 23.1 shows that there is good overlap and balance, that is, we have sufficient migrant and nonmigrant households that share similar background characteristics but that are different in their migration status. Once we have estimated the propensity score, we need to estimate the impact of migration on solidarity. Given that solidarity can be manifested in many different ways, we can run a multinomial regression for each category of solidarity, taking into account the number of times each observation was used in the estimation of the propensity score so that we can include the weight of matched controls. Once we have constructed the weights, we just include them in the multinomial regression model. In situations when there is no overlap between treatment and control units, regression analysis can be helpful and uncontroversial because we would be limiting our analysis to those areas of the distribution where there are treatment and control units that overlap without making inferences over parts of the distribution where we don't have data.

EMPIRICAL RESULTS

After matching migrant and nonmigrant households and after running the multinomial regression, the results suggest that migrant households are more likely to receive nonmonetary help from the community relative to nonmigrant households. In other words, the results indicate that on average, migration has a positive effect

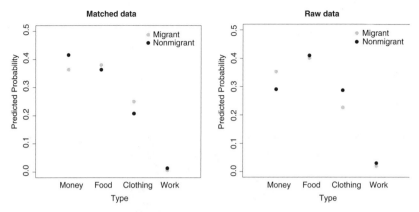

Figure 23.2. Predicted probabilities of receiving help for matched and raw data from the migration analysis.

on solidarity. But did we gain anything by implementing propensity score matching? In other words, how different would our results have been if we had not matched the data? If we hadn't matched the data, we might have arrived at a different conclusion regarding the effect of migration on solidarity. One way to illustrate how we could have arrived at an opposite conclusion is by comparing the results from the multinomial regression when using the matched versus the raw data.

Figure 23.2 shows the predicted probabilities for the matched data and for the raw data against each of the four categories of solidarity (receiving money, food, and clothing and helping out with daily work).

The matched data tell a story that is consistent with our initial hypothesis. That is, migrant households, on average, are more likely to receive nonmonetary solidarity relative to nonmigrant households. Now let's focus our attention on monetary transfers in order to illustrate why matching was, after all, a good idea.

Migration theories suggest that people migrate for many reasons, probably the most important one being to improve their economic situation and help those left behind by sending money home. It does not make much sense to give money to a migrant household that may already be receiving money (and most likely a lot more) from a migrant abroad or from a migrant living in another state. In other words, you don't give charity to the wealthy; however, if we had use the raw data, this would be our conclusion.

Why do the results of the matched data make sense? As mentioned, given that the traditional division of labor within the household changes as a by-product of mostly male migration, the women left behind may now perform some duties that were formerly carried out by men. If this is the case, they won't have much time for other activities, and this is when members of the community, such as close family members, neighbors, or friends, step in to help. We can test how each of our four categories of solidarity changes with the number of male migrants per household. We would expect to see an inverse relationship between monetary and nonmonetary solidarity. With more migrants abroad or in another state, a household would expect to receive more money and less nonmonetary solidarity, some sort of a substitution effect.

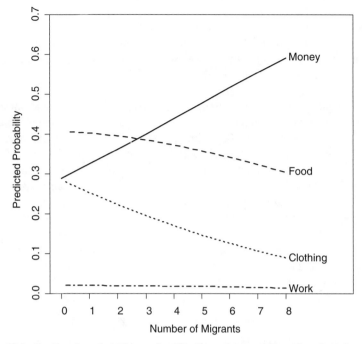

Figure 23.3. Predicted probabilities of solidarity versus number of male migrants per household.

Figure 23.3 shows the predicted probabilities for the four categories of solidarity. It is clear that as the number of male migrants per household increases, so does the probability of receiving a monetary transfer, while the probability of receiving nonmonetary help (food, clothing, and work) decreases.

Stated differently, if a migrant household has more potential remitters, then it makes sense that it will potentially receive more monetary transfers relative to a nonmigrant household. This, in turn, may indicate that migrant households are better off economically and thus send a signal to the community that they don't need substantial nonmonetary help, probably because they can now cover some expenses directly or simply by substituting labor with remittances.

This last example illustrates some of the advantages of using propensity-score matching and regression analysis in order to estimate the treatment on the treated. Propensity-score matching is not synonymous with problem-free data; however, at a minimum, it does guarantee (if done correctly) that we will be comparing apples with apples. Not doing so could lead us to make completely different conclusions about the phenomenon in question.

CONCLUDING REMARKS

In this last part of the book, I introduced some concepts and applications to help polish our causal arguments from a theoretical and an empirical perspective. By considering potential outcomes, we can use several different statistical tools to help us better understand the consequences of varying a treatment and the conditions under which that causal relationship holds.

Like the other parts of this book, this part is not intended to be a full methodological treatise or even an overview. Rather, I am describing some tools that have been useful to me in my own research, with the understanding that many other tools can be useful as well.

The potential-outcome framework mimics the conditions of randomness that we would expect if we were conducting an experiment. Obviously, there's a price that we have to pay. We must be willing to make some strong assumptions about how units are assigned to the experimental and control groups. However, if we are willing to make these assumptions, and if we have a solid theory that specifies the relationship between an outcome and a set of predictors, then we may be able to identify the underlying causal mechanisms.

We need to define explicitly what we mean by a causal effect to guide our model specification, selection of predictors, and causal mechanisms. When we find it difficult to define or estimate causal effects, we often find it helpful to go back to basics and consider potential interventions and how they could affect our outcomes of interest.

FURTHER READING FOR PART VII

For an excellent discussion of the pluralist versus unitary views of causal inference in the social sciences, see Gerring (2001, 2005), who argues that from a normative and, in my opinion, practical perspective, the pluralist view of causal inference is not very useful to create and advance knowledge. Unity, Gerring states, not differentness, should be the goal of any causal methodology.

For more on the Dehejia and Wahba example, see the series of articles by Jeffrey Smith and Petra Todd referred to at http://www.nber.org/~rdehejia/cvindex#0 along with Dehejia's comments. These articles provide a rare back-and-forth discussion of a methodological dispute and are worth reading for anyone interested in propensity-score matching for causal inference.

Michael Sobel (1995), Chistopher Winship (Winship and Sobel 2004), and Stephen Morgan (Morgan and Winship 2007) provide splendid critical examinations of the literature on causal inference in the social sciences. In addition, they offer accessible discussions of the potential-outcomes causal model and many of its assumptions, such as ignorability. For causal inference from an incomplete-data perspective, the volume edited by Andrew Gelman and Xiao-Li Meng (2004) offers a rich assortment of views on causal inference and observational studies. For example, the chapter by Jennifer Hill, Jerome Reiter, and Elaine Zanutto, in addition to comparing experimental and observational data analyses, reports an important finding regarding the usefulness of including geographic variables in propensity-score matching. As you might recall from our definition of causality, the context in which the causal relation takes place is important.

For a methodological discussion of experimental and quasi-experimental designs for causal inference, see the text by William Shadish, Thomas Cook, and Donald Campbell (2002), which offers a concise and clear idea of the main obstacles, challenges, and virtues associated with experiments for causal inference.

Exercises for Part VII

1. Explain what happens when ignorability and the stable unit treatment value assumption do not hold and how we can be sure that these assumptions hold when using observational data.
2. What are the implications of including posttreatment variables when estimating the propensity score?
3. Discuss how the potential-outcomes causal model could be thought of as a missing-data problem.
4. Create a counterfactual thought experiment of your own and specify:
   a. the potential causal relation between your cause and effect
   b. the potential outcomes
   c. the ideal research design in order to test the causal relation
   d. the steps needed and the assumptions you would have to make if you were using observational data
5. Download from http://www.nber.org/~rdehejia/nswdata.html Dehejia and Wahba's data subset that includes information on 1974 earnings (NSWRE74_CONTROL.TXT and NSWRE74_TREATED.TXT). Assume that the treatment assignment is ignorable conditional on all the pretreatment cofounders used by Dehejia and Wahba.
   a. Using any statistical software package (SPSS, Stata, R, etc.), estimate the propensity score using a logistic and probit regression with all the pre-treatment cofounders as main effects. Discuss whether there are any differences in the propensity scores and plot the propensity scores distributions.
   b. Estimate the propensity score using a logistic regression with all the pretreatment cofounders as main effects and the following interactions: Hispanic x Married, Hispanic x No Degree, Black x Married, Black x No Degree. Plot the propensity score distributions, compare them with the propensity-score distributions of (a), and discuss if there are any noticeable differences and why.

References

Aberbach, Joel D. *Keeping a Watchful Eye: The Politics of Congressional Oversight.* Washington, DC: Brookings Institution Press, 1991.
    "What's Happened to the Watchful Eye?" *Congress and the Presidency* **29**, no. 1 (2002): 3–23.

Acemoglu, Daron, Simon Johnson, and James A. Robinson. "Reversal of Fortune: Geography and Institutions in the Making of the Modern World Income Distribution." *Quarterly Journal of Economics* **117**, no. 4 (2002): 1231–94.

Achen, Christopher H. "Toward a New Political Methodology: Microfoundations and Art." *Annual Review of Political Science* **5** (2002): 423–50.

Ansolabehere, Stephen, and James Snyder. *The End of Inequality: One Person, One Vote, and the Transformation of American Politics, Issues in American Democracy.* New York: Norton, 2008.

Ashworth, Scott, and Ethan Bueno de Mesquita. "Monotone Comparative Statics for Models of Politics." *American Journal of Political Science* **50** (2006): 214–31.

Ashworth, Tony. *Trench Warfare 1914–1918: The Live and Let Live System.* New York: Holmes and Meier, 1980.

Athey, Susan, Paul Milgrom, and John Roberts. *Robust Comparative Statics.* Cambridge, MA: Harvard University, 1998.

Axelrod, Robert. *The Evolution of Cooperation.* New York: Basic Books, 1984.

Ayala, Cesar J., and Laird W. Bergad. "Rural Puerto Rico in the Early Twentieth Century Reconsidered: Land and Society, 1899–1915." *Latin American Research Review* **37** (2002): 65–97.

Babbie, Earl R. *The Practice of Social Research.* Belmont, CA: Wadsworth Publishing, 2003.

Bailey, Michael, and Kelly H. Chang. "Comparing Presidents, Senators, and Justices: Interinstitutional Preference Estimation." *Journal of Law, Economics, and Organization* **17**, no. 2 (2001): 477–506.

Bartels, Larry M. "What's the Matter with *What's the matter with Kansas?*" *Quarterly Journal of Political Science* **1**, no. 2 (2006): 201–26.

Baumgart, Winfried. "The Economic Theory of Imperialism." In *Imperialism: The Idea and Reality of British and French Colonial Expansion, 1880–1914*, 91–135. Oxford: Oxford University Press, 1982.

Baumgartner, Frank R., and Bryan D. Jones, eds. *Policy Dynamics.* Chicago: University of Chicago Press, 2002.

Baumol, William. "Productivity Growth, Convergence and Welfare: What the Long-Run Data Show." *American Economic Review* **76**, no. 5 (1986): 1072–85.

Beitz, Charles R. *Political Equality: An Essay in Democratic Theory*. Princeton, NJ: Princeton University Press, 1990.

Berger, Peter L. *Invitation to Sociology: A Humanistic Perspective*. New York: Knopf, 1963.

Berlin, Isaiah. *Three Critics of the Enlightenment: Vico, Hamann, Herder*, ed. Henry Hardy. Princeton, NJ: Princeton University Press, 2000.

Bermeo, Nancy G. *Ordinary People in Extraordinary Times*. Princeton, NJ: Princeton University Press, 2003.

Beveridge, Andrew A. "Local Lending Practice: Borrowers in a Small Northeastern Industrial City, 1832–1915." *Journal of Economic History* **45**, no. 2 (1985): 393–403.

Bloomfield, Arthur. *Monetary Policy Under the International Gold Standard, 1880–1914*. New York: Federal Reserve Bank of New York, 1959.

Blossfeld, Hans-Peter, and Gerald Prein, eds. *Rational Choice Theory and Large Scale Data Analysis*. Boulder, CO: Westview Press, 1998.

Boix, Carles, and Susan C Stokes. "Endogenous Democratization." *World Politics* **55** (2003): 517–49.

Bordo, Michael D. "The Bretton Woods International Monetary System: A Historical Overview." In *A Retrospective on the Bretton Woods System: Lessons for International Monetary Reform*, ed. Michael D. Bordo and Barry Eichengreen, 3–98. Chicago: University of Chicago Press, 1993.

Bordo, Michael D., and Barry Eichengreen, eds. *A Retrospective on the Bretton Woods System: Lessons for International Monetary Reform*, National Bureau of Economic Research Project Report. Chicago: University of Chicago Press, 1993.

Box-Steffensmeier, Janet M., and Bradford S. Jones. *Event History Modeling: A Guide for Social Scientists: Analytical Methods for Social Research*. Cambridge: Cambridge University Press, 2004.

Braudel, Fernand. *The Mediterranean and the Mediterranean World in the Age of Philip II*. Berkeley: University of California Press, 1996.

Brundage, W. Fitzhugh, ed. *Under Sentence of Death: Lynching in the South*. Chapel Hill: University of North Carolina Press, 1997.

Brush, Steven G. "Dynamics of Theory Change in the Social Sciences: Relative Deprivation and Collective Violence." *Journal of Conflict Resolution* **40**, no. 4 (1996): 523–45.

Cain, Bruce, John Ferejohn, and Morris Fiorina. *The Personal Vote: Constituency Service and Electoral Independence*. Cambridge, MA: Harvard University Press, 1990.

Cameron, Charles M., and B. Peter Rosendorff. "A Signaling Theory of Congressional Oversight." *Games and Economic Behavior* **5**, no. 44 (1993): 44–70.

Campbell, Donald T., and Julian C. Stanley. *Experimental and Quasi-Experimental Designs for Research*. Boston: Houghton Mifflin, 1963.

Campbell, James E. "Polls and Votes. The Trial-Heat Presidential Election Forecasting Model, Certainty, and Political Campaigns" *American Politics Quarterly* **24**, no. 4 (1996): 408–33.

Campbell, James E., and James C. Garand, eds. *Before the Vote, Forecasting American National Elections*. Thousand Oaks, CA: Sage, 1999.

Cantril, Hadley. *The Psychology of Social Movements*. New York: Wiley, 1941.

Carmagnani, Marcello. "Demografía Y Sociedad: La Estructura Social de Los Centros Mineros Del Norte de México, 1600–1720." *Historia Mexicana* **21** (1972): 419–59.

Chaunu, Pierre. "Histoire Quantitative Ou Histoire Sérielle?" *Cahiers des Annales*, **3** (1964): 165–76.

Chiang, Chin L. *Introduction to Stochastic Processes in Biostatistics*. New York: Wiley, 1968.

Clarida, Richard, Jordi Gali, and Mark Gertler. "Monetary Policy Rules in Practice: Some International Evidence." *European Economic Review* **42**, no. 6 (1998): 1033–67.

Cleveland, William S. "Robust Locally Weighted Regression and Smoothing Scatterplots." *Journal of the American Statistical Association* **74** (1979): 829–36.

The Elements of Graphing Data. Summit, NJ: Hobart Press, 1985.

Visualizing Data. Summit, NJ: Hobart Press, 1993.

Cobban, Alfred. *The Social Interpretation of the French Revolution*. Cambridge: Cambridge University Press, 1964.

Cole, Stephen, ed. *What's Wrong with Sociology?* New Brunswick, NJ: Transaction Books, 2001.

Coleman, James S. *The Adolescent Society: The Social Life of Teenagers and Its Impact on Education*. New York: Free Press, 1961.

Equality and Achievement in Education. Boulder, CO: Westview Press, 1993.

Costa, Dora L., and Matthew E. Kahn. "Changes in the Value of Life, 1940–1980." *Journal of Risk and Uncertainty* **29**, no. 2 (2004): 159–80.

Cox, Gary W., and Katz, Jonathan. "Why Did the Incumbency Advantage Grow?" *American Journal of Political Science* **40** (1996): 478–97.

Crafts, Nicholas F. R. "Quantitative Economic History. Working Paper 48." In *The Economic History Working Paper Series* London: London School of Economics, 1999.

Crosby, Alfred W. *The Measure of Reality: Quantification and Western Society, 1250–1600*. Cambridge: Cambridge University Press, 1997.

Cumby, Robert E., and Frederic S. Mishkin. "The International Linkage of Real Interest Rates: The European–U.S. Connection." *Journal of International Money and Finance* **5**, no. 1 (1986): 5–23.

Curtin, Philip D. *The Atlantic Slave Trade: A Census*. Madison: University of Wisconsin Press, 1969.

Dahrendorf, Ralf. "Social Science." In *The Social Science Encyclopedia*, 2nd ed., ed. Adam Kuper and Jessica Kuper, 800–2. New York: Routledge, 1995.

De Long, J. Bradford. "Productivity Growth, Convergence, and Welfare: Comment." *American Economic Review* **78**, no. 5 (1988): 1138–54.

Dehejia, Rajeev H. "Estimating Causal Effects in Nonexperimental Studies." In *Applied Bayesian Modeling and Causal Inference from Incomplete-Data Perspectives*, ed. Andrew Gelman and Xiao-Li Meng, 25–36. New York: Wiley, 2004.

Dehejia, Rajeev H., and Sadek Wahba. "Causal Effects in Nonexperimental Studies: Reevaluating the Evaluation of Training Programs." *Journal of the American Statistical Association* **94** (1999): 1053–62.

Desrosiers, Alain. *The Politics of Large Numbers: A History of Statistical Reasoning*. Cambridge, MA: Harvard University Press, 1998.

Diermeier, Daniel, and Timothy J. Feddersen. "Information and Congressional Hearings." *American Journal of Political Science* **44**, no. 1 (2000): 51–65.

Dilthey, Wilhelm. *Einleitung in Die Geisteswissenschaften: Versuch Einer Grundlegung Für Das Studien Der Gesellschaft Und Der Geschichte*. Leipzig: Dunker and Humblot, 1883.

Introduction to the Human Sciences: An Attempt to Lay a Foundation for the Study of Society and History. Detroit: Wayne State University Press, 1989.

Dimaggio, Paul, John Evans, and Bethany Bryson. "Have Americans' Social Attitudes Become More Polarized?" *American Journal of Sociology* **102**, no. 3 (1996): 690–755.

DiPrete, Thomas A., and Whitman T. Soule. "Gender and Promotion in Segmented Job Ladder Systems." *American Sociological Review* **53**, no. 1 (1988): 26–40.

"The Organization of Career Lines: Equal Employment Opportunity and Status Advancement in a Federal Bureaucracy." *American Sociological Review* **51**, no. 3 (1986): 295–309.

Dorman, Peter. *Markets and Mortality: Economics, Dangerous Work, and the Value of Human Life*. Cambridge: Cambridge University Press, 1996.

Dorman, Peter, and Paul Hagstrom. "Wage Compensation for Dangerous Work Revisited." *Industrial and Labor Relations Review* **52** (1998): 116–35.

Downs, Anthony. *An Economic Theory of Democracy*. Boston: Addison-Wesley 1957.

Easterly, William R. *The Elusive Quest for Growth: Economists' Adventures and Misadventures in the Tropics*. Cambridge, MA: MIT Press, 2002.

Edlin, Aaron S., Andrew Gelman, and Noah Kaplan. "Voting as a Rational Choice: Why and How People Vote to Improve the Well-Being of Others." *Rationality and Society* **19** (2007): 293–314.

Eells, Ellery. *Probabilistic Causality*. Cambridge: Cambridge University Press, 1991.

Eichengreen, Barry. *Golden Fetters: The Gold Standard and the Great Depression, 1919–1939*. Oxford: Oxford University Press, 1992.

Elster, Jon. *Nuts and Bolts for the Social Sciences*. Cambridge: Cambridge University Press, 1989.

   Explaining Social Behavior: More Nuts and Bolts for the Social Sciences. New York: Cambridge University Press, 2007.

Enelow, James M., and J. Melvin Hinich. *The Spatial Theory of Voting: An Introduction*. Cambridge: Cambridge University Press, 1984.

England, Paula. *Comparable Worth Theories and Evidence*. New York: Aldine Transaction, 1992.

Epstein, Lee, Andrew D. Martin, Jeffrey A. Segal, and Chad Westerland. "The Judicial Common Space." *Journal of Law, Economics, & Organization* **23**, no. 2 (2007): 303–25.

Erikson, Robert S. "The Advantage of Incumbency in Congressional Elections." *Polity* **3** (1971): 395–405.

Evans, Richard J. *In Defense of History*. New York: W. W. Norton, 2000.

Fair, Ray C. "An Estimate of the Uncertainty of Policy Effects in a Macro-Economic Model." In *Discussion Papers*, Cowles Foundation. New Haven, CT: Yale University, 1978.

Farber, Henry S., and Joanne Gowa. "Polities and Peace." *International Security* **20**, no. 2 (1995): 123–46.

Ferejohn, John, and Charles Shipan. "Congressional Influence on Administrative Agencies: A Case Study of Telecomunications Policy." In *Congress Reconsidered*, 4th ed., ed. Lawrence C. Dodd and Bruce I. Oppenheimer. Washington, DC: Congressional Quarterly Press, 1989.

Ferguson, Thomas. *Golden Rule: The Investment Theory of Party Competition and the Logic of Money-Driven Political Systems*. Chicago: University of Chicago Press, 1995.

Finch, Janet. *Married to the Job: Wives' Incorporation in Men's Work*. London: Allen and Unwin, 1983.

Fiorina, Morris P., Samuel J. Abrams, and Jeremy C. Pope. *Culture War? The Myth of a Polarized America*. New York: Longman, 2005.

Fiorina, Morris P., and Roger G. Noll. "Voters, Bureaucrats and Legislators: A Rational Choice Perspective on the Growth of Bureaucracy." *Journal of Public Economics* **9** (1978): 239–54.

Fisher, Ronald Aylmer. *Statistical Methods for Research Workers*. New York: Macmillan, 1925.

Fiske, Susan and Shelley Taylor. *Social Cognition, from Brains to Culture*. New York: McGraw-Hill, 2007.

Fogel, Robert W. *Railroads and American Economic Growth: Essays in Econometric History*. Baltimore: Johns Hopkins University Press, 1964.

Fogel, Robert W., and Stanley L. Engerman. *Time on the Cross: The Economics of American Negro Slavery*. Boston: Little, Brown, 1974.

Foucault, Michel. *Madness and Civilization: A History of Insanity in the Age of Reason*. New York: Vintage Books, 1965.

Discipline and Punish: The Birth of the Prison. New York: Vintage Books, 1975.

L'hermeneutique du Sujet: Cours au Collège de France Hautes Études. Paris: Seuil, 2001.

Fowler, James H. "Altruism and Turnout." *Journal of Politics* **68**, no. 3 (2006): 674–83.

Fox, John. *An R and S-Plus Companion to Applied Regression*. Thousand Oaks, CA: Sage, 2002.

Frank, Thomas. *What's the Matter with Kansas? How Conservatives Won the Heart of America*. New York: Metropolitan Books, 2004.

Freud, Sigmund. "The Dynamics of Transference." In *The Standard Edition of the Complete Pyschological Works of Sigmund Freud (Vol. 12)*, ed. Sigmund Freud. London: Hogarth Press, 1912.

Friedman, Jeffrey, ed. *The Rational Choice Controversy: Economic Models of Politics Reconsidered*. New Haven, CT: Yale University Press, 1996.

Friedman, Milton. *Essays in Positive Economics*. Chicago: University of Chicago Press, 1953.

Furet, François. *Penser la Revolution Française*. Paris: Gallimard, 1978.

Gelman, Andrew. "Voting, Fairness, and Political Representation (with discussion)." *Chance* **15**, no. 3 (2002): 22–6.

"Game Theory as Ideology: Some Comments on Robert Axelrod's 'The Evolution of Cooperation.'" *QA-Rivista dell'Associazione Rossi-Doria* (2008).

Gelman, Andrew, and Jennifer Hill. *Data Analysis Using Regression and Multilevel/ Hierarchical Models*. Cambridge: Cambridge University Press, 2007.

Gelman, Andrew, and Gary King. "Estimating Incumbency Advantage without Bias." *American Journal of Political Science* **34**, no. 4 (1990): 1142–64.

"Why Are American Presidential Election Campaign Polls So Variable When Votes Are So Predictable?" *British Journal of Political Science* **23**, no. 1 (1993): 409–51.

"A Unified Method of Evaluating Electoral Systems and Redistricting Plans." *American Journal of Political Science* **38**, no. 2 (1994): 514–54.

Gelman, Andrew, and Xiao-Li Meng, eds. *Applied Bayesian Modeling and Causal Inference from Incomplete-Data Perspectives*. New York: Wiley, 2004.

Gelman, Andrew, David Park, Boris Shor, Joseph Bafumi, and Jeronimo Cortina. *Red State, Blue State, Rich State, Poor State: Why Americans Vote the Way They Do*. Princeton, NJ: Princeton University Press, 2008.

Gerring, John. "Causation." *Journal of Theoretical Politics* **17**, no. 2 (2005): 163–98.

Social Science Methodology: A Criterial Framework. Cambridge: Cambridge University Press, 2001.

Geyl, Pieter. *Napoleon: Voor En Tegen in De Franse Geschiedschrijving*. Utrecht: A. Oosthoek, 1946.

Gibbons, Robert S. "Incentives in Organizations." *Journal of Economic Perspectives* **12**, no. 4 (1998): 115–32.

Godoy, Ricardo A. *Mining and Agriculture in Highland Bolivia: Ecology, History and Commerce among the Jukumanis*. Tucson: University of Arizona Press, 1990.

Góes, José Roberto. *O Cativeiro Imperfeito. Um Estudo Sobre a Escravidão No Rio De Janeiro Da Primeira Metade Do Século Xix*. Vitória, Vitória Lineart, 1993.

Goldthorpe, John H. *On Sociology*. Oxford: Oxford University Press, 2000.

Goodin, Robert, and Hans-Dieter Klingemann. "Political Science: The Discipline." In *A New Handbook of Political Science*, ed. Robert Goodin and Hans-Dieter Klingemann, 3–49. Oxford: Oxford University Press, 1996.

Graunt, John. *Natural and Political Observations Made Upon the Bills of Morality*. Baltimore: Johns Hopkins University Press, reprinted 1939.

Green, Donald, and Ian Shapiro. *Pathologies of Rational Choice Theory: A Critique of Applications in Political Science*. New Haven, CT: Yale University Press, 1994.

Greene, William H. *Econometric Analysis*. Upper Saddle River: Prentice Hall, 2007.

Groves, Robert M., Jr., Floyd J. Fowler, Mick P. Couper, James M. Lepkowski, Eleanor Singer, and Roger Tourangeau. *Survey Methodology*. Hoboken, NJ: Wiley-Interscience, 2004.

Gwartney, James, and Charles Haworth. "Employer Costs and Discrimination: The Case of Baseball." *The Journal of Political Economy* **82**, no. 4 (1974): 873–81.

Hamilton, James D. *Time Series Analysis*. Princeton, NJ: Princeton University Press, 1994.

Hanke, Steve, Lars Jonung, and Kurt Schuler. *Russian Currency and Finance: A Currency Board Approach to Reform*. Oxford: Routledge, 1994.

Hansen, Bruce E. "The New Econometrics of Structural Change: Dating Breaks in U.S. Labor Productivity." *Journal of Economic Perspectives* **15** (2001): 117–28.

Hardin, Garrett. "The Tragedy of the Commons." *Science* **162** (1968): 1243–8.

Harford, Tim. *The Undercover Economist: Exposing Why the Rich Are Rich, the Poor Are Poor – and Why You Can Never Buy a Decent Used Car!* New York: Oxford University Press, 2006.

Harvey, Andrew C. *Time Series Models*. Cambridge, MA: MIT Press, 1993.

Hastie, Reid, and Robyn M. Dawes. *Rational Choice in an Uncertain World: The Psychology of Judgement and Decision Making*. Thousand Oaks: Sage Publications, 2001.

Hastie, Trevor J., and Robert J. Tibshirani. *Generalized Additive Models*. London: Chapman & Hall, 1990.

Hayashi, Fumio. *Econometrics*. Princeton, NJ: Princeton University Press, 2000.

Heckman, James J. "The Scientific Model of Causality." *Sociological Methodology* **35** (2005): 1–97.

Heckman, James J., and Edward Vytlacil. "Structural Equations, Treatment Effects, and Econometric Policy Evaluation." *Econometrica* **73**, no. 3 (2005): 669–738.

Hedström, Peter, and Richard Swedberg, eds. *Social Mechanisms: An Analytical Approach to Social Theory Studies in Rationality and Social Change*. Cambridge: Cambridge University Press, 1998.

Henry, Louis. *Manuel de Démographie Historique*. Geneva: Libraire Droz, 1967.

Hobbes, Thomas. *Leviathan*. London: Touchstone, 1997.

Hoffmann, Carl, and John Shelton Reed. "Sex Discrimination? The Xyz Affair." *Public Interest* **62** (1981): 21–39.

Hotelling, Harold. "Stability in Competition." *Economic Journal* **39** (1929): 41–57.

Hovland, Carl I., and Robert R. Sears. "Minor Studies of Aggression: Correlation of Lynchings with Economic Indices." *Journal of Psychology* **9** (1940): 301–10.

Hudson, Pat. *History by Numbers: An Introduction to Quantitative Approaches*. New York: Oxford University Press, 2000.

Hull, David. "The Need for a Mechanism." In *Science as a Process: An Evolutionary Account of the Social and Conceptual Development of Science*, 277–321. Chicago: University of Chicago Press, 1988.

Hume, David. *An Enquiry Concerning Human Understanding*. New York: Oxford University Press, 2006.

Iyengar, Shanto. "Experimental Designs for Political Communication Research: From Shopping Malls to the Internet." Paper presented at the Workshop in Mass Media

Economics, London, 2002. Available at http://pcl.stanford.edu/common/docs/research/iyengar/2002/expdes2002.pdf.

Iyengar, Shanto, and Donald R. Kinder. *News That Matters*. Chicago: University of Chicago Press, 1987.

Jacobson, Gary C. *Politics of Congressional Elections,* 6th ed. Washington, DC: Longman, 2003.

Jaffary, Nora E. *False Mystics: Deviant Orthodoxy in Colonial Mexico*. Lincoln: University of Nebraska Press, 2004.

Jones, Alice Hanson. *Wealth of a Nation to Be: The American Colonies on the Eve of the Revolution*. New York: Columbia University Press, 1980.

Kahneman, Daniel, Paul Slovic, and Amos Tversky, eds. *Judgment Under Uncertainty: Heuristics and Biases*. Cambridge: Cambridge University Press, 1982.

Kahneman, Daniel, and Amos Tversky. "Prospect Theory: An Analysis of Decision Under Risk." *Econometrica* **47** (1979): 263–91.

Kanter, Rosabeth M. *Men and Women of the Corporation*. New York: Basic Books, 1977.

Kerner, Otto, John V. Lindsay, Fred R. Harris, Edward W. Brooke, James C. Corman, William M. Mcculloch, I. W. Abel, Charles B. Thornton, Roy Wilkins, Katherine G. Peden, and Herbert Jenkins. *Report of the National Advisory Commission on Civil Disorders*. New York: Bantam Books, 1968.

King, Gary, John Bruce, and Andrew Gelman. "Racial Fairness in Legislative Redistricting." In *Classifying by Race*, ed. Paul E. Peterson, 85–110. Princeton, NJ: Princeton University Press, 1995.

King, Gregory. *Two Tracts by Gregory King. (a) Natural and Political Observations and Conclusions Upon the State and Condition of England. (b) of the Naval Trade of England Ao. 1688 and the National Profit Then Arising Thereby*. Baltimore: Johns Hopkins University Press, 1936.

Klein, Herbert S. *The American Finances of the Spanish Empire, 1680–1809*. Albuquerque: University of New Mexico Press, 1998.

   The Middle Passage: Comparative Studies in the Atlantic Slave Trade. Princeton, NJ: Princeton University Press, 1978.

   "Peasant Communities in Rebellion: The Tzeltal Republic of 1772." *Pacific Historical Review* **35** (1966): 247–64.

Klein, Herbert S., and Francisco Vidal Luna. "Sources for the Study of Brazilian Economic and Social History on the Internet." *Hispanic American Historical Review* **84** (2004): 701–15.

Klein, Herbert S., and Edmund P. Willis. "The Distribution of Wealth in Late 18th Century New York City." *Historie Sociale/Social History* **18** (1985): 259–83.

Kleinbaum, David G. *Survival Analysis*. New York: Springer, 1996.

Kruskal, Joseph B., and Myron Wish. *Multidimensional Scaling*. Newbury Park, CA: Sage, 1978.

Kuhn, Thomas S. *The Structure of Scientific Revolutions*. Chicago: University of Chicago Press, 1962.

Labrousse, Ernest. *Esquisse du Mouvement des Prix et des RevenusaAu Xviiie Siecle*. Paris: Dalloz, 1933.

   La Crise de L'economie Française a la Fin de L'ancien Régime et au Début de la Révolution. Paris: PUF, 1944.

Lalonde, Robert J. "Evaluating the Econometric Evaluations of Training Programs with Experimental Data." *American Economic Review* **76** (1986): 604–20.

Laslett, Peter. *The World We Have Lost, Further Explored*. New York: Charles Scribner's Sons, 1984.

Levitt, Peggy. *The Transnational Villagers*. Berkeley: University of California Press, 2001.

Lewis, Oscar. *La Vida: A Puetro Rican Family in the Culture of Poverty*. New York: Vintage Press, 1966.

Lewis-Beck, Michael S. and Tom W. Rice. *Forecasting Elections*. Washington, DC: CQ Press, 1992.

Liebow, Elliot. *Tally's Corner: A Study of Negro Streetcorner Men*. Boston: Little, Brown, 1967.

Lohr, Sharon L. *Sampling: Design and Analysis*. Pacific Grove, CA: Duxbury Press, 1999.

López Beltrán, Clara. *Alianzas Familiares. Élite, Género y Negocios en La Paz, S. Xvii*. Lima: Instituto de Estudios Peruanos, 1989.

Luce, R. Duncan, and Howard Raiffa. *Games and Decisions: Introduction and Critical Survey*. New York: Wiley, 1989.

Maddison, Angus. *Phases of Capitalist Development*. New York: Oxford University Press, 1982.

Malinowski, Bronislaw. "Anthropology." In *Encyclopedia Britannica*. London: Encyclopaedia Britannica, 1936.

Magic, Science and Religion. Boston: Beacon Press, 1948.

Malthus, Thomas R. *An Essay on the Principle of Population, as It Affects the Future Improvement of Society. With Remarks on the Speculations of Mr. Godwin, M. Condorcet, and Other Writers*. London: Printed for J. Johnson, 1798.

Mankiw, N. Gregory. *Principles of Economics*. Mason, OH: Thomson South-Western, 2003.

Martin, Michael, and Lee C. Mcintyre, eds. *Readings in the Philosophy of Social Science*. Cambridge, MA: MIT Press, 1994.

Maurer, Stephen B., and Albert W. Tucker "An Interview with Albert W. Tucker." *Two-Year College Mathematics Journal* **14**, no. 3 (1983): 210–24.

Mayhew, David R. *Congress: The Electoral Connection*, New Haven, CT: Yale University Press, 1973.

Milgrom, Paul, and Chris Shannon. "Monotone Comparative Statics." *Econometrica* **62** (1994): 157–80.

Miller, Dale T. "The Norm of Self-Interest." *American Psychologist* **54** (1999): 1053–60.

Mintz, Alexander. "A Re-Examination of Correlations between Lynchings and Economic Indices." *Journal of Abnormal and Social Psychology* **41** (1946): 154–60.

Mishkin, Frederic S. *The Economics of Money, Banking, and Financial Markets*. New York: HarperCollins, 1995.

Mokyr, Joel, ed. *The Oxford Encyclopedia of Economic History*. London: Oxford University Press, 2003.

Morgan, Mary S. *The History of Econometric Ideas: Historical Perspectives on Modern Economics*. Cambridge: Cambridge University Press, 1990.

Morgan, Stephen L., and Christopher Winship. *Counterfactuals and Causal Inference Methods and Principles for Social Research*. Cambridge: Cambridge University Press, 2007.

Morton, Rebecca. *Methods and Models: A Guide to the Empirical Analysis of Formal Models in Political Science*. Cambridge: Cambridge University Press, 1999.

Nagel, Ernest. *The Structure of Science: Problems in the Logic of Scientific Explanation*. New York: Harcourt, Brace, and World, 1961.

Neal, Radford. *Bayesian Learning for Neural Networks*. New York: Springer, 1993.

Neyman, Jerzy. "On the Application of Probability Theory to Agricultural Experiments. Essay on Principles. Section 9." *Statistical Science* **5**, no. 4 (1990): 465–80 (translated from Polish original from 1923).

North, Douglass C., and Robert P. Thomas. *The Rise of the Western World: A New Economic History*. Cambridge: Cambridge University Press, 1973.

Nurkse, Ragnar. *International Currency Experience: Lessons of the Inter-War Period.* Geneva: League of Nations, 1944.

Olzak, Susan, and Suzanne Shanahan. "Deprivation and Race Riots: An Extension of Spilerman's Analysis." *Social Forces* **74** (1996): 931–61.

Olzak, Susan, Suzanne Shanahan, and Elisabeth H. McEneaney. "Poverty, Segregation, and Race Riots, 1960–1993." *American Sociological Review* **61** (1996): 590–613.

Ordeshook, Peter C. *Game Theory and Political Theory: An Introduction.* Cambridge: Cambridge University Press, 1968.

Page, Benjamin I., and Robert Y. Shapiro. *The Rational Public: Fifty Years of Trends in Americans' Policy Preferences.* Chicago: University of Chicago Press, 1992.

Pearl, Judea. *Causality: Models, Reasoning, and Inference.* Cambridge: Cambridge University Press, 2000.

Peña Sánchez de Rivera, Daniel, and Nicolás Sánchez-Albornoz. *Dependencia Dinámica Entre Precios Agrícolas: El Trigo en España 1857–1890, Estudios de Historia Económica.* Madrid: Banco de España-Servicio de Estudios, 1983.

Perlo, Victor. *The Negro in Southern Agriculture.* New York: International Publishers, 1953.

Pinson, Koppel. *Modern Germany, Its History and Civilization.* New York: Macmillan, 1966.

Pleck, Joseph H. "The Work–Family Role System." *Social Problems* **24**, no. 4 (1977): 417–27.

Poole, Keith T., and Howard Rosenthal. *Congress: A Political-Economic History of Roll Call Voting.* New York: Oxford University Press, 1997.

Portes, Alejandro. "Immigration Theory for a New Century: Some Problems and Opportunities." *International Migration Review* **31** (1997): 799–825.

    The Economic Sociology of Immigration: Essays on Networks, Ethnicity, and Entrepreneurship. New York: Russell Sage Foundation, 1998.

Prendergast, Canice. "The Provision of Incentives in Firms." *Journal of Economic Literature* **37** (1999): 7–63.

Przeworski, Adam, and Fernando Limogni. "Modernization: Theories and Facts." *World Politics* **49** (1997): 155–83.

Quiggin, John. "Egoistic Rationality and Public Choice: Critical Review of Theory and Evidence." *Economic Record* **63** (1987): 10–21.

Rabe-Hesketh, Sophia, and Brian S. Everitt. *A Handbook of Statistical Analyses Using Stata,* 3rd ed. London: CRC Press, 2003.

Radcliffe-Brown, A. R. *Structure and Function in Primitive Society.* London: Cohen and West, 1952.

Ramsey, Fred, and Daniel Schafer. *The Statistical Sleuth: A Course in Methods of Data Analysis,* 2nd ed. Belmont, CA: Duxbury Press, 2001.

Raper, Arthur F. *The Tragedy of Lynching.* Chapel Hill: University of North Carolina Press, 1933.

Ray, James Lee. "Does Democracy Cause Peace?" *Annual Review of Political Science* **1** (1998): 27–46.

Reynolds, Paul D. *Primer in Theory Construction.* New York: Allyn and Bacon, 2006.

Rhoads, Steven E. *The Economist's View of the World.* Cambridge: Cambridge University Press, 1985.

Robins, James M., and Sander Greenland. "Identifiability and Exchangeability for Direct and Indirect Effects." *Epidemiology* **3** (1992): 143–55.

Romer, Christina D. "Spurious Volatility in Historical Unemployment Data." *Journal of Political Economy* **94** (1986a): 1–37.

    "Is the Stabilization of the Postwar Economy a Figment of the Data?" *American Economic Review* **76** (1986b): 314–34.

Romer, Christina D., and David H. Romer. "Federal Reserve Information and the Behavior of Interest Rates." *American Economic Review* **90** (2000): 429–57.

Rosenberg, Gerald N. "Judicial Independence and the Reality of Political Power." *Review of Politics* **54** (1992): 369–98.

Rosenfeld, Rachel A. "Job Mobility and Career Proesses." *Annual Review of Sociology* **18** (1992): 39–61.

Rosenstone, Steven J. *Forecasting Presidential Elections.* New Haven, CT: Yale University Press, 1983.

Ross, Dorothy. *The Origins of American Social Science.* Cambridge: Cambridge University Press, 1991.

Ross, Sheldon M. *Introduction to Probability Models.* New York: Academic Press, 1985.

Rossi, Peter H., Richard Berli, David P. Boesel, Bettye K. Eidson, and W. Eugene Groves. "Between White and Black – the Faces of American Institutions in the Ghetto." In *Supplemental Studies for the National Advisory Commission on Civil Disorders*, 69–208. Washington, DC: Government Printing Office, 1968.

Rubin, Donald B. "Estimating Causal Effects of Treatments in Randomized and Non-randomized Studies." *Journal of Educational Psychology* **66** (1974): 688–701.

Rutkus, Denis Steven, and Maureen Bearden. "Supreme Court Nominations, 1789–2005: Actions by the Senate, the Judiciary Committee, and the President." In *CRS Report for Congress.* Washington, DC: Congressional Research Service–Library of Congress, 2005.

Sala-I-Martin, Xavier. "The World Distribution of Income: Failing Poverty . . . and Convergence, Period." *Quarterly Journal of Economics* **121** (2006): 351–97.

Salvatore, Dominick. *International Economics.* Englewood Cliffs, NJ: Prentice Hall, 1995.

Schickler, Eric. *Disjointed Pluralism: Institutional Innovation and the Development of the U.S. Congress.* Princeton, NJ: Princeton University Press, 2001.

Segal, Jeffrey A., and Albert D. Cover. "Ideological Values and the Votes of U.S. Supreme Court Justices." *American Political Science Review* **83** (1989): 557–65.

Shadish, William R., Thomas D. Cook, and Donald T. Campbell. *Experimental and Quasi-Experimental Designs for Generalized Causal Inference.* Boston: Houghton Mifflin, 2002.

Shapiro, David. *Neurotic Styles.* New York: Basic Books, 1965.

Shaughnessy, John J., Eugene Zechmeister, and Jeanne Zechmeister. *Research Methods in Psychology.* New York: McGraw-Hill, 2006.

Shepsle, Kenneth A., and Barry R. Weingast, eds. *Positive Theories of Congressional Institutions.* Ann Arbor: University of Michigan Press, 1995.

Smelser, Neil J. *Theory of Collective Behavior.* New York: Free Press, 1963.

Smith, Jeffrey, and Petra Todd. "Does Matching Overcome Lalonde's Critique of Non-experimental Estimators?": University of Maryland and University of Pennsylvania, 2003. Available at http://www.nber.org/~rdehejia/cvindex#0.

Snidal, Duncan. "Coordination versus Prisoners' Dilemma: Implications for International Cooperation and Regimes." *American Political Science Review* **79** (1985): 923–42.

Snyder, David, and William R. Kelly. "Conflict Intensity, Media Sensitivity and the Validity of Newspaper Data." *American Sociological Review* **42** (1977): 105–23.

Sobel, Michael E. "Causal Inference in the Social and Behavioral Sciences." In *Handbook of Statistical Modeling for the Social and Behavioral Sciences*, ed. Gerhard Arminger, Clifford C. Clogg, and Michael E. Sobel, 1–38. New York: Plenum Press, 1995.

"Discussion of the Scientic Model of Causality by James Heckman." *Sociological Methodology* **35** (2005): 99–133.

Southern Commission on the Study of Lynching. "Lynchings and What They Mean." Atlanta: Southern Commission on the Study of Lynching, 1931.

Spilerman, Seymour. "The Causes of Racial Disturbances: A Comparison of Alternative Explanations." *American Sociological Review* **35** (1970): 627–49.

———. "The Causes of Racial Disturbances: Tests for an Explanation." *American Sociological Review* **36** (1971): 427–43.

———. "Structural Characteristics of Cities and the Severity of Racial Disorders." *American Sociological Review* **41** (1976): 771–93.

Spilerman, Seymour, and David Elesh. "Alternative Conceptions of Poverty and Their Implications for Income Maintenance." *Social Problems* **18** (1971): 358–73.

Spilerman, Seymour, and Tormud Lunde. "Features of Educational Attainment and Job Promotion Prospects." *American Journal of Sociology* **97** (1991): 689–720.

Spilerman, Seymour, and Trond Petersen. "Organizational Structure, Determinants of Promotion, and Gender Differences in Attainment." *Social Science Research* **28** (1999): 203–27.

Spilerman, Seymour, and Harris Schrank. "Responses to the Intrusion of Family Responsibilities in the Workplace." *Research in Social Stratification and Mobility* **10** (1991): 27–61.

Spiller, Roger J. "S.L.A. Marshall and the Ratio of Fire." *RUSI Journal* **133** (Winter 1988): 63–71.

Stanovich, Keith E. *How to Think Straight about Psychology,* 7th ed. Boston: Allyn and Bacon, 2004.

Stecklov, Guy, and Joshua R. Goldstein. "Terror Attacks Influence Driving Behavior in Israel." *Proceedings of the National Academy of Sciences of the United States of America* **101** (2004): 14551–6.

Stigler, George J. "The Theory of Economic Regulation." In *Chicago Studies in Political Economy,* ed. George J. Stigler, 209–33. Chicago: University of Chicago Press, 1988.

Stinchcombe, Arthur L. *Constructing Social Theories.* New York: Harcourt and Brace, 1968.

Taylor, John. "Discretion Versus Policy Rules in Practice." *Carnegie-Rochester Conference on Public Policy* **39** (1993): 195–214.

Thernstrom, Stephan. *Poverty and Progress: Social Mobility in a Nineteenth Century City.* New York: Atheneum, 1970.

Tolnay, Stewart E.,, and E. M. Beck. *A Festival of Violence: An Analysis of Southern Lynchings, 1882–1930.* Urbana: University of Illinois Press, 1995.

Truman, David Bicknell. *The Governmental Process: Political Interests and Public Opinion.* Berkeley: University of California Press, 1993.

U.S. Census Bureau. "Twelfth Census of the United States, Manufactures," Vol VIII. Washington, DC: U.S. Census Bureau, 1900.

U.S. Congress, Subcommittee on Antitrust and Monopoly of the Committee on the Judiciary. "Hearings on Economic Concentration." Washington, DC: U.S. Government Printing Office, 1964–6.

Veblen, Thorstein. *The Theory of the Leisure Class: An Economic Study of Institutions.* London: Macmillan, 1912.

Verba, Sidney, Kay Lehman Schlozman, and Henry Brady. *Voice and Equality: Civic Voluntarism in American Politics.* Cambridge, MA: Harvard University Press, 1995.

Viscusi, W. Kip. "Risk Equity." *Journal of Legal Studies* **29** (2000): 843–71.

Viscusi, W. Kip, and Joseph E. Aldy. "The Value of a Statistical Life: A Critical Review of Market Estimates throughout the World." *NBER Working Paper No. 9487.* Cambridge, MA: National Bureau of Economic Research, 2003.

Weber, Robert P. *Basic Content Analysis: Quantitative Applications in the Social Sciences.* Thousand Oaks, CA: Sage, 1990.

Winship, Christopher, and Michael E. Sobel. "Causal Inference in Sociological Studies." In *The Handbook of Data Analysis*, ed. Melissa A. Hardy, 481–503. Thousand Oaks, CA: Sage, 2004.

Wittfogel, Karl. *Oriental Despotism: A Comparative Study of Total Power*. New Haven, CT: Yale University Press, 1957.

Wlezien, Christopher, and Robert S. Erikson. "The Fundamentals, the Polls and the Presidential Vote." *PS: Political Science and Politics* **37**, no. 4 (2004): 747–51.

Woodward, C. Vann. "Southern Slaves in the World of Thomas Malthus." In *American Counterpoint: Slavery and Racism in the North/South Dialogue*, 78–106. Oxford: Oxford University Press, 1983.

Wooldridge, Jeffrey M. *Introductory Econometrics: A Modern Approach*. Cincinnati: South-Western College Publishing, 2000.

Wrigley, Edward A., and Roger S. Scholefield. *The Population History of England, 1541–1871: A Reconstruction*: *Cambridge Studies in Population, Economy and Society in Past Time*. Cambridge: Cambridge University Press, 1989.

Zivot, Eric, and Donald W. K. Andrews. "Further Evidence on the Great Crash, the Oil-Price Shock, and the Unit-Root Hypothesis." *Journal of Business and Economic Statistics* **10** (1992): 251–70.

Index

Aberbach, Joel, 244
Abrams, Samuel, 207
Acemoglu, Daron, 212
Achen, Chris, 236
acting white, 159
actuarial, 295
Adams, Greg, 8
Africa, 36–8, 95
agent-based modeling, 221
Aldy, Joseph, 29
algebra, 248, 272
Alito, Samuel, 250
almanacs, 56
Americans for Democratic Action (ADA)
    scores, 209, 225
Amerindian societies, 87
anarchists, 54
Andrews, Donald, 218
animal training, 273
Annales, 45, 46, 49, 327
apples with apples, 308
Argentina, 76, 88
aristocracy, 56
Arkansas, 187
Ashworth, Anthony, 23, 24, 25, 28, 29, 247
Atlanta, 182
Atlanta Constitution, 177
Austro-Hungarian Empire, 53
autoregressive model, 113
average square error, 118
Axelrod, Robert, 20–9, 330
Ayala, Cesar, 84

Babbie, Earl, 31
Bailey, Michell, 251
balance, 320

balance of payments, 74
Bank of England, 77, 78
Bank of Japan, 147
Barcelona, 55
bargaining, 4
Baumol, William, 102
Bearden, Maureen, 250
Beck, E.M., 189
behavioral finance, 288
behavioral intention, 288
behaviorism, 276–80
Beitz, Charles, 29
Bentham, Jeremy, 43
Benthamite, 53
Bergad, Laird, 84
Berger, Peter, 30
Bergman, Karl, 95
Beveridge, Andrew, 86
biases, 16, 51, 56, 57, 85
bivariate scatterplots, 233
Black, Hugo, 250, 254, 263
Black Death, 37
Blackburn, Robin, 95
blip, 293
Bloch, Marc, 45
Bloomfield, Arthur, 80
Blossfeld, Arthur, 162
Boix, Carles, 211
Bolivia, 56
Booth, Booth, 43
Borah, Woodrow, 94
Borchardt, Knut, 96
Bordo, Michael, 64, 75, 76, 77, 79
Bork, Robert, 229, 240, 242, 250
Bourbon-type lynchings, 181
Box-Steffensmeir, Janet, 196, 203

ordinal, 188
ordinary least squares, 258
organizing, 36
orthogonality, 111
outcome variable, 104
outcomes, 303
overfitting, 237
overlap of pretreatment characteristics, 317, 320

padrone, 87
Page, Benjamin I., 8, 29, 213
Palm Beach County, 8
panel data, 106
Panel Study of Income Dynamics, 311
paradigms, 162
paradox, 219
parallel publics, 8
parametric models, 243
Park, Jee-Kwang, 226
partitioning the data, 261
party polarization, 209
patriarchal, 319
pauperization, 43
Pavlov, Ivan, 277
payoff matrix, 293
Pearl, Judea, 304
Peña Sánchez de Rivera, Daniel, 55
penicillin, 50
pension systems, 92
perceived qualifications, 234
  as proxy for bad news, 236
Perlo, Victor, 180
Petersen, Trond, 200, 202
philosophy of science, 275
physical environment, 291
Platonic absolute, 274
plausibility, 219
Pleck, Joseph, 198
Poisson model, 166–70, 216, 258
polarization, 207, 208, 209
political agenda and slave trade, 37
political arithmetic, 41
political elites, 208
political ideology, 4, 5
political organization, 36
political parties, 14
political psychologists, 213
political science, 8, 10, 11–31, 207–67
political survival hypothesis, 212
political system, 11, 16, 17, 18, 19, 21, 93

political theory, 213
Poole, Keith, 17, 209, 225, 251
Poor Law Commission, 43
Pope, Clayne, 94
Pope, Jeremy, 207
population growth, 41
positivism, 42, 49
post-modern, 49
potential outcomes, 303–8, 322
poverty rate, 171
pre-Columbian, 39
predetermined variables, 102, 104, 142
predictability, 274
predicted probabilities, 321
predictions, 7, 286
predictor variable, 142
predictors, 104, 303
pre-election polls, 7
Prein, Gerald, 162
Prendergast, Canice, 27
presidential election, 8, 16
pretreatment variables, 309, 317
price-specie-flow mechanism, 77
principal component analysis, 252
prisoner's dilemma, 21–9, 100
private sector, 120
probabilistic forecasting, 31
probability, 8
production function, 244
projection, 286
proletarian-type lynchings, 181
promotion, 191–203
  blockage, 199
promotion of employees, 4
promotion rate, 195
propensity scores, 215, 308–9, 314, 319
proportional representation, 14–16, 19
prosopography, 56
prospect theory, 287
Protestants, 38
proof, 274
Przeworski, Adam, 211
psychodynamic theory, 284–7
psychodynamics, 286
psychological experiments, 291
psychology, 100, 271–300
psychophysics, 291
psychosexual stages, 285
public granaries, 39
public health, 43
public opinion, 5, 207